Dangerous Memory in Nagasaki

On 9 August 1945, the US dropped the second atomic bomb on Nagasaki. Of the dead, approximately 8500 were Catholic Christians, representing over 60 per cent of the community. In this collective biography, nine Catholic survivors share personal and compelling stories about the aftermath of the bomb and their lives since that day.

Examining the Catholic community's interpretation of the A-bomb, this book not only uses memory to provide a greater understanding of the destruction of the bombing, but also links it to the past experiences of religious persecution, drawing comparisons with the 'Secret Christian' groups which survived in the Japanese countryside after the banning of Christianity. Through in-depth interviews, it emerges that the memory of the atomic bomb is viewed through the lens of a community which had experienced suffering and marginalisation for more than 400 years. Furthermore, the author argues that their dangerous memory confronts Euro-American-centric narratives of the atomic bombings, while also challenging assumptions around a providential bomb.

Dangerous Memory in Nagasaki presents the voices of Catholics, many of whom have not spoken of their losses within the framework of their faith before. As such, it will be invaluable to students and scholars of Japanese history, religion and war history.

Gwyn McClelland holds a Master of Divinity from the University of Divinity, Melbourne, Australia and a Doctorate of Philosophy in Japanese history from Monash University.

Asia's Transformations
Edited by Mark Selden, Cornell University, USA

The books in this series explore the political, social, economic and cultural consequences of Asia's transformations in the twentieth and twenty-first centuries. The series emphasizes the tumultuous interplay of local, national, regional and global forces as Asia bids to become the hub of the world economy. While focusing on the contemporary, it also looks back to analyse the antecedents of Asia's contested rise.

50 **The Making of Modern Korea**
   Adrian Buzo

51 **Danger, Development and Legitimacy in East Asian Maritime Politics**
   Securing the Seas, Securing the State
   Christian Wirth

52 **Denying the Comfort Women**
   The Japanese State's Assault on Historical Truth
   Edited by Rumiko Nishino, Puja Kim and Akane Onozawa

53 **National Identity, Language and Education in Malaysia**
   Search for a Middle Ground between Malay Hegemony and Equality
   Noriyuki Segawa

54 **Japan's Future and a New Meiji Transformation**
   International Reflections
   Edited by Ken Coates, Kimie Hara, Carin Holroyd and Marie Söderberg

55 **Dangerous Memory in Nagasaki**
   Prayers, Protests and Catholic Survivor Narratives
   Gwyn McClelland

For more information about this series, please visit: www.routledge.com/Asias-Transformations/book-series/SE0401

Dangerous Memory in Nagasaki

Prayers, Protests and Catholic Survivor Narratives

Gwyn McClelland

LONDON AND NEW YORK

First published 2020
by Routledge
2 Park Square, Milton Park, Abingdon, Oxon OX14 4RN

and by Routledge
52 Vanderbilt Avenue, New York, NY 10017

Routledge is an imprint of the Taylor & Francis Group, an informa business

© 2020 Gwyn McClelland

The right of Gwyn McClelland to be identified as author of this work has been asserted by him in accordance with sections 77 and 78 of the Copyright, Designs and Patents Act 1988.

All rights reserved. No part of this book may be reprinted or reproduced or utilised in any form or by any electronic, mechanical, or other means, now known or hereafter invented, including photocopying and recording, or in any information storage or retrieval system, without permission in writing from the publishers.

Trademark notice: Product or corporate names may be trademarks or registered trademarks, and are used only for identification and explanation without intent to infringe.

British Library Cataloguing-in-Publication Data
A catalogue record for this book is available from the British Library

Library of Congress Cataloging-in-Publication Data
Names: McClelland, Gwyn, author.
Title: Dangerous memory in Nagasaki : prayers, protests and Catholic survivor narratives / Gwyn McClelland.
Identifiers: LCCN 2019028161 (print) | LCCN 2019028162 (ebook) | ISBN 9780367217754 (hardback) | ISBN 9780429266003 (ebook) | ISBN 9780429556517 (adobe pdf) | ISBN 9780429565458 (mobi) | ISBN 9780429560989 (epub)
Subjects: LCSH: Catholic Church–Japan–History. | Catholics–Japan–Nagasaki-shi–Biography. | Atomic bomb victims–Japan–Nagasaki-shi–Biography. | Atomic bomb victims–Religious life–Japan–Nagasaki-shi. | Nuclear warfare–Religious aspects–Catholic Church. | Collective memory–Japan–Nagasaki-shi. | Nagasaki-shi (Japan)–History–Bombardment, 1945–Personal narratives.
Classification: LCC D767.25.N3 M33 2020 (print) | LCC D767.25.N3 (ebook) | DDC 940.54/252244092882–dc23
LC record available at https://lccn.loc.gov/2019028161
LC ebook record available at https://lccn.loc.gov/2019028162

ISBN: 978-0-367-21775-4 (hbk)
ISBN: 978-0-429-26600-3 (ebk)

Typeset in Times New Roman
by Wearset Ltd, Boldon, Tyne and Wear

To the *kataribe* of Nagasaki who told their dangerous memory. Thank you Miyake, Nishida, Fukahori Jōji, Konishi, Matsuo, Nakamura, Mine, Fukahori Shigemi, Kataoka, Nagase, Enju and Ozaki.

Gwyn McClelland

Contents

List of illustrations ix
Editorial notes xii
Foreword xiv
YUKI MIYAMOTO
Preface: 'dangerous' memory – political theology of
Johann Baptist Metz xix
Acknowledgements xxviii

PART I
Legacy of survival 1

1 Fissures 3
2 Survivors 18
3 Bodies 35

PART II
Reinterpreting the bomb: archetype, monument and cry 57

4 Providential atomic bomb? 59
5 A-bombed Mary 87
6 Urakami Cathedral: a fifth persecution 110
7 Water! Atomic cries and their echoes in the past 129

PART III
Memory's future 143

8 Dangerous hope 145

9 Lament, anger and protest 168

10 Conclusion 196

Appendix: notes on sources 201
Glossary: Japanese and theological terms 209
Index 213

Illustrations

Figures

0.1	Urakami Cathedral ruins, black and white drawing by Nagai Takashi, c.1946	xxix
1.1	Depiction of the 1622 martyrdom of Spinola (and others) at Nishizaka slopes, photograph, 6 July 2015	3
1.2	Urakami valley: valley of death, US Marine Corp, 1945	4
2.1	Montage-photographs of survivors, 2008–16	18
2.2	Nagai Takashi's painting of the Urakami Cathedral ruins	25
3.1	A modern monument to San Lazaro and San Joao Baptista Church at Nishizaka	39
3.2	Takagi Sen'emon, *ikinokori* (survivor) of the exile, 1898, 74 years	45
4.1	Nagai Takashi, 1946, mourning for Midori	60
4.2	Nagai Tokusaburō poses at the Nyokodō museum of his grandfather	65
4.3	Kataoka Chizuko, photograph supplied	73
4.4	Statue of Pope John Paul II, erected at Megumi no Oka Gembaku Hōmu on occasion of the Pope's visit in 1981	76
5.1	A 'dangerous' Maria Kannon, confiscated by the Nagasaki magistrate during the 1860s	92
5.2	Mary holds the body of Christ: a *fumi-e* (image for trampling), public domain, photograph, used by permission, National	94
5.3	Photograph of the Spanish grieving Mary at 9 August 2015 Mass at Urakami Cathedral	98
5.4	Nagase Kazuko	99
6.1	Stained-glass windows which depict the burning cathedral, photograph, Richard Flynn, 2006	110
6.2	From left: 深堀譲治 Fukahori Jōji (14 years), 暁郎 Akio (c.10 years), 待子 Machiko (5 years), 耕治 Kōji (c.12 years), in front of Urakami Cathedral 1944	112
6.3	The *yon-ban kuzure* returnees in front of Urakami Cathedral, 1930: Matsuo's grandmother, 西尾ワキ Nishio Waki, is in the third row, third from left	114

x *Illustrations*

6.4	23 November 1945, memorial service at the ruins of the Urakami Cathedral	120
6.5	February 1946 sketch of the ruins of the Cathedral, by Nagai Takashi	123
7.1	Urakami River on the occasion of the seventieth anniversary of the atomic bombing of Nagasaki	130
7.2	'The boy who cried for water', drawn by his son, Nakamura Kōji	133
8.1	Ozaki Tōmei, in his robes, 12 September 2018	146
8.2	Ozaki's sketch map of his journey home after the bombing, with annotations, Ozaki's blog	149
8.3	Full page proof from the manga by Shiōra, Ozaki finds the burnt rosary beads of his mother	151
9.1	Fukahori Jōji	169
9.2	'Hashigachi-machi and environs seen from Yamazato National School', taken by Shigeo Hayashi	171
9.3	Yamazato Kokumin Gakkō (Yamazato State School)	175
9.4	Matsuo Sachiko	181
9.5	Ozaki Tōmei's mother, Clara Wasa Tagawa	186
10.1	Urakami Cathedral stained-glass window	196

Maps

0.1	Approximate location of ten interviewees at 11:02 a.m. on 9 August 1945	xi
1.1	Panorama shiki Nagasaki kankō annai-zu Map 151 (1953)	8

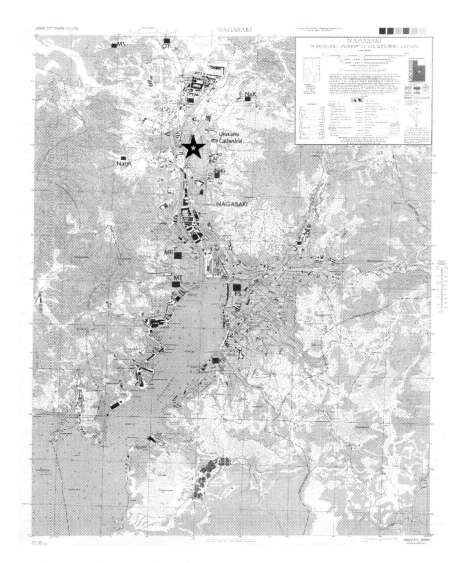

Map 0.1 Approximate location of ten interviewees at 11:02 a.m. on 9 August 1945, superimposed on a map from US survey of Nagasaki, June 1945, public domain, additions by the author.

Notes
Key: MS = Matsuo Sachiko; OT = Ozaki Tōmei; NaK = Nakamura Kazutoshi; NagK = Nagase Kazuko; NiKi = Nishida Kiyoshi; MR = Miyake Reiko; MT = Mine Tōru; FS = Fukahori Shigemi; FJ = Fukahori Jōji; KS = Konishi Shin'ichi; ☆ = Hypocenter/Ground Zero.

Editorial notes

I retain the Japanese order for names in the text, family name first. I will retain standard order in bibliography and footnotes. Japanese authors who predominantly publish in English will be included in the text in standard order. I base all Biblical references upon the New Revised Standard Version (NRSV) unless otherwise noted. I capitalise cities and names in Japanese, but otherwise leave all words non-capitalised.

I completed the translations in this monograph from the conversations in Japanese between myself as the interviewer and the interviewees. I initially developed transcriptions in Japanese from each conversation. The resulting texts include pauses, omissions, false starts, back loops and so on. I made decisions about translation and interpretation at each stage, conscious of the dilemma as to what extent literal translation may be employed and how much contextual translation may be used for readability as well as addressing the complexity of interpreting oral text. I have tended towards translating contextually and creatively rather than producing a formal and literal equivalent of texts. An ellipsis […] in the text indicates that I have edited some data from the original interview. Clarifications and editorial notes are included in square brackets []. I take full responsibility for final translations.

Apart from survivors, I interviewed the following community members: Nagai Tokusaburō, the grandson of Nagai Takashi; Miyazaki Yoshio, a Korean teacher at the Catholic Center; Takazane Yasunori, the Director of the Oka Masaharu Peace Museum; Matsuzono Ichijirō, the son of a bomb survivor, who was working at a Catholic institution.[1] I engaged with scholars including Paul Glynn, Shijō Chie, Nishimura Akira, Shiōra Shintarō, Takahashi Shinji and A'nan Shigeyuki, reflecting on the responses from these secondary interviews as well as the main evidence of the interviews and using them as a sounding board and primary resource.

An earlier version of Chapter 4 was published as 'Re-interpreting *hansai*: burnt offerings as the Nagasaki atomic bomb' in David W. Kim (ed.) volume, **Colonial Transformation and Asian Religions in Modern History**, Cambridge Scholars Publishing, 230–60, February 2018. Substantially reworked since then, an earlier paper based on some of the content of Chapter 5 was published as 'The Mother of Sorrows as *Hibakusha*', in Elena V. Shabliy (ed.),

Representations of the Blessed Virgin Mary in World Literature and Art, Lexington Books, 111–32, 15 August 2017. Also developed and refined, the material included in Chapter 6 was initially published in a journal article as follows: 'Remembering the ruins of the Urakami Cathedral: Providence or Fifth Persecution?' **Journal of Religion in Japan**, June 2016, 5 (1), 47–69.

Note

1 I use a pseudonym for Matsuzono.

Foreword

Yuki Miyamoto

Yuki Miyamoto is an ethicist whose work centres on nuclear discourse and environmental ethics, through the framework of comparative ethics. Her monograph **Beyond the Mushroom Cloud: Commemoration, Religion, and Responsibility after Hiroshima** *(Fordham University Press, 2011) examines the ways in which survivors of the atomic bombings of 1945 came to terms with the nuclear attacks within their religious understandings – Hiroshima with True Pure Land Buddhism; Nagasaki with Roman Catholicism – while critiquing the framework imposed by nation-states. She continues to work on nuclear discourse, marshalling the key concepts of commemoration, representation, and dark tourism in articles such as 'Gendered Bodies in Tokusatsu' in The Journal of Popular Culture (2016), and 'In the Light of Hiroshima' in the edited volume, Reimagining Hiroshima and Nagasaki (Routledge, 2017).*

Nagasaki has enjoyed its status as a city of firsts in Japan – the first city in which a trading company was established prior to the Meiji period by Sakamoto Ryōma, a beloved historical figure in Nagasaki. Nagasaki was the first city in Japan to have a trial run of a steam engine in 1863, brought by Thomas Glover, a Scottish merchant; the first to open a Western-style restaurant, Jiyūtei, and the first to institute marine telegraphic cables Nagasaki to Shanghai; Nagasaki to Vladivostok; even before the line from Nagasaki to Tokyo. Nagasaki's firsts cease when the atomic bomb was dropped; Nagasaki was the second city that suffered from an atomic bomb during the war.

A number of scholars have already pointed out that Hiroshima and Nagasaki have dealt with the historical event of the atomic bombings differently, which, as is quoted by the author of this monograph, is often summarised by the phrase *ikari no Hiroshima, inori no Nagasaki* ('Hiroshima rages, Nagasaki prays'). The difference is not just in how feelings are expressed. A scholar of communication, Fukuma Yoshiaki, notes that people in Nagasaki envied Hiroshima for its 'Peace Festival', even when Hiroshima's city officials frowned upon the festivities on the second anniversary of the bombing. In this festival, people sang the 'Hiroshima *ondo* [song]', danced to music and played drums while marching through the city. It was indeed a festival, rather than the solemn commemoration that we would expect and are used to observing. Nagasaki's envy was attributed not to its festivity but to the number of people who gathered in Hiroshima for the anniversary,[1] and the concern that commemorating the atomic bombing would not necessarily gather as many people in Nagasaki.

The difference cannot be explained by Nagasaki's being the second city to be attacked. The plutonium bomb that fell on Nagasaki was more powerful in its lethal capacity than the uranium bomb dropped on Hiroshima. The lesser death toll was only because of the geographical location of Ground Zero: the bomb was dropped about 3 kilometres (1.9 miles) from the city's centre and fell between the mountains of a less-residential area. Such conditions are in stark contrast to Hiroshima's hypocenter, where the affected area was a relatively flat plain that was densely populated as the residential and commercial centre of the city. Consequently, the death toll in Hiroshima amounted to 140,000 people, twice as many as in Nagasaki. In addition to geographical differences, demography must be mentioned: the Nagasaki bomb exploded over the marginalised areas of the Catholics and its neighbouring community of *buraku* (the outcastes that faced discrimination). Nagasaki's atomic bomb experiences may have been, in large part, seen as 'their' experiences for Nagasaki citizens.

Despite the politically and culturally underrepresented position of Nagasaki, a Catholic convert, Nagai Takashi's interpretation of the atomic bombing dominated the discourse of the bombing and represented Nagasaki's experiences in the period of the late 1940s and early 1950s – a time crucial to the formation of the narrative. This is largely attributed to the support of the Supreme Commander of the Allied Powers (SCAP), who was reigning over defeated Japan. Yet eventually, nonconforming voices such as those of Yamada Kan and Akizuki Tatsuichirō arose from the Catholic communities of Nagasaki and from outside Nagasaki in the person of Inoue Hisashi (playwright/novelist). I myself disagree with Nagai's theodicy, which obscures human agency and thus disregards the accountability of the US in dropping the nuclear bombs, while mystifying and glorifying the dead in Japan.[2] My dilemma is that, as much as I disagree with Nagai, invalidating his theory would disregard some survivors' needs at that time of despair. There is a need to acknowledge the community's yearning for an explanation, and in fact some *hibakusha* [survivors of the atomic bomb][3] tried to embrace Nagai's theory in their efforts to come to terms with the calamity and find hope in it.

This dilemma gives rise to questions of who authenticates memory and who can represent it. Nagai's interpretation was endorsed by SCAP and those who were in power at the time. Then, it was further disseminated through film to the general populace beyond the Catholic *hibakusha* of Nagasaki. The above example of Hiroshima's Peace Festival in 1947 also revealed a tension regarding the authentication of memory: some *hibakusha* thought it appropriate to celebrate their survival through songs and dances, while foreign correspondents, city officials and bereaved families found it tasteless and offensive.

This addresses the further question of where (and to whom) memory belongs. When Gwyn McClelland collects the personal accounts of Nagasaki *hibakusha*, their experiences are always situated in a larger framework than the storyteller's own. In other words, each experience – unique and distinctive – belongs to an individual, but the nature of such beyond-words experiences are put into words so as to become intelligible to oneself as well as to others. One's experience, on the one hand, must negotiate with frameworks that are available and convincing to the speaker. On the other hand, such frameworks in the milieu beyond oneself are the products of various power dynamics. Thus, memory, situated in a historical context, cannot be entirely free from the variables of power; at the same time, memory is always dialogical, a transaction between oneself and beyond.

Given the testimony's framework, Nagai's theology was indeed dominant,[4] with nationally successful books and a movie that set the tone for the atomic bomb discourse in Nagasaki. If Nagai's *hansai* (or Holocaust) theory became orthodoxy in post-war Japan, challenging his theory was understood as dissident and heretical. The voices included in this collective biography are indeed 'dangerous', as they disturb the order, calling into question the legitimacy of orthodoxy. As McClelland, drawing upon Johann Baptist Metz's concept of a dangerous memory, demonstrates in this monograph, such voices are worth studying, precisely because their memories make an opening into the continuity of history, driving a wedge into the monolithic architecture of a discourse. Only out of such disjuncture can a change for the future emerge.

By collecting personal accounts that do not necessarily cast direct criticism against the orthodoxy represented by Nagai's theology, McClelland shows that those stories do, nevertheless, undermine a romanticised and mystified popular narrative. For instance, many Catholic *hibakusha*, in coming to terms with their atomic bomb experiences, situate them in the history of suffering inflicted upon their community and ancestors. Historically, due to their faith and its practice, which was banned by the authorities of the time, the Urakami community underwent persecutions (at least) four times. Notably, the last *kuzure*, or attempted dismantling of the community, was executed at the largest scale by the Tokugawa shogunate that originally proscribed Christianity and the practice was continued by the newly established Meiji government for another four years. Due to this long-lasting expulsion in the Fourth Persecution, most members were displaced and the community vanished. When they were allowed to return to their community, they found only a wasteland where their community had once existed.

By linking the suffering from the atomic bombing to that of their ancestors' *kuzure* experiences, Nagasaki's Catholics' testimonies subvert a narrative that renders their plight a beautiful story of resilience, somewhat comfortable to the audience. Narrating the atomic bombing as not being the beginning of their suffering, their testimonies illuminate to readers their marginalised position throughout history. Their accounts, thus, offer a memory that is dissonant to the expectations of readers who look for an uplifting story in the tragic event and to those in power who want to dissociate themselves from the history of oppression.

Because a dangerous memory opens up and draws attention to this disjuncture in orthodoxy, it enables the audience to call into question (employing Judith

Butler's term of epistemology) the 'frame' – the frame that limits our recognition of the victim's precariousness.[5] Nagasaki's Catholics' accounts, by connecting their plight to their historical experiences, reveal their precarious place in history. When we fail to fully grasp their precariousness, we also fail, as Butler claims, to mourn the lives lost. Instead of mourning, we exploit their lives, which are now romanticised and mystified in popular narratives.

There are many others who have been excluded from the prevailing discourse for a long time, as the result of the failure to grasp their precariousness: people in *buraku*, Koreans, Chinese POWs (political dissidents), Dutch POWs (who were called 'dark Dutch' as a colonised population from Indonesia) and so on. Their testimonies often begin with their hardship prior to the bombing, unlike the popular accounts. Korean *hibakusha*, for instance, would talk about their suffering in the occupied Korean peninsula, their exploitation in coal mines and their experiences of other perilous jobs after migrating to Japan; and even after the bombing, discrimination against them would prevent their receiving proper medical treatment.[6] The dangerous memory of the *buraku* community allows us to wonder why a Catholic community was able to rebuild its community after the bombing and how a neighbouring community of *buraku* vanished. Those memories help us to resist the romanticising of the tragedy.

Yet the dangerous memories in this volume also provide a hope. Some Catholic *hibakusha* interviewees identify their experiences of the atomic bombing with those of Job. As McClelland shows, a dangerous memory channels their despair towards God; Job too challenged God. However, I believe that the chronology of the narrative is crucial. Job initially did not complain about his loss and misfortune. Only after his friends visited him and pointed to his misery did Job begin to confront God. Eventually, his loss was restored. But, here again, the reinstatement took place only after Job realised his place in relation to God and began to pray for his friends. When Job prayed for others, his heartbreak from the loss was healed as also his relationship with God. The story of Job, as I interpret it, does not impose perseverance of suffering as God's will, but the process of healing – healing to the victim as well as to victimisers and beyond. The interviewees, though some of them took a long time to talk openly about their experiences, decided to share their stories, so that no one would have to go through the same suffering. Like Job's prayers for his friends, *hibakusha* testimonies restore their dignity by their ownership of their stories and thereby serving as an invocation, appealing for the flourishing future of humankind.

Notes

1 Fukuma Yoshiaki, *Shōdo no kioku: Okinawa, Hiroshima, Nagasaki ni utsuru sengo* (Tokyo: Shin'yōsha, 2011), 373.
2 Yuki Miyamoto, *Beyond the Mushroom Cloud: Commemoration, Religion, and Responsibility After Hiroshima* (New York: Fordham University Press, 2011), 140–1.
3 I (Miyamoto) use the term 'survive' and 'survivor' for convenience, but in reality, one will never know if one has survived in the case of nuclear attack. Radiation sickness may appear ten or twenty years later, so one cannot be certain until one's death.

4 Chad R. Diehl also discusses this issue. For example, Chad R. Diehl, *Resurrecting Nagasaki: Reconstruction and the Formation of Atomic Narratives* (Ithaca, NY: Cornell University Press, 2018), 131.
5 Judith Butler, *Frames of War: When Is Life Grievable?*, 1st ed. (London, New York: Verso Trade, 2010).
6 See, for example, Soo-nam Park, *Mō hitotsu no Hiroshima: Ariran no uta*, 1987.

References

Butler, Judith. *Frames of War: When Is Life Grievable?*, 1st ed. London and New York: Verso Trade, 2010.
Diehl, Chad R. *Resurrecting Nagasaki: Reconstruction and the Formation of Atomic Narratives*. Ithaca, NY: Cornell University Press, 2018.
Miyamoto, Yuki. *Beyond the Mushroom Cloud: Commemoration, Religion, and Responsibility After Hiroshima.* New York: Fordham University Press, 2011.
Miyamoto, Yuki. 'Gendered Bodies in Tokusatsu: Monsters and Aliens as the Atomic Bomb Victims'. *Journal of Popular Culture* 49.5 (2016): 1086–106.
Miyamoto, Yuki. 'In the Light of Hiroshima: Banalizing Violence and Normalizing Experiences of the Atomic Bombing'. In *Reimagining Hiroshima and Nagasaki: Nuclear Humanities in the Post-Cold War*, eds N. A. J. Taylor and Robert Jacobs. New York: Routledge, 2018.
Park, Soo-nam. *Mō hitotsu no Hiroshima: Ariran no uta* [Documentary Film], 1987.
Yoshiaki, Fukuma. *Shōdo no kioku: Okinawa, Hiroshima, Nagasaki ni utsuru sengo*. Tokyo: Shin'yōsha, 2011.

Preface
'Dangerous' memory – political theology of Johann Baptist Metz

> *[...] staring at reality, after [the atomic bombing], it was the indestructible nature of God's existence which I saw. The Lord God who holds all created things, the source of love and life is the God I know.*
>
> (Ozaki Tōmei)[1]

The atomic bombing of Nagasaki as 'dangerous' memory is the focus of this book. I incorporate the testimony of survivors as they ultimately question how the wider world remembers the ending of a horrific war which is currently in the process of moving beyond living memory. Initially, though, I must introduce Johannes B. Metz (1928–), a Roman Catholic academic theologian, who was the originator of the term 'dangerous' memory as 'political theology', drawing on the work of Walter Benjamin. In his book *Faith in History and Society* (1979) he outlined in detail his conception of 'dangerous' memory.[2]

When Metz was a 16-year-old from Auerbach in Bavaria in 1944, the German army took him out of school and forced him into the army. A life-changing moment occurred at the end of the Second World War, when one night, near the frontline, he was sent by his company commander to take a message to battalion headquarters. Having wandered all night through destroyed, burning villages and farms, he returned to his company to find it also destroyed.

In engaging with his own memory of this traumatic encounter as a youth, Metz describes how he came to employ theology in engaging with history and faith. He argued that faith and theology must 'turn to the world'. He believed that above all else memory of 'Auschwitz' had been suppressed from German society, Christian faith and theology.[3] For Metz a solution lay in the pursuit of an authentic 'Job-like spirituality of lamentation and complaint'; and an addressing of his protest to God, rather than seeking a conceptual-systematic answer.[4]

Essentially, Metz was suggesting that Christian communities might use the term 'dangerous' memory as they remember in their meta-narrative the story of an innocent person condemned to death by a mob (representing ordinary people) and their execution by the authorities. For Metz the shocking and 'dangerous' memory of Auschwitz posed serious and disturbing questions about the complicity of the church and of the wider society alongside the Nazi regime. Jürgen

Moltmann, a compatriot of Metz, proclaimed, 'theology is not church dogmatics and not a doctrine of faith. It is *imagination for the kingdom of God* in the world and for the world in God's kingdom.'[5]

I did not expect to find an explicit connection to Auschwitz when I began to examine the possibility that Metz's 'dangerous' memory would be applicable in Nagasaki. However, a connection soon became evident. One survivor, Ozaki Tōmei, had visited Auschwitz and Poland multiple times and written in Japanese about the haunting affinity between the two places (I elaborate in Chapter 8). Up to and after the time of the atomic bombing, on the other hand, having heard of the many Japanese atrocities and aggressive acts in war, many people around the world proclaimed the Japanese people guilty and deserving of death.

The ancestors of the Catholics who lived around what became the site of Ground Zero were themselves frequently persecuted, maimed, exiled and executed by the Japanese authorities, over many years. Thus, a central motif of this religious group was their ongoing commemoration of the difficult narrative as raised by Metz of 'the death of an innocent person' condemned due to their challenge to the ruling class or to subsequent forces of violence and repression.

This book, in striving to remember the social nuances of Nagasaki, avoids the reduction of the bombings to a mere tale of how the Japanese were victimised and aims to bring out at least some of the deeper resonances which emerge from the Nagasaki experience of the atomic bomb. Looking closer into the dangerous memory of Nagasaki through the lens of the collective biography presented in this book, we discern ordinary people affected by extraordinary forces, representatives of a microcosm of a Japanese society in which some were favoured and others neglected. These recollections of the atomic bombing confront the memories of war, and by raising previous persecutions and repressions they put in words a 'dangerous' memory for the Japanese nation and the colonial context of the time. Nagasaki as an atomic city has often been forgotten in favour of Hiroshima. Therefore, the focus of this work is not on the justification or undermining of nuclear or atomic weapons: other scholars write more directly on this topic.

After the war, faced with an interpretation of the bombing as a divine gift, or 'providence', many Catholics avoided revisiting their memories of the bomb, because they only reminded them of the utter devastation. However, as the survivors testify in this writing, a new era in which Catholic survivors are able to be more open and candid has dawned. Through this book I aim to allow those ordinary people, as Catholic survivors, to narrate their memory and show how they join Hiroshima survivors and the peace activists of Nagasaki to today speak of anger as opposed to only prayer. Meanwhile, in remembering the bombing from the northerly Catholic suburb of Urakami, those who speak today are reminded of their community's and ancestors' long-held survivor status, of an exilic legacy of persecution and of longer memories of martyrdom in and around this city.

I promote Metz's concept of 'dangerous' memory as a powerful and apt framework for research about the experiences of the Christian community in

Nagasaki. The methodology I utilised in the research for this book intentionally crosses the boundary between secular and sacred, investigating a community identity informed by spirituality and developed in the marginalised village of Urakami. Critical methodology employs the framework of 'dangerous' memory, to ensure that the historian questions, plays with possibilities, pays attention to silences, unlikelihood, contradictions, lies and errors. Suspicion is the standpoint of the historian, but also of the political theologian.[6]

Resisting the status quo

Metz's conception of how memories become dangerous for those by whom they are remembered is not simply memory of something dangerous. Memories flare up and unleash dangerous new insights about the past for the present, impacting on the speaker personally, on those around them and on the wider community. 'Dangerous' memories question hegemonic powers.[7] Both the powerful who oppress others for their beliefs and those subjugated because of their beliefs experience these memories as 'dangerous'. Metz points out that totalitarian governments typically undertake the destruction of certain memories or narratives.[8] In the context of Nagasaki, respectful engagement with difference through theology is a way of understanding Christianity in Japan. On the other hand, remembered suffering subversively resists the 'prophets of historylessness' (such as those who adopt 'victor's justice' and exclude the vanquished from history).[9] For Metz, subjugation begins when memories are taken away. Peace or freedom cannot be at the expense of the repression or silencing of other groups of people. Rather, the history of suffering acts to unite all men and women.[10] As well, the danger in 'dangerous' memory signifies essentially for Metz that such memories have a future impact and that they demand change. The future suggested is, controvertibly, for the oppressed; for the hopeless; for the disabled.

In other words, Metz's 'dangerous' memory demands that suffering be remembered. This memory questions the dominant paradigm, with a provisional future viewpoint of achieving justice for the oppressed.[11] He argues that a 'dangerous' memory of suffering suggests an understanding of politics out of which new possibilities arise. It reduces the gap between inhumanity and a possible humanity.[12] His critique is of histories which emphasise the successful who 'made the present', with no way of talking about the forgotten, the vanquished, the repressed and defeated.[13]

Theology and history

Religion may offer insights to historical and social interpretation. The 'exceptional character of evil' (Ricœur) is a topic of considerable difficulty for those who attempt critical analysis and explanation: at the same time, however, there is reluctance to consider religion and spirituality as possible avenues of analysis of extreme events. As feminist theologian Jenny Daggers suggests, 'to a secularising mind, Christianity is an antiquated mind anchored in the stream of no further relevance to modern civilisation'.[14] Christianity, religion and folk religion have become de-legitimised at least in areas of secularised academic scholarship. When faced with extreme events of trauma, an approach which takes historical study beyond the secular is worth exploration.

A second reason for incorporating theology is for its expressiveness and ability to decode narrative frameworks. By deployment of theology within historical method I consider the expressions, symbols, terminology and imagination of the subjugated group in question. Theological or religious language allows for creative expression within specific communities. As Paul Ricœur notes, '... to say [that something is] untransmissible is not to say inexpressible'.[15] Survivors commonly experience the traumatic in a transcendent sphere, outside time and even space. As a result, representing the experience of the atomic bombing remains difficult, as has been noted. 'The Shoah' and nuclear 'apocalypse' may only be expressed partially. Written documents, pictures, even movies are expressive, but never quite 'properly' remember these experiences. In Nagasaki as well as Hiroshima, the experience of the bombing has often been expressed in religious Buddhist and Christian terms as hell on earth.[16] The Urakami community is a modern day Christian Catholic community, despite its previous isolation from the wider church over centuries.[17] In its historical context, this 'faith-expression' was marginalised from its Western origins and within its Japanese context it was situated on the edges of Japanese cultural, political and economic life.[18] The community's understanding of the devastation caused by the atomic bomb is expressed through the lens of a group that was marginalised and accustomed to suffering, making its response characteristic. This book explores how the Catholic community's particularised understanding of history demonstrates resilience in suffering ascribed to the hope and comfort brought by faith.

Third, an imaginative theology, with awareness of suffering, considers what it is to be human. Such a theology is not exclusive but illuminates what the Nagasaki Christian community shares with the wider secular, Buddhist and Shinto Japanese communities. The sociological or class aspect of the analysis also acknowledges the existence of so-called *burakumin* (low-caste group), class systems, economic disadvantage and non-religious expressions of marginalisation. A distinct history of *burakumin* presence may be traced back to the Tokugawa era when untouchables in the district were frequently also *kirishitan*. Around 260 households of *burakumin* were located in southern Urakami in 1945 when the US army dropped an atomic bomb and at the time, social, political and religious forces dichotomised Nagasaki into the harbour town area and the heathen or Christian-*buraku* Urakami. David Tracy ascribes to theology an 'analogical imagination', affirming plurality and ambiguity and sharing (but not avoiding the differences) with other minority groups.[19] Through analogy, a 'dangerous' memory contributes its critique to the wider community.

In addition, theology allows for appraisal of the future arising from history. The historian Michael Frisch wrote 'It is history ... that can provide the basis for shared re-imagination of how the past connects to the present and the possibilities this vantage suggests for the future.'[20] Here, I consider present, future and hopeful perspectives as a part of the community's expression. 'Analogical' imagination and future-orientation anticipate history's continuation, although without definitiveness. 'Dangerous' remembering draws on the 'horizon of expectation' or a vision of the future.[21] The sacred memory in the present draws the individual and the community into the future, through a past event. For Metz, 'dangerous' memory recalls the element of anguish in Jesus' cry on the cross and an element of hopefulness, which can never be final. Metz's compatriot, Jürgen Moltmann, writes similarly:

> ... when faith confesses Christ, this cannot be a final ontological or factual judgment ... it is an anticipatory judgment of trust and confidence and therefore ... provisional in an eschatological sense.[22]

A major academic area elided by Metz but relevant to Nagasaki is that of trauma and memory.[23] Metz is criticised for this omission by trauma studies scholars including Flora Keshgegian, Johann Vento and Candace McLean, who take 'dangerous' memory further and in a different direction, through trauma studies.[24] The 'black hole' of trauma, argues Keshgegian, denotes an 'impossible history' carried by survivors and contributes to an ambivalence experienced around memory and time. The memory is 'dangerous' for the survivors themselves. Trauma studies, like 'dangerous' memory, deals with the interruption of history by the genocides of 6 million Jews, the Armenian massacres, Hiroshima, the Gulag, Cambodia and Uganda and the often-unmentioned Nagasaki.[25] Paul Ricœur writes of the suffering of the 'unacceptable' in history (such as genocide and trauma) which interrupts the historical record due to the 'exceptional character of evil'. Here is a 'black hole', an 'untransmissible' event, out of reach, impossible to explain or understand. The traumatised carry an 'impossible' history within them.[26]

Keshgegian's criticism of Metz's 'dangerous' memory suggests that it does not allow 'room for the ambiguity and provisionality that seem to be the lot of those who deal with trauma'. In Chapter 9, by the testimony of Fukahori Jōji, I engage with the issue of ambiguity, the inability of the trauma survivor to make sense of what happened. Keshgegian urges the inclusion of the 'other' without restriction, embracing complexity. Although I focus on survivors, I aim in this project to demonstrate how the narrators are not defined by their suffering and how their identity transcends the Japanese label of *hibakusha* (an atomic survivor/irradiated person).

Keshgegian notes that when Metz writes positively of the benefits of danger and irruption of memory, he neglects to show that for survivors of trauma, irruptions of memories of violence are a profoundly negative occurrence.[27] In the philosophy of trauma, scholars comment on a dichotomy between the impossibility of meaning versus the impossibility of finding no meaning in suffering.[28] I suggest that the ruins of the Urakami Cathedral near the hypocenter[29] of the bombing of Nagasaki up to 1959 (Figure 1.1) could be analogous to the negative symbol of the cross for the trauma sufferer. For Keshgegian, 'Suffering violence at the hands of others ought not to be, nor is it, meaningful or good.'[30] Keshgegian does not discuss Nagasaki, but in this light, she might view the existence of the ruins as symbolic of a 'black hole' for this community, acknowledging personal injury – physical, emotional and psychic. The ruins for the survivors invite re-traumatisation and re-entry into a black hole. This is not to say that Keshgegian would believe there is nothing in the ruins of Urakami Cathedral for recovery for the *hibakusha*. She is suggesting that there is a need for remembrance of more than only suffering. The ruins are not in themselves redemptive. Pain and disruption are accompanied by ambivalence and a great sense of loss. Therefore, as a researcher investigating a socio-cultural and living community, acknowledgement of the community's ongoing feelings of ambivalence is vital.

While examining 'dangerous' memory, I acknowledge the inherent ambiguity of suffering, loss and the impact of generational trauma. As interviewer, I acknowledge my own presence including the limitations of my own biases and subjectivity and I promote the survivors' co-authorship of this collective biography, through an ongoing exchange of materials and shared attention to secondary, visual and symbolic sources. Through this monograph I seek to allow those living in the Urakami community to speak and to tell their own stories, anticipating powerful connections between their personal memory, communal and public consciousness of history.

Notes

1. Tōmei Ozaki, *Jūnanasai no natsu*, Seibo bunko (Nagasaki: Seibo no kisha-sha, 1996), 56.
2. Johann Baptist Metz, *Faith in History and Society: Toward a Practical Fundamental Theology* (London: Burns & Oates, 1980).
3. Peter Scott and William T. Cavanaugh, eds, *The Blackwell Companion to Political Theology*, 1 ed. (Malden, MA: Wiley-Blackwell, 2006), 243–4.
4. Scott and Cavanaugh,*The Blackwell Companion*, 249.
5. Devin Singh, 'Resurrection as Surplus and Possibility: Moltmann and Ricœur', *Scottish Journal of Theology*, 61.3 (2008): 251–69 (261). I use Moltmann's original emphasis in italics.
6. Paul Ricœur, *Memory, History, Forgetting* (Chicago and London: University of Chicago Press, 2009), 317.
7. Jenny Daggers, 'Thinking "Religion": The Christian Past and Interreligious Future of Religious Studies and Theology'. *Journal of the American Academy of Religion* 78.4 (1 December 2010): 978–9, https://doi.org/10.1093/jaarel/lfq078.
8. Metz, *Faith in History and Society*, 1980, 105.
9. Johannes Baptist Metz, *Faith in History and Society: Toward a Practical Fundamental Theology*, 2 ed. (New York: Crossroad Pub. Co., 2007), 106.
10. Metz, *Faith in History and Society*, 1980, 102.
11. If Jesus's cry of 'My God, My God, why have you abandoned me?' on the cross is anguished, but also has an element of hopefulness, without ontological or factual judgement – it leaves open a possible future.
12. Metz, *Faith in History and Society*, 1980, 107.
13. Metz, *Faith in History and Society*, 1980, 107.
14. Daggers, 'Thinking "Religion",' 973.

15 Ricœur, *Memory, History, Forgetting*, 452.
16 For example, classic medieval texts such as the early thirteenth century *Hōjōki* describe fractured images as evidence of *mappō*, the Buddhist apocalypse or 'latter days of Buddhist law'. John W. Dower, *Ways of Forgetting, Ways of Remembering: Japan in the Modern World*, Reprint ed. (New York: The New Press, 2014), 153.
17 A significant proportion of so-called 'Hidden Christians' did not return to the Catholic church when offered the opportunity to do so, during the Meiji Restoration. Only about half did so, according to Christal Whelan. Christal Whelan, *The Beginning of Heaven and Earth: The Sacred Book of Japan's Hidden Christians* (Honolulu: University of Hawaii Press, 1996), 14. They are called 'Crypto-Christians' by some translators in view of their altered or hybridic beliefs.
18 Haruko Nawata Ward, *Women Religious Leaders in Japan's Christian Century, 1549–1650*, Women and Gender in the Early Modern World (Farnham, England; Burlington, VT: Ashgate, 2009). Ward's insightful book examines women's religious leadership prior to and during the isolation and oppression of the Christian community.
19 David Tracy et al., 'Review Symposium: Plurality and Ambiguity: Hermeneutics, Religion, Hope'. *Theology Today* 44.4 (January 1988): 499. Teruo Kuribayashi has delineated a *buraku* liberation theology, considering the experience of the *buraku* underclass in Japan. In Japanese and English, see Teruo Kuribayashi, *A Theology of the Crown of Thorns: Towards the Liberation of the Asian Outcasts* (Union Theological Seminary, 1987); Teruo Kuribayashi, *Keikan no shingaku: hisabetsu buraku kaihō to kirisutokyō* (A Crown of Thorns: Burakumin liberation and Christianity), 1 ed. (Tokyo: Shinkyō Shuppansha, 1991).
20 Michael Frisch, *A Shared Authority: Essays on the Craft and Meaning of Oral and Public History* (Albany, NY: SUNY Press, 1990).
21 Miroslav Volf, *The End of Memory: Remembering Rightly in a Violent World* (Grand Rapids, MI: W. B. Eerdmans Pub. Co, 2006), 100.
22 Jürgen Moltmann, *The Crucified God: The Cross of Christ as the Foundation and Criticism of Christian Theology* (London: SCM, 2001), 106.
23 Candace Kristina McLean, '"Do This in Memory of Me": The Genealogy and Theological Appropriations of Memory in the Work of Johann Baptist Metz', unpublished dissertation (University of Notre Dame, 2012), 290.
24 Johann M. Vento, 'Violence, Trauma, and Resistance: A Feminist Appraisal of Metz's Mysticism of Suffering unto God'. *Horizons*, 29.1 (2002): 7–22; McLean, '"Do This in Memory of Me"'; Flora A. Keshgegian, *Time for Hope: Practices for Living in Today's World* (New York: Bloomsbury, 2006).
25 Tracy et al., 'Review Symposium', 498. Trauma studies theologians challenge the view of history as progressive or linear, which has often been hegemonic.
26 Cathy Caruth, *Trauma: Explorations in Memory* (Baltimore and London: JHU Press, 1995), 5.
27 Keshgegian is quoted in McLean, 'Do this in Memory of Me', 296. On the other hand, Metz's project claims 'dangerous' memory disrupts sanitised views of history and life, rather than ignoring the negativity of memory of violence for victims. Still, Metz does not directly engage with trauma studies in his writing.
28 See for example Sean Field, 'Loose Bits of Shrapnel: War Stories, Photographs, and the Peculiarities of Postmemory'. *The Oral History Review* 41.1 (2014): 108–31. Also, Michael Roper, 'The Unconscious Work of History'. *Cultural and Social History* 11.2 (2014): 169–93 (184).
29 I will refer to the centrepoint of the bombing as the hypocenter (US Spelling) as this is the common word used in Nagasaki in English, or alternatively I will designate it as Ground Zero.
30 Keshgegian, *Time for Hope*, 124.

References

Butler, Judith. *Frames of War: When Is Life Grievable?* 1st ed. London and New York: Verso Trade, 2010.
Caruth, Cathy. *Trauma: Explorations in Memory.* Baltimore and London: JHU Press, 1995.
Daggers, Jenny. 'Thinking "Religion": The Christian Past and Interreligious Future of Religious Studies and Theology'. *Journal of the American Academy of Religion* 78.4 (1 December 2010): 961–90. https://doi.org/10.1093/jaarel/lfq078.
Diehl, Chad R. *Resurrecting Nagasaki: Reconstruction and the Formation of Atomic Narratives.* Ithaca, NY: Cornell University Press, 2018.
Dower, John W. *Ways of Forgetting, Ways of Remembering: Japan in the Modern World.* Reprint ed. New York: The New Press, 2014.
Field, Sean. 'Loose Bits of Shrapnel: War Stories, Photographs, and the Peculiarities of Postmemory'. *The Oral History Review* 41.1 (1 January 2014): 108–31. https://doi.org/10.1093/ohr/ohu019.
Frisch, Michael. *A Shared Authority: Essays on the Craft and Meaning of Oral and Public History.* Albany, NY: SUNY Press, 1990.
Keshgegian, Flora A. *Time for Hope: Practices for Living in Today's World.* New York: Bloomsbury Academic, 2006.
Kuribayashi, Teruo. *A Theology of the Crown of Thorns: Towards the Liberation of the Asian Outcasts.* Union Theological Seminary, 1987.
Kuribayashi, Teruo. *Keikan no shingaku: hisabetsu buraku kaihō to Kirisutokyō.* 1st ed. Tokyo: Shinkyō Shuppansha, 1991.
McLean, Candace Kristina. '"Do This in Memory of Me": The Genealogy and Theological Appropriations of Memory in the Work of Johann Baptist Metz'. Unpublished doctoral dissertation, University of Notre Dame, 2012.
Metz, Johann Baptist. *Faith in History and Society: Toward a Practical Fundamental Theology.* London: Burns & Oates, 1980.
Metz, Johannes Baptist. *Faith in History and Society: Toward a Practical Fundamental Theology.* 2nd ed. New York: Crossroad Pub. Co., 2007.
Miyamoto, Yuki. *Beyond the Mushroom Cloud: Commemoration, Religion, and Responsibility After Hiroshima.* New York: Fordham University Press, 2011.
Moltmann, Jürgen. *The Crucified God: The Cross of Christ as the Foundation and Criticism of Christian Theology.* London: SCM, 2001.
Ozaki, Tōmei. *Jūnanasai no natsu.* Seibo bunko. Nagasaki: Seibo no kisha-sha, 1996.
Park, Soo-nam. *Mō hitotsu no Hiroshima: Ariran no uta* [Documentary Film], 1987.
Ricœur, Paul. *Memory, History, Forgetting.* Chicago: London: University of Chicago Press, 2009.
Roper, Michael. 'The Unconscious Work of History'. *Cultural and Social History* 11.2 (1 June 2014): 169–93. https://doi.org/10.2752/147800414X13893661072717.
Scott, Peter, and William T. Cavanaugh, eds. *The Blackwell Companion to Political Theology.* 1st ed. Malden, MA: Wiley-Blackwell, 2006.
Singh, Devin. 'Resurrection as Surplus and Possibility: Moltmann and Ricoeur'. *Scottish Journal of Theology* 61.3 (2008): 251–69. https://doi.org/10.1017/S003693060800402X.
Tracy, David, Mark Kline Taylor, Sallie McFague, Jeffrey Stout and Sharon Welch. 'Review Symposium: Plurality and Ambiguity: Hermeneutics, Religion, Hope'. *Theology Today* 44.4 (January 1988): 496–519.

Vento, Johann M. 'Violence, Trauma, and Resistance: A Feminist Appraisal of Metz's Mysticism of Suffering unto God'. *Horizons* 29.1 (2002): 7–22. https://doi.org/10.1017/S0360966900009695.

Volf, Miroslav. *The End of Memory: Remembering Rightly in a Violent World*. Grand Rapids, MI: W. B. Eerdmans Pub. Co, 2006.

Ward, Haruko Nawata. *Women Religious Leaders in Japan's Christian Century, 1549–1650. Women and Gender in the Early Modern World*. Farnham, England; Burlington, VT: Ashgate, 2009.

Whelan, Christal. *The Beginning of Heaven and Earth: The Sacred Book of Japan's Hidden Christians*. Honolulu: University of Hawaii Press, 1996.

Yoshiaki, Fukuma. *Shōdo no kioku: Okinawa, Hiroshima, Nagasaki ni utsuru sengo*. Tokyo: Shin'yōsha, 2011.

Acknowledgements

I am most grateful to my *sempai*, Yuki Miyamoto, a scholar who herself has spent a long period of time considering religious responses to the atomic bombings. Miyamoto asks an astute question, who actually owns memory, in the thoughtful foreword she contributed for this book. I wish to make special mention of my academic supervisor, Beatrice Trefalt (Monash University), for her incredible support of this project, her knowledgeable and astute advice and her continual encouragement of my writing. Thank you also to Series Editor Mark Selden, who gave generously of his time to offer astute advice and comments on the text.

Without the prodigious support of my wife and family I would not have been able to complete the research and writing involved in completing this manuscript. In 1999, I travelled to Nagasaki with my wife and daughter and was struck by this city and the atomic bomb museum. Nine years later, I went once more with my eight-year-old son, who asked two *hibakusha* about the experience of the atomic bombing, 'Was your family alright?' Keren, thank you for accompanying me along the entire journey, for your generous and ongoing thoughtfulness, ideas and creativity.

I have received significant support from Monash University and a 2015 Japan Studies grant from the National Library of Australia allowed me to consolidate my knowledge of the Japanese literature. Countless people generously gave of their time in assisting my research and writing, all of whom I have not mentioned here – thanks. Special thanks to my mother and father, to Jono, Lydia, Geordie, Paul Glynn, Ernest Koh, Christiaan Mostert, Ross Langmead, David Chapman, Mark Brett, Nishimura Akira (Tokyo University), Shijō Chie (Nagasaki University), Tokusaburō Nagai, Takahashi Shinji, Renzo De Luca, Takazane Yasunori, A'nan Shigeyuki, Kasai Kenta, Murayama Yumi, Roger Munsi, Hagimori Etsuko, Iwanami Chiyoko, Shiōra Shintarō and Miyazaki Yoshio. Also, thanks Kate Cregan, Alistair Thomson, Mayumi Shinozaki, Yayoi Nikakis, Jeremy Breaden, Basil De Caux-Casuhac, Jenny Hall, Richard Flynn, Fiona McCandless, Takuya Kojima and Levi Durbidge for your support. Finally, Mark Selden, Stephanie Rogers and Georgina Bishop have ably supported me at Routledge throughout the publishing process.

Figure 0.1 Urakami Cathedral ruins, black and white drawing by Nagai Takashi, c.1946, used by permission, Nagai Tokusaburō, 21 January 2019.

Part I
Legacy of survival

1 Fissures

Urakami hibakusha have it [the germs] [...] *so you shouldn't go near them* [...] *they said.*

(Matsuo Sachiko, 2014)

Introduction

When the United States dropped the second atomic bomb in wartime on 9 August 1945, its air force deployed it on an already 'fissured' place, divided by religion. Many years earlier in seventeenth-century Nagasaki, executions and persecutions aiming to expunge Christianity drove the believers underground (Figure 1.1). Hidden Christians remembered these persecutions by place: the Nishizaka slopes, on which the faithful had been executed, marked the stark

Figure 1.1 Depiction of the 1622 martyrdom of Spinola (and others) at Nishizaka slopes, photograph, 6 July 2015, used by permission, National Library of Australia, public domain.[1]

4 *Legacy of survival*

religious division of Nagasaki, with Urakami in the north and the harbour town in the south. In that sense, religion and the processes of marginalisation that came with it created a historic divide in Nagasaki. Those who held onto faith remembered executions by re-conceiving of the liminal Nishizaka slopes as a 'new kind of sacred space'.[2] For the Christians, Nishizaka symbolised the legendary biblical execution place of 'Golgotha'. Here was an accursed place, outside town, arousing 'dangerous' memories of death.[3] Through a new oral history in this book we may observe how Catholic survivors consciously and unconsciously associate the experience of the bomb with a long history of marginalisation and suffering. This history of the bomb, as a collective biography, presents new understandings about the specific nature of Catholic atomic bomb memory.

The United States bombing magnified the 'fissured' nature of Nagasaki. The citizens experienced the main impact of the bombing in the Urakami suburban area, the home to the Catholic minority, rather than the centre of town as in Hiroshima's case. The US bombing resulted in the wholesale destruction of the biggest Catholic community found in Japan at the time, largely situated around the hypocenter in the northern suburb of Urakami (see Map 0.1 in the preface and Figure 1.2). The bomb was said to have killed 8500 Catholics out of 12,000, destroying the community, flattening the cathedral and kindling questions about

Figure 1.2 Urakami valley: valley of death, US Marine Corp, 1945, public domain.

faith and survival.[4] Due to cloud cover limiting visibility and a dangerous lack of fuel, the pilots released the bomb not above the initial city target, but slightly earlier. The bomb exploded 1650 feet above the Urakami valley, exerting the equivalent force of 22,000 tons of TNT, compared to 12,500 tons of TNT in Hiroshima three days earlier.[5] Whereas people found casualties up to 3.5 kilometres from the hypocenter of the Hiroshima bombing, casualties in Nagasaki were scattered up to 4 kilometres from the blast.[6] Yet the harbour city of Nagasaki was not nearly as badly impacted as Hiroshima, owing to the hilly topography of the city which shielded substantial districts from the bomb. Therefore, recovery from the destruction was highly differentiated in the two regions of Nagasaki. By late 1945, a newspaper reported that people on one side of Nagasaki city were rejoicing and dancing in the Suwa shrine *o-kunchi* Festival, while those on the other (in Urakami) mourned at a church.[7]

Differentiated impacts

The atomic bombing accentuated Nagasaki's spatial differentiation. Urakami's landscape was obliterated. Pictures of the damage wrought by the atomic bomb show the main destructive power and the lesser impacts in the harbour town (Figure 1.2). Nagasaki citizens observed that Urakami, the northern suburb, was more devastated than Nagasaki city, which recovered at a faster rate. Given the contrasts experienced by the populace, understanding the bombing requires the elucidation of the socio-economic and religious distinctions. Yet there is very little written about how the Nagasaki Catholics understood the bombing, especially after the early years post-war. Most writers have not examined closely the connections between the atomic bomb and earlier Catholic experiences of persecution and marginalisation.[8]

The interactive online Nagasaki Archive reveals a vacant space in the centre, with few faces and testimonies – a lacuna which is representative of the widespread loss of Catholic narratives.[9] It was many years before those who survived from Urakami would speak of their experiences. On the outskirts of northern Urakami and in the southern region of the city, however, there are many witnesses' faces and comments. This writing turns to the emptiness around the hypocenter, symbolising as it does major silences and rupture within the Catholic remembering of the atomic bomb. The absence of witnesses reflects the disproportionate death toll of a large segment of the community, the damaged landscape and broken societal fabric and a long-lasting dearth of discourse and testimony in Catholic Urakami.

In this book, a focus on attempted meaning-making in the aftermath of trauma enables attention to be turned to these silences. I examine a variety of symbols and literary tropes which emerged from interviews and which demonstrate new and evolving forms of public memorialisation of an event such as this one.

The interviews I conducted with survivors of the atomic bombing between 2014 and 2018 centre on the historical experience of the community of Urakami which I describe in this book. I interviewed with the generous assistance of the Nagasaki Atomic Bomb Museum and contacts, in pre-arranged places, such as museums, libraries and Catholic institutions. Nine of the atomic bomb survivors interviewed in this project identified as Catholics and three did not. I began the interviews by asking about family backgrounds and pre-bombing memory and followed up by discussing the day of the bombing and subsequent experiences. I introduce the survivors in the next chapter.

The community recollection of a long history of trauma and persecution after 1597 extending throughout the Tokugawa period and beyond was important for the Catholic interviewees. Since the initiation of the Tokugawa proscription on Christianity, the Japanese authorities had often gagged the Secret Christian/Catholic community or blotted it out of the historical record. Representatives of the Tokugawa and later the Meiji regimes carried out persecutions, executions, massacres and exiles sporadically between 1597 and 1873. The community recalled these events orally and community historians wrote accounts of them. The persecutions became known as *kuzure*, indicating the crushing or crumbling of secret groups of Christians.[10] Researcher Tsuruta Bunshi dates four renowned Urakami persecutions sequentially to 1791, 1839, 1856 and finally 1867–73.[11] When the atomic bomb was dropped on Nagasaki, as my participants told me, the *yon-ban* (or Fourth) Persecution was still in living memory for the very oldest members of the community.

Many years after the practice of Christianity became legal during the Meiji regime, the history of violence and memory of discrimination continued to form a barrier between the people of the old Nagasaki city and the Urakami region.[12] The prohibition of Christianity was lifted in 1873 and the Urakami Christians returned, but religious stratification was still evident. Nagasaki city folk called the Urakami Christians names such as *Kurō*, *Kuroshū* (derivatives of 'cross') and *kirishitan* and the Catholics in turn called the townsfolk *Zenchō* (from the Portuguese *gentio* meaning Gentile).[13] A memoir retold by Japanese historian Shijō Chie recounts an incident in communal life in 1897 (thirtieth year of Meiji), 24 years after the prohibition on Christianity had been lifted:

> As a Christian brought vegetables in to the outskirts of Nagasaki city, from Urakami, a bystander yelled: '*Kurō ga kita! Kurō ga kita! Kuroshū da zo! Yankuro Jōmonji dazo.* [It's a cross! it's a cross! It's a cross! It's a Christ Cross!]' I thought, 'Christians are a weird species, sub-human' … And the Christian was chased away by the bystander throwing stones.[14]

The disjuncture between people of different religious or socio-economic backgrounds is still noted by interviewees. Survivor Konishi Shin'ichi discussed in his interview the discrimination against Urakami by those who considered the suburb to be 'Christian' and that it continued to be a backward region socio-economically. The city folk perceived Urakami as a rural backwater, where people were uneducated and not as wealthy as those in Nagasaki's town area:

> 裏ですね．裏の神であつてから，山，おくのほうに裏神ですね．
>
> *ura desu ne. ura no kami de atte kara, yama, oku no hou ni urakami desu ne.*

It is behind (Ura). Because it is the behind or 'bottom-god', the behind-side of the mountain or hill, (i.e. *ura – kami*. The Chinese characters used here are different to those used for the suburb of Urakami and indicate a god or spirit, *kami*).[15]

According to Konishi, the Nagasaki townspeople derided the Christians of Urakami and their worship of another god, calling the Christian god a 'bottom', or backward god. The townspeople's historic disparagement and religious discrimination against the country-folk, who lived in a 'backward' region and worshipped a god who lacked in strength, underpinned this statement.

'Two faces' of Nagasaki

Stark socio-economic realities in the post-war period are behind the ongoing depiction of 'two faces' of Nagasaki, consistent with the history of the Catholic populace and their links to a *burakumin* underclass. Writers proclaimed in post-war tourist publications that the old city of Nagasaki was the *akarui yu no Kao* (明るい湯の顔 warm, welcoming face of the hot springs) and the northerly location of Urakami was the *kage no kao* (影の顔 shadowy face).[16] Isomoto Tsunenobu, who lived in *burakumin* (outcaste) Urakami, wrote that 260 households of *burakumin* were located in southern Urakami (Urakami-chō) in 1945 when the US army dropped the atomic bomb (although no overlap with the Catholic population is recorded).[17] Takahashi Shinji, local academic, described old Nagasaki as a town split into what he calls *nijūkōzō* (二重構像), his own terminology to describe the two distinct areas, created alongside each other.[18] Into the twentieth century, social, political and religious forces dichotomised Nagasaki into two: the harbour town area and the heathen Christian Urakami, divided by the boundary marker of Nishizaka (see Map 1.1). The townspeople were still aware of these divisions even as Urakami was officially made a part of Nagasaki city after 1920, when the city boundaries were extended. Thus, Urakami was not a part of the city of Nagasaki in the Tokugawa period and at the time of the suppression of the Christians.

Cartographers marked the Urakami Cathedral, 26 martyrs' site, prefectural building and the United States' ABCC (Atomic Bomb Casualty Commission) office, as landmarks onto a map in 1953 (Map 1.1).[19] The city council no longer officially recognised Urakami town, although it is clearly labelled on the map, next to the international cemetery. The map shows topographical and geographical features which differentiated the impact of the bomb on places, including hills, harbour, rivers and valleys. Urakami is located on the left-hand side of the map, the main city to the right and Nishizaka close to the river mouth and the main railway station.

As we have seen, although the United States did not deliberately target Urakami, the action of dropping the atomic bomb on Nagasaki intensified the already outstanding fissure in Nagasaki. The atomic bomb's impact made the historic demarcation between Nagasaki city and the Urakami district more

Map 1.1 Panorama shiki Nagasaki kankō annai-zu Map 151 (1953) used by permission, Nagasaki History and Culture Museum, 21 December 2018.

noticeable.[20] Both the Catholic populace and other townspeople who lived in Nagasaki drew various religious conclusions about the nature of divine punishment and grace from the differences in impacts.

The tourist map (Map 1.1) reflects the ongoing perceptions of Nagasaki citizens about the city's post-war geography. Broken into a map and a topographical depiction of the city it shows the significance of the geographical features of mountains and harbour. The cartographers depicted two faces of the city, Urakami and Nagasaki 'harbour town'. The artists who drew the impression incorporate a picture of an almost innocuous mushroom cloud at the hypocenter in Urakami, contrasting with the action of ships evident in the harbour of the city. The Urakami River dominates the valley, the Urakami.

The cathedral is marked on the lower map (on the far-left side) and on the upper illustration the building ruins are vaguely visible behind the mushroom cloud. On the city side, as well as the boat routes, the train terminal next to Nagasaki station and the network of trams visible depict a more active region than Urakami. The northern region is portrayed by the mushroom cloud, the Peace Park and Peace Hall.

Cleansing Urakami

In the post-war period, Catholic interviewee Fukahori Jōji remembered how urban revitalisation and road-widening usurped a part of his family's land.[21] Residents felt that their needs were disregarded when the city's reconstruction of Urakami was implemented with disregard for their needs. It was not only the Catholics who were affected. City officials utilised the reconstruction to clean up the down-at-heel suburb of Urakami at the expense of the *hisabetsu burakumin* (lit. the discriminated against outcaste community). Dōmon Minoru writes that by this project, 'the Urakami *burakumin* were neutralised (dispersed)…'[22] Land acquired compulsorily and cheaply by the council forced the *burakumin* to take refuge elsewhere.[23] In the *burakumin* region, landlords put up 'no trespassing' signs and wire fences and sold the land where the community had lived. Before 1945, few roads led through Urakami, but a new network of roads was developed which required new space, streamlining Nagasaki's traffic through the down-at-heel neighbourhoods. The council purportedly erased the neighbourhood where those identified as *burakumin* had lived, by building these wide roads.

Shijō Chie (Research Center for Nuclear Weapons Abolition, Nagasaki) writes that the main difference between the two atomic bombs was the total destruction of Hiroshima versus the partial destruction of Nagasaki.[24] Due to the remarkable geographical differences in impacts of the bombing a large proportion of Nagasaki society emerged comparatively untouched, in contrast to the shattered Urakami region, which was impacted more intensely than any locality in Hiroshima (with the exception of Ground Zero).[25] After the 1957 establishment of medical compensation by the Japanese government, survivors in both Hiroshima and Nagasaki often defined themselves by relating the distance they were from the bomb's hypocenter.[26] Given the topography, in Nagasaki the contrast of the impacts is much greater between the absolute levelling experienced by those caught near the hypocenter, compared to the experience of those in the less affected areas of the city and beyond the hills.

Recognising the specific nature of Nagasaki's bomb experience in his 1995 book, *Writing Ground Zero*, John W. Treat described this city's 'atomic literature' as being also qualitatively distinct. The amount of writing about the atomic bombing in Hiroshima has tended to eclipse that about Nagasaki. Still, Nagasaki's historical sensitivity to social discrimination, Treat continued, was attested to by the tendency to locate the bombing in literary genres describing issues of class, racial, religious and gender differences.[27] In this book, I aim to add to the growing recognition of Nagasaki's specific atomic bomb experience, by examining the Catholic experience of the bombing.

I use the term Urakami to distinguish the largely Catholic area, and the *burakumin* populated town area, from the Nagasaki city region, although I note the city office officially allocated new names for the suburb in the post-war period. In modern times, city folk still know Urakami 'unofficially' as the area surrounding the Urakami River and Urakami station exists to this day. Townsfolk call the surrounding regions various names including Mezamemachi, Iwakawamachi, Hamaguchimachi and Heiwamachi (Peace-town). The historical record demonstrates how the Catholic community in Urakami survived and re-emerged after the bombing. Before and during the early Meiji period, *sempuku* (secret) Christians lived in the same region. Researchers relate that across Nagasaki Prefecture in 1873, after over 250 years of bans on Christianity, around 14,000 of 20,000 'Secret Christians' re-joined the Catholic Church.[28] A large number of the Catholic believers settled in the region where 'Secret Christians' had previously lived in Urakami, north of Nagasaki city.

Japanese Christianity and Urakami

Christian identity in Japan is broad, especially since the Second World War. The older name for Christian (*kirishitan*) in Japanese refers to the group who are descended from the first wave of Christian converts in the seventeenth and eighteenth centuries and is particularly relevant to the history of the Urakami Catholics. This group is also known today as *Katorikku* (Catholic). *Sempuku* refers to the hidden and secret believers, at the time when Christianity was officially banned in Japan, from whom the Urakami *kirishitan* are descended. *Kakure*, in addition, is the title given to those *sempuku* who did not return to Catholicism after the ban on Christianity was lifted, many of whom may have retained syncretistic Buddhist, Shinto and Catholic faith practices. The modern name in Japanese for Christian is *kurisuchan*.

In present-day Urakami landmarks testifying to both the A-bomb and Nagasaki's Catholic heritage are visible for those who walk through the region. Such landmarks are central to the narratives introduced in the text and worthy of brief introduction. The Nagasaki Atomic Bomb Museum is located alongside the Peace Park, which incorporates the hypocenter (Ground Zero) of the bombing of

9 August 1945. Ruins from the original Urakami Cathedral, built by the community after their return from exile in the early twentieth century, are found in the Peace Park (Chapter 6) and have been re-created in the Atomic Bomb Museum, while the rebuilt cathedral is a regional landmark on top of a small hill 500 metres to the north-east of the museum.

The liturgical and religious life of Urakami Catholicism reminds locals of their public history. When I visited the Urakami Cathedral in February 2016, the banner on the left-hand side at the front of the church stated: 'Emulate the strong faith which your ancestors showed towards the *tabi* (exile) and pass it on to your descendants.'[29] The public narrative remembered their past travail and the peoples' faith is recounted as pulling them through hard times. In the parish sheet, a sentence stated: 'Just as we have been carried in a history of martyrdom, so as God's people, even now we live in new persecution ...'.[30] The modern survivors are influenced by their communal history and by remembering their past, including martyrdoms, exile and suffering.

Another feature in the landscape is Nyokodō, to the north-west of the cathedral, a tiny preserved hut where the Catholic doctor Nagai Takashi spent his remaining days before his death in 1951. Nagai gained prominence in the post-war period both for his publication of memoirs and stories of the bombing and for a theology in which he designated the experience of the bomb a (burnt) sacrifice, made by Urakami inhabitants, for the benefit of humankind (Chapter 5). Nyokodō is 500 metres from Urakami Cathedral and tourists commonly visit this shrine to Nagai's memory.

Distinct from atomic memory, but a reminder of martyrdom, Nishizaka Hill is located in the direction of central Nagasaki from Urakami. The 26 martyrs' monument stands here in memory of the 1597 crucifixions of the foreign priests and Japanese Christians. The Urakami River, near the hypocenter, was devastated by the bombing and runs from north to south towards the old Mitsubishi factory and the harbour. Two schools which feature in survivor narratives are Yamazato Elementary School and Junshin Girls' High School to the north. Shiroyama Elementary School is on the western side of Matsuyama town tram stop.

Memory, public narrative and history

In this book, I explore an interplay in discourse on memory and history between personal memory, communal memorialising and layers of public narrative. In particular, I seek to elucidate ways in which this discourse both challenges and draws on official and privileged narratives of history, to contribute to a better understanding of the multiple processes of marginalisation of minority groups. I define memory as knowledge of the past, embodied and performed in interaction between individual and group, or self and society.[31] I will refer to Urakami Catholic narratives as wider communal lay remembering rather than official Catholic remembering. The Catholic Church put out official publications which referred to the atomic bombing, but was silent when it came to publishing atomic memoirs.[32] On the other hand, a small number of

12 *Legacy of survival*

Catholic survivors such as Akizuki Tatsuichirō published their own memoirs of the bombing.[33]

The book is organised into three main sections. I begin with the Catholic legacy of survival. I introduce the survivors and their varied contexts in Chapters 1 and 2. By August 1945 this community was characterised by a silenced landscape, rubble and remains. In Chapter 3, I describe how the opening up of the survivors' testimony necessarily engages in the difficult memory of bodies in a desecrated landscape. The *kataribe* (storytellers) task begins here. I explore the relevance of landscape to understand a public history of sociological and religious fissure in Nagasaki. 'Dangerous' memory of bodies in the landscape after 1945 superimposed a subsequent cleavage on the older public memorialisation of suffering and executions in Nishizaka and other locations. Centuries earlier, social and religious stratification through the authorities' historical persecution of the Christian and 'hidden Christian' communities began at the centre of town and proceeded to the margins. Over time, this persecution and its aftermath resulted in the dividing of Nagasaki by the northern slopes of Nishizaka into the old 'harbour' city and the outer valley of *kirishitan* Urakami.

The second section focuses on Catholic interpretations of the atomic bombing. Initially, the bombing was described as a 'burnt sacrifice' by Catholic doctor Takashi Nagai, tending to intensify 'survivor' guilt among the survivors. Silence was induced among many survivors as a result. After Nagai's death, scholars accused him of adopting the image of a violent God, who required the sacrifice of the people. He was also accused of exclusivism, honouring only the pure, innocent Urakami believer. The Catholic community and others in Nagasaki seldom spoke of their experiences, nor did they publish about the bombing for 40 years, but I examine how survivors challenge this initial interpretation. Eventually, many of the survivors (not all) openly protested about the violence of the bomb.

The Nagasaki visit of Pope John Paul II in 1981 and new levels of political engagement by atomic bomb survivors within the Christian community contributed to a gradual metamorphosis in the ways the Catholic people remembered the bomb, challenging Nagai's theory. The subversion of this interpretation or theology of a bomb that was required as a sacrifice by God continues.

An analysis of the alternative symbolic interpretations of the atomic bombing proved fruitful in the interviews. Chapters 5–7 engage with symbols which open up alternative narratives to a 'sacrificial' understanding. I discuss the 'trampled, hidden' archetypal Mary in Chapter 5 as a figure of veneration in historic persecution and how a new A-bombed Mary after the bombing was a symbol of life, survival and of holy presence. The articulation of Mary's symbolism in the aftermath of the bombing may be traced to a long veneration of Mary and traditions which assisted in keeping faith in the past. Mary, Mother of Christ, as divine presence in the aftermath of the bombing may be compared to *kannon* and *fumi-e* symbols which represented Mary for ancestral hidden Christians. Mary statues in the atomic rubble are described alongside memory of the *fumi-e* trampling pictures of the Edo period and Mary as *kannon*, a 'goddess' Buddha. Some of the interviewees revere 'fractured' Mary *hibakusha* statues recovered since the bombing and link Urakami's 'suffering Holy Mother' of the past, to the Peace-Mary of the present.

I move on from the representations of Mary to St Mary's Cathedral, the centre of worship for the community, which was destroyed and became an icon in ruins, only 500 metres from Ground Zero. Between 1945 and 1959, the monument of the ruins of the Urakami Cathedral was visited by many tourists and served as a visible representation of the ruin of Nagasaki. The replacement building for the Catholics, though, represented resilience and resistance. Today, an ongoing controversy in civil Nagasaki continues over the lost opportunity to retain the symbolic Urakami Cathedral ruins as a civic memorial. The loss of the ruins is lamented by secular citizens and non-Catholic authors as the missing 'atomic bomb dome' of Nagasaki. The Catholics razed the ruins of the cathedral in 1959, which had drawn many tourists up to that date. Today, Hiroshima has reserved the atomic bomb dome for posterity and it is known around the world, while Nagasaki lost this symbolic ruin. I revisit the debate about this building, incorporating added discussion by the survivors within this project. The survivors are reconciliatory, yet through personal photos from past eras their testimony contributes to a richer understanding of this building, which is to them not solely an atomic relic. The rebuilt cathedral recalls persecution and anticipates the future for the Catholics, showing resilience and resistance to victimhood for the marginalised Christian group. The cathedral as monument contributes to understanding the bombing from the perspective of Urakami.

The third symbol examined is a memory of audible pain, the trope of a suffering 'cry for water'. Nagasaki and Hiroshima narratives recall this 'cry for water' frequently and as part of this collective biography this cry represents 'dangerous' memory. The suffering 'cry for water' is also evident 70 years before 1945, in survivor Kataoka Chizuko's great-grandmother's account of the public narratives of the 'Fourth Persecution'. In Chapter 7, I initially analyse Miyake Reiko's experiences at the Urakami River alongside Nakamura Kazutoshi's memory of a boy who cried for water. Still, today the Urakami river invokes challenging scenes of the dying and suffering in 1945. As well as the human cost, atomic warfare wrenches the environment – represented especially by invisible radioactivity – and I add to the analysis the interpretation of the Urakami river as a symbol of cleansing in the modern landscape. The memory of the cry for water remembers impotence, broken through by the Catholic survivors' new role as *kataribe* and opening up the assertion of indignation and protest.

The final section of the book shows how lament and anger turn to protest in the voices of the *kataribe*, imitating Job of the biblical text. The community recalls the story of this survivor. The future content of the survivors' dangerous memory of the experience of atomic suffering incorporates their prophetic voice. Catholic survivors, traditionally reticent to be involved, are increasingly involved in peace activities and speak about their wartime experiences. Some acknowledge Japan's aggression in war and the Shōwa Emperor's complicity in the Second World War. I discuss how the orphaned Ozaki travelled to Auschwitz

14 *Legacy of survival*

and researched a link from Nagasaki to the Polish monk who instituted a Nagasaki orphanage and whose death is remembered as a narrative which stood against Nazi violence. In addition to Ozaki's explication of a direct connection from Nagasaki to the suffering experienced in Auschwitz, shattered statues of Mary have been exchanged between the Urakami and a Spanish Catholic community in Guernica, Spain.

In the final chapter, orphaned Fukahori Jōji laments the 'illogical' in his encounters with dead bodies and family members who perished due to the atomic bomb. His harrowing narrative of the death of his siblings prefaces the *hibakusha* protest against American and Japanese violence and implicitly questions the divine. Survivors in Nagasaki raise Job as a relevant story of survival and so I compare the Urakami survivors' narratives to Job's tale of suffering and loss. The emotional, caricatured figure of Biblical literature, Job, first praises God, before cursing the day of his own birth. The survivors' lament transforms into a 'rhetoric of protest'.[34]

Notes

1 Tokihide Nagayama, *Kirishitan shiryōshū*, Zōtei saihan (Nagasaki-shi, Tokyo: Taigai Shiryō Hōkan Kankōkai, 1927).
2 Carla Montane, 'Sacred Space and Ritual in Early Modern Japan: The Christian Community of Nagasaki (1569–1643)' (PhD diss., University of London, 2012), 115. See also Haruko Nawata Ward, *Women Religious Leaders in Japan's Christian Century, 1549–1650*, Women and Gender in the Early Modern World (Farnham, England; Burlington, VT: Ashgate, 2009), 325.
3 I use the term dangerous memory as introduced by Metz and describe how he uses this term in the preface. See Johann Baptist Metz, *Faith in History and Society: Toward a Practical Fundamental Theology* (London: Burns & Oates, 1980), 112.
4 Kyoko Iriye Selden and Mark Selden, *Atomic Bomb – Voices from Hiroshima and Nagasaki* (Armonk, NY: Routledge, 1990), xxi.
5 Michael Kort, *The Columbia Guide to Hiroshima and the Bomb* (New York: Columbia University Press, 2007), 4.
6 Yuko Matsunari and Nao Yoshimoto, 'Comparison of Rescue and Relief Activities Within 72 Hours of the Atomic Bombings in Hiroshima and Nagasaki'. *Prehospital and Disaster Medicine* 28.6 (2013): 536–42 (538).
7 Kazuhiko Yokote, *Nagasaki kyū Urakami tenshudō 1945–58: ushinawareta hibaku isan* (Tokyo: Iwanami Shoten, 2010), 74.
8 One reason is that historians have in the past avoided oral testimony, believing memory may play 'tricks' and jeopardise the credibility of research. In validation of oral history and memory, Dominick LaCapra writes that memory's tricks are themselves able to be validated through historical scrutiny and that memory adds to or corrects written histories. Dominick LaCapra, 'Trauma, History, Memory, Identity: What Remains?'. *History and Theory* 55.3 (2016): 375–400 (382).
9 Nagasaki Shinbun, *Nagasaki Archive*, Archive (Nagasaki: Nagasaki Shinbun, 2016), accessed 23 April 2019, http://e.nagasaki.mapping.jp/p/nagasaki-archive.html.
10 It is not clear when the magistrate began to call these persecution incidents *kuzure*, but the word in Japanese implies that Christianity was wiped out or decimated. Sunaaya Aoyagi, 'Sotome chiku ni okeru kakure kirishitan to chishukyo to no kakawari no henka: Karematsu jinja no sairei wo jirei ni', Chirigaku Fiirudowaaku

Fissures 15

Nagasaki no chiiku chousa (Tokyo: Ochanomizu University, Autumn 2009), 47, http://133.65.151.33/ocha/bitstream/10083/33478/1/gfw2008aoyagi.pdf.
11 Bunshi Tsuruta, *Seikai no kirishitan bunka souran: Amakusa, Shimabara, Nagasaki, gaikai, Ōmura, Hirado, Seitsuki, Goto, Nishikyushu Kirishitan shi nyumon* (Nagasaki: Seibo no kisha-sha, 1983), 143. The dates cited by Tsuruta have been corroborated in a recent book by Takayama Fumihiko, although Takayama records the first *kuzure* was in 1790, rather than 1791. Fumihiko Takayama, *Ikinuke sono hi no tame ni: Nagasaki no hisabetsu buraku to Kirishitan* (Ōsaka: Kaihō Shuppansha, 2016), 146.
12 Takahashi, *Nagasaki ni atte*, 196; Nobuo Takahashi, 'Nagasaki Peace Site: Nagasaki no shisō to Nagai Takashi' (Nagasaki: 1 August 2000), accessed 10 July 2017, www.nagasaki-np.co.jp/peace/2000/kikaku/nagai/nagai1.html.
13 Shinji Takahashi, *Nagasaki ni atte*, 200.
14 Yan refers to the kanji or Chinese characters for *yaso* or Christ (耶蘇). The author's translation from Chie Shijō, *Urakami no genbaku no katari: Nagai Takashi kara Rōma kyōkō e* (Tokyo: Miraisha, 2015), 40.
15 I have used *kanji* and hiragana characters to show how a play on homophones which use different characters is described. *Kami* means spirit or god in Japanese. Shin'ichi Konishi, interviewed by Gwyn McClelland, Nagasaki Atomic Bomb Museum, 1 October 2014.
16 This quote is taken from a publication of 1972 by Nihon Hosō Shuppan Dōkai, entitled '*Nagasaki ... bakushinchi katsuden no kiroku*' and described in Shijō, 38.
17 Nagasaki-ken buraku shi kenkyusho, ed., *1945.8.9 Nagasaki: Furusato wa isshun ni kieta: Nagasaki/Urakami cho no hibaku to ima* (Nagasaki: Kaihō Shuppansha, 1995), 2.
18 Shinji Takahashi, *Nagasaki ni atte*, 198.
19 The ABCC, a US research institution to study the results of the atomic bombing, was viewed by many Nagasaki locals with ambivalence, as it was not intended to assist the survivors, but for scientific research in the service of the United States. As a result, the commission was accused by some researchers of using human survivors as guinea pigs. Laura E. Hein and Mark Selden, eds, *Living with the Bomb: American and Japanese Cultural Conflicts in the Nuclear Age*, 3rd ed. (Armonk, NY: Routledge, 2014), 58.
20 Shijō, *Urakami no genbaku no katari*, 188.
21 Jōji Fukahori, interview by Gwyn McClelland, Nagasaki Atomic Bomb Museum, 10 January 2014.
22 Minoru Dōmon, 'Bundan sabetsu no rekishi wo koete wakai he [Ikinuke, sono hi no tame ni nagasaki no hisabetsu buraku to Kirishitan)', *Christian Today*, 12 May 2016, accessed 3 July 2017, www.christiantoday.co.jp/articles/20857/20160512/ikinuke-sonohinotameni.htm.
23 Kenta Mori, 'Genbaku wa hito ni nani mo tarashita no ka: chiriteki kankei kara nagasaki wo kaishaku suru', *Waseda shakai kagaku kenkyu*, 2008, 36, https://dspace.wul.waseda.ac.jp/dspace/bitstream/2065/32390/1/ShakaiKagakuSougoKenkyu_S_2009_Mori.pdf.
24 Shijō, *Urakami no genbaku no katari*, 54.
25 Shijō, *Urakami no genbaku no katari*, 54.
26 Lisa Yoneyama, *Hiroshima Traces: Time, Space, and the Dialectics of Memory* (Berkeley: University of California Press, 1999), 113.
27 John Whittier Treat, *Writing Ground Zero: Japanese Literature and the Atomic Bomb* (Chicago: University of Chicago Press, 1995), 302–8.
28 *The Cambridge History of Christianity: Volume 8, World Christianities c.1815–c.1914*, eds Sheridan Gilley and Brian Stanley (Cambridge, UK; New York: Cambridge University Press, 2005), 509.
29 The *tabi* which they remember was a part of the Fourth Persecution, during the 1860s and 70s. I explain this exile further in Chapter 3 of this book. As I will describe, over

16 *Legacy of survival*

    3000 men, women and children who were suspected to be hidden Christians, were transported to 22 different locations around Japan.
30 It is not immediately clear what is meant by a 'new persecution', or whether this is intended as a metaphor.
31 E. Byron Anderson, 'Memory, Tradition, and the Re-Membering of Suffering'. *Religious Education* 105.2 (2010): 124–39 (125). There are also specific features of traumatic memory, which have an impact on self-identity and relationships. See Elizabeth O'Donnell Gandolfo, 'Remembering the Massacre at El Mozote: A Case for the Dangerous Memory of Suffering as Christian Formation in Hope'. *International Journal of Practical Theology* 17.1 (2013): 75–9, https://doi.org/10.1515/ijpt-2013-0006. Marianne Hirsch, *The Generation of Postmemory: Writing and Visual Culture after the Holocaust* (New York: Columbia University Press, 2012).
32 Shijō, *Urakami no Gembaku no Katari*, 162.
33 Tatsuichirō Akizuki, *Nagasaki gembaku ki: hibaku ishi no shogen* (Nagasaki: Nagata, 1966).
34 The Old Testament scholar Walter Brueggemann writes of the Israelites' similar rhetoric which emerges from a 'matrix of hope'. Brueggemann also refers to 'dangerous memory' in his book, *Cadences of Hope*. Walter Brueggemann, *Cadences of Home: Preaching among Exiles* (Louisville, Kentucky: Westminster John Knox Press, 1997), 119.

References

Akizuki, Tatsuichirō. *Nagasaki genbaku ki: hibaku ishi no shogen*. Nagasaki: Nagata, 1966.
Anderson, E. Byron. 'Memory, Tradition, and the Re-Membering of Suffering'. *Religious Education* 105.2 (30 March 2010): 124–39.
Aoyagi, Sunaaya. 'Sotome chiku ni okeru kakure kirishitan to chishukyo to no kakawari no henka: Karematsu jinja no sairei wo jirei ni'. Chirigaku Fiirudowaaku Nagasaki no chiiku chousa. Tokyo: Ochanomizu University, Autumn 2009. http://133.65.151.33/ocha/bitstream/10083/33478/1/gfw2008aoyagi.pdf.
Brueggemann, Walter. *Cadences of Home: Preaching among Exiles*. Louisville, KY: Westminster John Knox Press, 1997.
Dōmon, Minoru. 'Bundan sabetsu no rekishi wo koete wakai he (Ikinuke, sono hi no tame ni nagasaki no hisabetsu buraku to Kirishitan)'. *Christian Today*, 12 May 2016. www.christiantoday.co.jp/articles/20857/20160512/ikinuke-sonohinotameni.htm.
Fukahori, Jōji. Interview by Gwyn McClelland. Nagasaki Atomic Bomb Museum. 10 January 2014.
Gandolfo, Elizabeth O'Donnell. 'Remembering the Massacre at El Mozote: A Case for the Dangerous Memory of Suffering as Christian Formation in Hope'. *International Journal of Practical Theology* 17.1 (2013): 62–87. https://doi.org/10.1515/ijpt-2013-0006.
Gilley, Sheridan, and Brian Stanley, eds. *The Cambridge History of Christianity: Volume 8, World Christianities c.1815–c.1914*. Cambridge, UK; New York: Cambridge University Press, 2005.
Hein, Laura E., and Mark Selden, eds. *Living with the Bomb: American and Japanese Cultural Conflicts in the Nuclear Age*. 3rd ed. Armonk, NY: Routledge, 2014.
Hirsch, Marianne. *The Generation of Postmemory: Writing and Visual Culture after the Holocaust*. New York: Columbia University Press, 2012.
Konishi, Shinichi. Interview by Gwyn McClelland. Nagasaki Atomic Bomb Museum. 1 October 2014.

Kort, Michael. *The Columbia Guide to Hiroshima and the Bomb*. New York: Columbia University Press, 2007.
LaCapra, Dominick. 'Trauma, History, Memory, Identity: What Remains?' *History and Theory* 55.3 (1 October 2016): 375–400. https://doi.org/10.1111/hith.10817.
Matsunari, Yuko, and Nao Yoshimoto. 'Comparison of Rescue and Relief Activities Within 72 Hours of the Atomic Bombings in Hiroshima and Nagasaki'. *Prehospital and Disaster Medicine* 28.6 (2013): 536–42. https://doi.org/10.1017/S1049023 X13008832.
Metz, Johann Baptist. *Faith in History and Society: Toward a Practical Fundamental Theology*. London: Burns & Oates, 1980.
Montane, Carla. 'Sacred Space and Ritual in Early Modern Japan: The Christian Community of Nagasaki (1569–1643)'. PhD diss., University of London, 2012.
Mori, Kenta. 'Genbaku wa hito ni nani mo tarashita no ka: chiriteki kankei kara nagasaki wo kaishaku suru'. *Waseda shakai kagaku kenkyu*, 2008. https://dspace.wul.waseda. ac.jp/dspace/bitstream/2065/32390/1/ShakaiKagakuSougoKenkyu_S_2009_Mori.pdf.
Nagasaki Shinbun. 'Nagasaki Archive'. Archive. Nagasaki: Nagasaki Shinbun, 2016. http://e.nagasaki.mapping.jp/p/nagasaki-archive.html.
Nagasaki-ken buraku shi kenkyusho, ed. *1945.8.9 Nagasaki: Furusato wa isshun ni kieta: Nagasaki/Urakami chō no hibaku to ima*. Nagasaki: Kaihō Shuppansha, 1995.
Nagayama, Tokihide. *Kirishitan shiryōshū*. Zōtei saihan. Taigai Shiryō Hōkan. Nagasaki-shi; Tokyo: Taigai Shiryō Hōkan Kankōkai, 1927.
Selden, Kyoko Iriye, and Mark Selden. *Atomic Bomb – Voices from Hiroshima and Nagasaki*. Armonk, NY: Routledge, 1990.
Shijō, Chie. *Urakami genbaku no katari: Nagai Takashi kara Rōma kyōkō e*. Tokyo: Miraisha, 2015.
Takahashi, Nobuo. 'Nagasaki Peace Site: Nagasaki no shisou to Nagai Takashi 3'. Nagasaki Shinbun Archive. 'Genbaku wa kami no setsuri ka', 1 August 2000. www. nagasaki-np.co.jp/peace/2000/kikaku/nagai/nagai1.html.
Takahashi, Shinji. *Nagasaki ni atte tetsugakusuru: kakujidai no shi to sei*. Shohan. Tokyo: Hokuju Shuppan, 1994.
Takayama, Fumihiko. *Ikinuke sono hi no tame ni: Nagasaki no hisabetsu buraku to Kirishitan*. Ōsaka: Kaihō Shuppansha, 2016.
Treat, John Whittier. *Writing Ground Zero: Japanese Literature and the Atomic Bomb*. Chicago: University of Chicago Press, 1995.
Tsuruta, Bunshi. *Seikai no kirishitan bunka souran: Amakusa, Shimabara, Nagasaki, gaikai, Ōmura, Hirado, Seitsuki, Goto, Nishikyushu Kirishitan shi nymon*. Nagasaki: Seibo no kisha-sha, 1983.
Ward, Haruko Nawata. *Women Religious Leaders in Japan's Christian Century, 1549–1650*. Women and Gender in the Early Modern World. Farnham, England; Burlington, VT: Ashgate, 2009.
Yokote, Kazuhiko. *Nagasaki kyū Urakami tenshudō 1945–58: ushinawareta hibaku isan*. Tokyo: Iwanami Shoten, 2010.
Yoneyama, Lisa. *Hiroshima Traces: Time, Space, and the Dialectics of Memory*. Berkeley: University of California Press, 1999.

2 Survivors

> […] *Whatever the case, I hold no grudge against God. It [the bomb] was a trial for humankind* […]
>
> (Nakamura Kazutoshi, 2016)

Introduction

Interviewees include eight men and four women, including a nun and a monk (Figure 2.1). All the interviewees experienced the bomb as children, teenagers or

Figure 2.1 Montage-photographs of survivors, 2008–16, top-left to right: Enju, Matsuo, Nagase; centre-left to right: Fukahori Joji, Fukahori Shigemi; bottom-left to right: Mine, Konishi, Kataoka, used by permission, the author.

young adults and remember the bomb through the lens of 70 years of post-war life. Five were aged between 15 and 20 years in 1945 and seven between six and eleven years old. Many were protected by the topography of Nagasaki, scattered as they were around Urakami at the time (see Map 0.1 prior to the Preface). Two of them were located less than 1 kilometre from the hypocenter and others returned soon after the bombing to find their destroyed houses in the space adjacent to Ground Zero. I draw in this book on the 12 survivors' varied experiences to understand their faith/non-faith view and to construct a collective biography. By discussing the often misunderstood and largely missing history of the Nagasaki Catholics in the post-war era, I draw on a multi-voiced, interpretive narrative, rather than a collection of individual stories.

Although I focus on Catholic remembering, the inclusion of non-Catholics and other community members allows for alternative perspectives highlighting the specificity of Catholic narratives.[1] Kataoka and Ozaki provide an occasional 'official voice', but the survivors are mostly 'unofficial' or 'ordinary' Catholics. Fukahori Jōji, Matsuo Sachiko, Nakamura Kazutoshi, Konishi Shin'ichi, Mine Tōru and Nagase Kazuko forthrightly represent the lay-person Catholic. The non-Catholic voices of Miyake Reiko, Nishida Kiyoshi and Enju Toshio provide important balance and alternative points of view. Oral historian Alessandro Portelli argues that oral sources are important for marginalised groups of people.[2] He also emphasises the need for a range of sources. Among the 12 *hibakusha*, or survivors, some have broken their silence about the bombing only recently, although others are more practised at speaking out.[3] Their life experiences are broad and they demonstrate varying emotional and intellectual reactions to the interview process.

Kataribe is a title given to witnesses of the atomic bombing in Japan with authority born of direct experience to tell their stories and the survivors can claim this role. They find prophetic agency by the narrative of witness and as *kataribe*.[4] The interviewees gain an opportunity to be change-agents by their speech, a role dependent on those listening. By allowing ordinary people to reflect on their memory, through an ongoing interaction and negotiation with public layers of history, I hope to contribute to the subverting of the status quo of the 'great men' of history.[5] I acknowledge the interviewees' testimonial and co-authoring role. Memory and emotion are 'troublesome ideas' in history and anger and rage empower, providing grounds for political activism and the space to contest unequal power relationships.[6] Scholars discuss testimony and witness at length in the literature of the Holocaust and in Latin American and African American church traditions. The Latin American *testimonio* appeals to truth, dependent on individual narration, from the position of group experience.[7]

It is significant that the survivors were children or youths at the time of the bombing. In the case of major experiences of war, however, the passing of time does not significantly impede their memories.[8] Nonetheless, their testimony should be considered carefully, weighing up the passing of time and the likely addition of other narratives to the 'composure' or interpretation of their history. Four were orphaned and of the others, three lost one parent, leaving them vulnerable and struggling for survival. Some show resilience, relying on peers and trusting adults and relatives to assist them during the especially difficult years immediately after the war. Others struggled, could not work and faced suicidal thoughts, despair and hopelessness. Many were supported by educational institutions, religious groups or figures and neighbourhood communities. I introduce the interviewees below.

Before the bombing

The survivors are of assorted ages and varying family backgrounds. Their testimony may be put into context by understanding better their situations prior to the bombing. Miyake Reiko was the eldest of the interviewees at the time, a 20-year-old non-Catholic teacher at *Shiroyama kokumin gakkō* (Shiroyama State School) in Urakami in 1945. Many Catholics were school children in this school, including interviewee Nagase Kazuko. The day before the bombing, Miyake had gone with other teachers to Nagayo village to weed a rice field the school rented to provide food for their pupils. Miyake remembers she had left some clothes at school, so returned to pick them up in the afternoon. Arriving at the school, she met some of the members of the young men's association carrying *tatami* mats to place in the school, for night watch. Although it was late, she helped them carry the mats inside. As she looked so tired after her busy day, another teacher told her to come in late the next day. If she had gone to school as usual, she would have been caught up in the bombing and would have become another statistic.[9]

Nagase Kazuko (seven years old in 1945) lived in the same suburb, Shiroyama, where Miyake's school was destroyed. Nagase had a disability which prevented her from walking and was born into a family who had recently moved to Nagasaki from the rural township of Hirado. She said in an earlier interview that people called her a lively little girl before the bombing, despite her condition.[10] She had nine brothers and sisters, although all but four had moved to other locations for work by 1945. In August, she was at home with her parents, an elder sister, two elder brothers and one younger brother, very close to Ground Zero at the time of the bombing.

Nishida Kiyoshi (aged 16 in 1945), student in the *shōgyō gakkō* (School of Commerce), was 700 metres away from the hypocenter in the Nagasaki hospital, with its attached medical school at the time of the bombing, on the first floor of the main building (*honkan*).[11] A total of 80 per cent of the patients and staff died in the hospital, but Nishida survived.[12] The bomb did not level the hospital completely as it was a large ferro-concrete structure. This hospital was the location where Nagai Takashi also survived the bombing, in his work as a doctor.

Fukahori Jōji's family had previously lived in Shimonoseki, the southernmost point of Honshū island, where his father was an administrator working for Japan Rail, but his father died when he was in Grade 6. Although his mother came from Kumamoto, he moved to the old city of Nagasaki with his siblings and his mother to be near his father's family three years prior to the bombing of

Nagasaki. In his interview, Fukahori says that in Shimonoseki there were not many Catholics and he remembers noticing the sizeable community when he moved to Nagasaki.[13] Fukahori attended confirmation classes at the church, but says he could not remember the content, because he could not concentrate. All he recalls now of these lessons are a few gospel stories. One year before the bombing, the family moved from the city centre of Nagasaki to rural Urakami, under the misconception they would be safer.

Mine Tōru grew up in Nagoya, where his father had moved to work for the arms company, Mitsubishi. Mine used to capture dragonflies with a friend at the Yada River there. He remembers visiting the Nagoya Higashi-yama zoo often. It had penguins, giraffes and elephants and Mine said that it was known as the top zoo in the East.[14] However, his father became sick and died in 1944. Therefore, when Mine was nine, his family moved back to their hometown of Nagasaki and he lived in Hirado district with his mother, older sister, little brother and two baby sisters. Mine's home at Hirado on Mount Inasa was 2.5 kilometres from Ground Zero of the bombing. On the morning of 9 August, Mine's mother set out to his aunt's place in Urakami, to fetch some food supplies. She went missing and was never found in the chaos after the bombing. Mine's older sister at the time was 12, his younger brother five and his two younger sisters were one and three years old.[15]

'Clara' Tagawa Wasa, Ozaki Tōmei's mother, was a descendant of the hidden Christians and told Ozaki about the path of the 26 martyrs of 1597. Ozaki's story recalls the colonial context of wartime Japan up until 1945, because he was born in a northern Korean coastal town in 1928, where his father was a butcher. When the Urakami Catholics returned from their exile in the 1870s, as the land was not sufficient for farming, a number of them turned to butchery, traditionally an occupation dominated by the Urakami *hisabetsu burakumin* (outcaste) community.[16] Ozaki's father died when the boy was ten years old.[17] His father had been born in Sotome, Nagasaki, a descendant of the *sempuku kirishitan* and his mother was also a descendant of the *kirishitan*. At 13 years of age, Ozaki contracted spinal tuberculosis, precipitating a move back to Japan with his mother. He was hospitalised for a period in Nagasaki, although he also remembers going to Mass at Urakami Cathedral. In 1945, at 17, having recovered, he travelled each day from Urakami to a tunnel factory in Akakō, north of Urakami, where he assisted in the war effort, building torpedoes and armaments.[18]

Several interviewees were members of large families and households. Matsuo Sachiko, 11 years old, lived in Ōhashi in a household with 20 people, including her parents, grandparents, brothers and sister and sisters-in-law. Matsuo's family were long-term locals in the Urakami area. She described her family's horse and cart business, started by her great-grandfather after the family's return to Nagasaki from the Fourth Persecution in the 1870s. She remembered life before the bombing as rich, describing abundant rice and vegetable fields around their big house, where she lived with many children.[19]

Nakamura Kazutoshi's ancestors openly became Catholics in the sixth year of Meiji (1873) at the end of the *kuzure* persecution, from their *sempuku* background.

Nakamura Kazutoshi was 11 years old in 1945 and remembered singing Latin songs at the cathedral before the bombing. He lived on a farm with a large family 500 metres from what would be Ground Zero.[20] He had two little brothers and two baby nieces who lived with his family. Nakamura recalls his mother and father were enthusiastic Catholics and he was happy to participate in church life as a child. On the day of the bombing, Nakamura set out on an errand with his mother in the morning to a locality known as Honbara ni-chōme, over the hill from home. A local boy invited Nakamura to stay on and play and he was therefore not in the Urakami Valley at the time of the bombing.

Fukahori Shigemi lived in his familial home immediately beside Urakami Cathedral as a child, though by age 15 he had moved to a dormitory at the Ōura Seminary, pursuing the possibility of becoming a priest.[21] Fukahori's mother died during the war, but his father and five brothers and sisters lived at home. Fukahori remembered living next to the Urakami Cathedral and that every day after school he and other children would not return home straight away but would go directly to the church and study there. The church was not just a place of prayer, but a place of education and of play. 'We really entertained ourselves there, at the church!' he said. At the time of the bombing, Fukahori was working in a Mitsubishi factory at the shipyard making torpedoes and his father was working in a tunnel factory. His older brother had been called up by the army to the war and was not in Urakami at the time.

Konishi Shin'ichi lived in a house near Ōura Cathedral in old Nagasaki, part of the fourth generation of Catholics there since the time of the *sempuku kirishitan*.[22] Born in 1939, Konishi was six years old at the time of the bombing. Ōura is south of the city of Nagasaki, so he was not as badly impacted by the atomic bomb as those survivors who came from Urakami.

Kataoka Chizuko, seven years old in 1945, prefers not to discuss her own family's experiences of the atomic bomb. She is willing, on the other hand, to discuss her impression of the community's recovery from the war. Her father, Yakichi (1908–80), was a prolific writer and historian of the *Sempuku Kirishitan* and the Catholics of Nagasaki. He was a professor at the Junshin Girls' 2-year University, where Kataoka Chizuko later became Principal. Yakichi wrote about the experiences of his grandmother, as recorded in a diary. She was caught up by the Fourth Persecution in Urakami and was exiled along with her four children. Kataoka Chizuko followed in her father's academic footsteps, authoring and co-authoring various books and articles before I interviewed her in 2016.

Along with Miyake and Nishida, Enju Toshio provides a non-Catholic perspective on experiences after the bombing. Enju was born in a Buddhist family in Inasa district and remembers the fear which beset him when he had to enter bomb shelters with his family, after hearing enemy aeroplanes.[23] Enju, along with Nagase Kazuko, is cared for today in the Catholic old people's home, the *Gembaku Hōmu* (Atomic Bomb Home) at Megumi no Oka.

Kataribe: voicing the horror

One reason the survivors speak and show their emotions is because they take on the role in Japan as *kataribe*, or storytellers. Becoming a *kataribe* is a challenging calling to a public, civil society role. The label *kataribe* originally described Japanese storytellers who travelled from place to place and recited tales for entertainment but came to be a term which described the *hibakusha* who remembered the atomic bombings. In the years after the war, Nakamura Kazutoshi tried and failed to forget his experiences. Laid low by radiation sickness and medical ailments, Nakamura considered suicide before he decided to speak. Eventually, prompted by his health problems, he decided not to stay mute, finally becoming a *kataribe* at the age of 71:

> Because I wanted to forget, after the war, I didn't talk to anyone. Still, I had a lot of sickness, which went on and on: heart sickness, liver [...] And then, when I thought I would die [...] to die without speaking out would be the worst. I had something I could say, in some shape or form [...] about the awful atom bombing [...] So [...] I decided to become a *kataribe* [...] Even the things you most don't want to talk about, better not to die silent, but to say how the atomic bomb was horrible and war is a terrible thing for little children [...] [so,] putting aside my 'not wanting to speak', I decided to talk.[24]

Nakamura talks for the sake of 'little children' to influence the future. Still, speaking about the atomic bomb is 'horrible' – a 'dangerous' memory also for his audience.

Other Catholic interviewees similarly took a long time to become *kataribe*, partly due to the danger which they ascribe to the role for themselves. Mine Tōru took up the role at 70 years old in 2006 and Fukahori Jōji at age 84 in 2009. Like Nakamura, Fukahori struggles with the 'dangerous' content of his narrative. He mentions the telling of 'horrible, painful things'. He implies that the content and manner of speaking for a *kataribe* is of importance and that his calling is to 'speak truth'. He describes his role:

> Listen. It is now only five years since I became one [a *kataribe*] [...] as much as possible, [speaking of] horrible things, painful things I [had] tried and tried to forget [...] And [...] [previously] I thought I would be able to forget. Already, it is sixty-five or seventy years that have passed [...] [To say] What happened, [with] no additions, nothing taken away, no lies. The reality [is made] believable [because it is] told by many people.[25]

Despite the horror and danger of discussing his memory, Fukahori hints that a collective narration is of importance in making reality 'believable'. He aims to share the danger, confronting his listener with the reality of what happened.

Four interviewees' styles of discussion were particularly eloquent, likely due to their differing educational opportunities. Three whose interviews were articulate and well-spoken included Miyake Reiko, the school teacher, Kataoka Chizuko, previous Principal of Junshin University, and Ozaki Tōmei, Brother in the *Seibo no Kishi* order. The latter two Catholics have previously contributed to scholarly work in Urakami Catholic public history, writing books about the bombing and their hidden Christian ancestry. They tend to refer to other books and their own writing in the interviews. As well as his own books, Ozaki has published in local, national newspapers, online and on his personal blog.

Intersubjectivity

Holocaust survivor Avraham Kimmelman said, 'I never had a problem, to talk, with the right people. I need a confidant. I need someone ... who I feel is worthy of hearing my story...'[26] Thus, the *kataribe* seek listeners: witnesses require an audience. The audience fulfils the requirement for a listener, someone who will accompany the speaker. Miyake, Matsuo, Fukahori Jōji, Nakamura and Nagase yearn for someone to listen, an audience for the memory (although the telling must proceed with care).[27]

In my interview with Ozaki Tōmei, he asked to photograph me, asking some questions and taking down notes. Coming across his blog a few days after the interview, I found the blog post which reflected upon his encounter with me, an Australian researcher. The photo shows me on the tatami mat floor next to his bed, in the Franciscan old people's home, where I conducted the interview. Researcher turned subject, Ozaki's post demonstrates his consciousness of my presence within the interview and his comprehension of details such as my age, Australian nationality, Japanese ability and perspective. Ozaki himself demonstrates how my own analysis of empirical knowledge about structures, contexts and meanings of 'others' is impacted by my 'locatedness' within the research, and the combination of my own subjective experience with the experiences of my research subjects.[28]

As Ozaki showed me, this collective biography incorporates my voice as the interviewer, a 'presence' in the room. My background as theologian suggests empathy and yet I am an outsider, a non-Catholic and a male, non-Japanese interlocutor. Oral history's subjectivity in the space between the interviewer and the interviewee becomes a strength, providing clues to meanings and relationships.[29] The emotional residues of the past shape unconscious transference from the informants, as well as my own responses to the data.[30] The interview process opens up relationships between the narrator and the audience as between events of the past and the narrative in the present.[31] In the case of Catholic Nagasaki, interviews reconstruct knowledge where archival records cannot describe aspects of life, including emotions and domestic experience.[32] My interpretations as historian consider layers of meaning in the stories of the Catholic survivors with whom I co-write.

I incorporate pictures and images in this book, although interpreting the visual record is not an easy task. I am grateful for Nagai Tokusaburō's permission to print three poignant pictures his grandfather painted/drew of the ruined Urakami

Cathedral. Nagai Takashi's paintings of the ruins of the Urakami Cathedral after the bombing provide a visual dimension not present in photographic images, nor in his spoken or written texts (Figure 2.2). The painting reprinted here he completed in early 1946 and is an example of how difficult it is to interpret visuals such as this. Nagai depicts a southerly view, towards Nishizaka and the mountains. Without the possibility of a primary interpretation by Nagai, the painting, which may be viewed imbued with colour in Urakami at the reading room Tokusaburō manages, may be viewed as putting a positive spin on a negative event, encouraging those left behind to look forward and move on, aligned to his theology of God's grace.

The intersubjective lens recognises Nagai's grandson, Tokusaburō, and his unfolding agency in co-constructing knowledge.[33] As a member of the second generation since the bombing, Tokusaburō's perspective adds the possibility of atomic post-memory, or generationally transmitted memory, in his interpretation of the painting.[34] I interviewed Tokusaburō in Urakami twice in this project, as the current museum director of Nyokodō, and I was aware of the haunting of memory across generations, not only through public history, but also through private and unspoken communication within families.[35] Discussing his grandfather's interpretation of the bombing, Tokusaburō says:

> As himself, [Nagai Takashi], he [intended] … encouraging words, I believe. For the sake of those who would always be disappointed by the loss of

Figure 2.2 Nagai Takashi's painting of the Urakami Cathedral ruins, used by permission, Nagai Tokusaburō, 21 January 2019.

26 *Legacy of survival*

people who had died. In other words, *Mae muite, arukou* ... [Look forward and walk] To those who say [he intended] otherwise, it was look forward, do your best and move on. That's what I think he wanted to say.[36]

Tokusaburō interprets his grandfather's words in a subjective and located context. Catholic communal narrative recalls Nagai Takashi's interpretation of the atomic bomb from the end of 1945 until his death in 1951. Nagai imagined God's 'providence' and grace even in the bombing of Urakami. Tokusaburō suggests his grandfather worked to encourage, out of the rubble of disappointment and death: 'Look forward, do your best', supporting the view that the picture drawn by Nagai encourages the community forward.

An alternative interpretation of Nagai's painting, however, subverts the interpretation I outlined above. When Nagai Takashi drew this picture he was likely reflective and ambivalent about the remains of the building, which represented death, and the wider communal mourning including for his wife, who died in the bomb. This picture of the ruins of the cathedral, therefore, may represent an alternative, rare and somewhat circumspect perspective for Nagai, the belief in war as the work of humanity, apprehension about God, and subverting the interpretation of the atomic bomb as a providential form of 'grace'.

Personal photographs and pictures convey an uneasy relationship between public and personal memory in the narrative of the interviewees. By analysis of a photograph or image I consider both the denotation (literal or manifest meaning) and the connotations (cultural associations, ideas and symbolic meanings) relevant in each case.[37] The point of view of the photograph, its audience, its context and explanation is of importance. For example, the atomic ruins of the cathedral, as well as the rebuilt cathedral and its representations, are understood from pictures, drawings and images, in varying ways.

Locating the interviewees

The map inserted prior to the Preface in this monograph illustrates the location of ten of the interviewees at the time of the bombing on 9 August 1945.[38] The survivors were spread around Urakami and the hypocenter, mirroring the religious community's focus in this area. The hilly topography of the north protected many of the interviewees. Fukahori Shigemi was working in the Mitsubishi factory at the time (Labelled FS). The main Nagasaki station is adjacent to this location. Nagase Kazuko was closest to the hypocenter (NagK) in Shiroyama. Six of the *hibakusha* were located on or behind hills, including Matsuo Sachiko (MS), at a high elevation on Mount Iwaya. Fukahori Jōji (FJ) was building armaments at his school in Nishizaka. Nakamura Kazutoshi (NaK) lived relatively close to the hypocenter but had gone out with his mother and stayed behind to play with a friend. He was protected from the blast by the undulations and hills behind the Urakami Cathedral. Mine Tōru and Miyake Reiko were both at their homes on the slopes of Mt Inasa, to the west (MT, MR). Only one interviewee, Konishi (KS), was in the old harbour city at the time of the bombing. He was standing in front of the Mary statue at the Ōura Cathedral, he remembers in his interview, after going to classes to prepare for his first communion.

Situations and subjectivities

Similarities and differences between interviewees were evident. Those who had reached a certain age by the time the bomb was dropped were employed. One, Miyake Reiko, was working as a teacher at Shiroyama National Elementary School. Three Senior High School age students, Fukahori Jōji, Fukahori Shigemi and Ozaki Tōmei, were working in 'war-service', producing armaments.

An important characteristic for their later life experience was the extent of injuries sustained by survivors, correlating to some degree with relative distance to Ground Zero (indicated by the star on Map 0.1). The bombing caused injuries to Nishida Kiyoshi and Nagase Kazuko and consequent issues plagued them in ensuing years. Nagase had a problem from birth with her legs, which left her in a wheelchair. However, her kidney ailments and symptoms of radiation sickness eventuated in her moving into an elderly people's home by her late 30s.[39] Nakamura Kazutoshi mentioned the burden of his sicknesses in his interview. Others, such as Miyake and Konishi Shin'ichi, suffered minor injuries, such as being struck with glass fragments which had to be removed. Family trauma and loss was a significant distinguishing factor for most Catholic survivors. At least three became orphans, five lost their mothers and Matsuo's father died. Faced with familial devastation, one survivor later in life tried to kill herself and three others talked or wrote in memoirs about the 'temptation' of suicide. There should be no assumption that all survivors were equally resilient and hopeful.

The genre of 'collective biography' provides knowledge about 'ways in which individuals are made social...', seeking not 'totalizing truths but particular, local and situated truths'.[40] Oral historian Valerie Raleigh Yow quotes psychologist Katherine Nelson's statement, 'Autobiographical memory ... is highly personal and idiosyncratic, but never escapes its social and cultural boundaries.'[41] This book engages in cultural exploration, pressing forward to elaborate on meaningfulness, with a wariness of the subjectivity of its findings. Private memory is overlaid with social and cultural codes and the ongoing 'sedimentation' of public narratives. To be thought of as historical, this biography will draw on both oral and written sources, in an exploration of how individuals relate to their specific society.[42]

Questions, faith and religion

After extreme traumatic events such as the atomic bombings and the Jewish Holocaust, people of faith question God's will or existence. This was also true of many Urakami Catholics. The atomic bombing raised questions about the nature and location of the divine. The nine I interviewed had various ways of understanding their own Catholic religious cosmology. Theology as 'faith seeking understanding' benefits from dialogue with universal themes crossing Catholic-Protestant, Buddhist-Shinto and secular delineations.[43] Such theology depends upon the motto of 'faith asking questions and struggling to find provisional answers'.[44] The *hibakusha* lay believers and those with church office seek to make sense of their experiences through reference to transcendence, even as their memories clash with or incorporate public history and authority.

Japanese and Western commentators have regularly compared the piety of Nagasaki Catholics to the bitterness and anger which emerged in Hiroshima, by quoting a Japanese popular saying, *ikari no Hiroshima, inori no Nagasaki*, or 'Hiroshima rages, Nagasaki prays.'[45] The assumption that Nagasaki symbolises passivity and prayer is problematised by the re-examination of Catholic public narratives.[46] Journalists and visitors to the city who have tried to understand a relative lack of resistance have concluded that the Nagasaki populace is more passive and tolerant, whereas citizens of Hiroshima more obviously protest the atomic bombs and angrily revisit the confronting past. Lisa Yoneyama discusses how in the 1970s, during the Vietnam war, the phrase *ikari no Hiroshima* was popularised. Peace activist protests turned violent upon the then Prime Minister Eisaku Satō's attendance at the Hiroshima commemoration of 6 August in 1971.[47] In contrast, Nagasaki Catholic survivors insist upon the precedence of prayer over protest. For this and other reasons, the 'Hiroshima atomic experience' has become the paradigmatic official history of the impact of the bomb in Japan, singularly dominant over Nagasaki in public histories of 'the atom bomb'.[48] Many of my interviewees openly challenge the slogan that Nagasaki prefers prayer. The survivors demonstrate an ambivalence about forgiveness, show anger and transmit a determination to resist the acceptance of the atomic bombing as inevitable.

Current and past church involvement and levels of adherence to Catholicism are variable, although two of the interviewees, namely Kataoka and Ozaki, joined Catholic orders, as a nun and monk respectively. Fukahori Shigemi describes how he had entered a seminary with a view to becoming a priest. This did not eventuate, but he held an ongoing semi-official role in the modern Urakami church as a lay-person. In the early twenty-first century, he was responsible for installing in the Urakami Cathedral a fragmented Mary statue which had survived the bombing, mentioned in Chapter 5.

As for connections with religious institutions, Mine Tōru and Ozaki Tōmei were assisted as orphans by the *Seibo no Kishi* monastery, an institution started by Polish monks. Ozaki (at 17 years) became a monk in October of 1945 and Mine (who was nine when the bomb was dropped) was in school there for ten years. This monastery, located in a different part of Nagasaki, survived the bombing and its monks assisted in looking after children and youths such as Mine and Ozaki following the bombing.

When I ask Nakamura Kazutoshi whether he understands the bombing as 'God's providence', he answers:

> I think that whatever the case, I hold no grudge against God. It [the bomb] was a *shiren* 試練 (trial) for humankind, I think. Do you know the word,

shiren? It was *shiren*, a trial from God, given to humanity, to survive through suffering.[49]

Carefully avoiding the word providence, which I used in the question, Nakamura's inference is that if God's providence caused or allowed the event of the atomic bomb, his task is to endure through the following trial. During the interview, he provides evidence of how he perceives the importance of his faith in God by giving me a photo of his shrine, where he had prayed that very morning. Second, Nakamura frames his statements by his faith-community's understanding of public history. Nakamura deflects the question, calling the bomb *shiren*: a spiritualised word for a trial from God (for the Urakami Catholics). *Shiren* is a word employed by his community in interpreting the atomic bomb, but also the persecutions of historic times. Nakamura's use of this vocabulary, *shiren*, shows his understanding of the connotations of its use in public history, shifting his own interpretation of the bombing to relate to the community's public history of persecution. Nakamura does not negate God's 'providence' completely, construing his life as a 'trial' or sacrifice, in view of his personal and traumatic experiences, but he demonstrates reluctance to state the term outright. Through the context of his interview, his view of his life may be understood as a 'living sacrifice' to God.

Nakamura's personal theologising, his knowledge of public Urakami interpretations (and public Nagasaki narratives) and his own personal context reflect a difficulty he has in coming to terms with his own narrative. 'Composure' is a term used in oral history to describe how narrators such as Nakamura seek to compose their memory about their past so that it makes sense and is meaningful, although, as historian Alistair Thomson writes, composure is never fully achieved and does not cure life's ills.[50] Nakamura's theologising and faith view seeks to 'find provisional answers', which match his experiences, his memory of the atomic bomb and public memory narratives. By his statement, Nakamura attempts to make sense of his memory of trauma, even as he incorporates wider public narratives, including those of his minority community and complex interrelated interpretations of the bombing.

Within the wider community of Nagasaki, interpretations of divine influence in Nagasaki were diverse. Multiple competing public narratives of the divine by various protagonists included (1) the Catholic narratives of God's providence; (2) the suggestion by devotees of Suwa Shrine that the gods of Japan wrought the bomb as punishment; and even (3) the wielding of 'God' in wartime by the US army. Nakamura's attempt to make sense of his personal narrative is achieved by analysing his memory alongside the experience of the community's suffering. The narratives of the interviewees explicitly challenge the earlier Catholic understanding that the atomic bomb could be understood as inflicted within God's providence. I will return to the communal formation of interpretations of the atomic bombing in Part II, examining how earlier interpretations must be negotiated and how individual narratives of the Catholic survivors are today understood.

Oral history

Oral history has expanded quickly, especially since the 1970s and survivor testimonies contributed to Holocaust studies, but also within the historiography of Hiroshima and Nagasaki. Oral history discloses more about the meaning than the details of events and equally the telling of Nagasaki and the atomic bomb illuminates polyphonic meanings for different individuals and groups.[51] Despite or due to their subjectivity, the narratives discussed here reveal the meaning of the speakers' relationships to their history. In interviews, meaning can be discerned in narrators' emotions and the way the story affects the person – meanings not as easily perceived in written texts. In writing and reflecting on the information given to me by my interviewees, visuals, photographic and material culture and secondary sources contribute to meaning. The interviewees act as co-writers in the conversation, achieving a shared labour between the narrators and the researcher, in the context of still unfolding and changeable narratives of the past. By the unusual synthesis of theology and oral history, I turn in this book to some 'forgotten' sources of Catholic remembering, among the very last survivors of the atomic bombing of Nagasaki and uphold their important contribution to understanding side-lined Nagasaki narratives.

Following on from this introduction of the survivors, I turn to the 'dangerous' memory of death in the landscape of atomic-bombed Urakami. The finding of remains and skeletons adds to a long history of bodies in the landscape and the concept of a 'fissured' Nagasaki, stratified by class, religion and origin.

Notes

1 Robert Perks and Alistair Thomson, eds, *The Oral History Reader* (London: Routledge, 1998), 64.
2 Alessandro Portelli, *Order Has Been Carried Out: History, Memory, and Meaning of a Nazi Massacre in Rome* (New York: Palgrave Macmillan, 2006), 17–18.
3 *Hibakusha* is the Japanese word for survivor of the atomic bombings, or for someone exposed to atomic radiation.
4 *Kataribe* are 'tribal narrators' in Japanese and *hibakusha* survivors of the atomic bomb have often been characterised in this role in Japan. This is a term which goes back to the time prior to literacy in Japan, when clans performed the role of recitation (*katari*) of genealogies and stories. John W. Treat discusses the *kataribe* and that being a *kataribe* in Nagasaki means speaking with authority and special responsibility for the future. John Whittier Treat, *Writing Ground Zero: Japanese Literature and the Atomic Bomb* (Chicago: University of Chicago Press, 1995), 318.
5 Paul Ricœur, *Memory, History, Forgetting* (Chicago: London: University of Chicago Press, 2009), 365.
6 Jenny Harding, 'Looking for Trouble: Exploring Emotion, Memory and Public Sociology: Inaugural Lecture, 1 May 2014, London Metropolitan University'. *Oral History* 42.2 (2014): 94–104 (97).
7 Ana Douglass and Thomas A. Vogler, eds, *Witness and Memory: The Discourse of Trauma* (New York: Routledge, 2003), 163.
8 Anika Walke, *Pioneers and Partisans: An Oral History of Nazi Genocide in Belorussia*, Oxford Oral History Series (Oxford and New York: Oxford University Press, 2015), 9.

9 Gen Okada, 'A Graduation Ceremony for Fourteen Students', *Asahi Shimbun* (Nagasaki, October 2008), am edn, accessed 20 April 2019, www.asahi.com/hibakusha/english/shimen/nagasakinote/note01-08e.html.
10 Kazuko Nagase, 'The Twenty-Nine Years I Have Lived Through', in *Voices of the A-Bomb Survivors* (Nagasaki: The Nagasaki Testimonial Society, 2009), 82.
11 Kiyoshi Nishida, interview by Gwyn McClelland, Nagasaki Atomic Bomb Museum, 19 July 2008.
12 Paul Glynn, *A Song for Nagasaki* (Grand Rapids, MI: Eerdmans, 1990), 99.
13 Jōji Fukahori, interview by Gwyn McClelland, Nagasaki Atomic Bomb Museum, 1 October 2014.
14 'Nagoya de chichi byōshi Nagasaki ni (Nagasaki nōto)', *Asahi Shimbun*, 15 June 2011.
15 Tōru Mine, interview by Gwyn McClelland, Nagasaki Atomic Bomb Museum, 24 February 2016.
16 Tomoe Otsuki, 'Reinventing Nagasaki: The Christianization of Nagasaki and the Revival of an Imperial Legacy in Postwar Japan'. *Inter-Asia Cultural Studies* 17.3 (2016): 395–415 (399). The so-called *buraku* community was, like the Catholics, decimated by the atomic bombing and I will mention some survivor recollections from this community within this monograph.
17 Ozaki said in his interview his father died when he was seven, but a journalist in a 2008 Asahi newspaper article stated he was ten years. See the newspaper article at his blogsite: Tōmei Ozaki, *Ozaki Tōmei no heya* [online blog] 'Kirishitan to watashi', accessed 6 June 2017, https://sites.google.com/site/tomaozaki/Home/05-kirishitan.
18 Tōmei Ozaki, interview by Gwyn McClelland, Francisco-en Hōmu, 27 February 2016.
19 Sachiko Matsuo, interview by Gwyn McClelland, Nagasaki Atomic Bomb Museum, 5 December 2014.
20 Kazutoshi Nakamura, interview by Gwyn McClelland, Nagasaki Atomic Bomb Museum, 23 February 2016.
21 Shigemi Fukahori, interview by Gwyn McClelland, Urakami Cathedral, 23 February 2016. Some names in Nagasaki were known for their prevalence among the *sempuku* and the modern Catholics and one such name was Fukahori; Kataoka and Tagawa were also common. Chie Shijō records an insult which seized upon the prevalence of Fukahori among the Catholics by a Nagasaki citizen: 'Urakami wa Fukahori to buta no kuso bakkashi!' 'Urakami is just Fukahori and pig shit!' Chie Shijō, *Urakami no genbaku no katari: Nagai Takashi kara Rōma kyōkō e* (Tōkyō: Miraisha, 2015), 40.
22 Shin'ichi Konishi, interview by Gwyn McClelland, Nagasaki Atomic Bomb Museum, 1 October 2014.
23 Toshio Enju, interview by Gwyn McClelland, Megumi no oka, Gembaku Hōmu, 25 February 2016.
24 Nakamura, 23 February 2016, McClelland.
25 Fukahori, 1 October 2014, McClelland.
26 Nathan Beyrak, *Oral History Interview with Avraham Kimmelman*, 2004, US Holocaust Memorial Museum Archives Branch, accessed 29 August 2017, https://collections.ushmm.org/search/catalog/irn518056.
27 Yet listening to a distressing narrative can re-traumatise the interviewee or sometimes traumatise the interviewer. Alyssa Boasso, Stacy Overstreet, and Janet B. Ruscher, 'Community Disasters and Shared Trauma: Implications of Listening to Co-Survivor Narratives'. *Journal of Loss and Trauma* 20.5 (2015): 397–409 (398).
28 Aitemad Muhanna, 'When the Researcher Becomes a Subject of Ethnographic Research: Studying "Myself" and "Others" in Gaza'. *Women's Studies International Forum* 45 (2014): 112–18 (118).
29 Alistair Thomson, *Anzac Memories: Living with the Legend* (Melbourne and New York: Oxford University Press, 1994), 227.

32 *Legacy of survival*

30 Michael Roper, 'Analysing the Analysed: Transference and Counter-Transference in the Oral History Encounter'. *Oral History* 31.2 (2003): 21.
31 Portelli, *Order Has Been Carried Out*, 15.
32 Walke, *Pioneers and Partisans*, 30.
33 Sean Field notes the 'transmission of trauma' model is problematic. Memory is not passed on like a 'disease' to the next generation. Sean Field, 'Loose Bits of Shrapnel: War Stories, Photographs, and the Peculiarities of Postmemory'. *The Oral History Review* 41.1 (1 January 2014): 126, https://doi.org/10.1093/ohr/ohu019.
34 See for example, Victoria Aarons and Alan Berger, *Third-Generation Holocaust Representation: Trauma, History, and Memory* (Evanston, IL: Northwestern University Press, 2017), 42.
35 Tina Wasserman, 'Constructing the Image of Postmemory', in *The Image and the Witness: Trauma, Memory and Visual Culture*, eds Frances Guerin and Roger Hallas, Nonfictions (London: Wallflower Press, 2007), 166.
36 Tokusaburō Nagai, interview by Gwyn McClelland, Nyokodō Museum, 29 September 2014.
37 Penny Tinkler, *Using Photographs in Social and Historical Research*, 1st ed. (Los Angeles: SAGE Publications Ltd, 2013), 27.
38 I created this map from information provided by the interviewees, drawing on secondary sources that provided enough information to locate the survivors at the time of the bombing. Two interviewees are not included here.
39 Karl Schoenberger, 'Seeks to Remember – and Forget: Nagasaki: Reluctant Actor in Role of Atomic Martyr', *Los Angeles Times* (Los Angeles, 6 August 1989), online archive ed., accessed 4 May 2016, http://articles.latimes.com/1989-08-06/news/mn-410_1_atomic-bomb-victims.
40 Bronwyn Davies, *Doing Collective Biography Investigating the Production of Subjectivity*, Conducting Educational Research (Maidenhead, England: Open University Press, 2006), 4.
41 Valerie Raleigh Yow, *Recording Oral History: A Guide for the Humanities and Social Sciences*, 2nd ed. (Walnut Creek, CA: Altamira Press, 2005), 36.
42 Joseba Agirreazkuenaga and Mikel Urquijo, 'Collective Biography and Europe's Cultural Legacy'. *The European Legacy* 20.4 (2015): 373–88 (379).
43 Brian Davies and G. R. Evans, eds, *Anselm of Canterbury: The Major Works*, Reissue ed. (Oxford and New York: Oxford University Press, 2008), 87.
44 Daniel L. Migliore, *Faith Seeking Understanding: An Introduction to Christian Theology* (Grand Rapids, MI: W. B. Eerdmans, 2004), 2.
45 Treat, *Writing Ground Zero*, 301.
46 For a recent example of the trope about Nagasaki as passive, see Susan Southard, *Nagasaki: Life after Nuclear War* (New York: Viking, 2015), 171. Southard argues the people of Nagasaki are associated with a passivity due to Nagai Takashi's writing. I will discuss at length Nagai's interpretation of the bombing in Chapter 4.
47 Lisa Yoneyama, *Hiroshima Traces: Time, Space, and the Dialectics of Memory* (Berkeley: University of California Press, 1999), 61.
48 For example, Hiroshima was the first atomic bomb in Japan, it is a city closer to Tokyo, it had many professional writers who had evacuated from Tokyo and Nagasaki is perceived as more regional and 'clannish'. See Treat's discussion of the differences between the two cities in Treat, *Writing Ground Zero*, 303.
49 Nakamura, 23 February 2016, McClelland.
50 Alistair Thomson, 'Anzac Memories Revisited: Trauma, Memory and Oral History'. *The Oral History Review* 42.1 (2015): 1–29 (23).
51 Perks and Thomson, *The Oral History Reader*, 67.

References

Aarons, Victoria, and Alan Berger, eds. *Third-Generation Holocaust Representation: Trauma, History, and Memory*. Evanston, IL: Northwestern University Press, 2017.

Agirreazkuenaga, Joseba, and Mikel Urquijo. 'Collective Biography and Europe's Cultural Legacy'. *The European Legacy* 20.4 (19 May 2015): 373–88. https://doi.org/10.1080/10848770.2015.1019216.

Asahi Shinbun. 'Nagoya de chichi byoushi Nagasaki ni (Nagasaki nooto)'. *Asahi Shimbun*. 15 June 2011.

Beyrak, Nathan. *Oral History Interview with Avraham Kimmelman*. DVCAM, 2004, accessed 29 August 2017, https://collections.ushmm.org/search/catalog/irn518056.

Boasso, Alyssa, Stacy Overstreet and Janet B. Ruscher. 'Community Disasters and Shared Trauma: Implications of Listening to Co-Survivor Narratives'. *Journal of Loss and Trauma* 20.5 (3 September 2015): 397–409. https://doi.org/10.1080/15325024.2014.912055.

Davies, Brian, and G. R. Evans, eds. *Anselm of Canterbury: The Major Works*. Reissue ed. Oxford and New York: Oxford University Press, 2008.

Davies, Bronwyn, ed. *Doing Collective Biography Investigating the Production of Subjectivity*. Conducting Educational Research. Maidenhead, Berkshire: Open University Press, 2006.

Douglass, Ana, and Thomas A. Vogler, eds. *Witness and Memory: The Discourse of Trauma*. New York: Routledge, 2003.

Enju, Toshio. Interview by Gwyn McClelland. Genbaku Hōmu, Megumi no Oka. 25 February 2016.

Field, Sean. 'Loose Bits of Shrapnel: War Stories, Photographs, and the Peculiarities of Postmemory'. *The Oral History Review* 41.1 (1 January 2014): 108–31. https://doi.org/10.1093/ohr/ohu019.

Fukahori, Jōji. Interview by Gwyn McClelland. Nagasaki Atomic Bomb Museum. 10 January 2014.

Fukahori, Shigemi. Interview by Gwyn McClelland. Urakami Cathedral. 23 February 2016.

Glynn, Paul. *A Song for Nagasaki*. Grand Rapids, MI: Eerdmans, 1990.

Harding, Jenny. 'Looking for Trouble: Exploring Emotion, Memory and Public Sociology: Inaugural Lecture, 1 May 2014, London Metropolitan University'. *Oral History* 42.2 (2014): 94–104.

Konishi, Shinichi. Interview by Gwyn McClelland. Nagasaki Atomic Bomb Museum. 1 October 2014.

Matsuo, Sachiko. Interview by Gwyn McClelland. Nagasaki Atomic Bomb Museum. 5 December 2014.

Migliore, Daniel L. *Faith Seeking Understanding: An Introduction to Christian Theology*. Grand Rapids, MI: W. B. Eerdmans, 2004.

Mine, Tōru. Interview by Gwyn McClelland. Nagasaki Atomic Bomb Museum. 24 February 2016.

Muhanna, Aitemad. 'When the Researcher Becomes a Subject of Ethnographic Research: Studying "Myself" and "Others" in Gaza'. *Women's Studies International Forum* 45 (July 2014): 112–18. https://doi.org/10.1016/j.wsif.2013.11.010.

Nagai, Tokusaburō. Interview by Gwyn McClelland. Nyokodō Museum. 29 September 2014.

Nagase, Kazuko. 'The Twenty-Nine Years I Have Lived Through'. In *Voices of the A-Bomb Survivors*, 82–5. Nagasaki: The Nagasaki Testimonial Society, n.d.

34 Legacy of survival

Nakamura, Kazutoshi. Interview by Gwyn McClelland. Nagasaki Atomic Bomb Museum. 23 February 2016.

Nishida, Kiyoshi. Interview by Gwyn McClelland. Nagasaki Atomic Bomb Museum. 19 July 2008.

Okada, Gen. 'A Graduation Ceremony for Fourteen Students'. *Asahi Shimbun*. October 2008, am ed. accessed 20 April 2019, www.asahi.com/hibakusha/english/shimen/nagasakinote/note01-08e.html.

Otsuki, Tomoe. 'Reinventing Nagasaki: The Christianization of Nagasaki and the Revival of an Imperial Legacy in Postwar Japan'. *Inter-Asia Cultural Studies* 17.3 (2 July 2016): 395–415. https://doi.org/10.1080/14649373.2016.1217631.

Ozaki, Tōmei. Interview by Gwyn McClelland. Francisco-en Homu, Sasaki. 27 February 2016.

Ozaki, Tōmei. 'Kirishitan to watashi: Ozaki Tomei no heya'. Blog. *Ozaki Toumei no Heya* (blog), n.d., accessed 6 June 2017, https://sites.google.com/site/tomaozaki/Home/05-kirishitan.

Portelli, Alessandro. *Order Has Been Carried Out: History, Memory, and Meaning of a Nazi Massacre in Rome*. New York: Palgrave Macmillan, 2006.

Ricœur, Paul. *Memory, History, Forgetting*. Chicago: London: University of Chicago Press, 2009.

Roper, Michael. 'Analysing the Analysed: Transference and Counter-Transference in the Oral History Encounter'. *Oral History* 31.2 (2003): 20–32.

Schoenberger, Karl. 'Seeks to Remember – and Forget: Nagasaki: Reluctant Actor in Role of Atomic Martyr'. *Los Angeles Times*. 6 August 1989, online archive edition, accessed 4 May 2016, http://articles.latimes.com/1989-08-06/news/mn-410_1_atomic-bomb-victims.

Shijō, Chie. *Urakami no genbaku no katari: Nagai Takashi kara Rōma kyōkō e*. Tōkyō: Miraisha, 2015.

Southard, Susan. *Nagasaki: Life after Nuclear War*. New York: Viking, 2015.

Thomson, Alistair. *Anzac Memories: Living with the Legend*. Melbourne; New York: Oxford University Press, 1994.

Thomson, Alistair. 'Anzac Memories Revisited: Trauma, Memory and Oral History'. *The Oral History Review* 42.1 (1 April 2015): 1–29. https://doi.org/10.1093/ohr/ohv010.

Thomson, Alistair, and Robert Perks, eds. *The Oral History Reader*. London: Routledge, 1998.

Treat, John Whittier. *Writing Ground Zero: Japanese Literature and the Atomic Bomb*. Chicago: University of Chicago Press, 1995.

Walke, Anika. *Pioneers and Partisans: An Oral History of Nazi Genocide in Belorussia*. Oxford Oral History Series. Oxford and New York: Oxford University Press, 2015.

Wasserman, Tina. 'Constructing the Image of Postmemory'. In *The Image and the Witness: Trauma, Memory and Visual Culture*, eds Frances Guerin and Roger Hallas, 159–72. Nonfictions. London: Wallflower Press, 2007.

Yoneyama, Lisa. *Hiroshima Traces: Time, Space, and the Dialectics of Memory*. Berkeley: University of California Press, 1999.

Yow, Valerie Raleigh. *Recording Oral History: A Guide for the Humanities and Social Sciences*. 2nd ed. Walnut Creek, CA: Altamira Press, 2005.

3 Bodies

> *From his point of view, it was once [my father] got to the Nagasaki station that there were dead bodies everywhere* [...]
>
> (Matsuzono Ichijirō, 2016)

Introduction

The survivors' recollections of remains in the landscape are intrinsic to the distressing and challenging narrative of the atomic bombing of Nagasaki. In the topography of this city, such bodies echo stories of Christian martyrdoms of the past. The survivors remember the bodies as 'dangerous' memory in a space doubly fissured by the atomic bombing on the one hand and by past instances of desecration and death on the other. Four survivor reflections are dispersed throughout this chapter on the presence of the deceased in the landscape. The reflections are related by Miyake Reiko, 20 years old at the time, Ozaki Tōmei, who was 17, Matsuo Sachiko, who was 11 and Mine Tōru, who was nine. Most were outside, or on the periphery of Urakami at the time of the bomb blast: in Map 1 in the first pages of this book, Miyake and Mine were in the vicinity of Mt Inasa (MR,MT); Ozaki Tōmei was at Asakō (OT); and Matsuo Sachiko (MS) was on Mt Iwaya in a temporary shelter. Consequent to the bombing, these survivors, apart from nine-year-old Mine, travelled towards and through Urakami, or returned to live there. The survivors' recollections of bodies in Urakami haunt their own remembering, are troubling to the listener and question the generalisation of the bombing as a Nagasaki city event. I also include Matsuzono's narrative of his father's memory of the bodies. Additionally, the memories of the dead recall older memories of executions, of suffering and of bones discarded on the outskirts of the city.

Some who returned after the Fourth Persecution of the community in 1873 saw the enormity of the impacts of the atomic bombing and called it the 'Fifth Persecution'. I connect a spatial divide to the differences in the experiences of impact on the city, due first to the weather which influenced the bombing on 9 August and second to a religious fissure created by Christian persecution since the Tokugawa period. The city in 1945 presented 'two faces': that of Nagasaki city and the northern suburb of Urakami.[1]

In the wake of the bombing, some Nagasaki city residents admonished their Urakami neighbours that the bombing of Urakami (not Nagasaki) resulted from the judgement of the Japanese gods on an impure area.[2] They said:

> It was thanks to *Suwa-san* [Suwa Shrine of the Autumn festival of *kunchi*] that the town was saved from the bombing;

> The judgement of the bombing against Christ and upon Urakami did not come to *Suwa-san;*

> The atomic bomb which fell on Nagasaki was because of the *kuroshū* [pejorative name for Christians] who lived in Urakami.[3]

Such comments based on religious particularity after the bombing accentuated existing fissures in Nagasaki.

Memories of bodies

Matsuzono Ichijirō's father was a survivor who had lived in Nagasaki's Chinatown. He only spoke once to his son about his experiences following the bombing, so it was as much his father's reticence to speak of this memory as the story which struck Matsuzono. His father travelled to Urakami from the city soon after the bombing. The second-hand description of his father's experience is an example of how memories of bodies haunt narratives across generations.

His father's narrative confirms the stark difference between damages experienced in the city and suburbs. After the bombing, Matsuzono's father travelled from Shinchi district (Chinatown in the city) to Nishizaka. He noticed the increasing visible impacts as he approached Urakami. Nagasaki station is where he became aware of bodies 'everywhere'. Matsuzono recalls his father's story:

> When the atomic bomb was dropped, my father had been injured [...] and so he had been back in Shinchi, resting. But when the bomb dropped [...] he had relatives and friends in Urakami so, wondering what had happened [...] From Shinchi, to Ōhato he went, although after the atom bomb was dropped, the fires were so bad, that he could not have gone through there, so I think it was the next day. From his point of view, it was once he got to the Nagasaki station that there were dead bodies everywhere.[4]

Matsuzono's account of his father's experience may be compared to a first-person account. He notes his father went home after the bombing, suggesting the difference in damages from Urakami to Shinchi in the city. He is not as visceral in his narration as Matsuo and Ozaki's remembering, which will come later. Matsuo and Ozaki include in their accounts the evocation of smells and visual images.

The destruction of more than 70 per cent of the Christian population has major implications for the recovery of this particular community. Matsuzono's father's memory shows how the landscape changed in the journey from the city, as his father entered the Urakami district and the presence of the bodies became more prominent. Even in this secondary account there is a sense of disbelief and horror over the images of the dead located specifically in Urakami. The atomic bomb killed an estimated 8500 of 12,000 Christians and 300 of 900 low-caste *burakumin* people, most of whom had lived in Urakami.[5] Damages were heaviest in Urakami and lighter in other parts of Nagasaki, deepening the already present societal fissure and adding an additional stigma due to the absorption of the major impacts of the *shingata* (new-style) bomb.[6]

Dancing Nagasaki, mourning Urakami

In 1945 some danced while others mourned, reflecting fissured Nagasaki. Those in Urakami continued to participate in the clean-up, grieved and sought refuge in outer regions, while in the city there were signs of resumption of normal life. To pay homage to *Suwa-san*, in late 1945, the people of Nagasaki resumed the religious celebration of the *o-kunchi* festival, which the city had halted during the war. The *o-kunchi* festival dated from the early Tokugawa period, to the attempted de-Christianisation of the region.[7] The people traditionally performed the dance of the *hono-odori* in the city square, in front of the Public Hall, a 'sacred resting place for gods during the festival parade'.[8] The city folk resumed the festival celebration in the city after the war had ended with considerable relief and excited activity.[9]

This aspect, the spatially uneven destruction of Nagasaki, was the major distinguishing factor between the atomic bombings of Hiroshima and Nagasaki.[10] Reporting on the phenomenon in late 1945 of 'Dancing Nagasaki' at the o-*kunchi* festival, a newspaper disclosed that in contrast, 'cave-dwellers' of Urakami were attending a Requiem Mass to grieve their dead.[11] These 'cave-dwellers' living in bomb shelters at the time included the interviewees Fukahori Shigemi, Nagase Kazuko and Matsuo Sachiko. Those from the *kage no kao* (shadowy face) of the city mourned, prayed and lived hand-to-mouth with their few remaining family members.

Contested 'sacred' spaces

However, it was not only the atomic bombing that led to the division between the two sides of the city. The physical and spiritual desecration of 1945 added to older existing stigmas, including those associated with stories of martyrdom. An oral historian, Dominick LaCapra, explains how 'land has memory', due to the perceived presence of the sacred in places of trauma.[12] Catholic survivors show awareness of the earlier history of persecution and so the new wave of destruction by the bomb was absorbed in a landscape already fissured by persecution and marginalisation. In particular, the Christians knew the Nishizaka slopes for

38 *Legacy of survival*

the desecrated bodies and bones found there in the past. It is necessary to refer to the early settlement of Nagasaki to understand how 'sacred space' and suffering were remembered over time.

From the first incursions of the Catholic mission, the clergy contested sacred spaces in the city. The mission established churches at the expense of pre-existing Buddhist and Shinto sites. In 1570, Nagasaki Jinzaemon, the Lord of the region, granted an abandoned temple to a Portuguese Jesuit, Father Gaspar Vilela, known for his work in the Jesuit mission to Miyako (Kyoto).[13] Vilela established a church of All Saints or *Tōdos os Santos*.

From its establishment as a settlement, Nagasaki was associated with both missional and colonial powers. Under the protection of the Christian Lord Ōmura Sumitada (Bartolemeu) in 1571, the Jesuits established a settlement at Morisaki cape and built the *Hishōten* (Ascension) Santa Maria church, as the symbolic centre of the town.[14] Ōmura assigned the Jesuits administrative rule over the town in 1580, which quickly became a merchant centre.[15] Their power was short-lived, but the missionaries and Christians in the city of Nagasaki created a myriad of Christian sacred spaces by the year 1613, including churches such as Santa Maria, Santo Domingo and San Francisco. Christians at Nishizaka burnt the icon of the local divine guardian, *Morisaki Gongen*, previously worshipped at Morisaki Cape. The Christians destroyed many temples and shrines in the area between 1570 and 1600, such as *Jingu-ji* near Nagasaki and *Jinzu-ji* found adjacent to the Urakami area.[16]

Although Christian sacred spaces were initially established in the centre of town, other missions located themselves on the margins during the process of settlement. The establishment of a leper hospital in Nishizaka reflected the marginal status of the northern region, supplemented by the arrival of Koreans in the neighbourhood. The Koreans were largely prisoners-of-war, who Japanese warriors had taken prisoner. Brought to Nagasaki after Hideyoshi's invasion of Korea from 1592, many subsequently became Christians. Jesuit historian Luis Fróis writes that the Jesuits met Koreans 'kneeling outside their church' in the year 1594.[17] Some Christians associated themselves with those of low social standing and the poor. Anan Shigeyuki writes about the occupations of the people who lived in *kawaya-chō*, who dealt with dead bodies and animal skins.[18] The confraternity called the Misericordia, established in 1583, led more Japanese villagers on the periphery to join in ministry to the poor, the sick and the foreign community. Missionaries established San Joao Baptista and the hospital of San Lazaro for assisting those with Hansen's disease (Figure 3.1), alongside the Nishizaka slopes. As Kawamura Shinzō states, the Nagasaki Misericordia was the most 'sophisticated, advanced and flourishing charitable confraternity in Japan'.[19] The Christians engaged by the Misericordia ministered to the poor, widows, orphans and sick, despite cultural norms which traditionally marginalised the lepers as *hinin* (sub-human) in Japanese society.[20] Members of the Misericordia were expected to bury the needy who died, whether Christian or not.[21]

Given the Catholic involvement in the operation of the house of Misericordia and San Lazaro, some of the early Christian workers were in close contact with

Figure 3.1 A modern monument to San Lazaro and San Joao Baptista Church at Nishizaka, photograph, the author, February 2016.

people from the outskirts of society. The Nishizaka region assumed the function of boundary marker of religious and societal difference, along the pathway to the area which would become the village of Urakami. So-called *hinin* and *eta* (subhuman, or 'filth') underclasses were associated with groups of the Christian believers from the time of the founding of Nagasaki.[22]

From the late 1500s, some of the low-caste *kawaya* or *eta* (more recently called *burakumin)* had also became Christian. The missionaries established a church among the *kawaya* themselves.[23] The Nagasaki magistrate's records of a *kuzure* persecution in Urakami in 1725 state that of the 55 Christians arrested, eight were *eta* or 'filth'.[24] Anan asserts that as late as the Kyōhō era (1716–36), *hisabetsu* (discriminated against) graves of those called the *eta* or *kawaya* were often Christian. Many *kawaya* people who were Christian became Buddhist after the proscription of Christianity, although others joined secret societies as *sempuku* or secret *Kirishitan*.[25]

Nishizaka martyrdoms

The Christians began to associate Nishizaka slopes closely with martyrs' dead bodies from the late sixteenth century, after the authorities commenced a crackdown on Christian activity. Preeminent *Daimyō* (feudal lord) Toyotomi Hideyoshi, increasingly concerned by the growing power of Christians in the Nagasaki region, began to repress the Christian organisations.[26] Hideyoshi ordered the execution of 26 priests and lay believers at Nishizaka after they had been forcibly marched from Kyoto to Nagasaki in the middle of the winter of 1597. In the days following this public martyrdom, many Japanese and Portuguese Christians visited the execution grounds to pay respect to the martyrs, ask for intercessions and gather relics. In some accounts, the Misericordia were called in to cover the dead bodies.[27]

In 1614, the first Tokugawa Shogun, Ieyasu, prohibited Christianity across Japan and expelled all priests. Nagasaki had grown to a population of 25,000 people by 1611 and the city included ten churches within eight parishes.[28] The systematic dismantling of the churches of Nagasaki commenced from the centre of the harbour town and radiated outwards.[29] The first church destroyed in Nagasaki after the exile of the missionaries was the central church of the Assumption on Morisaki Cape, where the Nagasaki magistrate's office was established for the administration of the town. The magistrate, or *bugyō*, levelled nine churches by the end of the year.

The magistrate carried out public executions in the in-between (mid-point between Nagasaki city and the outskirts) space of Nishizaka, which the Christians recalled as martyrdoms. The 1597 events were the first of a string of martyrdoms in desecrated Nishizaka. Officials performed executions in the same locality in 1622 (Chapter 1, Figure 1.1). On 10 September, at least 55 people, including lay Christians and 19 members of religious orders, were decapitated and burnt at the stake.

The Christians interpreted martyrdom as a mark of faith and this understanding persisted beyond the outlawing of Christianity. A surviving pamphlet, written by Andres de Parra in Madrid in 1624, entitled 'A Short Account of the Long and Rigorous Martyrdom…', describes the 1622 martyrdoms (Chapter 1, Figure 1.1). The authorities caught a ship smuggling priests into Nagasaki. The magistrate executed the priests, the sailors and the captain of the ship, along with many native Christian prisoners from Ōmura and Nagasaki. The authorities beheaded some and burnt others alive. The officials threw the bodies into a pit or dumped them into the sea. Don Seitz writes that the Christians present hailed the executed martyrs for their faithfulness and prayed.[30] After this time, the interpretation of martyrdom as the ultimate form of faithfulness was remembered even as the seclusion of the hidden Christians began. A Japanese text of 1793, written shortly after the first Urakami *kuzure* or persecution of 1790, included advice about the Christian ideal of and preparation for martyrdom.[31]

The unburied dead

The image of rotting bodies and bones left behind in the aftermath of the martyrdom of Christians in the seventeenth century has a dark resonance with the aftermath of the atomic bombing. When survivor Ozaki Tōmei faced the experiences of seeing many bodies in the landscape in 1945, he transformed himself by taking on the name of a martyr, a story to which I return in Chapter 8.

For now, though, I touch upon Ozaki's recollection of the aftermath of the bombing. He travelled after the bombing from a tunnel factory north of Urakami, to the burnt-out wreck of his home.[32] One body he saw on the way and which he could not forget was the corpse of a man, who sat on the foundation stone of a house, staring and mute. When he passed that way again three days later the body remained there, apparently unchanged. He writes he did not 'believe' this image in his memory, until much later when he saw something similar photographed from the devastation at Hiroshima, a 'standing' body. His dissonant memory of a baffling body in the landscape was confirmed by this later examination of a photograph. Ozaki also remembers in another moment, a survivor riding past him, carrying two dead bodies on a bicycle, the bodies smeared with dirt and blood. The most prominent aspect of the atomic bomb experience which remains with him is these multiple images of death seared in his memory including the piles of dead bodies.[33] The images of martyred bodies haunted the Christians in earlier times and the memory of the bodies after the atomic bombing stayed with Ozaki.

The confronting image of the corpses instigates Ozaki's ongoing reflections about the spiritual world and highlights the nature of the 'danger' inherent in these memories. Ozaki perceived a spiritual dimension to the 'dangerous' bodies he saw. In his autobiography, he writes he wondered where the spirits of so many dead would go. 'I wanted to pray for the forgotten spirits who would not be reached even by prayer', he remembers.[34] The corporeal presence of the bodies added a physical danger for those who viewed them like Ozaki, as they lay unburied.

It was not only for the Christian survivors that the presence of death in the landscape was 'dangerous'. In Catholic and Buddhist thought, where the souls of the dead and the abandoned may go is of importance. In Buddhist belief, the unwilling forfeiture of life was thought to result in angry and vengeful spirits, for whom ritual pacification was necessary.[35] As recently as 1995, a new memorial structure was created in the Nagasaki Peace Park for the departed spirits, as a 'Nagasaki City Atomic Bomb Memorial Hall for unknown Dead'.[36] The presence of bodies in the landscape was 'dangerous' for Ozaki and for Buddhist believers in Nagasaki after the bombing, and in earlier times during the savage initiation of persecution of the Christians described above.

Persecutions in the seventeenth century included the Governor's interference with Christian gravesites. The Tokugawa authorities allowed the Misericordia confraternity to continue its work in Nagasaki after the elimination of the central churches, possibly due to the credibility of its public service. Some organisations located near Nishizaka, such as Sao Lorenzo, chapel of the Korean community in Kōrai-machi, and Sao Miguel and Santa Clara in Urakami, at first survived the initial 1614 purge of churches. However, Hasegawa Gonroku (Fujimasa), governor of Nagasaki from 1606, renewed the razing of the churches on the outskirts of the city in late November 1619.[37] Christian hospitals in disparate locations around the city were destroyed, inmates evicted and the three houses for the lepers outside the city were burnt.[38] Hasegawa's officials dug up the cemeteries of the Misericordia, Santa Cruz and Santa Maria and re-interred the bones outside the city in Sao Miguel cemetery.

Interviewee Mine Tōru described a similar occurrence to Hasegawa's disposal of bones outside the city in the seventeenth century, but this time in the atomic narrative about the abandoned after the bombing. Mine's memory of discarded dead in 1945 adds to the contrast between Urakami and Nagasaki city, as bodies decomposed and became a part of the roads and soil of the 'polluted' suburb. Mine reported: 'The dead bodies were piled high in carts used for rubbish collection and dumped out in an outer area.'[39] As the border between purity and pollution had been marked with the bodies of those martyred in Nishizaka in the seventeenth century, the bomb reiterated the divide between Nagasaki and Urakami. The question of who disposed of the remains of the dead and in what circumstances was relevant in the earlier times, but also in 1945 and after. In Urakami 'Barrels [were] placed at intersections for the collection of ashes and bones.'[40] The American occupation forces also participated in the clean-up and an account by Uchida Tsukasa adds to Mine's description the following anecdote about the US occupation soldiers 'clearing' Urakami with bulldozers.

> There were still many dead under the rubbish. Despite that the Americans drove their bulldozers very fast, treating the bones of the dead just the same as sand or soil ... a person ... tried to take a picture of what they were doing. The MP pointed his gun and threatened to confiscate any picture taken.[41]

The role taken by the magistrate in the seventeenth century was transferred in this way to the US forces post-1945. Mine's and Uchida's anecdotes show how after the bombing the bodies of the dead literally became a part of Urakami's soil, a new layer metaphorically overlaying the martyrs carelessly discarded nearby in the early seventeenth century.

Religious and social exclusion

With the outlawing of Christianity from the early 1600s, the sacred spaces of Christians were reclaimed and the Christians themselves driven underground. The magistrate of Nagasaki in the early 1600s demolished many Christian sites to make way for Buddhist and Shinto institutions, attempting to stamp out the hold of Christianity by the re-establishment of temples and shrines. The magistrate allocated a *Nichiren* Buddhist priest the site of the Sao Joao Bautista church (Figure 3.1), alongside the Nishizaka slopes. The priest built a temple there in 1620, also uprooting the cherry trees marking the 26 martyrdoms of 1597 and throwing them into the sea.[42] In 1623, Aoki Kensei, *Shugendō* Shinto priest, received approval to establish a place of worship and enshrined the three deities, *Suwa Daimyōjin, Sumiyoshi Daimyōjin* and *Morisaki Gongen*, at the symbolic central location of the previous Catholic church, *Tōdos os Santos*.

Faced with severe persecution and the threat of death, many Christians gave up on faith and were driven to the margins by Hasegawa's demolishing of the churches from the centre of civic life. Some altered their practice from open religiosity to secret observance. The faithful developed new methods of religious practice within secret societies, despite Christianity's official outlawing. Driven wholesale to the margins and into rural seclusion, many Christians continued to remember the suffering and death imposed by the regime on their family and ancestors.

Societal and political forces altered the social composition of Nishizaka and the Urakami region. The magistrate moved the outcaste *kawaya* from their early location on the eastern side of the town, to live in Nishizaka by 1648.[43] Here, the magistrate hoped that they would contribute to reporting any Christian activity which they observed. In 1718, the magistrate again moved the *kawaya* closer to Urakami, to Magome, which the officials called *eta-machi* (filth-town).[44]

The Nagasaki magistrate required the outcast inhabitants of *kawaya* town to watch out for the Christians and new apostates and report any concerns back to the city office. Thus, the relocated *kawaya-chō* near Nishizaka became a 'breakwater' between the Buddhist society and the presence of the 'heathen-religion' (*jakyō*) apostates. Later, in the nineteenth century, members of a *tokushu burakumin* sub-group arrested and exiled the Christians, during the Fourth Persecution, known by the Christians as *tabi* (travel) and by the magistrate as a *kuzure* (demolishing), between 1867–73.[45]

Mission, hidden churches, persecution

Japan reopened to Western trade and French missionaries arrived in Nagasaki in the 1860s, purportedly to minister to the foreign religious community. French

Catholic priests constructed the Ōura Cathedral in 1864 south of the city centre and attracted the attention of the Japanese hidden Christian cult in Urakami. A group from Urakami travelled to the church in southern Nagasaki in 1865, putting themselves in considerable danger by making the journey and revealing their ongoing adherence to the Christian faith. The French priests did everything they could to support the 'return' to Catholicism of the faithful, providing illegal Holy Mass throughout the Urakami region. The foreign missionaries reconnected some Hidden Christians to Catholicism and reached out to the marginalised *kirishitan* communities. In the late Tokugawa period, the Christians and missionary priests created four 'hidden' churches in Urakami. The missionaries secretly baptised, celebrated mass and taught the hidden Christians in the four Urakami hidden churches named St Maria, St Joseph, St Clara and St Francisco Xavier between 1865 and 1868.[46] In response to the foreign interference and clandestine activity, the authorities renewed a harsh wave of persecutions.

The community's method of interment of dead bodies in the 1860s was the final straw, precipitating this new surge of marginalisation and repression. Prior to the installation of a new Meiji government in 1867, some of the Urakami Christians, influenced by French priests, refused to call in Buddhist priests for the burial of the dead.[47] Upon this act of defiance, the magistrate began to arrest groups of Christians in Gotō islands Ōmura and Nagasaki. The Shogun sent a letter to the French Emperor, Napoleon III, demanding that the priests' propaganda be stopped.[48]

Officials ordered the new repression of the Christians on 14 May 1867. The accompanying notice by the magistrate read:

> [...] Christianity has begun to spread again and is likely to do great harm to the state. We cannot allow this to continue [...] if they refuse to repent, we have no recourse other than to exile the rest to forced labor in other clans [...][49]

The Christians heard about initial reports of mass arrests and torture of Christians in the Gotō islands.[50] On 8 June 1868, officials identified a leadership group of 120 Christians from Urakami and forcibly exiled them, including the patriarch, Takagi Sen'emon (Figure 3.2).[51] Sen'emon survived the ordeal and is photographed in 1898, wearing a woollen kimono and gazing at what may be a medal image of Christ's body, attached to rosary beads.

The exile and persecution came to be known as the Urakami *yon-ban kuzure* (Fourth Persecution).[52] In a second stage of this persecution, the officer in charge of public order in Kyushu, Sawanobu Yoshi, exiled the entire village of Urakami in January 1870, including over 3000 men, women and children.[53] The people were transported to 22 different locations around Japan, as far north as Toyama and as far south as Kagoshima.[54] The Christians' final return from this exile in 1873 was of great significance for the community, as its members finally began to practise faith publicly.

Figure 3.2 Takagi Sen'emon, *ikinokori* (survivor) of the exile, 1898, 74 years, used by permission, Nichibunken, Kyoto, 25 December 2018.

Fifth Persecution

The community in Urakami compared their memory of the destructive events of the persecutions to the impact of the atomic bombing and some called the atomic bomb the *go-ban kuzure* (Fifth Persecution). In an essay published in 1983 in volume 15 of *Nihon no genbaku bungaku*, Kamata Sadao wrote that Nagai Takashi was greatly influenced by those Catholics he met after the bombing who used this term, the *go-ban kuzure*. He wrote in a memoir, *otome tōge* (Mountain pass lady) about the Christians returning after the bombing:

> The Urakami believers were one by one returning to the places they had come from [...] One of the people I remember at the time, who stayed there even after the atomic bombing [...] told me it appeared a lot like it was after they had returned from exile.[55]

In his book entitled 'Job of the atomic field', Itō Akihiko traces the descendants of Sene'mon (Figure 3.2) in a family tree and shows how 18 per cent of his family died or disappeared in the Fourth Persecution. Later, in an impact which decimated their social group, 80 per cent of Sene'mon's descendants died in the atomic bombing of Nagasaki, including the priest who had baptised Nagai Takashi.[56] Incorporating in the family tree of Sen'emon both those who died/disappeared in the Fourth Persecution and the casualties of 1945, Itō showed how like in the story of Job, familial and generational experiences of trauma extended over time. Itō writes that this kind of annihilated family line after the bombing was not unusual for Urakami people.[57]

The clean-up of bodies within Urakami began from central Nishizaka in 1946. After the US forces' bulldozing in Urakami in the early stage of the occupation a later concerted effort to retrieve remains by a local civil society group occurred in early 1946. A 2009 newspaper article described how women from the Ladies' Association at the Buddhist Higashi Honganji temple in Nishizaka began the clean-up of the suburb of Urakami and the river six months after the bombing and retrieved up to 20,000 abandoned bodies. Many who had wanted water after the bombing ended up in the river (see Chapter 7). By the time the clean-up began all that remained were rotted remains and whitening bones.[58]

As described, Nishizaka was itself remembered for the earlier presence of bodies due to martyrdoms. After the ancient martyrdoms and the bombing, Christians planted cherry trees in remembrance of those who died and for the beautification of the region.[59] In the early 1950s, Nagai Takashi donated royalties from the sales of his books towards the planting of cherry trees, in memory of those who died in 1945. These cherry trees in the Urakami valley, planted as memorials of the atomic bomb, subtly marry the Catholic public narratives of the presence of death to the recollections of desecration after the martyrdoms in Nishizaka.

'Please finish me off!'

The scenes of the dying which survivors encountered in Urakami after the bomb were extreme. Miyake Reiko's account is specific to Urakami's devastation and contrasts with the resumption of normal life in Nagasaki. The aftermath of the bombing she recalls focuses in detail on the injured, as well as those who died. Miyake arrived at Shiroyama Gakuin, the school where she was a teacher, the next day, on 10 August 1945. Here, approximately 1400 students died immediately or soon after the atomic bomb blast, as well as 28 of 33 staff members.[60] In her interview, Miyake describes her journey into Urakami.

> I went back to the school, the day after the bomb had dropped [...] There were fourteen or fifteen girls lying there. Some of them were still moving [...] and half of them were not moving at all [...] From the second and third floor, [having] fallen, there were many dead people. The children on the second floor made it to the stairs. And the third floor children made it to the stairs. And there was no staircase. What do you do if there is no staircase? You jump from the window [...] They jumped and because the ground was

concrete rocks, they hit the rocks [...] some had died immediately upon jumping and some had jumped, but were still breathing. There were around fifteen children and approximately half had died.[61]

There were dead bodies, but for Miyake the vivid suffering of those still alive is animated. In many cases, death was by no means instantaneous. The numbers are important to Miyake, who struggles to relate exactly how many children were still moving and how many had died. Miyake knew some of the dead and some who had survived:

> At the entrance, there was a 24-year-old male teacher called Mr. Miyamoto. After the atomic bomb was dropped, he had apparently been saying things like, 'It hurts!', 'Please finish me off', or 'Mother!' [...] On the 10th, at around six o' clock in the morning, when I arrived there, he was saying nothing. When I went, his breath had already [...] [stopped]. He couldn't say anything and was lying sideways [...][62]

Miyake's memory is composed by her reference to what others have told her about this man. She recollects the slow process of death for the severely injured, as recorded about Mr Miyamoto. Miyake focuses on the contrast between his cries and his silence.

A mother and child

Aged 11 years in 1945, Matsuo Sachiko lived in Ōhashi, near Mt Iwaya, just North-West of Urakami, and survived because her family escaped to the mountain the night prior to the bombing. Matsuo also had strong memories of the bodies in the landscape of Urakami.[63] Sensate memory overpowers narrative memory for her in her discussion of an incident of encounter with remains. Matsuo's fragmentary sense of memory is probably due to her state of shock induced by the experiences. Two bodies, a mother and child, exemplify the challenging scenes in Matsuo's memory:

> They were burying the bodies and burning them and there was a terrible smell. Amidst the bones of many dead bodies, I could see a perished baby inside the womb of a dead mother. It stayed like that for a long time. You could see the mother's skull and the baby's tiny skull and bones until Autumn. It rotted – I can't forget the condition of that baby.[64]

She describes physical pollution, the rotting bodies and a pungent smell. The physical presence of the bodies added to the dangers of disease. The potential for disease and pests to descend, as decomposition occurred, made them physically dangerous. She was haunted by this image of an unborn baby and his or her mother, representative of the bomb's indiscriminate killing of all people, regardless of age, gender or status. The killing of a pregnant mother encapsulates the desecration after the bombing to 80-year-old Matsuo and her memory of when she was 11. She adds, 'It stayed like that for a long time.' For some Christians, the images Matsuo mentions recall Mary with child, the Mother of Christ long revered by this community. Imagining Mary might also recall the A-bombed Mary statues discussed in Chapter 5, or the Buddhist *kannon*, used by hidden Christians to remember the Catholic faith.[65] The jarring experience of blemished bodies (multiplied in atomic literature) materially adds to the perception of Urakami as a tainted and 'dangerous' space, a literal place of apocalyptic otherness.

Urakami returnees

For Matsuo and the other interviewees, their grandparents' lineage as returned exiles form a fundamental piece of their identity. Early in her interview, Matsuo showed me photographs of her grandparents who were survivors of an exile which the Catholics remember as the 'Fourth Persecution' (see Chapter 6, Figure 3.2), arranged in front of the Urakami Cathedral.

> This [pointing to picture] is my grandmother, Nishio Waki. She was born in Keiō 2nd year [1866] on the 9th March. Then she died in the 34th year of Shōwa [1959], or the 33rd [1958] [...] She was taken to Tsuwano [on the exile] [...] And this is my grandfather. I know that he died when I was in primary school in Shōwa 18th year [1943] [...] His name was Kichirōji.[66]

Matsuo shows that modern Christians in Urakami understand their origins, from a marginalised community, in a divided city. The Christians circulate photos like these and take pride in their ancestral identity.

Other aspects of the older 'fissured' geography of Nagasaki and Urakami emerge in the interviewees' discussions. Fukahori Shigemi mentions the four 'secret' churches co-created with the missionaries, in Urakami district in the second half of the nineteenth century.[67] Matsuo indicates Santa Clara, a 'hidden church', memorialised next to Urakami River, north of the Peace Park.[68] The Governor of Nagasaki initially destroyed St Clara in 1619. The Christians reinstated this church when the French missionaries arrived, evidencing the importance of continuity of sacred space for the Christian narratives and for their practice. The Christians continue to venerate their ancestors by placing flowers here today, remembering by place. Santa Clara and the hidden and destroyed churches hint at the haunting, through social and group narrative, of the older history of fissure. A 'dangerous' memory of suffering is reiterated today after the decimation of the community in the atomic bombing, repeating ancestral experiences of the sixteenth and seventeenth centuries.

Gabriele Schwab writes that the consequence of 'secret family, communal or national histories' is how they haunt the stories that are told by the next generation, especially recalling those who lay unburied, or who died an abnormal death.[69] Thus, I began this chapter with Matsuzono's description, representative of the future of memory in Nagasaki, as the eyewitness numbers dwindle. There are traces of affect in memory after the eyewitnesses disappear, Schwab continues, which children receive in the memories or stories of parents.[70] I have also introduced memories of communal stories in the remaining Catholic and non-Catholic survivors' testimony. The specific social and religious context surrounding memory of the atomic bombing in Nagasaki traces earlier impacts of suffering and death. The Catholics inscribe through cross-generational processes memory of suffering of the bombing of Nagasaki onto a complex religious geography, reflecting their older narratives of martyrdom and persecution.

Memory of the atomic bombing and of the bodies of those who died is refracted through the community lens of older memory of suffering. The atomic bombing of 1945 created a situation in which the townspeople's perception of Urakami as tainted was intensified. The social history of Nagasaki included the development of early links between the Christian and apostate communities and outcast groups. Nishizaka evolved as a sacred space and narratives about the martyrs contributed to the discussions about recovery after the bombing. Eventually, a small *burakumin* or outcaste community was enlisted by the magistrate to guard and spy on the hidden Christian groups. Survivors today relate their experiences after the bombing to public persecutions, including the Fourth Persecution. In 1945, both the Catholics and the *burakumin* groups were decimated by the bombing.

Bodies abandoned in the landscape after the atomic bombing are an important example of 'dangerous' memory and have a long and traumatic impact on survivors Miyake, Ozaki, Mine and Matsuo. There are implicit and explicit connections from the survivors' memory of bodies in Urakami, to earlier iterations of bodies, including in the executions of Christians. Such connections evoke public narratives of repression and religious division and subvert the long existence of a divided Nagasaki.

Human bodies haunt the landscapes, especially in Nishizaka and Urakami and in the next section we investigate how the Catholics struggled after this traumatic event to make any sense of the devastation left by the atomic bombing. Soon after, religiously themed reactions to the bomb resonated and one in particular approached a hegemony for the Urakami Catholic surviving community, as we will see in the following chapter. Subsequently, I introduce the three significant symbols which emerged in interviews, one archetypal, one monumental and one a remembered cry. All have contributed to ongoing and renewed efforts to reinterpret and commemorate the atomic bomb, and the Catholic *kataribe* were attentive to them in their testimony.

Notes

1 Chie Shijō, *Urakami no genbaku no katari: Nagai Takashi kara Rōma kyōkō e* (Tōkyō: Miraisha, 2015), 38. Shijō quotes a 1972 publication which describes two faces of the city: one dark (of persecution and the atomic bombing) and one bright, represented by the hot springs (hot water).

50 *Legacy of survival*

2 Higashi Honganji, 'Hisabetsu buraku ni ochita genbaku', *Dōseki* newsletter, 6, 6.44 (2010).
3 Higashi Honganji, 'Hisabetsu buraku ni ochita genbaku', *Dōseki* newsletter, 6, 6.44 (2010).
4 Mori cites two sources, one a Nishi-Nippon Shinbun website of 2002 and the other a news article written in 1970 entitled 'Nagasaki no hibakusha: buraku, chōsen, chūgoku' in Kenta Mori, 'Genbaku wa hito ni nani mo tarashita no ka: chiriteki kankei kara nagasaki wo kaishaku suru', *Waseda shakai kagaku kenkyu*, 2008, 35, accessed 2 February 2016, https://dspace.wul.waseda.ac.jp/dspace/bitstream/2065/32390/1/ShakaiKagakuSougoKenkyu_S_2009_Mori.pdf.
5 Ichijirō Matsuzono, interview by Gwyn McClelland, Nagasaki, 26 February 2016.
6 Outcasts in the Edo period were known by other names, including *eta* (filth), *hinin* (non-human) and *kawaya(cho)* (people who dealt with skins). Shigeyuki Anan, 'Kirishitan hakugai to hisabetsu buraku – Urakami yonban kuzure jiken no kenshō o tōshite (tokushū Nagasaki no Kirishitan dan'atsu to buraku mondai)'. *Buraku Kaihō* (2004): 40–51 (40–2).
7 Initially, the survivors did not know what the bomb was and they called it a *shingata* (new-style) bomb. In interviews, survivors Enju Toshio, Fukahori Jōji and Ozaki Tōmei all mentioned this name given to the bomb before it was revealed by the authorities to have been an atomic bomb. Yokote also refers to the new-style bomb: Kazuhiko Yokote, *Nagasaki kyū Urakami tenshudō 1945–58: ushinawareta hibaku isan* (Tōkyō: Iwanami Shoten, 2010), 74.
8 Reinier H. Hesselink, 'The Two Faces of Nagasaki: The World of the Suwa Festival Screen'. *Monumenta Nipponica* 59.2 (1 July 2004): 186–9.
9 Japan National Tourism Organisation, 'Nagasaki Kunchi Festival', Japan National Tourism website, 2016, accessed 7 December 2017, www.jnto.go.jp/eng/location/spot/festival/nagasakikunchi.html.
10 Kazuhiko Yokote writes that a newspaper report in the Nagasaki Shimbun of 8 October 1945 reported on the Kunchi festival celebrations resumed as well as a mass attended by '1000 faithful living in cave shelters'. At one event the people were joyful and at the other they grieved, he writes. *Nagasaki kyū Urakami tenshudō 1945–58*, 74.
11 Chie Shijō, *Urakami no genbaku no katari: Nagai Takashi kara Rōma kyōkō e* (Tōkyō: Miraisha, 2015), 54.
12 Yokote, *Nagasaki kyū Urakami tenshudō 1945–58*, 74.
13 Dominick LaCapra, 'Trauma, History, Memory, Identity: What Remains?'. *History and Theory* 55.3 (2016): 375–400 (384).
14 Carla Montane, 'Sacred Space and Ritual in Early Modern Japan: The Christian Community of Nagasaki (1569–1643)' (PhD diss., University of London, 2012), 54–5.
15 Ōmura is believed to be the first Japanese Lord or daimyo to convert to Christianity. Derek Massarella, 'Envoys and Illusions: The Japanese Embassy to Europe, 1582–90 and the Portuguese Viceregal Embassy to Toyotomi Hideyoshi, 1591'. *Journal of the Royal Asiatic Society* (2005): 335.
16 John Whitney Hall, *The Cambridge History of Japan*, vol. 4, Cambridge History of Japan (Cambridge: Cambridge University Press, 1991), 329.
17 Montane, 'Sacred Space and Ritual in Early Modern Japan', 58–60.
18 By 1614, Fróis reported that the community of Korean converts to Catholicism, prisoners-of-war, men, women and children numbered 300. Christopher Wong, 'Jesuits, Korean Catholics, and the State: Narratives of Accommodation and Conflict to 1784' (PhD diss., St John's University, 2015), 46–7.
19 Shigeyuki Anan, *Hisabetsumin no Nagasaki gaku: boueki to Kirishitan to hisabetsu buraku* (Nagasaki: Nagasaki jinken kenkyu sho, 2009).
20 Shinzo Kawamura, 'Making Christian Lay Communities During the "Christian Century" in Japan: A Case Study of Takata District in Bungo' (PhD diss, Georgetown University, 1999), 126.

21 Montane, 'Sacred Space and Ritual in Early Modern Japan', 92–3.
22 Takayama Fumihiko lists the seven obligations of the Misericordia lay workers, as a priest described them from the Gospel of Matthew. They were to: (1) Give food to the starving; (2) Give water to the thirsty; (3) Clothe the naked; (4) Visit the sick; (5) Give travellers lodging; (6) Visit those in prison and (7) Dedicate those who had died. Fumihiko Takayama, *Ikinuke sono hi no tame ni: Nagasaki no hisabetsu buraku to Kirishitan* (Ōsaka: Kaihō Shuppansha, 2016), 311.
23 *Hinin* and *eta* were associated with the *kawaya* and these outcaste groups overlapped in Edo society.
24 *Kawaya* is a reference to the skins which *buraku* dealt with and which resulted in discrimination against them. Anan, Shigeyuki 'Kirishitan hakugai', 45–6.
25 *Eta* was a derogatory name for those who were excluded from societal life.
26 See Honganji Higashi, 'Hisabetsu buraku ni ochita genbaku', *Dōseki* newsletter, 6, 6.44 (2010).
27 Reinier H. Hesselink, 'Ideology and Christianity in Japan. By Paramore Kiri. Abingdon and New York: Routledge, 2009'. *International Journal of Asian Studies* 8.2 (July 2011): 236, https://doi.org/10.1017/S1479591411000131.
28 It is possible that the members of the confraternity buried the bodies. However, some sources indicate the authorities buried the bodies and others that they were not buried immediately. Haruko Nawata Ward, *Women Religious Leaders in Japan's Christian Century, 1549–1650*, Women and Gender in the Early Modern World (Farnham, England and Burlington, VT: Ashgate, 2009), 325. See also Montane, 'Sacred Space and Ritual in Early Modern Japan', 133–4.
29 João Paulo Oliveira e Costa, 'The Brotherhoods (Confrarias) and Lay Support for the Early Christian Church in Japan'. *Japanese Journal of Religious Studies* 34.1 (2007): 77.
30 Reinier H. Hesselink, *The Dream of Christian Nagasaki: World Trade and the Clash of Cultures, 1560–1640* (Jefferson, NC: McFarland, 2015), 158.
31 Don C. Seitz, 'The Nagasaki Martyrs'. *The Catholic Historical Review* 13.3 (1927): 504.
32 Yuki Miyamoto, 'Narrative Boundaries: The Ethical Implications of Reinterpreting Atomic Bomb Histories' (PhD diss., University of Chicago, 2003), 275.
33 Tōmei Ozaki, interview by Gwyn McClelland, Francisco-en Hōmu, 27 February 2016.
34 Tōmei Ozaki, *Jūnanasai no natsu*, Seibo bunko (Nagasaki: Seibo no kisha-sha, 1996), 17–19.
35 Ozaki, *Jūnanasai no natsu*, 46.
36 John Nelson, 'From Battlefield to Atomic Bomb to the Pure Land of Paradise: Employing the Bodhisattva of Compassion to Calm Japan's Spirits of the Dead'. *Journal of Contemporary Religion* 17.2 (2002): 155. John Nelson has also written about how since 1995, the Nagasaki Council of religious leaders (*shūkyōsha konwakai*), including Buddhist, Catholic, Episcopalian, Shinto and new religion representatives, has performed an *ireisai* ritual to comfort departed spirits in the Nagasaki Peace Park. The religious ceremony (held on the evening of 8 August each year) reclaims a religious role in remembering the atomic bombing, divested by the avowedly secular ceremonies on 9 August. John Nelson, 'Traversing Religious and Local Boundaries in Postwar Nagasaki: An Interfaith Ritual for the Spirits of the Dead', in *Multiculturalism in the New Japan: Crossing the Boundaries Within*, eds Nelson H. H. Graburn, R. Kenji Tierney and John Ertl, vol. 6, Asian Anthropologies (New York: Berghahn Books, 2008), 202.
37 Nelson, 'From Battlefield to Atomic Bomb to the Pure Land of Paradise', 151.
38 Hesselink, *The Dream of Christian Nagasaki*, 174.
39 Couros quoted in Hesselink, *The Dream of Christian Nagasaki*, 186.
40 Mainichi Shinbun, 'Hibaku de hahaushinai koji ni', *Mainichi Shinbun*, 3 May 2015, accessed 9 September 2015, http://doshisha39.blog130.fc2.com/blog-entry-406.html.

52   Legacy of survival

41 Susan Southard, *Nagasaki: Life after Nuclear War* (New York: Viking, 2015).
42 Quoted in Monica Braw, *The Atomic Bomb Suppressed: American Censorship in Occupied Japan* (Armonk, NY: Routledge, 1991), 6.
43 Hesselink, *The Dream of Christian Nagasaki*, 187.
44 Anan, *hisabetsumin no Nagasaki gaku*, 13.
45 Yuki Diego, 'Catholic Gathering for the Solution of the "Buraku" Problem', *Bulletin*, Jesuit Social Center (Tokyo: 26 Martyrs' Museum, 11 August 2000), www.jesuitsocialcenter-tokyo.com/eng/bulletin/no098/iss098_2.html; Nagasaki-ken buraku shi kenkyusho, ed., *1945.8.9 Nagasaki: Furusato wa isshun ni kieta: Nagasaki/Urakami cho no hibaku to ima* (Nagasaki: Kaihō Shuppansha, 1995), 8.
46 Nagasaki-ken buraku shi kenkyusho, *Furusato wa isshun ni kieta*, 8. The Christians were split up and sent to many different locations around Japan, as far as Kanagawa in the north and Kagoshima in the south.
47 Yakichi Kataoka, *Urakami yonban kuzure Meiji seifu no kirishitan dan'atsu.*, Tokyo: Chikuma Shobo, 1963, 57–8.
48 Thomas W. Burkman, 'The Urakami Incidents and the Struggle for Religious Toleration in Early Meiji Japan'. *Japanese Journal of Religious Studies* 1.2/3 (1974): 157.
49 Burkman, 'The Urakami Incidents', 163.
50 Burkman, 'The Urakami Incidents', 181–2.
51 Burkman, 'The Urakami Incidents', 186.
52 Stephen R. Turnbull, *Japan's Hidden Christians, 1549–1999*, vol. 1 (Richmond, Surrey: Japan Library and Edition Synapse, 2000), 185.
53 Sadao Kamata, 'Nagasaki no inori to ikari', in *Nihon no genbaku bungaku 15: hiron/essei*, vol. 15, Nihon no genbaku bungaku (Tōkyō: Horupu Shuppan, 1983), 412–13.
54 According to Takagi, there were 3404 exiles, of whom 660 died, 176 went missing and 1981 returned. Kazuo Takagi, *Meiji katorikku kyōkai shi* (Tōkyō: Kyōbunkan, 2008), 285.
55 Takashi Gonoi, Renzo DeLuca SJ, and Rumiko Kataoka, 'Maria-zō' ga mita kiseki no Nagasaki: Nagasaki no Urakami, Sotome, Gotō no Kirishitan wa 250-nen taeta, Kirishitan bunka, IV (Nagasaki-shi: Nagasaki Bunkensha, 2006), 7.
56 Kamata, 'Nagasaki no inori to ikari'.
57 Akihiko Itō, *Genshiya no 'yobu ki': katsute kakusenso ga atta* (Tokyo: Komichi Shobo, 1993), 260.
58 Itō, 260–1.
59 Nagashuu Shinbun, 'Amari shirarenu 2 man tai no ikotsu hibaku 1 nengo ni shuushuu shi maisou', Newspaper, Higashi Honganji Nagasaki, 18 May 2009, accessed 7 September 2016, www.h5.dion.ne.jp/~chosyu/amarisirarenu2manntainoikotu%20hibaku1nenngonisyuusyuusimaisou.html.
60 The cherry trees planted in the seventeenth century are mentioned in Hesselink, *The Dream of Christian Nagasaki*, 187.
61 Gen Okada, 'A Graduation Ceremony for Fourteen Students', Asahi Shimbun (Nagasaki, October 2008), am ed, accessed 22 April 2019, www.asahi.com/hibakusha/english/shimen/nagasakinote/note01-08e.html.
62 Reiko Miyake, interview by Gwyn McClelland, Nagasaki Atomic Bomb Museum, 19 July 2008.
63 Miyake, 19 July 2008, McClelland.
64 Sachiko Matsuo, interview by Gwyn McClelland, Nagasaki Atomic Bomb Museum, 5 December 2014.
65 'Nagasaki Atomic Bomb Survivor Tells Her Story' (Vienna: CTBTO Preparatory Commission, 2013) accessed 3 March 2017, www.youtube.com/watch?v=2aLU-3Z-r-g.
66 I will describe in Chapter 5 the *hibaku* Mary statues and how the hidden Christians used the *kannon* to remember the figure of Mary during the period when Christianity was proscribed.
67 Sachiko Matsuo, 5 December 2014, McClelland.

68 Shigemi Fukahori, interview by Gwyn McClelland, Urakami Cathedral, 23 February 2016.
69 Matsuo, 5 December 2014, McClelland. The church of Santa Clara was one of those built in the sixteenth and seventeenth centuries, until Gonroku, the Nagasaki Governor, destroyed the building.
70 Schwab, Haunting Legacies, 52. Quoted in LaCapra, 'Trauma, History, Memory, Identity', 378–9.

References

Anan, Shigeyuki. 'Kirishitan hakugai to hisabetsu buraku – Urakami yonban kuzure jiken no kenshō o tōshite (tokushū Nagasaki no Kirishitan dan'atsu to buraku mondai)'. *Buraku Kaihō* 540 (October 2004): 40–51.
Anan, Shigeyuki. *Hisabetsumin no Nagasaki gaku: boueki to Kirishitan to hisabetsu buraku*. Nagasaki: Nagasaki jinken kenkyu sho, 2009.
Braw, Monica. *The Atomic Bomb Suppressed: American Censorship in Occupied Japan*. Armonk, NY: Routledge, 1991.
Burkman, Thomas W. 'The Urakami Incidents and the Struggle for Religious Toleration in Early Meiji Japan'. *Japanese Journal of Religious Studies* 1.2/3 (1974): 143–216.
Costa, João Paulo Oliveira e. 'The Brotherhoods (Confrarias) and Lay Support for the Early Christian Church in Japan'. *Japanese Journal of Religious Studies* 34.1 (2007): 67–84.
Diego, Yuki. 'Catholic Gathering for the Solution of the "Buraku" Problem'. Bulletin. Jesuit Social Center. Tokyo: 26 Martyrs' Museum, 11 August 2000. www.jesuitsocialcenter-tokyo.com/eng/bulletin/no098/iss098_2.html.
Fukahori, Shigemi. Interview by Gwyn McClelland. Urakami Cathedral. 23 February 2016.
Gonoi, Takashi, Renzo DeLuca SJ and Rumiko Kataoka. *'Maria-zō' ga mita kiseki no Nagasaki: Nagasaki no Uragami, Sotome, Gotō no Kirishitan wa 250-nen taeta*. Kirishitan Bunka, IV. Nagasaki-shi: Nagasaki Bunkensha, 2006.
Hall, John Whitney. *The Cambridge History of Japan*, vol. 4. 6 vols. Cambridge History of Japan. Cambridge: Cambridge University Press, 1991.
Hesselink, Reinier H. 'The Two Faces of Nagasaki: The World of the Suwa Festival Screen'. *Monumenta Nipponica* 59.2 (1 July 2004): 179–222.
Hesselink, Reinier H. 'Ideology and Christianity in Japan. By Paramore Kiri. Abingdon and New York: Routledge, 2009'. *International Journal of Asian Studies* 8.2 (July 2011): 235–7. https://doi.org/10.1017/S1479591411000131.
Hesselink, Reinier H. *The Dream of Christian Nagasaki: World Trade and the Clash of Cultures, 1560–1640*. Jefferson, NC: McFarland, 2015.
Higashi Honganji. 'Hisabetsu buraku ni ochita genbaku'. *Douseki* newsletter 6.44 (30 June 2010): 4–7.
Itō, Akihiko. *Genshiya no 'yobu ki': katsute kakusenso ga atta*. Tokyo: Komichi Shobo, 1993.
Japan National Tourism Organisation. 'Nagasaki Kunchi Festival'. Japan National Tourism website, 2016, accessed 7 December 2017, www.jnto.go.jp/eng/location/spot/festival/nagasakikunchi.html.
Kamata, Sadao. 'Nagasaki no inori to ikari'. *Nihon no genbaku bungaku 15: hiron/essei* 15: 408–17. Nihon no genbaku bungaku. Tōkyō: Horupu Shuppan, 1983.
Kataoka, Yakichi. *Urakami yonban kuzure Meiji seifu no kirishitan dan'atsu*. Tokyo: Chikuma Shobo, 1963.

54 Legacy of survival

Kawamura, Shinzo. 'Making Christian Lay Communities During the "Christian Century" in Japan: A Case Study of Takata District in Bungo'. PhD diss., Georgetown University, 1999.

LaCapra, Dominick. 'Trauma, History, Memory, Identity: What Remains?' *History and Theory* 55.3 (1 October 2016): 375–400. https://doi.org/10.1111/hith.10817.

Mainichi Shinbun. 'Hibaku de hahaushinai koji ni'. *Mainichi Shinbun*. 3 May 2015. http://doshisha39.blog130.fc2.com/blog-entry-406.html.

Massarella, Derek. 'Envoys and Illusions: The Japanese Embassy to Europe, 1582–90, and the Portuguese Viceregal Embassy to Toyotomi Hideyoshi, 1591'. *Journal of the Royal Asiatic Society* 15.3 (5 December 2005): 329–50.

Matsuo, Sachiko. Interview by Gwyn McClelland. Nagasaki Atomic Bomb Museum. 5 December 2014.

Matsuzono, Ichijirō. Interview by Gwyn McClelland. Nagasaki institution. 26 February 2016.

Miyake, Reiko. Interview by Gwyn McClelland. Nagasaki Atomic Bomb Museum. 19 July 2008.

Miyamoto, Yuki. 'Narrative Boundaries: The Ethical Implications of Reinterpreting Atomic Bomb Histories'. PhD diss., The University of Chicago, 2003.

Montane, Carla. 'Sacred Space and Ritual in Early Modern Japan: The Christian Community of Nagasaki (1569–1643)'. PhD diss., University of London, 2012.

Mori, Kenta. 'Genbaku wa hito ni nani mo tarashita no ka: chiriteki kankei kara nagasaki wo kaishaku suru'. *Waseda shakai kagaku kenkyu*, 2008. https://dspace.wul.waseda.ac.jp/dspace/bitstream/2065/32390/1/ShakaiKagakuSougoKenkyu_S_2009_Mori.pdf.

Nagasaki Atomic Bomb Survivor Tells Her Story. Video. Vienna: CTBTO Preparatory Commission, 2013. www.youtube.com/watch?v=2aLU-3Z-r-g.

Nagasaki-ken buraku shi kenkyusho, ed. *1945.8.9 Nagasaki: Furusato wa isshun ni kieta: Nagasaki/Urakami cho no hibaku to ima*. Nagasaki: Kaihō Shuppansha, 1995.

Nagashuu Shinbun. 'Amari shirarenu 2 man tai no ikotsu hibaku 1 nengo ni shuushuu shi maisou'. Newspaper. Higashi Honganji Nagasaki, 18 May 2009. www.h5.dion.ne.jp/~chosyu/amarisirarenu2manntainoikotu%20hibaku1nenngonisyuusyuusimaisou.html.

Nelson, John. 'From Battlefield to Atomic Bomb to the Pure Land of Paradise: Employing the Bodhisattva of Compassion to Calm Japan's Spirits of the Dead'. *Journal of Contemporary Religion* 17.2 (2002): 149–64.

Nelson, John. 'Traversing Religious and Local Boundaries in Postwar Nagasaki: An Interfaith Ritual for the Spirits of the Dead'. In *Multiculturalism in the New Japan: Crossing the Boundaries Within*, eds Nelson H. H. Graburn, R. Kenji Tierney and John Ertl, vol. 6. Asian Anthropologies. New York: Berghahn Books, 2008.

Okada, Gen. 'A Graduation Ceremony for Fourteen Students'. *Asahi Shimbun*. October 2008, am ed. www.asahi.com/hibakusha/english/shimen/nagasakinote/note01-08e.html.

Ozaki, Tōmei. *Jūnanasai no natsu*. Seibo bunko. Nagasaki: Seibo no kisha-sha, 1996.

Ozaki, Tōmei. Interview by Gwyn McClelland. Francisco-en Hōmu, Sasaki. 27 February 2016.

Schwab, Gabriele. *Haunting Legacies: Violent Histories and Transgenerational Trauma*. New York: Columbia University Press, 2010.

Seitz, Don C. 'The Nagasaki Martyrs'. *The Catholic Historical Review* 13.3 (1927): 503–9.

Shijō, Chie. *Urakami no genbaku no katari: Nagai Takashi kara Rōma kyōkō e*. Tōkyō: Miraisha, 2015.

Southard, Susan. *Nagasaki: Life after Nuclear War*. New York: Viking, 2015.
Takagi, Kazuo. *Meiji katorikku kyōkai shi*. Tōkyō: Kyōbunkan, 2008.
Takayama, Fumihiko. *Ikinuke sono hi no tame ni: Nagasaki no hisabetsu buraku to Kirishitan*. Ōsaka: Kaihō Shuppansha, 2016.
Turnbull, Stephen R. *Japan's Hidden Christians, 1549–1999*, vol. 1. 2 vols. Richmond, Surrey: Japan Library and Edition Synapse, 2000.
Ward, Haruko Nawata. *Women Religious Leaders in Japan's Christian Century, 1549–1650*. Women and Gender in the Early Modern World. Farnham, England and Burlington, VT: Ashgate, 2009.
Wong, Christopher. 'Jesuits, Korean Catholics, and the State: Narratives of Accommodation and Conflict to 1784'. PhD diss., St John's University, 2015.
Yokote, Kazuhiko. *Nagasaki kyū Urakami tenshudō 1945–58: ushinawareta hibaku isan*. Tōkyō: Iwanami Shoten, 2010.

Part II
Reinterpreting the bomb
Archetype, monument and cry

4 Providential atomic bomb?

> *Professor Nagai [...] [said] [...] 'God's providence' [...] generally we couldn't accept it, 'God would do that?' [...]* [Laughs].
>
> (Konishi Shin'ichi, 2014)

Introduction

The post-war legacy of Catholic doctor, Nagai Takashi (Figure 4.1, 1908–51), still reverberates in Nagasaki and Urakami. Locals remember Nagai for his major contributions to recovery, symbolised by cherry trees that line the streets of Urakami, donated from the proceeds of his books. The photograph in Figure 4.1 portrays Nagai in the manner of a Christian patriarch, who has come through trial (his stance is similar to survivor Sen'emon after the Fourth Persecution: see Figure 3.2, Chapter 3). The unshaven Nagai is in mourning for his wife, Midori, who was killed by the bomb and he holds his rosary beads in prayer. Local Nagasaki philosopher Takahashi Shinji writes, 'Nagai was like Job [the biblical figure], refusing to shave or cut his hair for half a year.'[1] Nagai was a charismatic and influential figure, whose work between 1945 and his death in 1951 was dedicated to the rebuilding of Urakami after devastation.

Nagai survived the bombing in Nagasaki University Hospital and initially conceived an interpretation of the atomic bombing as providential suffering. Nagai's interpretation became influential in the public narrative for the Catholic survivors but has been challenged since. His interpretation built on the Catholic public history of martyrdom and yet reflects nationalist tropes. Nagai's writing characterised the bomb in religious terms as a sacrificial *hansai* (or a burnt offering), required by God, emphasising three religious concepts: *hansai* (sacrifice), *shiren* (trials) and *go-setsuri* (providence). Takahashi later called Nagai's interpretation the *hansai-setsu* (Burnt Offering Theory).[2] Japanese sources frequently translate *hansai* into English as holocaust which is strictly correct. However, holocaust suggests the Jewish 'Holocaust', also known as the Shoah.[3] I will translate the word as 'burnt offering' or refer to the *hansai*, to distinguish its use here.

Nagai argued that *hansai* (sacrifice) occurs as *go-setsuri* (providence or divine gift) from God, in the context of the ongoing *shiren* (trials) of the community.

60 *Reinterpreting the bomb*

Figure 4.1 Nagai Takashi, 1946, mourning for Midori, public domain.

RECNA (Research Center for Nuclear Weapons Abolition, Nagasaki University) researcher Shijō Chie summarises Nagai's theory as universalising, or sublimating an 'absurd violence' into the expression of Catholic faith through its 'Old Testament' style theology and in so doing, inducing a communal silence among the Catholics.[4] A range of other Japanese commentators, including Catholic and academic writers, have challenged his characterisation of the bomb as providential sacrifice. The narrative I draw on from the interviews in this project demonstrates that rather than accepting the bombing as a burnt offering, many Catholic survivors now openly protest the violence of the bombing they experienced and implicitly critique the spiritualised theory of a burnt offering.

Family life, military service, conversion

Nagai was born in a samurai family in 1908 in Matsue City, Shimane prefecture.[5] The Confucianist values of his parents and their esteem for the nearby

Izumo Shinto shrine exerted a strong influence on Nagai as a child, but by the time Nagai had reached Senior High School, his teachers and other students influenced him to become an atheist.[6] In 1931, as a university student of medicine in Nagasaki, Nagai sought board in Urakami and went to live with the Catholic Moriyama family. Nagai admired the close-knit Catholic community which he observed around him at Urakami.

After his graduation, the authorities conscripted Nagai for an initial term as a military doctor to Manchuria. His war experiences form an important context for his later framing of the bombing of Nagasaki. After the bombing, Nagai would often sign *shikishi* poem cards with the sentiment *heiwa wo* (For peace). Takahashi suggests the reason Nagai desired peace rather than war was not only the experience of the atomic bombings, but also his experiences of the horrific war in China.[7] Some scholars focus, additionally, on his military service to speculate that his previous support of the war effort clashes with his image of wanting peace after the war. Japanese Studies scholar Tomoe Otsuki writes that as a young doctor in the 1930s, Nagai showed his loyalty to Imperial Japan when he returned to Nagasaki and wore a military uniform at the hospital.[8] This may be so, but it was common during the war to wear uniforms in the way Nagai did and in any case, strident opposition to the war was, at that time, associated with jail terms.[9] Nagai's subsequent conversion to Catholicism, after he returned to Nagasaki, was a development which informed his own perception of his second tour supporting the Japanese army to Manchuria.

As well as finding out about the history of the Catholics and observing the community, Nagai's reading of the French scientist and theologian Blaise Pascal also swayed him to become a Christian.[10] He converted to Catholicism in 1934 and was baptised in the community.[11] Before travelling to Manchuria a second time, Nagai spent many hours in Urakami discussing religious matters in depth with a priest, Father Moriyama. Moriyama's father Jinzaburō was a compatriot of Sen'emon Takagi and also an esteemed survivor of the Urakami Fourth Persecution. Nagai was impressed deeply by the fervour and everyday fellowship of the Catholic community and by their tenacity which had led them through such torrid historical experiences. Nagai later married Moriyama Midori, the daughter of the couple with whom he had boarded as a student. She became a teacher at Junshin High School from 1939 to 1941. Yuki Miyamoto writes that due to his experiences in Manchuria, combined with his conversion to Catholicism, Nagai became increasingly negative about the war effort. She notes that he reflected in his diaries on the expansion of colonialist Japan and wrote at one point: '... why do we justify war, in which a group kills members of another group on a mass scale? Is there any truth to just war...?'[12]

In February 1940, Nagai returned from his second term in China and began work at Nagasaki University Hospital.[13] He heard about the bombing of Hiroshima and he and his wife Midori decided to send their two children to Matsuyama, 6 kilometres away in the countryside.[14] On 9 August, Nagai went to work as usual at the university hospital in Urakami and was badly injured by the atomic blast. Driven by his strong sense of duty, he remained there and assisted many survivors after the bombing. Midori was killed by the initial blast, but Nagai did not know this until he returned home two days later and found her remains.[15]

Nagai wrote his memoirs after he discovered he was slowly dying from the effects of radiation. This was not only due to the bombing, but also because of his work as a radiologist. As a scientist and after his own close encounter with the atomic bombing, Nagai sought to engage in a meaningful way with Urakami's recovery. His books about his experiences of the atomic bomb were some of the first survivor publications allowed by the US military occupation censor and the public read them avidly throughout Japan. *The Bells of Nagasaki* was the second top national best seller in 1949.[16] The Occupation heavily censored all reports about the impact of the bomb in Japanese medical journals at the time and prohibited all Japanese research into nuclear physics. Nagai's scientific papers published posthumously include the *Atom Bomb Rescue and Relief Report* (*genshibakudan kyūgo hōkokusho*).[17] His fame after the publication of his memoirs was such that American deaf-blind activist Helen Keller visited him in 1948 and the Shōwa Emperor in 1949.[18] Keller visited Nagai in his hut and walked through the hospital ruins where he had been at work at the time of the bomb blast.[19] Nagai died in 1951.

'Spiritualising' the atomic bomb

On 23 November 1945, well before he became bedridden, Nagai was chosen to speak at a funeral mass held at the ruins of Urakami Cathedral, in front of around 150 survivors.[20] He was an articulate and highly educated doctor, teacher and a public figure in Urakami, at a time when most people in the neighbourhood were unable to gain higher qualifications and this may explain why the priests chose him from among the parishioners to make a speech as representative of the laity. In addition, Midori had been the daughter of a *chōkata*, a designated leader among the hidden Christians and Nagai himself had been injured in the bombing. He was a good representative of the surviving, fractured community. The state of the crumbling cathedral ruins at the time, in the flattened landscape of Urakami (Figure 1.2, Chapter 1), and the actual presence of bodies in the landscape, facilitates an understanding of his distinct interpretation.

Nagai directed his speech specifically to those in the immediate location of 'fissured' Nagasaki, intimately aware of the Catholic microcosm around the hypocenter. He referred to Urakami nine times in the speech, speaking of Urakami destruction, Urakami slaughter, Urakami ruins and chosen Urakami. Because it focused on Urakami alone, his interpretation would be later criticised as 'exclusivist' and exclusionary, forgetful of those outside the Catholic community.[21] However, given the nature of the fissured community and the bombing in this valley, his attention to Urakami is understandable.

When Jesuit missionary William Johnston (1925–2010) translated Nagai's book into English, he replaced 'Urakami' with 'Nagasaki' in the transcription of Nagai's speech, possibly because the term Urakami was difficult for Western readers to understand.[22] Such conflation of Urakami with Nagasaki is problematic, in view of the stratified city described in the previous chapter. In Johnston's translation, Nagai is understood to be speaking of wider Nagasaki and his interpretation intended for the Catholics is inappropriately extended to the whole town.

The burnt offering theory of Nagai drew deeply on the public history of the Urakami Catholics, including the Edo period martyrdoms and persecutions at the hands of the Japanese officials and the magistrate. The past trials of the Urakami believers had been extended by the bombing and Nagai wrote: 'So many martyrdoms, uninterrupted persecution and the atomic bomb … these are the trials (*shiren*) that tell of the glory of God … on the "holy ground" of Urakami.'[23] Nagai recalled God's providence, or *go-setsuri*, which in his view, led to Urakami becoming the 'chosen' place where the bomb was dropped.

> Was not Urakami – the most sacred place in all Japan – chosen as a victim, a pure lamb that had to be slaughtered and burned on the altar of sacrifice (*hansai*) to expiate this sin of humanity, the World War?[24]

Elaborating, Nagai explained that for the Hebrews, the Old Testament 'sacrifice', translated into Japanese as *hansai*, involved an 'unblemished lamb being burnt on an altar and offered as a sacrifice to the Lord'. Relating the practice to the atomic bombing, he said: 'On that day, the fire burnt for world peace for humanity as a huge *hansai* … and the people who died were all unblemished lambs.'[25] Those who survived, according to Nagai's theory, were the sinners not the innocent and therefore had to endure the aftermath.[26] Chad Diehl writes that Nagai commented to a friend that the survivors had failed their entrance exam to heaven and had to stay on earth and continue their studies through suffering.[27] The implications for the survivors was a necessary stoicism.

The context of the fissured city by which Urakami was perceived as distinct from Nagasaki city assists in making clear Nagai's conceptualisation of a burnt offering.[28] Nagai's interpretation rebuts the suggestion made by other citizens of Nagasaki that the Suwa god allowed the people of Urakami to be punished for worshipping a foreign god. Nagai exonerated the Catholics from placing guilt on their dead, proclaiming the people who died as innocent 'lambs' and their sacrifice as valuable for humanity. The bombing as a religious sacrifice or *hansai* was 'providential' and the people who survived experienced a new time of communal *shiren*, or trials and tribulations. By *hansai*, Nagai suggested that the Christians who had died 'atoned' for the sins of humanity and their sacrifice bore the guilt for Japan, considering the Japanese crimes of the war.

The silenced landscape

The power of Nagai's interpretation was that he spoke to an utterly shattered society, in a 'spiritual vacuum' and an emptied-out landscape. Figure 2.2 in Chapter 2 shows an overhead view in 1945 of Urakami Valley, a photograph taken by the US army and annotated by an oblique biblical reference to Psalm 23, in this place which the Americans bombed.[29] The cathedral is in the left-hand foreground and a prison was located close to the hypocenter on the right front foreground. Bodies are not visible at this scale, but at the time of Nagai's speech, the human remains recalled in the previous chapter were visible in the landscape. In her own book, Kataoka Chizuko remembered that when Nagai spoke, white bones still lay untouched across the 'atomic field'.[30] In the intervening months, many more died and many others lay on their death beds. The final number of dead will never be known due to the combined results of the level of destruction, chaos and censorship. A UCLA website collated by James Yamazaki estimates the number of dead in Nagasaki at 60–80,000 by December 1945.[31] The Japanese government provided no special treatment for the welfare of survivors for 12 years.[32] Most survivors were left without many of their family members, friends, neighbours, homes, workable fields, their schools, workplaces and the cathedral at the centre of their communitarian faith practice.[33] Nagai's audience wanted to make some sense of what appeared inexplicable and Nagai provided a spiritualised explanation.

The 'silence' of the landscape reflected a spiritual vacuum and some abandoned their Catholic faith, as they had done during the *kuzure* persecutions. For a couple of weeks after the bombing, orphaned interviewee Ozaki Tōmei lived out in the open close to central Urakami. He reflects that those who were injured, or scarred, were also some of those who found it most difficult to continue believing. An example is Kataoka Tsuyo, a Catholic survivor who described how she was so shattered by her experience of being injured in the bombing and her facial scarring, that she seriously considered committing suicide. It was not until the coming of the Pope in 1981 that she experienced a transformation, becoming a *kataribe* (storyteller), talking about her experiences and explicitly rejecting the idea of the bomb as providence.[34] Ozaki was conscious that he himself was not injured. Faced with the dilemma of belief versus non-belief, he chose faith, but he understands why those injured had doubts:

> [...] people who had keloid [atomic] scars, for them, is there a God? They would say, 'Why would God do this? I don't believe in God' [...] 'I can't believe in God's providence.' There were people like that [...][35]

Nagai preached to the scarred community that God's providence allowed for the bombing, although some survivors, as Ozaki describes, called such providence into question even at that time.

Nagai's influence

Nagai Tokusaburō (Figure 4.2), grandson of Nagai Takashi, suggested in his interview that his grandfather himself believed war was the work of humanity.[36] Nagai Takashi had personal experience of war and may indeed have understood war and the bombing as human problems, but such a perspective was not easily reconciled with the popularised *hansai-setsu* interpretation.

Figure 4.2 Nagai Tokusaburō poses at the Nyokodō museum of his grandfather, photograph, the author, September 2014.

As well, Motoshima Hitoshi, Catholic Mayor of Nagasaki, wrote many years later that Nagai argued the war initiated by the Japanese was unjust. Motoshima believed this view of Nagai's is notable at a time when the Japanese broadly claimed victimisation.[37] Nagai argued against Japanese aggression, but the community may have at least partially misunderstood his intention. In the decades after the bombing, many Catholics accepted the bomb should be understood as a part of God's plan, that providence and sacrifice were an appropriate interpretation of the bombing and that avoiding protest, and accepting new *shiren* (trials) from God, was inevitable.

The authority of Nagai's interpretation grew within the community, especially after the successful publishing of his first books from 1948. Despite reactions by those who renounced the church, others welcomed Nagai's *hansai* interpretation. For those wrestling with the idea of the dead as guilty, as suggested by the taunts of Nagasaki townspeople mentioned in Chapter 3, Nagai's interpretation inverted this view. On the contrary, the *hansai* understanding of sacrifice indicated a 'special role' for the dead.[38]

An example of how the influence of Nagai's interpretation spread is in the way Junshin Girls' High School, a Catholic mission school, commemorated its dead, as Shijō Chie has explained. This school was located 1.4 kilometres from

66 *Reinterpreting the bomb*

the hypocenter and 206 students and seven staff members were killed by the bombing.[39] The school leadership took on the language of *setsuri* (providence), *shiren* (trials), *hansai* (burnt offering) and martyrdom from Nagai's writings and leadership.[40] The history of Catholic martyrdom and aspects of nationalistic rituals were drawn upon by school authorities at Junshin, as they were by Nagai. Junshin's modern day website records Nagai Takashi as a first-generation founder of the institution. After the war, according to the webpage, Nagai lined up with the Prefectural representative, Mayor Ōmura, at the first graduating ceremony held after the atomic bombing in March 1946. He spoke as a guest.[41]

The frequent executions of Christians between 1597 and 1873 had conflated Japanese and Catholic understandings of martyrdom as virtuous. Atomic historian Yuki Miyamoto argues that in his similar speeches and writing Nagai employed and even at times exploited the community's narratives of persecution and martyrdom to explain the bombing. Miyamoto shows that the Japanese concept of *junshi*, or virtuous (voluntary) death was likely associated with the Christian community's understanding of death by martyrdom. In Japanese voluntary death, one atoned for one's defilement. For the Catholics killing yourself was a sin but allowing yourself to be killed could potentially be understood in a similar way to the concept of *junshi*.[42] When Nagai spoke and wrote of martyrdom, the association between public communal history, national narratives of sacrifice and the atomic devastation was evidenced.

Nagai and school leaders mourned the Junshin girls' deaths, weaving combined Catholic and nationalistic aspects into interpretive narratives, calling the girls 'martyrs for the fatherland'.[43] Nationalist ways of remembering the war influenced Catholic concepts of martyrdom in mission school documents such as those published by Junshin Girls' school.[44] Religion and piety were emphasised by tropes which recalled the singing of holy songs rather than the national anthem in Catholic memorialising. Nagai wrote a *tanka* poem about some of the Catholic girl victims from Junshin High School, who sang 'Christ, the Lamb' as they went to their death, arriving at the Urakami River.[45] Nagai's *tanka* is today listed on the school website. A short excerpt reads:

燔祭の炎の中に歌いつつ *hansai no honō no naka ni utaitsutsu*
白百合乙女燃えにけるかも *shirayuri otome moe nikeru kamo*

Maidens like white lilies
Consumed in the burning flames
As a whole burnt sacrifice
And they were singing [[…]][46]

An interpretation of the 'Burnt Offering Theory', the girls in the poem sing about Christ the innocent sacrificial lamb as they take Christ's place. Those who died took on a special status as 'lambs', reflected in the school's construction of a memorial. Direct references to the girls as 'unblemished lambs' after Nagai, in the literature and in commemorations at the grave, approach a cliché. The school authorities preserved bones and hair at the Junshin 'school grave', following the widespread Catholic practice of revering relics of martyrs. Shijō writes this kind of grave is not found in Hiroshima nor elsewhere in Nagasaki.[47] The school engraved Nagai's poem onto the grave and on 9 August each year, the school population sings the '*hansai* song' to music.[48]

Unblemished lambs

The chief problem with Nagai's interpretation was that *hansai* provided consolation only for the select. The *hansai* did not inclusively remember all of those who died, nor those who had survived. The idea of the victims of the atomic bombing as sacrificed, 'unblemished lambs', excluded non-Catholics and anyone who did not correspond to the narrative of the innocent. What of the 'spirits' whom Ozaki invoked after seeing piles of bodies; the loved ones never found including Ozaki and Nakamura's mothers; those unburied who Matsuo and Mine referred to; those who became a part of the soil or ended up in the river? Where 'purity' was not experienced in death and instead bodies were defiled, did Nagai's language about pure and unblemished martyrdom ignore the 'other' or consign them to hell? Nagai's interpretation apparently excluded the impure, the blemished, those who died 'violent' deaths and those cremated. 'Sinful' survivors including the angry, the non-Catholic and those who committed suicide were excluded or left behind to endure the ruins of the city.

According to Johann Metz in his critique of exclusivist theologies which did not combat Nazi policies against the Jews during the Holocaust, 'dangerous' memory must incorporate the 'other', the forgotten and the non-Christian. For Christians in the early years, however, the *hansai* as an exclusivist theory discouraged discussion of the atomic bombing experiences with the non-Catholic populace and those on the fringes of the community. Theological implications of this theory about the nature of God led to a long and problematic communal silence about the bombing.

Religion which fails to acknowledge the surrounding world and suffering like the *hansai* theory is critiqued by 'dangerous' memory.[49] Johann Metz criticises theologies which lack a historical and political consciousness. Those who adhere to theology such as this are complicit, Metz argues, in the midst of silence about suffering.[50]

Meanwhile, for the survivors, if God would allow the bomb to kill (and maim) many in the community, there was no point in speaking publicly about it. In her interview in 2016, survivor Kataoka Chizuko recalled the shyness of the community. Her personal silence on the topic of the atomic bombing was due to a belief that it was 'something which God did…'

> […] 'Not wanting to talk' was the initial thing I think. To talk about 'that experience' […] was out of the question. I also didn't want to talk. Therefore, there were a lot of people who didn't want to talk [about] something which God did […] they couldn't talk […][51]

The silence of the people was because of the notion that the believers could not be upset at God.

A mute community

However, the *hansai* was not the only reason for silence. The Catholics were descended from *sempuku* (silent) Christians. The modern Catholics followed the intuition of their ancestors, the *sempuku Kirishitan*, and kept their heads down. Theirs was a community accustomed to taboo and silence in a 'politically dangerous' climate, especially where they were accused of blame and guilt by association with foreign religion. Further, the survivors had experienced trauma-induced silence and some described an absolute inability to speak. For many years to come, devastated survivors, including those such as Nakamura Kazutoshi and Fukahori Jōji, had 'no words' and avoided all speech about the bombing.

The official institution of the Nagasaki Diocesan (later Archdiocesan) Church stayed virtually silent about the event of the bombing. The official Church hierarchy exacerbated the communal tendency to avoid speech or writing about the bomb, rarely mentioning the bomb in official publications prior to the 1980s.[52] Apart from publications of Junshin Girls' school and a Catholic old people's facility called *Gembaku Hōmu* which produced some memoirs, Catholic believers only participated in the production of individual accounts.[53] In the 70 years after the bombing, the Nagasaki Urakami Church and the Nagasaki archdiocese produced the smallest number of publications about the bombing of any official organisations in Nagasaki.[54] Between 1937 and the 1980s, the Catholic conference of Japan put out just one title in publications with the word 'peace' in it. There were no articles at this time with the title *genbaku* 'atomic weapon'. From the 1980s, a gradual change in the Catholic discourse is demonstrable by the output of seven articles including the word 'peace' and eight including the word 'atomic weapon'.[55] Shijō writes, however, that more church publications were produced about the atomic bombing by the Catholic archdiocese of Hiroshima than Nagasaki. The current Catholic population of Hiroshima is 0.3 per cent of the total population, compared to 5 per cent in Nagasaki.[56] The Catholic survivors accepted the silence of the official church about the atomic bombing in the early years as emblematic of the need for oneself to avoid protest and accept one's fate.

Catholic ambivalence about politics and 'peacemaking' also contributed to the silences. The Catholic Church in Japan is known as an arch-conservative institution with a dislike of communism. *Katorikkukyō-hō*, a Catholic newspaper, included articles on the dangers of communism from as early as the 1920s.[57] When Catholics were involved in political activities, other Christians sometimes called them 'dirty' and *aka* (Red-Communist).[58]

Nagai himself wished to differentiate the Catholic movement for Peace from communist movements in the years leading to 1950. At the time, revolutionary and anti-American Communists were some of the only groups condemning the bomb. 'Angry shouting in the streets about peace often cloaked very un-peaceful hearts', wrote Nagai.[59] He employed anti-communist rhetoric and warned that any peace movement that was 'merely political' or ideological was unseemly.[60] He had written of Communism's dangers in China and Japan and published an article in 1949, describing his critique of Communism in the Tokyo Newspaper.[61] Nagai's comments broadly reflected the conservative Catholic community's religious concerns about political activism.

Given myriad reasons for silence, Nagai's *hansai* interpretation provided a transitory hope. The explanation of the bomb did not relieve the survivors' lingering discomfort and pain. Nakamura relates he was badly depressed during the long period when he did not speak of his experiences. He explains if it were not for his religious beliefs, he would have committed suicide. He fled with his father to the Gotō archipelago (an island group around 100 kilometres off the coast from Nagasaki) after the bombing and did not qualify for high school. His lack of access to education due to his seclusion on the islands contributed to his feelings of hopelessness. Talking of this time in his life, he states in the interview:

> [...] if I hadn't been Catholic, I would have jumped from somewhere and wouldn't be here [...] I most definitely felt like 'I want to die; I want to die'. I had no hope at all [...] [about his dream to go to Kaisei Senior High School] I had talked to the priests in this way [about going to school] and my mother, however that [dream] was crushed [Nakamura's mother died] and all [these people died] and I had no hopes.[62]

Nakamura appears to be impacted by the *hansai* sacrificial theory still today. He perceives of his own life as a type of trial, using the word *shiren* (trial), also used by Nagai (Chapter 1). For the survivor such as Nakamura 70 years on, the words *hansai* combined with *shiren* imply a required enduring obedience to God, a 'living sacrifice'.

Critiquing *hansai*

Gradually, though, strong challenges to the language of Nagai emerged. The spiritual language was initially critiqued by commentators around 15 years after his death. One reason for the timing of this critique is the Catholic demolition of the Urakami Cathedral ruins in 1959 and the rebuilding of the cathedral, which occurred despite significant protest from Nagasaki city's non-Catholic population (Chapter 6). Critics asserted that the *hansai* theory had subverted the Peace Movement in this city. In 1965, Tadokoro Tarō wrote an *Asahi Journal* article entitled 'sengo no besutoserā monogatari' (best seller stories of the post war), using the example of Nagai Takashi's book, *kono ko wo nokoshite* (*The Children I Leave Behind*), to claim that Catholics refused to participate in anti-war activities which would have indicated dissatisfaction with God's plan.[63] Tadokoro's was among the first of several posthumous public and academic critiques of

Nagai.[64] Tadokoro's major concerns with the *hansai-setsu* were its abrogation of political responsibility and its implied exoneration from guilt of both the United States and the Japanese military. Tadokoro took issue with Nagai's reference to atomic bomb victimhood as *setsuri*, or God's providence, arguing this interpretation offered no 'resistance to the bombing'.[65] He wrote: 'the fact that Nagai's books sold so well were a disadvantage to Nagasaki [and its peace movement]'.[66]

Another early critic was a medical doctor, Akizuki Tatsuichirō, who wrote that Nagai's religious interpretation was the reason for the ineffectiveness of the nuclear disarmament movement in Nagasaki (1972).[67] Akizuki himself converted to Catholicism in October 1953. Akizuki avoided spiritual language and implicitly challenged Nagai's theology. He wrote about his conversion: despite becoming a Catholic he could not accede to either Nagai's *hansai-setsu* interpretation of the bombing as 'God's will', nor to the Buddhist interpretation of the bombing as 'karma'. As one of few Catholic *hibakusha* activists, Akizuki described Nagai as overly religious:

> That literary talent, poetic sentiment, artistic heart; these were the soul of the teacher, whose decline, on the other hand, was unstoppable [...] However, he was too sentimental and I did not care for such brimming religiosity. Consequently, [...] the bombing of Nagasaki was only perceived through the recollections of Nagai Takashi [...] and he employed only religiosity in dealing with the atomic bomb [...] The firstly radiation-affected and secondly injured teacher had no other way to deal with the atomic bomb, except for the religious [...][68]

Akizuki was insistent about the extent of Nagai's influence: 'the bombing of Nagasaki was only perceived through the religious recollections of Nagai Takashi'. Later Akizuki added his own theological interpretation, asserting in 1972 that it was not that God was silent or acceded to the bombing. Rather, God lamented the destruction.[69]

Local Nagasaki poet Yamada Kan labelled Nagai an uninvited 'mouthpiece and saint' for Nagasaki. Yamada had personal reasons for criticising the exclusive claims of the *hansai* theory: when his sister, a fervent Catholic, committed suicide, the church refused to permit her funeral in a church.[70] Yamada may have felt personally excluded by Nagai's theology and due to the circumstances of his sister's death, rejected by the official Church. Nagai's shadow, wrote Yamada, enforced a long silence on the *hibakusha* masses, non-Catholic as well as Catholic. Yamada agreed that the criticising of Nagai was taboo in Nagasaki. For Yamada, the American occupation encouraged religiosity and doctrine and, therefore, allowed Nagai to be published.[71] Yamada interrogated Nagai's 'spiritual' vocabulary, reflecting that providence as doctrine allowed for no doubt, dissent or criticism. At the heart of the issue was Nagai's theology of the divine. If the bomb was God's providence and represented God's love as religious dogma, wrote Yamada, nothing further could be argued about the impact of the bombing on the Catholics, or other bomb victims.[72]

The taboo on speaking out against Nagai's spiritual interpretation was increasingly destabilised as time passed and the Catholics who remained silent were challenged to speak about their experiences of the atomic bomb. At the fortieth anniversary of the bombing in 1985, Akizuki spoke to a group of assembled Catholics at a meeting held over three days in Nagasaki city, saying:

> Believers of Nagasaki, as a people who have been persecuted for 300 years you are not accustomed to going into the midst of non-believers and people who have opposed you. Also, up to now, you haven't spoken much about the experiences of the atomic bomb. That is because you were afraid of it being used in a political fashion.

One of the assembled believers replied:

> In the Nagasaki bombing, most of those who experienced it from short range were Catholic believers. Therefore, rather than talking about the suffering with other people, there is a trend of enduring it amongst ourselves. The idea of saying something and that being used politically is a possibility we hate.[73]

Understanding 'fissured' Nagasaki makes sense of the Christians' ongoing perceptions about avoiding participation in politics and their identity as a minority devastated by the atomic bomb. Protesting the bomb might have revealed one's identity as a Catholic from stigmatised Urakami, opening oneself to societal discrimination and rejection. The people knew that if they discussed their experiences, others from Nagasaki would also know that they had worked at Mitsubishi plants, building armaments and participating in the war effort.

The concept of an ongoing stigma in this divided city is confirmed by modern *hibakusha* who reframe what occurred after the bombing from the perspective of the downtrodden and poor. Interviewee Matsuo Sachiko's recollections may be seen as 'dangerous', because her experience of living in Urakami after the war 'interrupts' the 'history of the successful and the established' in the 'fissured' city.[74] Matsuo suggests that it was not until compensation was paid to *hibakusha* (from 1957 onwards) that the atomic bomb was spoken of dropping on Nagasaki and not just Urakami.

> Yes, in Urakami there was [discrimination]. As I say, at first, if you mentioned the atomic bomb, you said it [fell on] Urakami. And then, later, the area [of reference] expanded and so that comment was less common. People stopped saying it was exclusively an attack on Urakami. After all, for those affected, as *hibakusha*, we received compensation. It was a long time though […] [that they described the region affected as Urakami].[75]

Recent critics

Criticisms of Nagai's avowed apolitical interpretation continue to circulate to the present day. Nagasaki philosopher Takahashi Shinji casts Nagai as sweetly sentimental, recounting Yamada's arguments and repeating the charge that the religious interpretation exonerated the United States from blame.[76] Takahashi writes that Nagai also directed attention away from the guilt of the Emperor of Japan (who visited Nagai) and the Japanese people who participated in the military aggression of the Second World War, implying Nagai himself may have wished to deflect attention from his own military participation as a doctor in Manchuria.[77]

Alternatively, according to Shijō Chie, it was the occupation by the United States that created the 'atomic saint', Nagai.[78] Shijō wrote in 2015 that Nagai did not pursue the guilt of the United States for dropping the bomb and that he conceptualised an 'abstract' peace, which led to the Occupation forces' support for his publishing activities. The American influence on Nagai was significant.

Shijō argues convincingly that Nagai's interpretation was not the only factor which affected the meaning given to the bombing. The United States may have encouraged the veneration of Nagai as a saint, although other factors also resulted in a perceived passivity towards the United States about the bombing in Nagasaki. Critiques of Nagai have been generally in Japanese, so that in English he is generally non-critically remembered as the 'Saint of Nagasaki'. There was also a call for 'internationalisation'.[79] Historian Chad Diehl argues that designating Nagasaki an 'International Cultural City' took away from its remembrance of the atomic bombing, in contrast to the more publicised narratives of Hiroshima, known as the 'Peace City'.[80]

Catholic responses

Spokespeople for Catholic institutions responded to criticisms by defending Nagai's legacy. A member of the Urakami Catholic group, Kataoka Yakichi, historian of the hidden Christians and father of Chizuko, argued that Nagai's interpretation did not prevent Nagasaki *hibakusha* from participating in the antinuclear movement.[81] Yakichi cited other reasons for why the peace movement in Nagasaki had been stymied and weak. He argued Nagasaki was the only port open to the West during much of the Edo period and as its citizens had an optimistic openness to the future, they tended to put the past behind them more quickly. Yakichi added a reference to 'fissured' Nagasaki, noting the city centre was not badly damaged, but the Urakami valley was devastated. Therefore, he wrote, *hibakusha* consciousness was not evenly experienced and was geographically stratified.[82] Those less affected in Nagasaki (harbour city), he said, avoided dwelling on the bombing as a central historical event for the city.

As Yakichi's daughter and a previous principal of Junshin University, the interviewee Kataoka Chizuko similarly defended the public legacy of Nagai Takashi. She acknowledged her personal connection through her father's legacy to the debate about Nagai.

Figure 4.3 Kataoka Chizuko, photograph supplied, used by permission, February 2016.

According to Kataoka, Nagai was speaking exclusively to the Christians of Urakami:

> [...] because he [Nagai] was talking to the Urakami people, if you were a believer from Urakami you could understand it but, other people couldn't follow it. There were a lot of phrases and words [...] There were a lot of expressions.[83]

Kataoka argues believers should understand Nagai's interpretation as embedded in the framework of Catholic faith and that his expressions are apt to be misunderstood by those without this faith. The language Kataoka utilises is of interest.

When speaking in the interview, she does not use the word *hansai* or 'burnt offering', but when writing she did. Kataoka referred me to her own writing about Nagai in a book published with her sister, Rumiko. In a chapter entitled 'Nagai Takashi to Nagasaki no kane (Nagai Takashi and The Bells of Nagasaki)', Kataoka Chizuko writes that Nagai's published works may be divided into those produced about 'life in the atomic field' and those where he discusses his energies in assisting the recovery effort.

Kataoka also suggested that Nagai's words were meant for those who held faith and as elements of a communal, spiritual conversation and should not be critiqued from a political perspective.[84] She argues *hansai-setsu* is only explicable for the Urakami believers and not to a foreign, non-Catholic like myself. In addition, non-Catholic Nagasaki citizens will not understand and therefore cannot criticise. Kataoka's response asserts a theology understandable and relevant only to Urakami believers.

When she discusses the Urakami Catholic use of the word *setsuri*, or providence, Kataoka asserts that Nagai's use of this word may not be understood by those who do not have 'this' faith.

> The understanding of the people from the home (*Gembaku Hōmu*) of *setsuri* (God's providence) and the Urakami [Catholic] people's understanding of *setsuri* and Nagai Takashi's use of *setsuri* [...] pre-supposes a deep faith [and] is not able to be understood by those who do not have this faith. [...] When something happens in daily life, we will say, 'that was God's providence, wasn't it!' So, we use it in everyday scenarios, or we use it about the atomic bomb. So, for Nagai to use the word *setsuri*, it was quite different to the meaning given by 'these people' [critics] [...] These words are known through faith. So, in [the word] *setsuri* [...] there is this deep [...] knowledge, a scholarly way, which [...] implies a true psychology of God present, offering praise [...] it is in that place where we have faith [...] by the grace of belief in God's significant grace, only possible itself via belief [...] Nagai Takashi's writing uses an extreme shorthand (*tanraku*) expression [...][85]

Kataoka brushes over the use of the word *setsuri*, 'about the atomic bomb'. Rather, she says, this is an everyday 'Urakami Catholic' word, understood in the context of faith. She re-defines the word as 'God's ongoing presence', avoiding the difficulty of the interpretation of the bomb as providence.

In her book Kataoka elaborated on the interpretation of the word *hansai*. Repeating Nagai's words about the uniqueness of Urakami, she expressed the bombing as the burnt sacrifice of Christ where God is present. According to Kataoka the 'wartime sins of humankind' were dissipated by the bomb:

> In Catholic faith the meaning of these words is expressed in the following way. By participating (*awaseteiru*) ourselves (*watashitachi*) with the sacrifice (*gisei*) of Christ's cross, we perceive how to offer up the wartime sins

Providential atomic bomb? 75

of humankind by way of atonement through the unprecedented horror (pain) of the atom bomb, at the same time, recognising God in Urakami together with Christ as the redeemer of humanity.[86]

Within this discussion, Kataoka reiterated from Nagai's interpretation that Urakami bore the 'wartime sins of humankind by way of atonement', explaining that he had used these words for the encouragement of survivors, in an apolitical, religious way.

Kataoka emphasises Urakami's trials and the communal identity of the Catholic group. Her interpretation presumes similar experiences for all believers and that those who died in the bombing joined (*awaseru*) with Christ's suffering and the death of Christ:

> Therefore, at the time for the believers, Christ's suffering as experienced at the place of the cross allowed for endurance, by way of offering up their own pain, regarding the largest physical and psychological damages which they had absorbed from the atom bomb [...] Therefore, they put together/gathered up (*awaseru*) their own suffering with that experienced by Christ and offered them up to God and then wanted to die or went to die as believers in Christ.[87]

Speaking as a public figure, Kataoka's articulation of the experiences of suffering are differentiated from the survivors who described their more personal torments and narratives. Messy and personal details of trauma are excluded (or hidden) from her abstract explanation of how survivors 'put together' their own suffering with Christ's and the suffering of 'others'. Similar to Nagai, Kataoka's theology does not explicitly address survivors, but focuses on those who died.

A paradigm shift

A significant impetus for a renewed conversation about how the Catholics might reinterpret God's response to the atomic bombing took place in 1981, on the visit and message of Pope John Paul II (Figure 4.4) to Japan. John Paul II began his speech at Hiroshima with these words: 'War is the work of humanity (*ningen no shiwaza*); war is destruction of human life; war is death.'[88] The Pope's speech influenced the transformation of the religious community's interpretation of the memory of the bombing.[89] Nagai's grandson, Tokusaburō, agreed that the community understood and were significantly impacted by the Pope's words, as they were also increasingly uneasy about the use of the words *setsuri* and *hansai* about the atomic bombing. As a brother at the *seibo no kishi* (Knights of the Holy Mother) monastery, interviewee Ozaki Tōmei greeted Pope John Paul II in 1981 and in his interview, paraphrases the Pope's words:

> Papa-sama ('Esteemed Dad' [The Pope]) said, 'War is the work of humanity. The atomic bomb is the work of humanity. It is not the providence of God'[90]

Figure 4.4 Statue of Pope John Paul II, erected at Megumi no Oka Gembaku Hōmu on occasion of the Pope's visit in 1981, photograph, the author, February 2016.

Ozaki remembers the speech in a way showing how important the meaning was for him and its role in dismissing the *hansai-setsu*, and the atomic bomb as providence. The Pope did not openly say, 'The atomic bomb is not the providence of God.' Ozaki's understanding of Nagai's legacy is of a different complexion to Kataoka, due to his work as a brother in the order of the *seibo no kishi*. He was taught by Nagai briefly at the monastery following the end of the war. Ozaki repeats in the interview the criticisms of Takahashi and Tadokoro that Nagai associated himself with the American occupation army, with negative implications for the Urakami Catholics. He states:

> [...] Nagai Takashi played up to the US army [...] and therefore we were oppressed [because of Nagai's work]. [Urakami] was discriminated against. And, the wounds which Urakami people took in because of this kind of thing happening were extremely painful. [...] For people who had keloid scars [...] 'Is there a God?' They would say, 'Why would God do this?', 'I don't believe in God' [...] or 'I can't believe in God's providence'. There were people like that. And then the Pope came and clearly said, 'This is the work of humanity, not God's providence' [...] [Some of them] opened their eyes and some of these people came back to the church.[91]

The *hibakusha* response

For other survivors, the struggle to understand the spiritualised vocabulary used by Nagai continues. Ozaki's own understanding of the atomic bomb is influenced by the local history of martyrdom and persecution. He referred frequently to the stories of the Fourth Persecution and exile when discussing the bombing. He reinterprets Nagai's spiritual language by returning to the theme of the struggle for faith, a common one in the discussion of the persecutions, as a valid response to the public narrative of past suffering. Rather than using providence to explain why the bomb fell on the community, Ozaki's interpretation of Nagai's *setsuri* was as 'strength to proceed'.

> To put it simply, [*setsuri* is] strength to proceed forward (*mae ni mukatte susumu chikara*) [or] strength and hope [...] so even when something inconceivable happens, or is a reality, we absorb it and face forward [...] That is God's providence, the ability to absorb [...] [the bombing]. The Pope said, War is the work of humanity. The atom bomb is the work of humanity. It is not God's providence [...][92]

Ozaki's theology of providence is distinguished from Nagai's because of the revelation from the Pope in 1981 that the atomic bombing had nothing to do with God. He suggests God's providence is rather understood by the people to assist them in absorbing damages and recovering from the atomic bomb. The bomb was an act of war and a human-induced disaster. Ozaki recalls the Fourth Persecution exile and how through faith the people returned and built the

78 *Reinterpreting the bomb*

Urakami Cathedral, suggesting Nagai understood providence in the same way. Many people lost their homes and had to rebuild in 1873 after release from exile. Similarly, they rebuilt in 1945. For Ozaki, faith is required to see God's hand, in equally difficult times (*shiren*).

Kataoka Chizuko also reflects upon the Pope's visit of 1981 and the changed attitudes which broke through walls of silence. Gradually, the Catholic community became more vocal. She remembers the Pope's specific appeal to the Catholic communities to contribute to the work of peace and tell their stories.

> [...] but after the Pope stated 'that' [war is the work of humanity], he said [we] must talk about it [...] This was what changed. [...] There were a whole lot of people who as victims [...] [had experienced this pain of ours] [...] [which] we (*jibun-tachi*) hadn't talked about it, [pain] concealed within us [...] However, the Pope urged [...] that we had to work more for the sake of world peace, so if the Pope says so, even if it is painful, alright, our experiences should be added to the discussion [...] I think this was the kind of change you see.[93]

Importantly, for Kataoka, the Pope told the survivors to speak out. The community found a new freedom to speak out and to break through silences. The Pope's appeal not only changed the interpretation of the bombing but broke down some of the walls of silence and drew forth testimony.

Among the survivors, others strongly reject Nagai and his interpretation. Fukahori Jōji is doubtful about God and his own ongoing faith as a Catholic. He is openly angry about the bombing and laments the loss of his own siblings (Chapter 9). Fukahori does not reinterpret providence or *hansai* and instead dismisses the legacy of Nagai Takashi outright.

> I've had very little to do with 'that guy': he became a Christian after he got married to a Catholic, so I don't know about him. Anyway, what would you say, he was a 'difficult' person, his way of thinking and he was a doctor, wasn't he? [...] Nagai Takashi from Urakami probably didn't really think like the average person [...] He went to Manchuria with the army. And [...] he was a teacher at the university. So, the university students of the time argued he was strict.[94]

Without a personal relationship with the historic Nagai, Fukahori aims to demonstrate Nagai's outsider-status on several fronts in Urakami. Urakami Catholics sometimes suggest that if a Catholic does not trace their lineage to the 'hidden Christians', they are categorically outsiders. Fukahori notes how Nagai became a Christian when he got married and has no *sempuku* ancestors. Fukahori is disparaging of Nagai's intellectual capacity, as a highly educated man and doctor, a class of person distinguished from the average Urakami believer. Nagai was of samurai class, which distinguishes him from the average believer in the Urakami community and the people's associations with the *burakumin* outcastes and marginalised. By noting he went to Manchuria, Fukahori, like scholars Otsuki and Takahashi, raises Nagai's participation in the aggressive Japanese war. Fukahori's antipathy to Nagai demonstrates one aspect of the emergence of a new Catholic resistance to the 'sacrificial' theory of the atomic bomb. Fukahori does not engage with Nagai's interpretation but shows clearly his dissatisfaction with Nagai's authority.

Konishi Shin'ichi is another who contests the idea of God's providence allowing the bombing. He states that neither he nor his community believe in Nagai Takashi's *setsuri* or providence. The community's response to the Pope's call to speak out, as mentioned by Kataoka, included, he says, participation in 'peace' activities, a form of political protest against the bomb.

> Professor Nagai [...] [said] [...] 'God's providence' [...] generally we [Oura community] couldn't accept it, 'God would do that?' [...] [Laughs] [[...]] 56 years later [Pope] John Paul first went to Hiroshima and stated, 'War is the work of humanity', 'the work of the devil' [...] [speaking of] [...] God's providence (*setsuri*) [...] to cause war, it wouldn't happen. Nagasaki people agreed with that [...] [Asked as to how church people agree with Nagai] [...] We don't agree or disagree really. [As for the notion of] *setsuri*, we didn't believe in it but [it did raise the question of] how did the United States do it? [...] We don't hate but accept it [the bomb] [...] it is faith by prayer. Anyway [...] peace activities are still rare, but now, they are increasing.[95]

Konishi links his community's dissatisfaction with Nagai's interpretation to the Pope's visit in 1981. Konishi equivocates when asked whether he concurs with Nagai's overall interpretation: 'We don't agree or disagree really.' Konishi is definitive, though, that the atomic bomb was a human-made weapon, with no connection to the providence of God.

Konishi reports an increase in peace-work involvement which he is also engaged in, by the Christians, a subtle alteration in political and community stance. An integral part of such peace-work is the *kataribe* tribal narrator role, by which Konishi, Miyake, Nakamura, Nishida and others speak to community groups, children and schools. Konishi's response indicates a new and emerging Catholic antipathy to the *hansai* sacrificial interpretation of the atomic bombing.

The *hansai-setsu* was a complex but pious response to the atomic bombing, in a context of utter deprivation and in the 'valley of death'. The burnt sacrifice theory initially resonated among Catholic mourners, appealing to both nationalist and Christian tropes of martyrdom. As a result and alongside apolitical attitudes, reticence and trauma, the believing community remained largely silent for many years. Critics suggested that even as Nagai Takashi interpreted the bombing as a religious sacrifice, he detracted from resistance and peace movements and exonerated US and Japanese war crimes. Later, after Pope John Paul II's visit to Japan, a paradigm shift in Catholic discourse about the atomic bomb was achieved.

Perhaps more significant than the Pope's visit, though, are the survivors' challenges to the Nagai 'burnt offering' interpretation of the bombing, emerging lucidly from their own attempts to understand their experiences and acknowledge the reality of deprivation and oppression. The *kataribe* reject theodicies which 'reconcile themselves and collude with the almighty God behind the back, so to speak, of nameless suffering'. 'Dangerous' memory recalls all those who have died in suffering, including believers, but also the 'other', forgotten and excluded people.[96] Metz suggests, 'humanity rebels against the God of the theologians' and against explanations of suffering which over-emphasise human guilt.[97] Still, the contesting of *hansai* today in Nagasaki is partial and not always coherent.

As I have foregrounded, the next chapters consider the superseding of *hansai* by symbolic memory of the atomic bombing. I initially examine an archetypal symbol which was significant for the Catholic community struggling to understand what had happened to them, in iconic and statue form, broken and haunting in the torn-up landscape after the bombing. Prior to the bombing, the symbol of Mary was already a constant for the people of Urakami – even as the Buddhist *kannon* – and the symbolic and transcendent Mary would be of significance for the community in recovery and for the survivors. She (Mother Mary) signified God's compassion and presence, but was also depicted as a 'dangerous', fractured and confronting icon.

Notes

1 Shinji Takahashi, 'Listening to the Wishes of the Dead: In the Case of Dr Nagai Takashi', trans. Brian Burke-Gaffney, *Crossroads*, 5. Autumn (1997), 23–32.
2 Shinji Takahashi, *Nagasaki ni atte tetsugakusuru: kakujidai no shi to sei*, Shohan (Tōkyō: Hokuju Shuppan, 1994), 198–9.
3 Using the term Holocaust about the twentieth century Nazi mass murder of Jewish people may be offensive, given the origin of the word: some prefer to use the term Shoah for this historic event.
4 Shijō refers to Jobian readings in the community which support this 'sublimation of violence' into Catholicism and writes that not only the atomic bombing, but also sickness and natural disaster would be considered a part of this understanding of God. The suggestion that Nagai used an 'Old Testament' theology, however, could be characterised as simplistic and lacking in nuance. Indeed, the Hebrew scriptures are a polyphonic collection of writings with various purposes and incorporating multiple genres. Nagai did refer to Job 1:21 in the final lines of his funeral speech. In her description of 'Old Testament' theology, Shijō may herself be influenced by other writers including John W. Treat, who wrote of Nagai as influenced by the idea of an 'Old Testament story of a wrathful God and a New Testament promise of delivery by the same God'. Chie Shijō, *Urakami no genbaku no katari: Nagai Takashi kara Rōma kyōkō e* (Tōkyō: Miraisha, 2015), 48. (Research Centre for Nuclear Weapons Abolition, Nagasaki [RECNA] *kakuheiki kenkyū sentā*, Nagasaki University). Shijō is today working in another part of Nagasaki University). Kevin Doak considers the suggestion that Nagai was influenced by 'Old Testament theology' in his recent book chapter in *When the Tsunami Came to Shore*. Kevin M. Doak, 'Hiroshima Rages, Nagasaki Prays: Nagai Takashi's Catholic Response to the Atomic Bombing', in *When the Tsunami Came to Shore*, ed. Roy Starrs (Leiden: Brill, 2014), 249–71 (261).

5 Yuki Miyamoto, *Beyond the Mushroom Cloud: Commemoration, Religion and Responsibility after Hiroshima* (New York: Fordham University Press, 2012), 119.
6 Paul Glynn, *A Song for Nagasaki* (Grand Rapids, MI: Eerdmans, 1990), 8.
7 Shinji Takahashi, 'Listening to the Wishes of the Dead: In the Case of Dr Nagai Takashi'.
8 Tomoe Otsuki, 'Reinventing Nagasaki: The Christianization of Nagasaki and the Revival of an Imperial Legacy in Postwar Japan'. *Inter-Asia Cultural Studies* 17.3 (2016): 395–415 (402).
9 Emiko Ohnuki-Tierney, *Kamikaze, Cherry Blossoms and Nationalisms: The Militarization of Aesthetics in Japanese History* (Chicago: University of Chicago Press, 2010), 7.
10 Glynn, *A Song for Nagasaki*, 59.
11 Glynn, *A Song for Nagasaki*, 156–7.
12 Miyamoto, *Beyond the Mushroom Cloud*, 123.
13 Yakichi Kataoka, *Nagai Takashi No Shōgai*, 2nd ed. (Tokyo: San Pauro, 1961), 156.
14 Glynn, *A Song for Nagasaki*, 92.
15 Glynn, *A Song for Nagasaki*, 98–107.
16 Under the orders of SCAP – Supreme Commander for the Allied Powers (General Douglas MacArthur). Takashi Nagai, *The Bells of Nagasaki* (Tokyo: Kodansha International, 1994) was published through the US Occupation's censor on condition that it included a description of Japanese war crimes in Manila in its preface. Nagai added in the preface that he was very thankful about the resultant book, making clear, says Treat, that he thought both events should be judged as war atrocities. John Whittier Treat, *Writing Ground Zero: Japanese Literature and the Atomic Bomb* (Chicago: University of Chicago Press, 1995), 315.
17 Takashi Nagai, *Atomic Bomb Rescue and Relief Report* (Nagasaki: Nagasaki Association for Hibakushas' Medical Care, 2000), accessed 27 April 2016, www.nashim.org/e_pdf/atomic_bomb/.
18 Kim E. Nielsen, *The Radical Lives of Helen Keller*, ed. Harvey J. Kaye, History of Disability Series (New York: NYU Press, 2004), 93; *The Emperors of Modern Japan*, ed. Ben-Ami Shillony (Leiden and Boston: Brill Academic Publishers, 2008), 95. Shillony writes the Shōwa Emperor showed a special interest in Catholicism, having visited a church in 1947 and sent a photograph to Pope Pius XII in 1948. When the Emperor visited Nagasaki to tour the atomic bomb ruins, he called on Nagai Takashi, who was sick with radiation sickness in hospital. Shillony, *The Emperors*, 175.
19 Nielsen, *The Radical Lives*, 93.
20 Chizuko Kataoka and Rumiko Kataoka, *Hibakuchi Nagasaki no saiken* (Nagasaki: Nagasaki Junshin Daigaku, 1996), 73. Shijō, *Urakami no genbaku no katari*, 43.
21 Critics included poet Yamada Kan, medical doctor Akizuki Tatsuichirō and others. I will enlarge on their criticisms later in this chapter.
22 Nagai, *Bells of Nagasaki*.
23 Takashi Nagai, *Rozario no kusari* (Tokyo: Romansusha, 1948).
24 Doak, 'Hiroshima Rages, Nagasaki Prays', 260. Doak revised Johnston's English translation of *The Bells of Nagasaki* (*Nagasaki no kane*) by Nagai, replacing Johnston's Nagasaki with Nagai's original Urakami.
25 Shijō, *Urakami no genbaku no katari*, 106.
26 Miyamoto, *Beyond the Mushroom Cloud*, 113. Chad Richard Diehl, *Resurrecting Nagasaki: Reconstruction and the Formation of Atomic Narratives* (Ithaca: Cornell University Press, 2018), 72.
27 Diehl, *Resurrecting Nagasaki: Reconstruction and the Formation of Atomic Narratives*, 72.
28 As for the US choice of Nagasaki as a target, there is some evidence that United States Secretary of State Henry Stimson chose Nagasaki as an alternative for Kyoto, due to the concern that the bombing of Kyoto would have long implications for the

82 Reinterpreting the bomb

relationship between Japan and the United States. Stimson was worried about civilian deaths and sought refuge in the idea that the US air force was engaged in precision bombing, according to Barton J. Bernstein, 'The Atomic Bombings Reconsidered'. *Foreign Affairs* 74.1 (1 February 1995): 135. According to Harry Truman's diary, Bernstein also notes that Nagasaki and Kokura were substituted for Kyoto as 'military objectives and soldiers and sailors are the target and not women and children [...] the target will be purely a military one'.

29 Psalm 23:4 'Even though I walk through the valley of the shadow of death [...]', NRSV, footnote a.
30 Kataoka and Kataoka, *Hibakuchi Nagasaki*, 73.
31 James Yamazaki, 'Hiroshima and Nagasaki Death Toll', *Children of the Atomic Bomb*, 2016, accessed 13 May 2016, www.aasc.ucla.edu/cab/200708230009.html.
32 Shijō discusses at length the difficult conditions in which the Urakami Christian community found themselves after the bombing. See Shijō, *Urakami no genbaku no katari*, 187–91.
33 Shijō, *Urakami no genbaku no katari*, 191. The Catholic community in Urakami was very much found around the hypocenter (estimated 8500 of 12,000 killed) and the Urakami Cathedral was located 500 m from the hypocenter and destroyed in the bombing.
34 Shōmei Tōmatsu, *Nagasaki 11:02, August 9, 1945; Photographs by Shōmei Tōmatsu*, 1st ed. (Tokyo: Shinchosha, 1995), 154–5.
35 Keloid scars do not only form in atomic bomb survivors, but are characterised by an irregular protruding scar tissue which forms during the healing process from burns experienced by many of the atomic bomb survivors. Excerpt from interview: Tōmei Ozaki, interview by Gwyn McClelland, Francisco-en Hōmu, Sasaki, 27 February 2016.
36 Tokusaburō Nagai, interview by Gwyn McClelland, Nyokodō Museum, 2014.
37 Yuki Miyamoto, 'Rebirth in the Pure Land or God's Sacrificial Lambs? Religious Interpretations of the Atomic Bombings in Hiroshima and Nagasaki'. *Japanese Journal of Religious Studies* 32.1 (2005): 131–59 (142).
38 Shijō argues that in the silent landscape, the *hansai-setsu* enabled survivors to deal with the great losses of the community, giving certain hope and meaning to atomic death. Shijō, *Urakami no genbaku no katari*, 191.
39 Shijō, *Urakami no genbaku no katari*, 100.
40 Shijō's book expands on how Junshin used Nagai's interpretation to describe their memory of the bombing. Shijō, *Urakami no genbaku no katari*, 45–8.
41 Junshin Junior High and High School website, 'Junshin Junior High/Girls Senior High: Junshin Gakuen to Nagai Takashi Hakase', *Junshin Girls School*, 2017, accessed 22 November 2017, www.n-junshin.ed.jp/modules/gakkou/index.php?content_id=9.
42 Yuki Miyamoto, 'Narrative Boundaries: The Ethical Implications of Reinterpreting Atomic Bomb Histories' (PhD diss., University of Chicago, 2003), 259–303.
43 Shijō, *Urakami no genbaku no katari*, 108.
44 Shijō, *Urakami no genbaku no katari*, 100–3.
45 Stephanie Houston Grey, 'Writing Redemption: Trauma and the Authentication of the Moral Order in Hibakusha Literature'. *Text & Performance Quarterly* 22.1 (2002): 1–23 (16).
46 The author's translation. I acknowledge this is not a poetic rendering of the poem – I have translated the poem more directly than Paul Glynn does in his book. See Glynn, *A Song for Nagasaki*, 116.
47 Shijō, *Urakami no genbaku no katari*, 106–8.
48 Shijō, 105. Junshin Junior High and High School website, 'Junshin chūgakkō junshin joshi kōtō gakkō kosho kōka'.
49 Daniel A. Rober, 'Ricœur, Metz and the Future of Dangerous Memory'. *Literature and Theology* 27.2 (2013): 196–207 (203) https://doi.org/10.1093/litthe/frt010.

50 Rober, 'Ricœur, Metz', 197.
51 Chizuko Kataoka, interview by Gwyn McClelland, Junshin University Library, 24 February 2016.
52 Shijō, *Urakami no genbaku no katari*, 190.
53 Shijō, 161–2. For example, Catholic survivors were interviewed by Robert Lifton in 1962. Robert Jay Lifton, *Death in Life: Survivors of Hiroshima* (Chapel Hill: The University of North Carolina Press, 1991). Nagai Takashi wrote about the testimony of Catholic survivors as well, before 1951. However, these were not official church publications which discussed experiences of the bombing. Takashi Nagai, *We of Nagasaki: The Story of Survivors in an Atomic Wasteland* (New York: Duell, Sloan and Pearce, 1951).
54 Shijō, *Urakami no genbaku no katari*, 190.
55 Shijō, *Urakami no genbaku no katari*, 190.
56 Shijō, *Urakami no genbaku no katari*, 180.
57 Shijō, *Urakami no genbaku no katari*, 190.
58 Shijō, *Urakami no genbaku no katari*, 162.
59 Shijō, *Urakami no genbaku no katari*, 162.
60 Miyamoto, 'Narrative Boundaries', 373.
61 Miyamoto, 'Narrative Boundaries', 373.
62 Kazutoshi Nakamura, interview by Gwyn McClelland, Nagasaki Atomic Bomb Museum, 23 February 2016.
63 Tadokoro is quoted in Miyamoto, 'Rebirth in the Pure Land or God's Sacrificial Lambs?', 165.
64 Yamaguchi also discusses the taboo and the disruption of this taboo by Yamada and Takahashi Shinji. Kenichiro Yamaguchi, *Kokusaku to gisei: gembaku gempatsu soshite gendai iriyou no yukue* (Tokyo: Shakai Hyoronsha, 2016), 316.
65 Kataoka and Kataoka, *hibakuchi Nagasaki*, 62.
66 Tadokoro is quoted in Miyamoto, 'Rebirth in the Pure Land or God's Sacrificial Lambs?', 146.
67 Miyamoto, *Beyond the Mushroom Cloud*, 134.
68 Tatsuichiro Akizuki, *Shi no doshinen: Nagasaki hibaku ishi no kiroku* (Tokyo: Kodansha, 1972), 194.
69 Miyamoto, 'Narrative Boundaries', 376.
70 Yamaguchi, *kokusaku to gisei*, 290.
71 Nagai's *Bells of Nagasaki* was the first survivor tale allowed through the American occupation censor in 1949.
72 Kan Yamada, 'Gizensha: Nagai Takashi e no kokuhatsu'. *Ushio* (1972): 231–7.
73 Lecture, 'Hankaku heiwa Kirisutosha no inori to kōdō', cited in Shijō, *Urakami no genbaku*, 185.
74 Michael Iafrate, '"We Will Never Forget": Metz, Memory and the Dangerous Spirituality of Post-9/11 America (Part II)', *Vox Nova*, 2009, accessed 21 August 2013, http://vox-nova.com/2009/09/12/we-will-never-forget-metz-memory-and-the-dangerous-spirituality-of-post-911-america-part-ii/.
75 Sachiko Matsuo, interview by Gwyn McClelland, Nagasaki Atomic Bomb Museum, 5 December 2014.
76 Shinji Takahashi, *Nagasaki ni atte tetsugakusuru*, 203.
77 Shinji Takahashi, *Nagasaki ni atte tetsugakusuru*, 200.
78 Shijō, *Urakami no genbaku*, 99. Chad Diehl, on the other hand, in his recently published book writes that for a Communist party leader, Kamiyama Shigeo, it was the capitalists who created the 'atomic saint of Urakami' as a political tool to appease the working class. He describes Kamiyama's arguments about Nagai Takashi at length. Diehl, *Resurrecting Nagasaki: Reconstruction and the Formation of Atomic Narratives*, 86–90.
79 Shijō, *Urakami no genbaku no katari*, 94.

80 Diehl, 'Resurrecting Nagasaki'.
81 Kataoka Yakichi died in 1980 and this paper, 'Nagasaki wa naze damatte iru noka', was published posthumously in Kataoka and Kataoka, 139–46.
82 Kataoka is quoted in Miyamoto, 'Narrative Boundaries', 379–80.
83 Kataoka, 24 February 2016, McClelland.
84 Nobuo Takahashi, 'Nagasaki Peace Site: Nagasaki no shisō to Nagai Takashi', *Nagasaki Shinbun* (Nagasaki: 1 August 2000), accessed 10 July 2017, www.nagasaki-np.co.jp/peace/2000/kikaku/nagai/nagai1.html.
85 Kataoka, 24 February 2016, McClelland.
86 Kataoka and Kataoka, *hibakuchi Nagasaki*, 75, author's translation.
87 Kataoka, 24 February 2016, McClelland.
88 To view the Pope's statement at Hiroshima see the following website: 'Pope John Paul II, Peace Memorial Hall, 25 February 1981', *Atomicbombmuseum.Org*, 2006, accessed 2 May 2016, http://atomicbombmuseum.org/6_5.shtml.
89 Shinji Takahashi, 'Hansai theory and Nagai Takashi', personal email 25 March 2016.
90 Ozaki, 27 February 2016, McClelland.
91 Ozaki, 27 February 2016, McClelland.
92 Ozaki, 27 February 2016, McClelland.
93 Kataoka, 24 February 2016, McClelland.
94 Jōji Fukahori, interview by Gwyn McClelland, Nagasaki Atomic Bomb Museum, 1 October 2014.
95 Shin'ichi Konishi, interview by Gwyn McClelland, Nagasaki Atomic Bomb Museum, 1 October 2014.
96 See for example, Johann Baptist Metz, *A Passion for God: The Mystical-Political Dimension of Christianity* (New York: Paulist Press, 1998), 144–8.
97 Janice Allison Thompson, 'Theodicy in a Political Key: God and Suffering in the Post-Shoah Theology of Johann Baptist Metz' (PhD diss., University of Notre Dame, 2004), 165.

References

Akizuki, Tatsuichiro. *Shi no doshinen: Nagasaki hibaku ishi no kiroku*. Tokyo: Kodansha, 1972.
Bernstein, Barton J. 'The Atomic Bombings Reconsidered'. *Foreign Affairs* 74 (1995): 135–52.
Diehl, Chad Richard. 'Resurrecting Nagasaki: Reconstruction, the Urakami Catholics and Atomic Memory, 1945–1970'. PhD diss., Columbia University, 2011.
Diehl, Chad Richard. *Resurrecting Nagasaki: Reconstruction and the Formation of Atomic Narratives*. Ithaca: Cornell University Press, 2018.
Doak, Kevin M. 'Hiroshima Rages, Nagasaki Prays: Nagai Takashi's Catholic Response to the Atomic Bombing'. In *When the Tsunami Came to Shore*, ed. Roy Starrs (Leiden: Brill, 2014), 249–71.
Fukahori, Jōji. Interviewed by Gwyn McClelland, Nagasaki Atomic Bomb Museum, 1 October 2014.
Glynn, Paul. *A Song for Nagasaki*. Grand Rapids, MI: Eerdmans, 1990.
Grey, Stephanie Houston. 'Writing Redemption: Trauma and the Authentication of the Moral Order in Hibakusha Literature'. *Text & Performance Quarterly* 22 (2002): 1–23.
Iafrate, Michael. '"We Will Never Forget": Metz, Memory and the Dangerous Spirituality of Post-9/11 America (Part II)'. *Vox Nova*, 2009, accessed 21 August 2013, http://vox-nova.com/2009/09/12/we-will-never-forget-metz-memory-and-the-dangerous-spirituality-of-post-911-america-part-ii/.

Junshin Junior High and High School website. 'Junshin chūgakkō junshin joshi kōtō gakkō kosho kōka', 2017 www.n-junshin.ed.jp/modules/gakkou/index.php?content_id=12.
Junshin Junior High and High School website. 'Junshin Junior High/Girls Senior High: Junshin gakuen to Nagai Takashi hakase', *Junshin Girls School*, 2017, www.n-junshin. ed.jp/modules/gakkou/index.php?content_id=9.
Kataoka, Chizuko. Interview by Gwyn McClelland, Junshin University Library, 24 February 2016.
Kataoka, Chizuko, and Rumiko Kataoka. *hibakuchi Nagasaki no saiken*. Nagasaki: Nagasaki Junshin Daigaku, 1996.
Kataoka, Yakichi. *Nagai Takashi no shōgai*, 2nd ed. Tokyo: San Pauro, 1961.
Konishi, Shinichi. Interview by Gwyn McClelland, Nagasaki Atomic Bomb Museum, 1 October 2014.
Lifton, Robert Jay. *Death in Life: Survivors of Hiroshima*. Chapel Hill: The University of North Carolina Press, 1991.
Matsuo, Sachiko. Interview by Gwyn McClelland, Nagasaki Atomic Bomb Museum, 5 December 2014.
Metz, Johann Baptist. *A Passion for God: The Mystical-Political Dimension of Christianity*. New York: Paulist Press, 1998.
Miyamoto, Yuki. 'Narrative Boundaries: The Ethical Implications of Reinterpreting Atomic Bomb Histories'. PhD diss., University of Chicago, 2003.
Miyamoto, Yuki. 'Rebirth in the Pure Land or God's Sacrificial Lambs? Religious Interpretations of the Atomic Bombings in Hiroshima and Nagasaki'. *Japanese Journal of Religious Studies* 32 (2005): 131–59.
Miyamoto, Yuki. *Beyond the Mushroom Cloud: Commemoration, Religion and Responsibility after Hiroshima*. New York: Fordham University Press, 2012.
Nagai, Takashi. *Rozario no kusari*. Tokyo: Romansusha, 1948.
Nagai, Takashi. *We of Nagasaki: The Story of Survivors in an Atomic Wasteland*. New York: Duell, Sloan and Pearce, 1951.
Nagai, Takashi. *Bells of Nagasaki*, trans. William Johnston. Tokyo: Kodansha International, 1994.
Nagai, Takashi. *Atomic Bomb Rescue and Relief Report*. Nagasaki: Nagasaki Association for Hibakushas' Medical Care, 2000. www.nashim.org/e_pdf/atomic_bomb/.
Nakamura, Kazutoshi, Nagasaki Atomic Bomb Museum, 2016.
Nielsen, Kim E. *The Radical Lives of Helen Keller*, ed. Harvey J. Kaye, History of Disability Series. New York: NYU Press, 2004.
Ohnuki-Tierney, Emiko. *Kamikaze, Cherry Blossoms and Nationalisms: The Militarization of Aesthetics in Japanese History*. Chicago: University of Chicago Press, 2010.
Otsuki, Tomoe. 'Reinventing Nagasaki: The Christianization of Nagasaki and the Revival of an Imperial Legacy in Postwar Japan'. *Inter-Asia Cultural Studies* 17 (2016): 395–415 https://doi.org/10.1080/14649373.2016.1217631.
Ozaki, Tōmei. Interview by Gwyn McClelland, Francisco-en Homu, Sasaki, 27 February 2016.
'Pope John Paul II, Peace Memorial Hall, 25 February 1981'. *Atomicbombmuseum.Org*, 2006. http://atomicbombmuseum.org/6_5.shtml.
Rober, Daniel A. 'Ricœur, Metz and the Future of Dangerous Memory'. *Literature and Theology* 27 (2013): 196–207. https://doi.org/10.1093/litthe/frt010.
Shijō, Chie. *Urakami no genbaku no katari: Nagai Takashi kara Rōma kyōkō e*. Tōkyō: Miraisha, 2015.

Shillony, Ben-Ami, ed. *The Emperors of Modern Japan*. Leiden and Boston: Brill Academic Publishers, 2008.
Takahashi, Nobuo. Nagasaki Peace Site: Nagasaki No Shisou to Nagai Takashi 3. *'Genbaku Wa Kami No Setsuri' Ka*, 2000. www.nagasaki-np.co.jp/peace/2000/kikaku/nagai/nagai1.html.
Takahashi, Shinji. *Nagasaki Ni Atte Tetsugakusuru: Kakujidai No Shi to Sei*, Shohan. Tōkyō: Hokuju Shuppan, 1994.
Takahashi, Shinji. 'Listening to the Wishes of the Dead: In the Case of Dr Nagai Takashi', trans. Brian Burke-Gaffney. *Crossroads* 5 (1997): 23–32.
Thompson, Janice Allison. 'Theodicy in a Political Key: God and Suffering in the Post-Shoah Theology of Johann Baptist Metz'. PhD diss., University of Notre Dame, 2004.
Tomatsu, Shomei. *Nagasaki 11:02, August 9, 1945; Photographs by Shomei Tomatsu*. 1st ed. Tokyo: Shinchosha, 1995.
Treat, John Whittier. *Writing Ground Zero: Japanese Literature and the Atomic Bomb*. Chicago: University of Chicago Press, 1995.
Yamada, Kan. 'Gizensha: Nagai Takashi e no kokuhatsu'. *Ushio* (1972): 231–7.
Yamaguchi, Kenichiro. *Kokusaku to gisei: gembaku gempatsu soshite gendai iriyou no yukue*. Tokyo: Shakai Hyoronsha, 2016.
Yamazaki, James. 'Hiroshima and Nagasaki Death Toll'. *Children of the Atomic Bomb*, 2016. www.aasc.ucla.edu/cab/200708230009.html.

5 A-bombed Mary

> [...] *even when I cried 'wanwan', the assistant would say to me with a meaning beyond words, 'Nagase-san, you are held by Mary like a baby'* [...]
> (Nagase Kazuko, 2016)

Introduction

The figure of Mary is a bridge for generational survivors of trauma, traversing the periods from the times of persecution to the memory of the atomic bombing, as an archetypal and powerful symbol of Urakami. Her figure is today often remembered as an 'A-bombed Mary' (*hibaku-Maria*). From the time of the Jesuits' arrival in Japan, Mary, Mother of Christ, comprised a figure of veneration among the kirishitan classes.[1] Many years later, the survivors interviewed for this project evoked her frequently.

Archetypal Mary's presence was a constant during the trauma of persecutions, martyrdoms and suffering. After the bombing, damaged Mary statues resembled human bodies and remains in the landscape, becoming both unsettling icons of Catholic *hibakusha* and a vehicle or an imagery for protest. In interviews, the survivors remember the icons of Mary in the rubble, they relate to her due to the loss of their own mothers and they speak of Mary as an anti-war image, encouraging prayer. In the wider Catholic narrative, Mary as a *hibakusha* was subjected to the 'Fifth persecution' (kuzure) of the bombing and survived. Although St Mary's, the monumental cathedral, was destroyed, Mary statues survived – or were in some way recoverable. Survivors suggest the statues bear the same 'keloid' atomic scars they suffered on their own bodies.[2]

Mary, peasant woman, symbolises the marginality of 'fissured' Nagasaki and bonds the trauma of the bomb to older narratives of persecution in individual and public Catholic history. In this chapter, I discuss how she was 'hidden', 'trampled' and 'dangerous', represented as Buddhist in *Maria Kannon* form and created by the magistrate as *fumi-e* icons during the period of the *sempuku kirishitan* (underground Christians). The worship of Mary signalled subversion for the Nagasaki magistrate and danger for the hidden Christians who stepped on iconic depictions of Mary and her son to avoid persecution. In contrast to virtuous compassion and gentleness, the symbolic Urakami Mary has been a 'dangerous' reminder of faith in this place.

Mary the Nazarene peasant

As a co-survivor Urakami Mary witnesses and demonstrates against the devastation of the atomic bomb. A-bombed Mary invokes the ancient story of the archetypal poor villager Mary, herself a witness and co-sufferer of violence. In Mary's 'Magnificat', a song in Luke 1:47–55, the pregnant Mary in the biblical text remembers God's deeds in the past and imagines a future for the abused and suffering: '[God] has brought down the powerful from their thrones and lifted up the lowly; he has filled the hungry with good things and sent the rich away empty' (vs. 52–53). Feminist theologian Gale Yee writes Mary in Nazareth would have observed brutal and horrifying Imperial Roman violence against rebellious Jews and witnessed the torture and crucifixion of her own son.[3] The icon of A-bombed Mary in Urakami Cathedral stands as a visual witness, on the side of those devastated by the atomic bomb. Mary protests the results of modern warfare and its indiscriminate impacts on civilians.

Mary 'survives'

The *hibakusha* are survivors of the A-bomb who imagine symbolic Mary surviving the bombing. The orphaned Fukahori Jōji described in his interview how he uncovered *hibaku-shita* (atomic-bombed) Mary and other religious symbols in his ruined house after the bombing. Ambivalent, he titles the material items he found memories and evidence.

> In my own house, in the burnt out remains, I found rosary beads, some Mary statues and the remains of Christ statues. And people collected these also [...] I'm not sure what for, as they were burnt up, but they treasure them.
>
> People still have them and are treasuring them [...] for memories, as evidence (*shōkōhin*).[4]

Damaged Mary statues and figurines crystallised Mary's symbolic presence in broken Urakami and especially around the broken-down Urakami Cathedral, denoting survivors, imitating the bodies in the landscape, evoking unsettling destruction and grief to the Catholic and non-Catholic community, the statues were dislocated from familiar context. *Hibakusha* Mary was highly visible in statue form at the site of the destroyed cathedral at Urakami. The statues evoked suffering, remembered an exotic 'other' and yet suggested resilience and continuity for the surviving community. As a child, Matsuo Sachiko remembers playing at the cathedral ruins once a week. She recollects seeing many 'beautiful' statues of grieving Mary, including damaged statues in the grass. Matsuo says:

> Mary(s), there were a lot, many around there. Mary and John [...] [statues] [...] They were beautiful Marys. But after the war, they were changed. They were so broken up and damaged [...] [laughs][5]

Pointing out Mary's brokenness like the survivors themselves, Matsuo introduces a sacred fractured Mary, who symbolised the people's relatedness with God, surviving the bombing in statue form. Mary is Mater Dolorosa, the Mother of Sorrows, a 'participant' in suffering at the cross. The damaged and broken Mary statues after the bombing show the Mater Dolorosa, present with the people in suffering; suffering herself. Matsuo's laugh at the end of the above interview excerpt seems to indicate an embarrassment about the state of the statues, which lay about for a long time in disrepair.

Kataribe Fukahori Shigemi participated in the restoration of the icon of *hibaku-Maria*, representing 'material' atomic history. Fukahori placed her in a shrine in the church.

> [...] in 2005, we made that [...] [altar]. Finally, [in Urakami Cathedral] properly. We put it there. Previously, she was on top of the old altar [...] A congregant made the altar in the same way [as the old altar]. So, in a way, it has a bit of the old image [...] I was the person in charge and it was an *hibaku-Maria* [...][6]

Remembering the atomic bomb history and the persecution narratives were both significant in this restoration. Fukahori and the parishioners of Urakami built the shrine for the A-bombed icon (Figure 5.1). The placement of the icon with its previous accoutrements was of importance, he said. In an Agence France-Presse (AFP) news article, Fukahori Shigemi states: '... it's as if the Virgin Mary is telling us about the misery of war by sacrificing herself'.[7] In this state, Mary statues are inclusive of memory of both the dead and survivors of atomic devastation.

The Japanese calligraphic *kanji* characters for peace are written on the shrine, showing an emerging understanding of an anti-war, anti-nuclear Mary, who protests the bombing. As mentioned in the last chapter, the Urakami Catholics tended to avoid overt 'peace demonstrations' and Nagai Takashi opined that those who participated in 'peace activity' were misled. On the other hand, Nagai signed his artworks with the calligraphy for 'Peace', signifying 'Peace to the world'. Fukahori elaborated, 'This is a significant symbol of peace which should be preserved forever.'[8] A-bombed-*Maria*, scarred and broken – remembers, laments and protests the atomic bombing.

Catholic survivor Konishi Shin'ichi refers in his interview to the eyes of A-bomb-*Maria*. Her fractured status embodies sacred and secular meaning, he says, as he ascribes to the icon an expression of grief:

> [...] this one was particularly damaged [...] and when you look at this Mary, it has a piercing gaze, it's burnt and it has this 'grieving' Mary look [...] [telling us] you shouldn't do war. Be peaceful. It's a different/transformed

(*kawatta*) symbol [...] [in a] burnt out state, [it is] a Peace statue which points to prayer [...][9]

The atomic-bombed 'icon of Mary' represents a grieving Mary who suffered with the people and who calls for peace. By holding up the icon of Mary as an anti-war symbol, Konishi shows a simultaneous anti-war and faith interpretation.

The Urakami Christian Museum published a picture of the same A-bomb-Maria in the modern Urakami Cathedral, suggesting the symbolic Mary, comforter and fellow sufferer, expresses otherwise incommunicable extreme experience for this community. A spokesperson commented:

> It is impossible to tell the things of the atomic bomb which she can see. Her expression speaks of the impossibility of telling the immensity of the horror. Anyway, both [this and another] Mary statues come alongside our pain and sadness and teach us (*watashitachi*).[10]

As the spokesperson writes, the symbolic A-bombed Mary helps survivors express sentiments otherwise impossible to turn into words. Paul Ricœur wrote, 'The limit facing the historian ... – lies ... in the untransmissible part of extreme experiences ... However, ... to say untransmissible is not to say inexpressible.'[11] The museum suggests the icon 'teaches' and comes alongside 'pain and sadness', using watashitachi to express an inclusive 'us' in Japanese, of the wider Japanese community, potentially exhorting secular and civic atomic memory.

Urakami Mary

Marian liturgy, devotion and imagery in Urakami is traced back to early Christianity.[12] Nun and academic Oka Ritsuko confirms that 'one of the characteristics of the Christian community of Nagasaki ... is the sincere and filial veneration towards the Maria, Mother of God'.[13] This archetype represents compassion, tradition, watchfulness but also challenges and endangers. Mary was not one of the educated upper class, but a humble Palestinian peasant, in a context in Nazareth that resembled the social situation of people in the community of Urakami in 1945, the lowest social strata of society.[14]

Several writers developed Johann Baptist Metz's ideas on 'dangerous' memory in a feminist direction, considering biblical Mary. Mariology, or the theological discipline of the study of Mary, is 'a liberating symbol for women only when it is seen as a radical symbol of a new humanity freed from hierarchical power relations, including that of God and humanity', writes feminist theologist Rosemary Ruether.[15] Theologian Elizabeth Johnson writes Mary of Nazareth is 'dangerous' to complacency and despair. She continues:

> the vital memory of this woman of Spirit has the quality of 'danger' insofar as it births wisdom, awakens resistance and inspires active hope for a just

and peaceful world in which poor people, women, indeed all human beings and the earth can flourish as beloved of God.[16]

Japanese Mariologies developed at a distance from the official Church after the Tokugawa shogunate banned Christianity and Nagasaki was cut off from Rome in the early seventeenth century. The symbol of Mary evolved and adapted variously according to localised interpretations as those who held on to their faith secretly developed an oral liturgical tradition.[17]

The 26 Martyrs' Museum in Nishizaka holds another *hibaku-Maria* (atom-bombed Mary), but this one is a *Maria Kannon* statue, venerated by the *sempuku kirishitan* ancestors of the modern Catholics. During the seventeenth and eighteenth centuries, outwardly, Buddhism and local religion swamped Christianity and yet the hidden Christians' faith was only partially submerged. The clandestine use of a Buddhist goddess of mercy, *kannon*, to portray Mary, was a new and dramatic development. The origin of the *Maria Kannon* was in Chinese representations of *guanyin*, or *kannon* (*Avalokitesvara*: the Buddha of Mercy) in Japan.[18]

Some might call the adaptability of the Hidden Christians syncretism, although given the pejorative understanding of this term, Robert Schreiter has called for 'cultural hybridity' as an alternative description. Cultural hybridity enabled the preservation of Christian faith, maintaining the outward appearance of Buddhism.[19] And so the *Maria Kannon* statues were used effectively by the *kirishitan* to characterise Mary with the baby Christ, following the tradition of a compassionate, femininised image of *kannon*, known as *jibo* or *hibo kannon*.[20] The small statue at the 26 Martyrs' Museum, in Nishizaka, is one such representation. In Japan, artisans produced more statues of *kannon* than any other deity and the *kannon* popularly represented compassion, in male androgynous and female form (Figure 5.1).[21] Artists in Japan depicted feminised *kannon* images with a child, to assist women in praying for the blessing of child-birth.[22] The *jibo* (compassionate mother) in this tradition is a symbol of compassionate and maternal love, much like Mary in the biblical narrative. Other *kannon* were depicted without child. Those used by the hidden believers were later named *Maria kannon* in scholarly literature describing the practices of worship of these groups.

Mary was central to some of the hidden Christian liturgies. Maruya (the Virgin Mary) is mentioned 45 times in a rare hidden Christian text entitled the *tenchi hajimari no koto* (Concerning the Creation of Heaven and Earth) and *Deus*, or God is mentioned 66 times.[23] Maruya was associated with the Holy Spirit as a feminine aspect of the Divine.[24] This particular text, the *tenchi hajimari no koto* of the oral tradition, was committed to paper in 1820 and consisted of 16,000 characters divided into 15 chapters.[25] Fujiwara Ken shows that Maruya's function in this text was as 'an intercessor, a helper; the Heavenly Father is *Pater*, the Son is *Filio* and the Holy Mother is *Spirito Santo*'.[26] Thus, at least one early Japanese Christian interpretation describes the Holy Trinity, including Mary as the Holy Spirit. Another early Christian text, the *Myōtei Mondō* (the

92 *Reinterpreting the bomb*

Figure 5.1 A 'dangerous' Maria Kannon, confiscated by the Nagasaki magistrate during the 1860s, Tokyo National Museum catalogue, public domain, photograph used by permission of the National Library of Australia, 2015.

Myōtei dialogue, a refutation of Buddhism by Fukansai Habian), argued that Adam and Eve brought original sin and that the Virgin Mary heralded the redemption of humankind by giving birth to Christ.[27] The community of 'hidden Christians' studied by Christal Whelan assigned Mary a place in the Trinity, in a culturally hybrid fusion of Buddhism and Christianity, which presented the community as Buddhist believers. The equation of Mary as 'Spirit' by at least one hidden Christian tradition underscores her importance in early Japanese-Catholic-Hidden Christian theology.

Hidden Christian groups were not singular, but there were several isolated groups, meaning theologies and oral traditions were distinct in different places.

Roger Munsi is one scholar who is currently investigating further and in an interview he described the modern groups as diverse, with various Buddhist and Shinto influences. In Christianity, everything is filled with the 'breath' or Spirit of God and Buddhists believe everything is enabled by *ki* (Spirit). The 'Tenchi' which Whelan translated describes how Mary, filled with the breath of the Holy Spirit, conceived Jesus.[28] Communities adapted a religious hybridity to allow the preservation of a Christian faith while maintaining the outward appearance of Buddhism. One Hidden Christian interviewed by the magistrate's office explained he worshipped a Buddhist deity named '*Deus tecum Virgin Santa Maruya*'.[29] Mary was of central importance for the *sempuku kirishitan* to perhaps even a greater degree than in the originating Catholic tradition.

Trampled Mary

Apart from the *Maria Kannon*, there was another source of images of Mary as physically and spiritually 'dangerous' for the *sempuku kirishitan* during the 'secret Christian' period. Items called *fumi-e* were used by the *bugyō* (magistrate) to prove apostasy. Ironically, the symbolic *fumi-e* created by the magistrate may have 'dangerously' reminded the hidden Christians of the meaning of their faith.[30] These 'pictures for stepping on' (Figure 5.2) included mainly Mary and Christ images. *Fumi-e* were initially copied from sacred medals and images taken from the Christians and were later made by the civic authorities. The Tokugawa authorities observed the centrality of Mary to the hidden Christians' faith and subsequently used her image (and Christ's) to test the Christians and force apostasy, triggering new pain and torment. The shogunate instituted an office of *shūmon aratame yaku*, or inquisitors, to perform this task from 1640.

The *fumi-e* in Figure 5.2 is an artistic depiction, known as a *pietá*. Mary at the scene of crucifixion confronts and laments death. The *pietá* image was popularised by Michelangelo in around 1498, depicting Mary holding the dead Christ at Golgotha. By trampling these images with their feet, Christians may have understood themselves as inflicting suffering on Mary and Christ. The *fumi-e* trampled Mary offers no explanation to make sense of the violence done to her son. Images of sorrowful Mary capture inexpressible sadness in the moment of death, and in a double meaning the *fumi-e* recall the Urakami Christian community's public humiliation over generations. Johnson wrote about the grieving Mary of the Cross: 'One never really gets over the pain when someone you love is a victim of violence.'[31] Meanwhile, each time they stepped on the images the hidden Christians were reminded of their unfaithfulness. Reports stated that groups of hidden Christians flagellated themselves for their sins following these ceremonies.[32] The Urakami populace stepped on the *fumi-e* each year for seven generations, over 230 years. The Tokugawa authorities finally relinquished the use of *fumi-e* for the Urakami locals in 1857, just as they also ended the *sakoku* (closed country) policy. Around the same time, a new persecution, an exile and repression began.

Figure 5.2 Mary holds the body of Christ: a *fumi-e* (image for trampling), public domain, photograph, used by permission, National Library of Australia, 2015.

The record of the 'Third *kuzure*', or Persecution, halfway through the nineteenth century, shows that the use of the *Maria Kannon* for faith practices by some groups endured throughout the period of proscription. In 1857, the Nagasaki magistrate interrogated a farmer *chōkata* (leader of a group of *sempuku*) named Hayashi no Kichizō and Kichizō described the practice of the use of these icons. Hayashi told the Nagasaki magistrate he made a practice of reciting the '*Gracia Ave Maria*' (Hail Mary in Latin), learnt orally from his parents in front of the statue of a Buddhist *kannon*, for a good harvest, a long life and to be reborn in *paraiso* (paradise) with his family.[33] The Tokugawa officials recorded that the *Maruya* Kichizō identified was a 'white ceramic *kannon*', known as a *koyasu kannon*, or child bearing *kannon*.[34] The magistrate received Kichizō's confession with great seriousness and on 15 July 1859, an official recorded that the villager died after his long confinement and interrogation.[35]

Later, the public history of the Fourth Persecution of Urakami adds to what we know of the symbol of Mary as an evolving symbol for the *sempuku kirishitan* communities. As I described in Chapter 3, new foreign influences arrived in Nagasaki by 1863 and the Tokugawa government allowed French missionaries to enter Japan on the proviso that they did not proselytise. French priest Bernard Petitjean became aware through the Urakami *kirishitan* of the survival of faith in hidden communities.

'Where is Santa Maria?'

In March 1865, the word that 'a statue of Mary was in the French Temple', spread to the Hidden Christian community and a group travelled to Petitjean's church in Ōura.[36] The very first question three women from this group are recorded as asking Petitjean was, 'where is the statue of *Santa Maria*?' Although the reported meeting of the missionary and villagers is difficult to verify, the description of the women's enthusiasm emphasises the resilient significance of the archetypal Mary for the community.[37] The women wanted to see the foreign statue, despite the potential danger to themselves. The women's personal memories were informed by *fumi-e* trampled Mary images and the usage of *Maria Kannon* figurines. However, due to the revival of Christian fervour, the magistrate initiated the *yon-ban kuzure* by the late 1860s, the devastating Fourth Persecution, which impacted the community greatly.

Surviving *Maria Kannon* statues such as the one found in the atomic ruins (Figure 5.1) were important for the community, because so many similar statues were confiscated during the exile by the state, up to 1873 (Figure 5.3). The use of these *Maria Kannon* demonstrates that for those caught up in the *kuzure*, Mary symbolised both compassion and danger.[38] Items confiscated during the Fourth Persecution included 45 charms (such as Mary statues), 199 rosaries, 27 prayer books, ten calendars, three picture portraits and 17 medals.[39] Today, most of these statues and artefacts are held by the Tokyo National Museum. They show a variety of elaborate artistry, sometimes hiding a cross on the back or underneath, reminding the people of their distinctive faith.[40]

Interpreting Mary of Urakami

Miyazaki Yoshio, an academic and official of the Catholic Center in Nagasaki, discussed the interplay of 'trampled' Mary and the clandestine *Maria Kannon* in the community's history. He also mentioned author Endō Shusaku's novels. The *fumi-e* and *Maria Kannon* figures are emblematic of the survival and resistance of the hidden Christians: images central to the drama described in Endō's novel, *Silence (Chinmoku)*.[41]

> [...] they had to step on the *fumi-e* and [...] [It was] a gentle forgiving Mother image, [...as] Endō Shusaku wrote about [...] And [it was unclear regarding the *kannon*] whether it was Mary or the *koyasu kannon*, as in, a god holding a child [...] Even if exposed [...] it was a Buddhist item, so it wasn't suspected at all.[42]

Although Miyazaki says the *koyasu kannon* were not suspected of supporting *kirishitan* worship, as I have shown above, there were periods when such icons were perceived as a sign of subversion. Miyazaki mentions the *fumi-e* and *kannon* images of Mary and how the *kannon* presented a Buddhist front for the *kirishitan*. He stresses the Mother-image's compassion.

> So therefore [...] [the people were able] to transmit the faith through generations [...] But rather than a punishing, tough father God, a forgiving Mother Mary was [central] in Endō Shusaku's way of thinking [...][43]

Miyazaki allows that the compassionate 'Mother Mary' in the form of *Maria Kannon* icons sustained faith for at least a period of time, despite the trampling on Mary and Christ images. The supplication of the forgiving mother, or *koyasu kannon*, enabled the hidden Christians to overcome their own guilt, more so than by a potentially vengeful 'Father' God. Remembering that he depicts the early period after proscription, Endō too portrayed Mary as highly influential for the sempuku kirishitan, representative of a forgiving God. On the other hand, Miyazaki understands the hidden *kirishitan* use of Buddhist icons as eschewing Christianity over the longer period of seclusion and declares the *Maria Kannon* did not represent Mary at all. Miyazaki is ambivalent about how a forgiving mother God could help the *sempuku*, perhaps because of the implication of a contradiction with Catholic orthodoxy.

In another interview, Matsuzono Ichijirō, who reported his father's memory of coming across bodies after the atomic bombing, also discussed the novel by Endō and opined that stepping on the *fumi-e* was forgivable.[44] Matsuzono became a (Protestant) Christian as a young boy and later worked at a Catholic institution in Nagasaki. His father had mixed racial heritage and *sempuku* ancestors and Matsuzono grew up in China town with a Chinese step-grandfather. Due to his mixed heritage and time in Chinatown, Matsuzono's father suffered discrimination in the wartime period. Matsuzono, nevertheless, saw himself as a quintessential 'child of Nagasaki' and was fascinated by the narratives of ancestral hidden Christians and Endō's writing:

> [...] at the time of the persecutions, for those people who had to step on the *fumi-e* [...] [We must consider] whether they followed God's lead, or [not] [...] Still [...] God's love saves weak people, so [...] God forgives for stepping on the *fumi-e* and that's my view.[45]

In the view of Matsuzono and Miyazaki, the hidden Christians of the late nineteenth century seem to have known God at least partly through the image of Mother Mary, subversive, forgiving and omnipresent for the weak and persecuted. Matsuzono perceives God's compassion as an important element of Nagasaki Christian theology. He frames the 'hidden Christians' as weak, due to their stepping on the *fumi-e* images *and* their social fragility and marginal status. There is a personal element evident in his reflection about the hidden Christians, hinting at his own perception of himself and his understanding of God. He also says as he discusses the stepping on the *fumi-e*, '... in my own thinking as a Protestant, God's love saves weak people ...' Is there a difference between Protestant and Catholic tradition in thinking about ritual and the incarnate? Here, Matsuzono, who acknowledges his own hidden Christian ancestors, suggests there is a difference in thinking about the ritual of stepping on the images.

From Urakami to Guernica

One aspect of danger for the Hidden Christians was Mary's inciting of subversion through a clandestine faith. The transformation after the bombing of Mary into *hibakusha* Mary led to new aspects of challenge including an increased awareness of other marginalised communities around the world. One restored atom-bombed Mary was transported in 2010 from Nagasaki to Guernica in Spain, as part of an exchange between the two groups of faith communities. Archbishop Joseph Mitsuaki Takami of Nagasaki (2003-) visited Spain with the Nagasaki 'Atomic-bombed Mary' and the statue was displayed in the city's Peace Museum. In 2015, for the seventieth anniversary of the bombing of Nagasaki, a surviving head of a Mary statue, recovered from a church in Guernica that had been bombed indiscriminately by German planes in 1937, was starkly displayed at the front of the Urakami Cathedral (Figure 5.3). The Spanish head of a Mary statue was placed in front of the crucifix. For the Urakami Catholics, familiar with their own *hibaku-Maria*, the Guernica broken statue of Mary associates the Urakami narrative with a wider universal narrative of suffering. Bombed Mary images starkly protest indiscriminate and inexplicable violence and war and through them, the faith communities reach out to the secular world. On the seventieth anniversary of the Nagasaki bombing, the children of Nagasaki (from Junior High and Elementary schools) painted a 70-metre mural 'Guernica' painting.[46] The Catholic and non-Catholic populace of Nagasaki seek new connections to the wider narrative of other communities.

98 *Reinterpreting the bomb*

Figure 5.3 Photograph of the Spanish grieving Mary at 9 August 2015 Mass at Urakami Cathedral, used by permission, Iwanami Chiyoko, Kirishitan Museum, Urakami, 29 January 2019.

In a burgeoning literature of 'trauma' and genocide, places of trauma such as Guernica, Auschwitz and Nagasaki are existentially connected.[47] The people of Guernica extend their sympathies to Nagasaki by the exchange of the fractured Mary statues. An emerging symbolism of *hibakusha Maria*, a friend of the poor, innocent and scarred, links from Nagasaki to Auschwitz and the Jewish Holocaust. Atom-bombed Mary opens up new and varied ways of imagining the 'other', peace protest and theology.

The tradition of the fractured *hibaku-Maria* demonstrates the connections made between the Fourth Persecution of the community and the so-called Fifth Persecution of the atomic bombing. Nagai Takashi wrote the story of 'Kiku', a woman transported to Tsuwano, a mountainous region of western Honshu, in the Fourth Persecution.[48] Today, a Catholic church is found in Tsuwano and Fukahori Shigemi told me there was a yearly pilgrimage back to this place to remember the trials of the ancestors. In his 2016 interview, Fukahori explained how the Catholic community in Tsuwano asked him to bring the *hibaku-Maria* on the yearly pilgrimage back to Tsuwano for the commemoration of the *yon-ban kuzure*.[49]

Compassionate Mary

The Catholic *hibakusha* also refer to more personal dimensions of Mary. People readily relate to Mother Mary, an image especially poignant for those who lost mothers. Nakamura Kazutoshi connects Mary's presence to his memory of his own mother, lost to the atomic bomb. Like Ozaki, he never found his mother's body. She was on her way home, between houses when the bomb dropped and Nakamura states, 'I searched together with my father for about three days, not knowing where she was, but we couldn't find her.' One of ten children, Nakamura tells me he is the only surviving child to this day. His mother, he says, was 'not very strong', but provided well for their large family:

> She raised so many children that [...] at the time, you [only] got a certain amount each, [...] a ration of just a little rice [...] there was not enough for everyone [and therefore, my mother missed out] [...] She would go so far[...] to the country, even though she would get only a little [food] [...] So, death [...] was experienced [by her] as blessing, although [...] it was sad, but Mary called her, don't you think? I do anyway [...] On the other hand, maybe my mother is like Mary and just went up to heaven directly.[50]

Nakamura appeals to religious meaning, to make sense of his belief in the 'assumption of Mary' to heaven.[51] He manages his sadness by associating his mother with Mary. Nakamura imagines Mary provides solace to his mother and 'called her' to heaven. Having never found his mother, he envisages she 'just went up to heaven like that'.

Nagase Kazuko (Figure 5.4) describes the loss of her own mother, who did not die immediately and then suggests Mother Mary was her own comfort. Nagase's story emanates from a point closest to the hypocenter of all interviewed

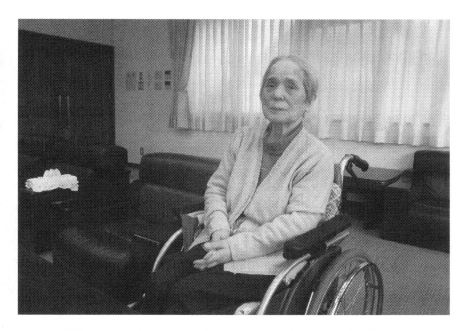

Figure 5.4 Nagase Kazuko, photograph, the author, used by permission, February 2016.

100 *Reinterpreting the bomb*

in this project, perhaps 500–700 metres away. At seven years of age, Nagase saw her mother transformed into someone unrecognisable, a memory which still alienates and terrorises her. During the interview, she was caught up by raw emotion as she remembered the death and funeral of her own mother. Nagase frequently paused, stopped to cry and her voice broke. On seeing her mother after the bomb, Nagase says:

> Someone was sitting next to me. I didn't notice, but then, 'Kazuko!!' they cried out. And I looked over and it was my mother. But, 'This could not be my mother', I thought. She was completely naked [...] Perched down there, she was utterly burnt, her whole body [...] I knew it was Mum but it couldn't be! Outside, the atmosphere was fearsome [whoa! (*ou!*)] [...] Aggrieved, I watched on [...][52]

Nagase's stress is evident in her testimony, by her exclamations and recycling of phrases. The emotional force of her testimony shows repeated disorientation by trauma, agitation and confusion.[53] Her cry of 'whoa!' [*ou!*] indicates her discomfort, as she imagines her mother, repeating a phrase she used previously in the interview: 'outside the atmosphere was fearsome/terrible' and stating her feelings as: 'Aggrieved'. She continues the narrative by explaining about her mother's death and funeral:

> [...] On that bright day, the 10th August, my mother died. As well as our house having been destroyed, mother [voice breaks] died [...] so in order to build a fire to cook us food, my mother had gone up to the mountains and collected firewood, frequently and piled it up. Taking that firewood, we took it to the river, all of us and laid it out and on top of that, on top of that wood [...] we lit a fire [...] and burnt [her]. [Cries and moans].[54]

The family's work to cremate the body on firewood which was ironically collected by her mother is remembered poignantly by Nagase. The swiftly erected funeral pyre is confronting in her discourse. Nagase's moaning cry resists and deplores the makeshift and perfunctory manner by which her family carried out the cremation at the time.

Soon after discussing this scene, talking about her religious belief, Nagase states that Mary was the most important symbol to her. She names Mary as Mother, a pious term, which she uses with feeling, evoking an embrace.

> My faith was helpful for me [...] It was Mother Mary. And Christ. When my stomach was ill and even when I would cry *wanwan*, the assistant would say to me with a meaning beyond words, 'Nagase-san, you are held by Mary like a baby' [Nagase cries audibly].[55]

Mary's compassionate presence after the bombing was palpable and circulated in wider Nagasaki and Japanese circles. Following the war, as Konishi indicated, symbolic Mary was understood as invoking peace and secular Nagasaki took notice. Artists such as Ueno Makoto and photographer Takaharu Itaru depicted symbols of Mary and the cathedral (St Mary's) which stood out in the 'silenced' landscape of Urakami, publicising them for wider civic consumption. In a photo of the ruins of the cathedral, Takaharu melds the 'grieving Mary' watching over the scene in the background as children like interviewee Matsuo Sachiko play in 1951.

Non-Catholic artist Ueno Makoto perceived symbolic Mary as remonstrating against death and suffering. Having spent the summer of 1961 in Nagasaki, Ueno created a series of 61 small prints, including, as an 'important element in the overall impression', eight of statues of Mary.[56] Scholar Chiyo Wakabayashi writes that, for Ueno, the symbol of Mary is less an interrogation of humanity about war, than an attempt to understand suffering and confront death, similar to the pieta Mary holding her dead son. Ueno drew Mary after seeing statues in 1961 near the newly built Urakami Cathedral. Wakabayashi describes Ueno's Mary as being without tranquillity or piousness:

> She stares fixedly forward with the engaged, deeply compassionate and caring face of a woman who stood fast at Ground Zero [...] It is a new representation of Mary.[57]

This Mary, writes Wakabayashi, accords with the liberation theology of Latin American societies and that of the Philippines, a 'peasant woman', during a people's movement.[58] For Wakabayashi, Ueno recalls Miriam of Nazareth, a 'dangerous' symbol for the powerful in her very divine presence with the downcast and poor. On the other hand, for Ueno Mary is also a symbol of the human suffering of the atomic bombing.

It is instructive to examine how Mary as *hibakusha* is depicted in popular literature and performance, recalling the bombing and earlier persecutions. The recent Japanese Noh drama '*Nagasaki no seibo*' (Holy Mother in Nagasaki), by Tada Tomio, integrates Mary of Urakami. The play was performed for the first time in 2005, in Urakami Cathedral and in New York in 2015.[59] In an apocryphal narrative, Mary, the Mother of Christ appears to the injured and dying faithful, after the bombing at the hypocenter. A pilgrim reaches the cathedral and learns from a priest the details of what happened. Virgin Mary, incarnated as a bomb survivor (one of the community), recounts her role in helping and comforting those hurt in the bomb blast.[60] A simple crucifix hangs on an upstage wall and the Virgin Mary is dressed in red with gold embroideries. Other scenes allude to the Urakami Christian history and to the persecutions of the Christians from the early seventeenth century until 1873. The play evinces *hibakusha* Mary, who bridges the sacred and secular divide. A reviewer, Samuel Leiter, writes the play encapsulates 'a requiem for those killed in 1945 and a call to world peace and nuclear disarmament'.[61]

Redeeming Mary

An older play, '*Maria no kubi*: A Nagasaki fantasia', by local playwright Tanaka Chikao, describes a narrative in which the protagonists work to restore the fractured Mary, as an allegorical restoration of the surviving community. The play was first performed in 1959, the year the old cathedral ruins were razed.[62] In this play, the 'keloid Madonna' is 'the eternal witness of our suffering'.[63] Mary is an ultimate *hibakusha* survivor and a witness of the devastation of the bombing. The play shows the living conditions of post-war Nagasaki, concluding in the ruined Urakami Cathedral.[64] The play takes on a dreamlike sensibility and *hibakusha* Mary is a broken statue, 'mother of the long suffering common people ... burned black'.[65] Protagonist Shika is a nurse and prostitute who understands herself as broken like fractured Mary, living a double-sided life.[66] Shika prays:

> Holy Mary [...] we know that we somehow have the right to pray to you [...] Mary [...] with your own keloid scar, you who must serve as eternal witness to the wind and flames of that day in August. We pray that we may take you to that hidden room [...][67]

Shika wishes to take Mary to the 'hidden room' (perhaps reminiscent of *sempuku* hidden practices of worship), to extricate her from desecration and ruin. Hiding or removing Mary from the place of death is a faithful attempt to re-sacralise this scarred symbol. This act to hide away Mary by Shika and the Catholics could reflect the tendency of the Catholics to hide her away and the wish to take repossession of Mary, stolen by the magistrate. The abuse, or destruction, of Mary associated her with the violent action of the atomic bombing, but re-sacralising this symbol means making her once more 'innocent', beautiful or redeemed. Taking her away from the ruins symbolically repossesses and purifies Mary, enabling 'transcendent' hope for those who died and who still suffer. Shika equates the elimination of the ruins of the cathedral and the loss of Mary with forgetting the bombing.

> Eventually it's going to get torn down! Eventually the head of Mary's going to get lost somewhere, that's what! And then every trace of what happened will disappear and the city will revert to its peacetime appearance [...][68]

A Nagasaki city council-man visiting Shika as a prostitute in this scene of the play is unaware she is also a Christian. Shika recognises a political opportunity and interrogates the 'righteous' council-man about the potential preservation of the cathedral ruins: 'They say they'll preserve it, but nobody has the slightest idea how and they're not doing anything!'[69]

The Catholics in the play cannot save the ruined Cathedral, but they can re-erect a Mary statue. Shika's profound wish for Mary's restoration is to resurrect this symbol from death-liness to hopefulness. In the final scene, one of the actors cries out:

The Church got fed up with the foot-dragging city council and finally decided to remove this image of blood and death and hate, [Mary statue] from this real and eternal place. We sacrificial victims of war must repossess her, the eternal witness of our suffering.[70]

The author of the play, Tanaka, shows the repossession of Mary by the Catholics is important due to their history of persecution. Re-sacralisation of this place and of this archetypal figure is intrinsic to the community's need for restoration.

By way of conclusion, A-bombed Mary as symbol challenges a simplistic interpretation of this figure as 'compassion' – she is dangerous herself. In the Catholic meta-narrative, Mary subversively protests imperialist violence and mourns death, in the 'song' attributed to her in biblical Luke when she was pregnant and at the crucifixion of Christ. Faithful devotion to compassionate Mary comforts the sick and injured. Urakami's potent icon of Mary overturns the *hansai* logic of required sacrifice and reframes 'God with us'. Today's bomb survivors retain ancestral links through suffering to the '*sempuku*' community (who were also survivors). The hidden Christians remembered Mary using *Maria kannon* figures, the *kannon* itself personifying compassion in Japan.

The Mater Dolorosa memorialised the crucifixion of Christ as well as acting as conduit for the Holy Spirit or as *ki*, sustaining faith. Mary was perceived by the Hidden Christians as a feminine aspect of God and the peoples' beliefs resulted in wholesale arrest, confessions and long persecution. The *fumi-e* depicted Mary in scenes such as the *pietá* and people gazed on them as they apostatised. Later, *kannon* were confiscated, and post-exile returnees named their new cathedral after their beloved Mary.

Statues of Mary, found in the atomic aftermath, bear symbolic atomic 'keloid scars' like the survivors and appear to protest the violence of the atomic bombing. Meanwhile, the statues and images of Mary also powerfully connect the suffering of the bombing to the haunting remembering of past persecution. Like the survivors themselves, Mary of Urakami suggests solidarity with suffering and acknowledges the common humanity of the 'other'. Shika, in Tanaka's play, wished to restore Mary and retain the ruins of the cathedral. The second symbol of the destruction of the Catholic community was the ruins of the cathedral, which stood out on a hill, just 100 m from Ground Zero.

In the next chapter, I explain how this building which was constructed as the largest cathedral in East Asia was destroyed and its ruins later claimed by the wider community as a 'dangerous' sign of the excesses of war. If Mary was a symbol for the community of Catholics itself, St Mary's Cathedral in Urakami became a contested civic space and vestige. Yet, for the Catholics, this was a place by which they did not only remember their recovery from the bomb but much more.

Notes

1 John W. O'Malley, *The First Jesuits* (Cambridge, London: Harvard University Press, 1995), 76.
2 Keloid scars result from the atomic blast's burns on humans. A Nagasaki manga humanises the Mary statues in this way: Yuka Nishioka, *Hibaku maria no inori: manga de yomu sannnin no hibaku shougen* (Nagasaki: Nagasaki Bunkensha, 2015).
3 Gale A. Yee, 'The Silenced Speak: Hannah, Mary and Global Poverty'. *Feminist Theology* 21.1 (1 September 2012): 51, https://doi.org/10.1177/0966735012451819.
4 Jōji Fukahori, interview by Gwyn McClelland, Nagasaki Atomic Bomb Museum, 10 January 2014.
5 Sachiko Matsuo, interview by Gwyn McClelland, Nagasaki Atomic Bomb Museum, 5 December 2014.
6 Shigemi Fukahori, interview by Gwyn McClelland, Urakami Cathedral, 23 February 2016.
7 Shingo Itō, 'Miracle Statue at Atom Bomb Site', *Sydney Morning Herald*, 8 August 2010, accessed 8 April 2017, https://tinyurl.com/la77ve5.
8 Itō, 'Miracle Statue'.
9 Shin'ichi Konishi, interview by Gwyn McClelland, Nagasaki Atomic Bomb Museum, 1 October 2014.
10 The author's translation: Christian Museum Urakami, 'Urakami Christian Museum' [Facebook post] 9 August 2015, accessed 24 May 2017, https://tinyurl.com/n3ulgs6.
11 Paul Ricœur, *Memory, History, Forgetting* (Chicago: London: University of Chicago Press, 2009), 452.
12 Sarah Jane Boss, *Mary: The Complete Resource*, 1st ed. (London, New York: Oxford University Press, 2007), 359.
13 Ritsuko Oka, 'The Motherly Presence of the Virgin Mary in the Local Church of Nagasaki', in *Asia Oceania Mariological Conference* (AOMC, Lipa City, Philippines: University of Dayton, 2009), accessed 10 September 2016, http://campus.udayton.edu/mary/VirginMaryinNagasaki.htm. Mary is named *Maria* in Japanese and *Maruya* in the *sempuku kirishitan* (Hidden Christian) text which Christal Whelan translated (see footnote 27).
14 Johnson, *Dangerous Memories*, 20. Johnson does not refer to Urakami or Japan.
15 Manfred Hauke, *God Or Goddess? Feminist Theology: What Is It? Where Does It Lead?* (San Francisco: Ignatius Press, 1995), 189.
16 Johnson, *Dangerous Memories*, 30.
17 Toshio Ikeda discusses the development of a secret society in Urakami after 1614 by believers who had previously worshipped at St Clara's. A monument to St Clara's church may now be found on the Urakami River and a photo of this monument was included in Chapter 4. Toshio Ikeda, *Kirishitan No Seiei* (Tokyo: Chuo Shuppansha, 1972), 48.
18 *Maria Kannon* is the name given by researchers to the phenomenon of the clandestine use of this statue as Mary and is not necessarily the name given by the Hidden Christian communities. *Kannon* is dealt with in the Lotus Sutra (Japanese *Hokekyo*), Fumon Chapter in which the *bodhisattva* uses 33 different manifestations to bring salvation to the believer. Shinjo Mochizuki, 'The Compassionate and the Wrathful'. *Japan Quarterly; Tokyo* 13.3 (1 July 1966): 341. Jeff Wilson has noted the 'rise of *kuan-yin* [guanyin]' worship as a 'female bodhisattva' in Western regions, whose worship, he writes, now is found in temples and homes in Northern America and Europe. Jeff Wilson, '"Deeply Female and Universally Human": The Rise of Kuan-Yin Worship in America', *Journal of Contemporary Religion* 23.3 (1 October 2008): 285, https://doi.org/10.1080/13537900802373270. Wilson writes that the *Kuan-Yin* is attractive to women who have left Catholicism as a reminder of the Virgin Mary. (289) The American insistence that she is female is 'reversing the arrow of history', writes Wilson

and clashes with the Buddhist insistence that the *bodhisattva* is masculine (290). On the other hand, at least some scholars claim that the Chinese have generally depicted the *Kuan-Yin* as feminine. See Chün-fang Yü, 'Feminine Images of Kuan-Yin in Post-T'ang China'. *Journal of Chinese Religions* 18.1 (1 January 1990): 61–89, https://doi.org/10.1179/073776990805307937. And Cathryn Bailey calls the *Kuan-Yin* the Trans *Bodhisattva*, suggesting that the figure transcends male and female. Cathryn Bailey, 'Embracing the Icon: The Feminist Potential of the Trans Bodhisattva, Kuan Yin'. *Hypatia* 24.3 (2009): 178–96.

19 Hebrew Testament scholar Mark Brett (Whitley College, Melbourne) suggested I consider Schreiter's idea of cultural hybridity as a more neutral term than syncretism as syncretistic is usually perceived as a negative. For further discussion of cultural hybridity and religion, see Robert Schreiter, 'Cosmopolitanism, Hybrid Identities and Religion'. *Exchange* 40.1 (2011): 30–2, https://doi.org/10.1163/157254311X550713.

20 In a book produced in Japanese and English in Tokyo about art history, the authors discuss the possibility that Hōgai was influenced in the early Meiji period in his painting of a Kannon by Christian images of Mother Mary and child. Sato Doshin writes that '... it seems certain that the Virgin and Child motif overlapped with that of Hōgai's own representation of Kannon and child'. Hogai Kano, *Kano Hogai: the track to Avalokitesvara as a merciful mother*, eds Tokyo Geijutu Daigaku and Shimonoseki Shiritu Bijutukan (Tokyo: Geidai Bijutukan Myujiamu shoppu, 2008), 172.

21 Mochizuki, 'The Compassionate and the Wrathful', 341.

22 Kano, *Kano Hogai*, 183.

23 Maria Reis-Habito, 'Maria-Kannon: Mary, Mother of God, in Buddhist Guise'. *Marian Studies* 47.1 (1 January 1996): 61.

24 Reis-Habito, 62.

25 Roger Munsi suggests that there at least two versions of documents like the *tenchi hajimari no koto*. Roger Vanzila Munsi, interview with Gwyn McClelland, Nagoya, 25 June 2017. Whelan has written this recent English translation of one of the *Tenchi Hajimari no Koto*. Christal Whelan, *The Beginning of Heaven and Earth: The Sacred Book of Japan's Hidden Christians* (Honolulu: University of Hawaii Press, 1996). The document captures a spirituality of a community at a time in history. Groups of Hidden Christians, who were separated by geography, had various beliefs and oral traditions.

26 Cited in Reis-Habito, 67.

27 The Myōtei Mondō was likely written in 1605 by Fukansai Habian, a former Zen monk. James Baskind, '"The Matter of the Zen School": Fukansai Habian's "Myōtei Mondō" and His Christian Polemic on Buddhism'. *Japanese Journal of Religious Studies* 39.2 (2012): 307–31; Haruko Nawata Ward, *Women Religious Leaders in Japan's Christian Century, 1549–1650*, Women and Gender in the Early Modern World (Farnham, England and Burlington, VT: Ashgate, 2009), 64–7.

28 Reis-Habito, 'Maria-Kannon', 62.

29 Reis-Habito, 'Maria-Kannon', 59–60.

30 There is a difference between the dangerousness of the *fumi-e* for the faith of the Christians, which may have resulted in passivity and/or despair, and the questioning or subversion of violence which could be interpreted of Mary in the *pietá*. The latter connotes 'dangerous' memory for this community which questions the status quo. In this book I aim to distinguish Metz's conception of 'dangerous' memory from memories of danger.

31 Johnson, *Dangerous Memories*, 155.

32 Turnbull writes that there is evidence that flagellation may have continued and in 1865, Father Petitjean gave a straw whip to a Christian named Michael and noted the zeal with which he used it. In the late twentieth century, Turnbull wrote that in Ikitsuki the kakure whip was no longer used for ritual flagellation. Stephen R. Turnbull, *The Kakure Kirishitan of Japan: A Study of Their Development, Beliefs and Rituals to the Present Day* (Richmond, Surrey: Japan Library, 1998), 86–7.

33 Reis-Habito, 'Maria-Kannon', 59.
34 Naoko Frances Hioki, 'Deconstructing Maria-Kannon: A New Look at the Marian Image for Urakami Crypto-Christians, ca. 1860'. *Japanese Religions* 40 (2015): 38–9.
35 Hioki studied the record of 'A case of unorthodox sectarians', fourth year of Ansei, 1857, original volume now in Nagasaki Prefectural Library. Hioki, 25–7.
36 Reis-Habito, 'Maria-Kannon', 63.
37 Ikeda, *Kirishitan no seiei*, 61.
38 The *fumi-e* were used by the magistrate in Nagasaki up until eight years before this event in 1865.
39 Yakichi Kataoka, *Urakami yonban kuzure Meiji seifu no kirishitan dan'atsu* (Tokyo: Chikuma Shobo, 1963), 70.
40 Eva Zhang, 'Kannon – Guanyin – Virgin Mary: Early Modern Discourses on Alterity, Religion and Images', in *Transcultural Turbulences*, eds Christiane Brosius and Roland Wenzlhuemer, Transcultural Research – Heidelberg Studies on Asia and Europe in a Global Context (Berlin, Heidelberg: Springer, 2012), 177.
41 Shusaku Endo, *Silence*, trans. Johnson, William (New York: Taplinger Pub. Co., 1980). Martin Scorsese, *Silence* (IMDb, 2016) www.imdb.com/title/tt0490215/, accessed 20 February 2018.
42 Yoshio Miyazaki, interview by Gwyn McClelland, Catholic Center, Nagasaki, 9 October 2014.
43 Miyazaki, 9 October 2014, McClelland.
44 I employ a pseudonym for privacy reasons for Matsuzono.
45 Ichijirō Matsuzono, interviewed by Gwyn McClelland, Nagasaki Institution, 26 February 2016.
46 Takuya Kaneda, 'Kids Guernica: 70 Meter Long Huge Kids' Guernica in Nagasaki', Otsuma Women's University, Kids Guernica, 27 June 2015, http://kids-guernica.blogspot.com.au/2015/07/70-meter-long-huge-kids-guernica-in.html.
47 See for example, Robert Seitz Frey, *The Genocidal Temptation: Auschwitz, Hiroshima, Rwanda and Beyond* (Oxford: University Press of America, 2004); Eric Kligerman, *Sites of the Uncanny: Paul Celan, Specularity and the Visual Arts* (Berlin: Walter de Gruyter, 2007), 146. Max Silverman, *Palimpsestic Memory: The Holocaust and Colonialism in French and Francophone Fiction and Film* (New York; Oxford: Berghahn Books, 2013), 69. Robin Adèle Greeley, *Surrealism and the Spanish Civil War* (New Haven, London: Yale University Press, 2006), 147.
48 Sadao Kamata, 'Nagasaki no inori to ikari', *Nihon no genbaku bungaku 15: hiron/ essei* 15, Nihon no genbaku bungaku (Tōkyō: Horupu Shuppan, 1983), 413. Kiku's Prayer, by Shusaku Endō, is a novel in which one character is also called Kiku and is transported to Tsuwano in the persecutions. Shusaku Endo, *Kiku's Prayer: A Novel* (New York: Columbia University Press, 2012).
49 Tsuwano is one place among many where Urakami hidden Christians were taken by the authorities in the Fourth Persecution. Today, a Catholic church is found also here and Fukahori told me there was a yearly pilgrimage back to Tsuwano to remember the trials of the ancestors.
50 Kazutoshi Nakamura, interview by Gwyn McClelland, Nagasaki Atomic Bomb Museum, 23 February 2016.
51 *Doing Emotions History*, eds Susan J. Matt and Peter N. Stearns (Urbana, Chicago and Springfield: University of Illinois Press, 2014), 155.
52 Kazuko Nagase, interview by Gwyn McClelland, Genbaku Homu, Megumi no Oka, 24 February 2016.
53 Michael Roper, 'The Unconscious Work of History'. *Cultural and Social History* 11.2 (1 June 2014): 184, https://doi.org/10.2752/147800414X13893661072717.
54 Nagase, 24 February 2016, McClelland.
55 Nagase, 24 February 2016, McClelland.

56 Chiyo Wakabayashi, 'When the Darkness Is Set Free: Woodcut and Ueno Makoto's Palm-Sized Series: The Atomic Bombing of Nagasaki'. *Inter-Asia Cultural Studies* 13.1 (2012): 88–121 (104).
57 Wakabayashi, 'When the Darkness Is Set Free', 105.
58 Wakabayashi, 'When the Darkness is Set Free', 107.
59 Kanji Shimizu, 'NY Koen "Nagasaki No Seibo" "Kiyotsune" Koen No Goannai to Bokin No Onegai', *Nou Raku Shi Shimizu Kanji*, accessed 8 November 2015, www.shimikan.com/1/post/2015/01/ny.html.
60 'Remembering Nagasaki', *Presbyterian Record*, February 2006, Academic OneFile.
61 Samuel L. Leiter, *Theatre's Leiter Side*, [online blog], 'Theatre's Leiter Side: 9 (2014–2015): Review of New and Traditional Noh (May 15, 2015)', accessed 8 November 2015, http://slleiter.blogspot.com.au/2015/05/9-2014-2015-review-of-new-and.html.
62 Chikao Tanaka, *The Head of Mary: A Nagasaki Fantasia*, trans. David G. Goodman, Current Theatre Series (Sydney: Melbourne: Currency Press; Playbox Theatre Centre, Monash University, 1995).
63 Tanaka, *The Head of Mary*, 61.
64 J. Thomas Rimer, 'Four Plays by Tanaka Chikao'. *Monumenta Nipponica*, 31.3 (1976): 275–98 (284).
65 Tanaka, *The Head of Mary*, 59.
66 Stanley Vincent Longman, *Crosscurrents in the Drama: East and West* (University of Alabama Press, 1998), 131.
67 Rimer, 'Four Plays', 289.
68 Goodman's full alternative translation of 'The Head of Mary' is included in the following collection. David G. Goodman, ed., *After Apocalypse: Four Japanese Plays of Hiroshima and Nagasaki*, Cornell East Asia Series 71 (Ithaca, NY: East Asia Program, Cornell University, 1994), 133.
69 Goodman, *After Apocalypse*, 132.
70 Tanaka, *The Head of Mary*, 61.

References

Bailey, Cathryn. 'Embracing the Icon: The Feminist Potential of the Trans Bodhisattva, Kuan Yin'. *Hypatia* 24.3 (2009): 178–96.
Baskind, James. '"The Matter of the Zen School": Fukansai Habian's "Myōtei Mondō" and His Christian Polemic on Buddhism'. *Japanese Journal of Religious Studies* 39.2 (2012): 307–31.
Boss, Sarah Jane. *Mary: The Complete Resource*. 1st ed. London and New York: Oxford University Press, 2007.
Endo, Shusaku. *Silence*, trans. William Johnson. New York: Taplinger Pub. Co., 1980.
Endo, Shusaku. *Kiku's Prayer: A Novel*. New York: Columbia University Press, 2012.
Frey, Robert Seitz. *The Genocidal Temptation: Auschwitz, Hiroshima, Rwanda, and Beyond*. Oxford: University Press of America, 2004.
Fukahori, Jōji. Interview by Gwyn McClelland, Nagasaki Atomic Bomb Museum, 10 January 2014.
Fukahori, Shigemi. Interview by Gwyn McClelland, Urakami Cathedral, 23 February 2016.
Goodman, David G., ed. *After Apocalypse: Four Japanese Plays of Hiroshima and Nagasaki*. Cornell East Asia Series 71. Ithaca, NY: East Asia Program, Cornell University, 1994.
Greeley, Robin Adèle. *Surrealism and the Spanish Civil War*. New Haven and London: Yale University Press, 2006.

Hauke, Manfred. *God Or Goddess?: Feminist Theology : What Is It?: Where Does It Lead?* San Francisco: Ignatius Press, 1995.
Hioki, Naoko Frances. 'Deconstructing Maria-Kannon: A New Look at the Marian Image for Urakami Crypto-Christians, ca. 1860'. *Japanese Religions* 40 (2015): 24–43.
Ikeda, Toshio. *Kirishitan No Seiei.* Tokyo: Chuo Shuppansha, 1972.
Ito, Shingo. 'Miracle Statue at Atom Bomb Site'. *Sydney Morning Herald*, 8 August 2010. https://tinyurl.com/la77ve5.
Johnson, Elizabeth A. *Dangerous Memories: A Mosaic of Mary in Scripture.* Annotated ed. New York: Bloomsbury Academic, 2004.
Kamata Sadao. 'Nagasaki no inori to ikari'. In *Nihon no genbaku bungaku 15: hiron/essei* 15: 408–17. Nihon no genbaku bungaku. Tōkyō: Horupu Shuppan, 1983.
Kaneda, Takuya. 'Kids Guernica: 70 Meter Long Huge Kids' Guernica in Nagasaki'. Otsuma Women's University. Kids Guernica, 27 June 2015. http://kids-guernica.blogspot.com.au/2015/07/70-meter-long-huge-kids-guernica-in.html.
Kano, Hogai. *Kano Hogai: The Track to Avalokitesvara as a Merciful Mother*, eds Tokyo Geijutu Daigaku and Shimonoseki Shiritu Bijutukan. Tokyo: Geidai Bijutsukan Myujiamu shoppu, 2008.
Kataoka, Yakichi. *Urakami yonban kuzure Meiji seifu no kirishitan dan'atsu.* Tokyo: Chikuma Shobo, 1963.
Kligerman, Eric. *Sites of the Uncanny: Paul Celan, Specularity and the Visual Arts.* Berlin: Walter de Gruyter, 2007.
Konishi, Shinichi. Interview by Gwyn McClelland, Nagasaki Atomic Bomb Museum, 1 October 2014.
Leiter, Samuel L. 'Theatre's Leiter Side: 9 (2014–2015): Review of New and Traditional Noh (Seen 15 May 2015)'. *Theatre's Leiter Side* (blog), 17 May 2015. http://slleiter.blogspot.com.au/2015/05/9-2014-2015-review-of-new-and.html.
Longman, Stanley Vincent. *Crosscurrents in the Drama: East and West.* Tuscaloosa: University of Alabama Press, 1998.
Matsuo, Sachiko. Interview by Gwyn McClelland, Nagasaki Atomic Bomb Museum. 5 December 2014.
Matsuzono, Ichijirō. Interview by Gwyn McClelland, Nagasaki Institution, 26 February 2016.
Matt, Susan J., and Peter N. Stearns, eds. *Doing Emotions History.* Champaign: University of Illinois Press, 2014.
Miyazaki, Yoshio. Interview by Gwyn McClelland, Catholic Center, Nagasaki, 9 October 2014.
Mochizuki, Shinjo. 'The Compassionate and the Wrathful'. *Japan Quarterly; Tokyo* 13.3 (1 July 1966): 340–51.
Munsi, Roger Vanzila. Interview by Gwyn McClelland, Nagoya, 25 June 2017.
Nagase, Kazuko. Interview by Gwyn McClelland, Genbaku Homu, Megumi no Oka, 24 February 2016.
Nakamura, Kazutoshi. Interview by Gwyn McClelland, Nagasaki Atomic Bomb Museum, 23 February 2016.
Nishioka, Yuka. *Hibaku maria no inori: manga de yomu sannnin no hibaku shougen.* Nagasaki: Nagasaki Bunkensha, 2015.
Oka, Ritsuko. 'The Motherly Presence of the Virgin Mary in the Local Church of Nagasaki'. In *Asia Oceania Mariological Conference.* Lipa City, Philippines: University of Dayton, 2009. http://campus.udayton.edu/mary/VirginMaryinNagasaki.htm.

O'Malley, John W. *The First Jesuits*. Cambridge and London: Harvard University Press, 1995.
Reis-Habito, Maria. 'Maria-Kannon: Mary, Mother of God, in Buddhist Guise'. *Marian Studies* 47.1 (1 January 1996): 50–64.
'Remembering Nagasaki'. *Presbyterian Record*, February 2006. Academic OneFile.
Ricœur, Paul. *Memory, History, Forgetting*. Chicago and London: University of Chicago Press, 2009.
Rimer, J. Thomas. 'Four Plays by Tanaka Chikao'. *Monumenta Nipponica* 31.3 (1 October 1976): 275–98. https://doi.org/10.2307/2384212.
Roper, Michael. 'The Unconscious Work of History'. *Cultural and Social History* 11.2 (1 June 2014): 169–93. https://doi.org/10.2752/147800414X13893661072717.
Schreiter, Robert. 'Cosmopolitanism, Hybrid Identities, and Religion'. *Exchange* 40.1 (2011): 19–34. https://doi.org/10.1163/157254311X550713.
Scorsese, Martin. *Silence*. Drama. IMDb, 2016. www.imdb.com/title/tt0490215/.
Shimizu, Kanji. 'NY Koen "Nagasaki No Seibo" "Kiyotsune" Koen No Goannai to Bokin No Onegai'. Nou raku shi Shimizu Kanji, accessed 8 November 2015, www.shimikan.com/1/post/2015/01/ny.html.
Silverman, Max. *Palimpsestic Memory: The Holocaust and Colonialism in French and Francophone Fiction and Film*. New York and Oxford: Berghahn Books, 2013.
Tanaka, Chikao. *The Head of Mary: A Nagasaki Fantasia*. Trans. by David G. Goodman. Current Theatre Series. Sydney, Melbourne: Currency Press; Playbox Theatre Centre, Monash University, 1995.
Turnbull, Stephen R. *The Kakure Kirishitan of Japan: A Study of Their Development, Beliefs and Rituals to the Present Day*. Richmond, Surrey: Japan Library, 1998.
Urakami, Christian Museum. 'Urakami Christian Museum Social Media'. Blog. Facebook, 9 August 2015. https://tinyurl.com/n3ulgs6.
Wakabayashi, Chiyo. 'When the Darkness Is Set Free: Woodcut and Ueno Makoto's Palm-Sized Series. The Atomic Bombing of Nagasaki'. *Inter-Asia Cultural Studies* 13.1 (1 March 2012): 88–121. https://doi.org/10.1080/14649373.2012.636876.
Ward, Haruko Nawata. *Women Religious Leaders in Japan's Christian Century, 1549–1650*. Women and Gender in the Early Modern World. Farnham, England and Burlington, VT: Ashgate, 2009.
Whelan, Christal. *The Beginning of Heaven and Earth: The Sacred Book of Japan's Hidden Christians*. Honolulu: University of Hawaii Press, 1996.
Wilson, Jeff. '"Deeply Female and Universally Human": The Rise of Kuan-Yin Worship in America'. *Journal of Contemporary Religion* 23.3 (1 October 2008): 285–306. https://doi.org/10.1080/13537900802373270.
Yee, Gale A. 'The Silenced Speak: Hannah, Mary, and Global Poverty'. *Feminist Theology* 21.1 (1 September 2012): 40–57. https://doi.org/10.1177/0966735012451819.
Yü, Chün-fang. 'Feminine Images of Kuan-Yin in Post-T'ang China'. *Journal of Chinese Religions* 18.1 (1 January 1990): 61–89. https://doi.org/10.1179/073776990805307937.
Zhang, Eva. 'Kannon – Guanyin – Virgin Mary: Early Modern Discourses on Alterity, Religion and Images'. In *Transcultural Turbulences*, eds Christiane Brosius and Roland Wenzlhuemer, 171–89. Transcultural Research – Heidelberg Studies on Asia and Europe in a Global Context. Berlin, Heidelberg: Springer, 2012.

6 Urakami Cathedral
A fifth persecution

I would sit and watch the cathedral, in the darkness, with no electric lights, blackness [...] each day and night [...] I would cry. Around that cathedral – there were 12,000 Catholic believers and 8,500 people died.

(Ozaki Tōmei, 2016)

Introduction

The ruins of Urakami Cathedral after the atomic bombing signified 'crippling memories' of the profound negative of death and the quashing of the Christian community.[1] The Catholics viewed the debris with grief. The broken walls and rubble, dominating their vision, were an ongoing reminder of the destruction the

Figure 6.1 Stained-glass windows which depict the burning cathedral, photograph, Richard Flynn, 2006, used by permission, 7 January 2019.

community had faced. The landscape of burnt wreckage represented the death of priests and parishioners at mass at the time and God's silence in the aftermath. The huge bells tumbled down and still lie alongside the cathedral today.

As in the case of the A-bomb-*Maria* of Urakami, the cathedral promptly bonded the trauma of the bomb to older memory of persecution in individual and public Catholic narratives, creating a justification for removing the ruins and erecting a new structure. Trauma studies writers suggest that remembering only loss and suffering condemns people to victimhood. By rebuilding the church in 1959 – against the opposition of other groups – the community re-enacted their struggle for autonomy in their return from exile building the initial cathedral of 1925. In this chapter, I draw upon the narratives described from two pre-bomb photographs, the persecution stories in public literature, and on the study of trauma via theology to examine the symbol of the cathedral.

Twentieth century cross

The ruined cathedral as symbol crossed into the civic life of the city outside Urakami more so than Mary, arousing even the non-Catholic community – and was heralded as a dangerous memory for the planet as a whole.[2] Soon after the war, the ruins transformed into a draw-card for tourism and became a well-known civic icon of the recovering city. When the removal of the detritus and the rebuilding of the cathedral occurred in 1959, many citizens believed Nagasaki was robbed of an anti-war symbol of peace – a reminder of the danger of nuclear warfare.[3] Regret for the loss of the ruins is today still remarked upon: in 2009, a Nagasaki non-Catholic council member from the 1950s, Iwaguchi Natsuo, said of the ruins of the Urakami Cathedral after 1945 that they:

> represented a [Christian] 'Cross' of the 20th Century ... A country which believed in Christianity dropped an atomic bomb right over Urakami, where lived Catholics of the same belief ... I have no doubt the ruins would have become World Heritage ... Yet our strength as 'citizens' [to ensure the ruins' survival] was not enough'.[4]

For the Catholics, there were alternate narratives about the cathedral which were equally valid and significant. The cathedral's visual and material symbolism was not limited to atomic ruin. Instead, returnees from the exile of the 1860–70s (the Fourth Persecution *kuzure*, or literally destruction) believed the bombing of Urakami exemplified the community's Fifth Persecution (or a *go-ban kuzure*).[5]

Biggest church in the East

To begin to understand the alternate narratives, I incorporate two photographs which *hibakusha* interviewees discussed, showing the Urakami Cathedral in its earlier iteration as the pre-1945 church. These photographs show how the church

112 *Reinterpreting the bomb*

in pre-war and wartime days already symbolised a memory for the Catholics of resilience and resistance against oppression. Fukahori Jōji's photograph (Figure 6.2) is of his 14-year-old self with his three siblings, killed soon after the bombing. The cathedral is a backdrop for the family portrait, after their recent move to Urakami. Fukahori showed me the photograph, pointed out the church and then mentioned his family.

> This [...] is the pre-war cathedral. You can't see it clearly, but [...] this is me. [I was in] Junior high, third year and this is my brother, who was in first year of junior high. And this is my brother who was in fifth year of primary school and my younger sister and apart from this I have another little brother [who survived] [...] my mother died together with these three in the atomic bomb.[6]

Fukahori mentioned his family's return to Urakami and his grandfather's internment in the 1870s Fourth Persecution. Returning with family to Urakami was significant for Fukahori, his mother and siblings. In the 'Fourth Persecution', Fukahori's grandfather was displaced to Ishikawa prefecture on the Japan Sea, north-west of Kyoto. Fukahori's photograph affirms the narratives of his deceased siblings (see Chapter 9) and his family's survival and return to this parish, where the community built the biggest church in East Asia. The cathedral

Figure 6.2 From left: 深堀譲治 Fukahori Jōji (14 years), 暁郎 Akio (*c.*10 years), 待子 Machiko (5 years), 耕治 Kōji (*c.*12 years), in front of Urakami Cathedral 1944, used by permission, Fukahori, 17 January 2019.

in the photograph signals identity and a connection to those lost due to the atomic bomb.

After the survivors of exile returned, the Urakami Cathedral was constructed between 1895 and 1925 as the largest church in East Asia.[7] The Nagasaki Catholics funded the building and Paul Glynn's biography of Nagai Takashi, *A Song for Nagasaki*, describes Nagai's first visit to this monument in around 1932. The people recall the original construction process, a narrative which denotes the determination of the community through hardship and pain. The established church emphasises the communal effort of the people, their rising above poverty, exile and persecution.

> Nagai […] was taken on a guided tour of the cathedral. It was seventy metres long, making it the biggest in the Far East. It accommodated five thousand worshippers and its two bell-towers were thirty metres high. The bell-ringer […] was just a boy in 1872 [sic] when they came home to Urakami from years of privation in the camps scattered all over Japan […] They had their eyes on the spacious house overlooking Urakami that had belonged to the government official responsible for interrogating their leaders and sending them all off to the prison camps […] women and children worked in shifts to make hundreds of thousands of red bricks […] It was all done by people just above poverty level and any number of times they ran out of money […][8]

The Christians turned the tables so that they occupied the place where their tormenter, the village headman, had previously lived. The people's collective purchase of this specific land and corporate fervour in building the initial church here symbolise redemption, agency and their outlasting of the persecutions. There are reports that the construction at the time was paid for by each parishioner's donation of a portion of their wages. Some Catholics reportedly went to town to sell vegetables and purchased bricks on the way back with money they had earned. Others manually carved stones and piled up the bricks.[9] Pope Pius XI donated a 160-pound stone lantern for use on the altar of the Cathedral.[10] A Mary statue donated from Spanish Catholics and treasures from the Hidden Christians were destroyed in the bombing.

Commemorating survival

A second treasured photograph records – not Matsuo Sachiko's atomic survival (as *hibakusha*) – but her grandparents' old familial narrative of survival after exile (*ikinokori*). Matsuo's photograph from 1930 (Figure 6.3, 60 years after the exile) represents the cathedral more sharply and the returnees are carefully arranged in their ceremonial black kimonos at its front door. The men wear *kuro montsuki*, black kimono, with *haori* and *hakama* (coats and trousers/skirts), the most formal of kimono, with five *mon*, or family crests, on them.[11]

Matsuo's attentiveness to women among the *ikinokori* survivors is noticeable. She mentions two, her grandmother and a woman named Tsuru. Some of the

114 *Reinterpreting the bomb*

Figure 6.3 The *yon-ban kuzure* returnees in front of Urakami Cathedral, 1930: Matsuo's grandmother, 西尾ワキ Nishio Waki, is in the third row, third from left, public domain.

women wear the *kuro montsuki* and the *mon* are visible on their coats. Matsuo's photograph associates the cathedral personally and immediately with memory of the Fourth Urakami persecution (destruction) and exile.

The return of foreign priests to Japan in 1858 led to the persecution, called a *kuzure* (collapse/demolishing/destruction) by the magistrate and the *tabi* (travels), by the Christians.[12] There were two stages to the Fourth Persecution. The first involved a small group exile in 1867, when the Tokugawa Shogunate was still in place. In the second stage, after the establishment of the Meiji government, the authorities made a wholescale example of the community by rounding up more than 3000 Christians and exiling them. During the exile, the Christians were forced to detention camps in 21 different places around Japan as far north as Toyama and Yokohama and as far south as Kagoshima.[13] Accounts about the persecutions narrate the progress of the women and men in their attempts to keep faith and avoid apostasy. Only 1900 of the Urakami community, including Matsuo's grandmother, Nishio Waki, and grandfather, Kichirōji, were eventually repatriated.[14] The text on Matsuo's photo describes the group as survivors (*ikinokori*) from three detention camps, Tsuwano, Matsue and Tottori. Matsuo says:

Yes [...] my grandmother was one of the Urakami Fourth Persecution survivors and at that time there were still some of those survivors who were alive [...] these people still believed, everyone was able to stick at it and get through [...] Within their testimony, they didn't talk about their pain.[15]

Matsuo focuses on the faith of the survivors. In the photograph (Figure 6.3), five years after the completion of the original cathedral and 60 years after the beginning of the *kuzure*, 12 men and 27 women returnees are in the photograph, around 10 per cent of those who were transported (39 of the original 335 people exiled to these three places). The Urakami *kirishitan* history, collated in 1943, lists 64 men and 271 women and children exiled to Tsuwano, Matsue and Tottori, of around 3000 people deported from Urakami on 6 January 1870.[16] Officials and *burakumin* (outcasts) sent by the Nagasaki magistrate's office (*bugyō*) separated family members from each other and confiscated religious paraphernalia, including Mary statues and religious medals.[17] Matsuo speaks of her grandmother (born 9 March 1866) with warmth, as a double survivor. Her grandfather died prior to 1945, but her grandmother, Nishio, endured the Fourth Persecution as a child and the 'Fifth' as an adult, having taken refuge with the family at the shelter on the mountain. Matsuo connects Nishio's recollection of the exile with resilience and faithfulness and says it gave her encouragement to endure following the bombing:

> My grandmother was a survivor [*ikinokori*] of the Fourth persecution and at the [time of the atomic bombing] there were still some of these surviving people of the persecutions. So, looking at these people [...] if people like this have believed and gone on living, if they can do their best and live on, then [I can endure] [...][18]

Matsuo's photograph of the handful of survivors makes sense of the temporary naming of the atomic bombing as the *go-ban kuzure* (Fifth Persecution). *Hibakusha* Konishi Shin'ichi gives another perspective about the return of the *ikinokori*:

> The Fourth Persecution [...] was the final persecution. The believers made up around 3600 people [...] sent to many places throughout Japan [...] [some] disappeared, were killed and escaped [...] And they returned [...] [losing their] homes [...] there were feuds (*izakoza*) over common property and some quickly gave up their faith [...][19]

A fractured community

Konishi adds to Matsuo's account by remembering those who gave up faith and the arguments among survivors when they returned, highlighting how the shogun's dividing of the people into apostate and faithful had long-lasting negative impacts. Even the experience of returning from exile led to some giving up faith.

116 *Reinterpreting the bomb*

The community was further fractured by division, apart from those tortured, killed or missing. A long-lasting societal rupture occurred due to the magistrate's pressing of the low-caste group, later to be known as the *burakumin*, into service, as police and jailers of the *Kirishitan*.

The initial building of the Urakami Cathedral following the return from exile was a significant and symbolic process representing the transformation of the broken community into a more unified group, evidenced by the two above photographs which show how the Catholic *hibakusha* incorporate the church building into the remembering of their personal community and family histories. Both survivors' narratives of atomic survival connect to Hidden Christian public history. Others claim the exilic history which both Fukahori and Matsuo acknowledge as a vital part of their own ancestral story. The Fourth Persecution traces a lineage to an older history and the older persecutions and martyrdoms of the sixteenth and seventeenth centuries.[20] The two photographs show the original church building as evidence of wholesale communal survival and resilience, despite persecution.

A torture stone and the cathedral

When I ask Matsuo about other places of significance, she mentions a second woman, known simply as Tsuru, whose record is included in the Catholic public history of the Fourth Persecution. 'There was a rock which a woman was forced to sit on and she was ordered to stop believing in Catholicism and to convert to Buddhism.'[21] The rock (*gōmonseki* or torture stone) which Matsuo referred to is today located in front of the cathedral, a memorial of the persecutions. The rock mnemonically links the so-called Fifth Persecution (atomic bombing) to the Fourth, adjacent to the A-bomb damaged statues as atomic memorials.

The 'torture' stone mentioned by Matsuo is accompanied by a stone tablet engraved with the story of Tsuru. 'The Resistance of Tsuru' (*Tsuru no teikō*) narrates Tsuru's torture by officials and a Shintō priest.[22] Tsuru, a 22-year-old woman, in 1869 reportedly resisted apostasy and physical abuse for 18 days.[23] Her miraculous survival demonstrates redemption in the Catholic public narrative from exile and torture. Officials made her kneel in *seiza* position (sitting with legs tucked under) on this rock, stripped to the waist. After a week elapsed she sunk unconscious into the snow, a victim of physical and public humiliation. She recovered, however, and returned to Urakami to take up a nun's habit in a religious order, assisting orphans at the Urakami Cross Society Convent. Tsuru's death in 1925 coincided with the community's proud completion of the original cathedral and the raising of two giant bells. The community memorialised her resistance by placing the 'torture stone' alongside the cathedral. Today, the rock is surrounded by atomic memorials, associating the public history of the community to hardship, from the atomic narrative, to the persecutions and to the *fumi-e* trampling on icons.

By reference to heroines Nishio and Tsuru, Matsuo engages in finding moments which transform her memory about her own experience of the atomic bombing. As in the narrative of the initial building of the cathedral, Tsuru's story demonstrates agency in the public history of the Catholics and their transcending of experiences of past persecution. Remembering only suffering and loss existentially imprisons people as victims, according to the trauma studies theologian Flora Keshgegian. She writes, 'the authenticity and effectiveness of Christian witness[ing] is to be measured by the capacity of the Christian story to be faithful to those victimized'.[24] The key to transforming memory is finding the instances of resistance and agency and incorporating them.[25]

The story of 'Tsuru's resistance' and of Matsuo's grandmother, Nishio, engages with aspects of liveliness and redemption, which Keshgegian wishes to add to Johann Baptist Metz's notion of 'dangerous' memory. The building of the cathedral symbolised the lifeblood of the resurrected community including Tsuru and those like Nishio, who returned from exile. Tsuru's story is mnemonically reinvigorated by the placement near the renewed cathedral of the torture stone, redeeming a 'dangerous' memory of victimisation and suggesting hope for the bereft. The connection of the Fourth Persecution to atomic victimisation is not wholly about remembering trial, but reminds the people of their communal agency in history, despite the all-too-real past and ongoing experiences of oppression or marginalisation.

The profound negative

Twenty years after the cathedral bells were raised for the first time, in the 'Fifth Persecution' of the atomic bombing, they were thrown violently to the ground on 9 August 1945 and the building burnt for days afterwards. The Catholics are criticised for rebuilding the cathedral and turning their backs on the disaster, and yet the stained-glass windows in the new cathedral depict the community's lasting memory of the burning cathedral (see Figure 6.1). Interviewee Ozaki Tōmei, whose adoption of the name of one of the 26 martyrs redeems his memory of victimisation (Chapter 8), reflects on the sight of the burning cathedral after the bomb, 'the biggest shock'. Aged seventeen, he remembers:

> [...] the destruction of the Urakami Cathedral was the biggest shock [for me]. It was said to be the largest church in the East. And [with the bombing], that church was destroyed in one moment, a [...] place of prayer[...] it burned for a long time. [...] I would sit and watch the cathedral, in the darkness, with no electric lights, blackness [...] each day and night [...] I would cry. Around that cathedral – there were 12,000 Catholic believers and 8500 people died. So, for the Catholics, there was awful suffering.[26]

Watching the church day and night, Ozaki associates his memory of the flames and the surrounding blackness to the Catholic death toll and the 'awful suffering' for those who remained – a 'profound negative'.

This symbol of the Christians' resistance, faithfulness and resilience was torn down by the atomic bomb and burnt to cinders. Nagai Takashi himself had great discomfort in drawing the ruins and a sense of deep ambivalence about the scene. The black and white drawing by Nagai on the Contents page of this book appropriates the same aspect as the first painting of the ruins in Chapter 2, although it appears especially stark and sombre. The sharp lines of the cathedral ruins fade out to the smoky rubble of Urakami valley and the buildings of Nagasaki in the hazy distance.

After war ended and reconstruction began, the broken-down relics of the building became a site of contest within Nagasaki, viewed across the social fissures of the city. From the Urakami Catholic perspective, the rubble which lay there from 1945 until 1958 represented the large-scale devastation of this specific 'holy' landscape, community and town. Referring to those who died there, including priests and parishioners, informant Miyazaki Yoshio of the Catholic Center maintained, 'you can understand that it seems it would be a wonderful memorial, but also empathise with how they [the believers] felt [about the need to remove the ruins]'.[27] The ruins were a memory to avoid, what Keshgegian terms a 'profound negative', or a 'crippling memory' (*fujiyuu na omoi*), in survivor Matsuo's words.[28]

Exile was not the only narrative of past persecutions. The cathedral itself was a neighbourhood and playground for Fukahori Shigemi, located as it was alongside his home. He says:

> This is important land. For 250 years, they were made to [step] on the *fumi-e*, they did that each year right here. So, there was nowhere else where the church could be built. If it was broken, we had to re-build. And at the time, there was the problem that people wanted to save the ruins. However, for the Urakami believers, there are many places which are important [...] basically the feeling was that we needed a place of worship here. In which case, if it was broken, then we had to re-build [...] Also, our ancestors had experienced persecution here. So, there was life here.[29]

Fukahori refers to absolutely 'dangerous' memory of suffering, of abandoned faith, through the magistrate's (or village headman's) enforced stepping on the *fumi-e*, the sacred images, in the public history. The Catholic and Hidden Christian public narrative proclaimed the building was erected specifically on this location where the people had been forced to step on Mary and Christ images in front of the headman in the *fumi-e* ceremonies (see Chapter 5). And so, says Fukahori Jōji, the cathedral was placed here.

> Yes, yes, that was the place where they stepped on the *fumi-e* (*fumi-e o shiteta basho*). [...] So [...] definitely [...] they really exerted themselves to make it [there].[30]

The dedication by the people of Urakami Cathedral as St Mary's sought an absolution for the actions of the believers' ancestors – for what had occurred over 250 years.

Naming the destruction of Urakami Cathedral a 'Fifth Persecution' also recalls an older history of violent and imposed destruction of churches. There was a cycle of destruction and of rebuilding of churches in the city over time (see Chapter 3). The warlord Toyotomi Hideyoshi first ordered churches destroyed in Nagasaki in 1587. Up to 1619, these churches were destroyed and rebuilt, before their ultimate demise.[31] Later, Urakami Hidden Christians secretly visited and worshipped at the site of St Clara's in Urakami, maintaining a façade as Buddhist believers. An early narrative recorded by Japanese historian Ikeda Toshio depicts two enthusiastic members at St Clara's, who started a secret society of *Kirishitan* in Urakami, 50 years after the banning of the religion in the seventeenth century.[32]

Debating reconstruction

Despite the Catholic history of exile, destruction, persecution and redemption in the location of the cathedral, others from Nagasaki city wanted to save the ruins. After the bombing destroyed the cathedral in 1945, debate began just weeks later about whether to reconstruct the church or to preserve the ruins. On 6 October 1945, Nagasaki City council-man Kunitomo said the city ought to 'preserve all important research material, such as factory ruins, scorched trees and the ruined Urakami Cathedral'.[33] Between 1949 and 1958, Nagasaki's Committee for the Preservation of Atomic Bombing Materials voted nine times in favour of preserving the rubble of Urakami Cathedral.[34] On the other hand, by July of 1954, the Urakami Catholic community, led by Fr Nakashima Banri and Morita Kijirō, had formed the Urakami *Tenshudō Saiken i'in Kai* (Association for the Reconstruction of Urakami Cathedral).[35] Chad Diehl has reported on the debate of the 1950s at length, with the 'Catholics' seeking reconstruction on one side and the Nagasaki city officials and residents seeking preservation of the ruins on the other. The potential of the ruins as a tourist destination was one aspect of the push for preservation, while the growth of the community in Urakami to 4319 by 1948 was a reason to rebuild.[36] The Catholics cited the 'guardian of Urakami, the Immaculate Mother Mary and our ancestors in heaven', admonishing the faithful to reconstruct.

For other citizens, older tropes of persecution and retribution were unknown and irrelevant for this building on the hill. The symbol of the cathedral ruins haunted the city, reaching from sacred Urakami into the secular, non-Catholic Nagasaki.[37] As icons of Mary represented the call for peace, the cathedral ruins became meaningful for others as a means to recall the devastation of the war. They constituted a major civic symbol of memory of the futility of war and encapsulated the American-led destruction. The idea of Urakami Cathedral as a 'sacred space' for wider atomic memory refracts interpretations of the atomic bombing and understandings of 'peace protest'. Survivors pushed for the ruins to be preserved as civic memorial. *Hibakusha* peace-activists argued, 'The ruins were no longer just the possession of the Catholics...'[38]

In the past 10 to 15 years, Japanese writers have continued to deplore the Catholic rebuilding as thwarting the ruins' potential use as a peace symbol, a

120 *Reinterpreting the bomb*

universal symbol like the 'atomic dome' of Hiroshima. Journalistic accounts lament the loss of the ruins as relics, by the publishing of books such as *Nagasaki kieta mō hitotsu no genbaku dōmu* (The Other Atomic Dome of Nagasaki which Vanished).[39] The narrative suggests the rebuilding has contributed to the predominance of Hiroshima or the slighting of Nagasaki in the historiography of the atomic bombings. Rather than keeping a memento which demonstrates the folly of war and promoted 'world peace', the razing of the relics put the tragedy behind the Christians, hand-in-hand with a passive 'burnt sacrifice' acceptance of the bombing as God's providence (Chapter 4).[40] The removal of the ruins left Nagasaki city with 'empty symbols'.[41] The silencing of Nagasaki as an atomic city, in this rendering, began from the rebuilding of the cathedral.

Rethinking the ruins and the previous building from the Catholic perspective, however, presents another side to the issue of rebuilding. A postcard from the post-war period depicts the 'mourning' face of Nagasaki (Figure 6.4). In the November 1945 photograph, a Requiem Mass surrounds the ruined cathedral on the hill, a month after the *o-kunchi* festival resumed in the old city. The postcard presents the Catholics as exotic 'other' for tourists, their grief muted by the view from behind. For tourists who purchased this postcard, the religious group represented a curious aspect of atomic history. Like their ancestors' treasured religious icons and 'flags of Mary', stripped from them in the Fourth Persecution and today displayed in Tokyo National Museum, the modern Catholics became an exoticised object of 'dark tourism'. A parishioner decried the sightseers pointing their cameras 'at believers who are holding mass' and taking their photos,

Figure 6.4 23 November 1945, memorial service at the ruins of the Urakami Cathedral, postcard, Nagasaki City Office, photograph public domain.

'as if looking in a zoo ... snap-snap (*pachipachi*)'. Community historian Kataoka Yakichi said in March 1958, 'To ... insist on using the present state [of the cathedral] as a billboard for tourism is religious sacrilege'.[42] Many of the mourning Catholic populace represented in the picture including interviewees Ozaki, Fukahori and Matsuo had not yet had a chance to rebuild and still lived day-to-day in bomb shelters, or shacks.

Tagawa Tsutomu, mayor of Nagasaki, sought to ensure the ruins were preserved, from his inauguration in 1951 until 1956.[43] In 1953, he cited tourist promotion as a priority, allocating 5 million yen of city funds to restore the main gate at Kofukuji temple, as well as money towards Sofukuji temple, repairs to the Takashima Shuhan residence and towards restoration of the Dutch factory at Dejima.[44] It seemed that the cathedral ruins would be preserved for future communal remembering.

Pearl Harbour, 'town affiliations' and US fundraising

Meanwhile, the Catholic community began to work towards rebuilding. After asking for donations from Catholic congregations around Japan in the early 1950s, the 30 million yen the Association for Reconstruction of Urakami Cathedral were able to raise was insufficient.[45] The Cathedral website writes that the lack of funds led to Bishop Yamaguchi's six month *saikon shikin bokin* (reconstruction fundraising) trip from May 1955 to the United States, visiting St Paul, Chicago, New York, Washington DC, New Orleans, Los Angeles, San Francisco and Honolulu.[46]

In 1955, on the anniversary of the Japanese bombing of Pearl Harbour, 7 December, city officials in St Paul, Minnesota announced the first relationship between a US city and a Japanese municipality (initially known as a town affiliation – later a sister-city relationship), namely St Paul and Nagasaki. A local newspaper back in Nagasaki wrote that St Paul was chosen for a 'town affiliation' due to its large Catholic community (Nagasaki Nichi Nichi Shinbun, 4 September 1955).[47] Bishop Yamaguchi was in St Paul and preached on the following Sunday at the Catholic St Paul's Cathedral.[48] In what was a significant turning point for the rebuilding process, the Mayor of St Paul invited Nagasaki's mayor to visit and Mayor Tagawa Tsutomu decided to visit the US in 1956. The journalist Takase Tsuyoshi wrote an implied result of the town affiliation was that the citizens ought to 'forget the event of the past that is the atomic bombing' because 'we are no longer concerned with Pearl Harbour'.[49] Ironically, the story indicates the Catholics relied upon the support from the United States, which had dropped the atomic weapon, in order to rebuild.

After his visit to the United States in the late 1950s, non-Catholic Mayor Tagawa sided with the Catholics and asserted the ruined cathedral was 'not appropriate' to display the tragedy of the atomic bomb. The Catholics were allowed to remove the remnants and begin the building of a new church.[50] The new cathedral's construction was completed by 1959. In the words of Fukahori Jōji:

Yes, that's right. People who weren't Catholic strongly sought to keep the ruins there, like the Hiroshima *genbaku dōmu* (atomic bomb dome). However, [laughs], for the Catholics that was the place where [...] they suffered their persecutions and where they put up a church, you see.[51]

Nowadays, Fukahori Jōji agrees that the city could have preserved the ruins as a memory of the bombing:

It's not that I don't understand the idea of leaving it there in remembrance of the war, of this horrific thing that happened; to treasure and to leave it there after such a tragedy had happened. Yes [...] my thought is that they could have put [the ruins] where they wanted to. Even keeping old things, we would understand Catholic history, wouldn't we? Even if it wasn't pretty.[52]

Similarly, Konishi Shin'ichi says, 'It would have been good to keep the ruins as a memorial, like the *genbaku dōmu* (Atomic Bomb Dome) of Hiroshima and as a testimony to the war.'[53] Konishi and Fukahori are reconciliatory, but also note the importance of the cathedral for the surviving community.

The ongoing debate about rebuilding pitted peace activist *hibakusha* against the Catholics, a dichotomy forgetful of the Catholic *hibakusha* community themselves.[54] The removal of the ruins was a 'silencing' for other citizens but rebuilding the cathedral was an understandable and desirable outcome for the Catholics. There may have been division among at least some of the Catholics. Still, by rebuilding the church in the late 1950s, the community was reminded of their original struggle for autonomy in building the 1925 cathedral. Survivors (*ikinokori*) of persecution built the original cathedral and survivors (*hibakusha*) of the atomic bombing assisted in building the new structure. The rebuilding advocated a future, recalling the suffering of the persecutions, exile, *fumi-e* and destroyed churches and evinced 'resurrection' and new life. For the Catholics, the bomb event was not forgotten – it could not be. The bombing was gradually subsumed into their wider story of survival and resilience. The rebuilt cathedral is viewed by the Catholic *hibakusha* for its atomic legacy and ongoing significance for perseverance. The people re-established the church building, moving beyond victimhood, towards future life.

There were also mundane yet persuasive reasons for rebuilding. When I interviewed atomic survivor Matsuo Sachiko, she said a temporary church building was raised, but it was too cramped and worshippers had to stand at mass. In earlier days, for Matsuo, the ruins were associated with the discomfort of standing in the rain for mass, or in the blazing heat for those who could not fit inside.

For us, it was uncomfortable. It was awful. I mean, we couldn't fit in. Even if it rained, we had to stand outside. A temporary church was built, an American semi-circular building like a barracks. It was made of wood [...] but it wasn't big enough for the number of people [...] In the summer heat we had to stand up [...] so our feeling was, even if it is small, building something would be better than this.[55]

Urakami Cathedral: a fifth persecution 123

The growth of the Catholic population added to the practicality of a new building.

A living community

Visitors and tourists are welcome to visit today's rebuilt cathedral, where parish life goes on day-to-day. As you walk up to the front of the church, you see on the left-hand side some of the statues which were broken in the bombing, as well as an unblemished statue of Mary, the guardian of the cathedral. Next to the atomic memorials is the torture stone where Tsuru was forced to stand. Around the corner, on the north side of the cathedral, the youngest of the 26 martyrs, St Ludoviko Ibaraki, stands in statue form. Mass is held each morning for parishioners and next to the building are a few other facilities, including offices and a hall. Across the street is the Catholic Center, including offices, a café and youth hostel and on the other corner, the Catholic archbishop's residence. Alongside the Catholic Center community facilities is a Catholic kindergarten.

The large bell from the original cathedral today lies where it fell in 1945, overlooking a residential quarter. A third painting (Figure 6.5) by Nagai Takashi,

Figure 6.5 February 1946 sketch of the ruins of the Cathedral, by Nagai Takashi, used by permission Nagai Tokusaburō, 21 January 2019.

of February 1946, shows a small rehung bell. The sound of even this small bell, breaking the silence in the landscape of Urakami, by Christmas 1945 – signalled a call to restoration for the region. Nagai's more colourful drawing of the ruins incorporates this diminutive sign of the fractured community picking up the pieces, despite the apparent 'Fifth Persecution', deadlier than any before.

The civic debate which lingers to the present day over the rebuilding of Urakami Cathedral reiterates the monument as a 'dangerous' recalling of atomic destruction and arouses memory of lesser known political and religious fissure within Nagasaki. Many citizens still regret the loss of the ruins, a quashing of the call for peace. Recent public histories question the motives behind US donations to the Urakami building project, as covering up the devastating results of the atomic bombing, an act which is itself still largely supported by US citizens. Hiding the ruins obstructs remembering the 'crucifixion' of the Catholic community (and Nagasaki) and the absolute devastation visited upon this place, tangible memory of death. The suggestion that the Urakami Catholics 'forgot' the atomic bombing by rebuilding is understandable but misguided. Catholic survivors are sensitive to the lost ruins as a connection to atomic memory and some show a sense of regret about their removal.

The cathedral links to an older public narrative through familial connections, manifesting historic symbolisms of resilience and resistance. Survivors remember wider stories of suffering and connections from Fourth, to Fifth communal Persecution. Locating the cathedral in the exact geographic location where the headman of Urakami lived, the people redeem sombre public stories of apostasy. They navigate a way forward, incorporating the past. The cathedral in three forms, pre-war monument, rubble and rebuilt: associates the experiences of the bombing with previous grief. When the ruins were demolished in 1958, one corner of the ruins was saved and the city paid 1,000,000 yen to move the remnant to the Peace Park. This single corner of the original cathedral ruins was placed alongside the Ground Zero Monument at the centre of remembrance of the bombing. The tiny broken-down corner of the old cathedral is a motif for the utter destruction which impacted the city and decimated a marginalised Catholic community.

Next to the concretised memorial in the Peace Park is a reminder of the third symbol which became evident from the interviews. Past the Ground Zero memorial flows a stream, a tributary of the Urakami River, a symbol for life as elemental water, polluted by irradiation in 1945. More than the water, though, in the next chapter I consider the silenced cries of people for water, as a memory which still pains the *kataribe* today.

Notes

1 Matsuo Sachiko called the ruins *fujiyuu na omoi*, which I translate here as 'crippling memories'. In an article about the cathedral published by the *Journal of Religion in Japan*, I link this saying to Flora Keshgegian's 'profound negative'. Flora A. Keshgegian, *Redeeming Memories: A Theology of Healing and Transformation* (Nashville: Abingdon Press, 2000), 121. Gwyn McClelland, 'Remembering the Ruins of the

Urakami Cathedral: a fifth persecution   125

Urakami Cathedral'. *Journal of Religion in Japan* 5:1 (1 June 2016): 47–69, https://doi.org/10.1163/22118349-00501007.
2 Scholars have discussed Hiroshima in respect of such symbolism. Yoneyama writes that 'we can conceive of historical agency in terms of the power to renarratize and recite past events and experiences'. In this way, the ruins of the cathedral were a form of 'dangerous' memory. Lisa Yoneyama, *Hiroshima Traces: Time, Space, and the Dialectics of Memory* (Berkeley: University of California Press, 1999), 33. Stefanie Schäfer has separately discussed the atomic bomb 'memorial artefacts', which boosted 'dark tourism' in Hiroshima from 1948. A debate regarding whether to keep the iconic atomic bomb dome in Hiroshima continued through to the 1960s. Stefanie Schäfer, 'From Geisha Girls to the Atomic Bomb Dome: Dark Tourism and the Formation of Hiroshima Memory'. *Tourist Studies* 16.4 (2016): 351–66 (354).
3 Tomoe Otsuki, 'The Politics of Reconstruction and Reconciliation in US–Japan Relations – Dismantling the Atomic Bomb Ruins of Nagasaki's Urakami Cathedral'. *The Asia-Pacific Journal: Japan Focus* 13.32 (2015): 1–33.
4 Tsuyoshi Takase, *Nagasaki kieta mō hitotsu no 'genbaku dōmu'* (Tōkyō: Heibonsha, 2009), 141. Tsuyoshi describes how Iwaguchi first made a similar statement in response to Mayor Tagawa's decision to allow the demolishing of the ruins during the 1950s debate, 154–5.
5 Kamata Sadao, 'Nagasaki no inori to ikari'. *Nihon no genbaku bungaku* 15: hiron/essei, 15 vols (Tōkyō: Horupu Shuppan, 1983), xv, 408–17 (413). One of my interviewees, Kataoka Chizuko, insisted *go-ban kuzure* (Fifth Persecution) was an inappropriate appellation of the bombing. As indicated above, though, a book has also been published with this name by Shinpei Nagami, *Go-ban kuzure* (Nagasaki: Nagasaki Bunkensha, 1974). Chizuko Kataoka, interview by Gwyn McClelland, Junshin University Library, 24 February 2016.
6 Jōji Fukahori, interview by Gwyn McClelland, Nagasaki Atomic Bomb Museum, 1 October 2014.
7 Chad Richard Diehl, 'Resurrecting Nagasaki: Reconstruction, the Urakami Catholics, and Atomic Memory, 1945–1970' (PhD diss., Columbia University, 2011), 187.
8 Paul Glynn, *A Song for Nagasaki* (Grand Rapids, MI: Eerdmans, 1990), 33–4.
9 Tomoe Otsuki, 'Ghostly Remnants of the Urakami Cathedral in Itaru Takahara's Photographs', *Evening Will Come: A Monthly Journal of Poetics* (August 2015), 56, www.thevolta.org/ewc56-totsuki-p1.html.
10 Diehl, 'Resurrecting Nagasaki', 188.
11 I am grateful to the anthropologist, Dr Jenny Hall, Monash University, who assisted me in describing the traditional clothing the survivors wear in these photos.
12 Yakichi Kataoka, *Urakami yonban kuzure Meiji seifu no kirishitan dan'atsu.* (Tokyo: Chikuma Shobo, 1963), 162.
13 See Chapter 3 of this book for the dating of the earlier persecutions. Yakichi Kataoka, *Urakami yonban kuzure Meiji seifu no kirishitan dan'atsu* (Tōkyō: Chikuma Shōbō, 1963), 52. Wasaburō Urakawa, *'Tabi' no hanashi* (Nagasaki: Katorikku Urakami Kyōkai, 2005, 1938).
14 Kazuhiko Yokote, *Nagasaki kyū Urakami tenshudō 1945–58: ushinawareta hibaku isan* (Tōkyō: Iwanami Shoten, 2010), 69.
15 Sachiko Matsuo, interview by Gwyn McClelland, Nagasaki Atomic Bomb Museum, 1 December 2014.
16 The numbers of those exiled is recorded differently in varying accounts and Urakawa's numbers of the total exiled was 2810, lower than that of Yokote above. Stephen Turnbull agrees that there were a larger number, citing 3300 Christians exiled. Stephen R. Turnbull, *Japan's Hidden Christians, 1549–1999*, vol. 1 (Richmond, Surrey: Japan Library and Edition Synapse, 2000), 186. Kazuo Takagi is another historian who lists 3404 people exiled, of whom 660 died, 176 went missing and 1981 returned. Kazuo Takagi, *Meiji Katorikku kyōkai shi* (Tōkyō: Kyōbunkan,

2008), 285. A different date was used in Japan at the time, as the Gregorian calendar was not used until the sixth year of the Meiji period. Wasaburō Urakawa, *Urakami Kirishitan shi* (Tōkyō: Kokusho Kankōkai, 1973), 290.
17 Urakawa, *Urakami Kirishitan shi*, 284.
18 Matsuo, 1 December 2014, McClelland.
19 Konishi cites a yet higher number of people exiled. Shin'ichi Konishi, interview by Gwyn McClelland, Nagasaki Atomic Bomb Museum, 1 October 2014.
20 *Handbook of Christianity in Japan*, ed. Mark R. Mullins, Handbook of Oriental Studies; Handbuch Der Orientalistik. Section Five, Japan, v. 10 (Leiden; Boston, MA: Brill, 2003).
21 Matsuo, 1 December 2014, McClelland.
22 Also found in Yakichi Kataoka, *Urakami yonban kuzure*, 183.
23 Kataoka, *Urakami yonban kuzure*, 183–4.
24 Keshgegian, *Redeeming Memories*, 235.
25 Keshgegian, *Redeeming Memories*, 121.
26 Tōmei Ozaki, interview by Gwyn McClelland, Francisco-en Homu, Sasaki, 27 February 2016.
27 Yoshio Miyazaki, interview by Gwyn McClelland, Catholic Center, Nagasaki, 9 October 2014.
28 See footnote 1. Keshgegian, *Redeeming Memories*, 121. Keshgegian critiques Johann B. Metz's conception of 'dangerous memory' as lacking in life affirmation and transformation. Focusing too much on suffering at the expense of survival, renewal and resistance would trap the victim in 'victimhood', she says. If all that is remembered is suffering and loss, then those who remember are still caught in the victimisation, says Keshgegian.
29 Shigemi Fukahori, interview by Gwyn McClelland, Urakami Cathedral, 23 February 2016.
30 Jōji Fukahori, 1 October 2014, McClelland.
31 Haruko Nawata Ward, *Women Religious Leaders in Japan's Christian Century, 1549–1650, Women and Gender in the Early Modern World* (Farnham, England; Burlington, VT: Ashgate, 2009), 321, 330.
32 Toshio Ikeda, *Kirishitan no seiei* (Tōkyō: Chūō Shuppansha, 1972), 48.
33 Urakawa, *Urakami Kirishitan shi*, 284.
34 Diehl, 'Resurrecting Nagasaki', 222.
35 Yokote, *Nagasaki kyū Urakami tenshudō*, 85.
36 Diehl, 'Resurrecting Nagasaki', 223.
37 Diehl, 'Resurrecting Nagasaki', 232.
38 Non-Catholic residents appreciated its aesthetic from earlier times as well. For example, novelist Kamohara Haruo in 1931 wrote the following as quoted in Diehl: 'red-bricked Urakami Cathedral, which greets us not with its religiousness but its beauty'. Diehl, 'Resurrecting Nagasaki', 189.
39 Takase, *Nagasaki kieta mō hitotsu no 'genbaku dōmu'*. See also Yokote, *Nagasaki kyū Urakami tenshudō*.
40 Diehl, 'Resurrecting Nagasaki', 216–18.
41 Diehl quotes an article from 2002 in *Nishi Nippon Shimbun* to back up this claim. Chapter 5 of his dissertation goes into more depth regarding the discussion of lack of atomic symbols and the reconstruction of Nagasaki. Diehl, 'Resurrecting Nagasaki', 233. His recently published book includes a chapter entitled 'Ruins of Memory: The Urakami Cathedral and the Politics of Urban Identity'. Chad Richard Diehl, *Resurrecting Nagasaki: Reconstruction and the Formation of Atomic Narratives* (Ithaca: Cornell University Press, 2018), 145–68.
42 Diehl, 'Resurrecting Nagasaki', 225.
43 Otsuki, 'Ghostly Remnants of the Urakami Cathedral in Itaru Takahara's Photographs'.

44 Yokote, *Nagasaki kyū Urakami tenshudō 1945–58*, 79.
45 Yokote, 85. The amount collected from the congregation is not cited clearly on the Urakami Cathedral website. The website states that the congregation could not raise very much and therefore decided to collect 300 yen per month (from each person?) to put towards the fund. The forecast cost according to the Urakami Cathedral website was 60 million yen and the final cost was 80 million yen. Nagasaki Archdiocese, Urakami Cathedral Website (17) *Urakami tenshudo saiken* (Cathedral Renewal), Church website, Urakami Cathedral, 2018, accessed 23 April 2019, http://www1.odn.ne.jp/uracathe/saiken.htm.
46 Diehl, 'Resurrecting Nagasaki', 224.
47 As quoted in Otsuki, 'Ghostly Remnants of the Urakami Cathedral in Itaru Takahara's Photographs'.
48 Sister City Committee Webpage, '40TH Anniversary | SPNSCC', St Paul-Nagasaki, 2018, accessed 23 April 2019, www.stpaulnagasaki.org/history/40th-anniversary/.
49 Takase, *Nagasaki kieta mō hitotsu no 'genbaku dōmu'*, 126.
50 Diehl, 'Resurrecting Nagasaki', 228–9.
51 Jōji Fukahori, 1 October 2014, McClelland.
52 Jōji Fukahori, 1 October 2014, McClelland.
53 Konishi, 1 October 2014, McClelland.
54 See for instance, Chad Diehl, who mainly categorises the Nagasaki citizens into three distinct groups including city officials, Catholics and the *hibakusha*. However, it is important to remember that many Catholics were among the most highly impacted *hibakusha*. Diehl limits the 'Catholic view', possibly due to his sources, to Nagai Takashi's opinions and the priests' views. The ordinary parishioners are elided from this discussion. Diehl, 'Resurrecting Nagasaki'. Diehl likely aims to differentiate the politically active *hibakusha* from the Catholic community, who did not tend to be involved in *hibakusha* peace movements.
55 Matsuo, 1 December 2014, McClelland.

References

Diehl, Chad Richard. 'Resurrecting Nagasaki: Reconstruction, the Urakami Catholics, and Atomic Memory, 1945–1970'. PhD diss., Columbia University, 2011.

Diehl, Chad Richard. *Resurrecting Nagasaki: Reconstruction and the Formation of Atomic Narratives*. Ithaca: Cornell University Press, 2018.

Fukahori, Jōji. Interview by Gwyn McClelland, Nagasaki Atomic Bomb Museum, 10 January 2014.

Fukahori, Shigemi. Interview by Gwyn McClelland, Urakami Cathedral, 23 February 2016.

Glynn, Paul. *A Song for Nagasaki*. Grand Rapids, MI: Eerdmans, 1990.

Ikeda, Toshio. *Kirishitan no seiei*. Tokyo: Chuo Shuppansha, 1972.

Kamata Sadao. 'Nagasaki no inori to ikari'. In *Nihon no genbaku bungaku 15: hiron/essei* 15: 408–17. Nihon no genbaku bungaku. Tōkyō: Horupu Shuppan, 1983.

Kataoka, Chizuko. Interview by Gwyn McClelland, Junshin University Library, 24 February 2016.

Kataoka, Yakichi. *Urakami yonban kuzure Meiji seifu no kirishitan dan'atsu*. Tokyo: Chikuma Shobo, 1963.

Keshgegian, Flora A. *Redeeming Memories: A Theology of Healing and Transformation*. Nashville: Abingdon Press, 2000.

Konishi, Shinichi. Interview by Gwyn McClelland, Nagasaki Atomic Bomb Museum, MP3 file, 1 October 2014.

Matsuo, Sachiko. Interview by Gwyn McClelland, Nagasaki Atomic Bomb Museum, 5 December 2014.
McClelland, Gwyn. 'Remembering the Ruins of the Urakami Cathedral'. *Journal of Religion in Japan* 5.1 (1 June 2016): 47–69. https://doi.org/10.1163/22118349-00501007.
Miyazaki, Yoshio. Interview by Gwyn McClelland, Catholic Center, Nagasaki, 9 October 2014.
Mullins, Mark R., ed. *Handbook of Christianity in Japan*. Handbook of Oriental Studies; Handbuch Der Orientalistik. Section Five, Japan, v. 10. Leiden and Boston, MA: Brill, 2003.
Nagami, Shinpei. *Go-ban kuzure*. Nagasaki: Nagasaki Bunkensha, 1974.
Nagasaki Archdiocese. 'Urakami Cathedral Website (17) Urakami tenshudo saiken (Cathedral Renewal)'. Church website. Urakami Cathedral, 2018. http://www1.odn.ne.jp/uracathe/saiken.htm.
Otsuki, Tomoe. 'Ghostly Remnants of the Urakami Cathedral in Itaru Takahara's Photographs'. *Evening Will Come: A Monthly Journal of Poetics* 56 (August 2015). www.thevolta.org/ewc56-totsuki-p1.html.
Otsuki, Tomoe. 'The Politics of Reconstruction and Reconciliation in US–Japan Relations – Dismantling the Atomic Bomb Ruins of Nagasaki's Urakami Cathedral'. *The Asia-Pacific Journal: Japan Focus* 13.32 (2015): 1–33.
Ozaki, Tōmei. Interview by Gwyn McClelland, Francisco-en Homu, Sasaki, 27 February 2016.
Schäfer, Stefanie. 'From Geisha Girls to the Atomic Bomb Dome: Dark Tourism and the Formation of Hiroshima Memory'. *Tourist Studies* 16.4 (1 December 2016): 351–66. https://doi.org/10.1177/1468797615618122.
St Paul-Nagasaki, Sister City Committee Webpage. '40TH Anniversary | SPNSCC'. St Paul-Nagasaki, 2018. www.stpaulnagasaki.org/history/40th-anniversary/.
Takagi, Kazuo. *Meiji katorikku kyōkai shi*. Tōkyō: Kyōbunkan, 2008.
Takase, Tsuyoshi. *Nagasaki kieta mō hitotsu no 'genbaku dōmu'*. Tōkyō: Heibonsha, 2009.
Turnbull, Stephen R. *Japan's Hidden Christians, 1549–1999*, vol. 1. 2 vols. Richmond, Surrey: Japan Library and Edition Synapse, 2000.
Urakawa, Wasaburō. *'Tabi' no hanashi*. Nagasaki: Katorikku Urakami Kyoukai, 2005 (1938).
Urakawa, Wasaburō. *Urakami kirishitan shi*. Tōkyō: Kokusho Kankōkai, 1973.
Ward, Haruko Nawata. *Women Religious Leaders in Japan's Christian Century, 1549–1650*. Women and Gender in the Early Modern World. Farnham, England and Burlington, VT: Ashgate, 2009.
Yokote, Kazuhiko. *Nagasaki kyū Urakami tenshudō 1945–58: ushinawareta hibaku isan*. Tōkyō: Iwanami Shoten, 2010.
Yoneyama, Lisa. *Hiroshima Traces: Time, Space, and the Dialectics of Memory*. Berkeley: University of California Press, 1999.

7 Water!
Atomic cries and their echoes in the past

I heard the [boy's] voice saying, 'Ni-chan, mizu wo chōdai – water please!'
(Nakamura Kazutoshi, 2016)

My God, why have you forsaken me?
(Jesus, Mark 15: 34)

Introduction

A 'cry for water' rang out again and again in the 'atomic field' after the bombing. Such a cry, abruptly silenced by death, is a common theme within many testimonies from both Hiroshima and Nagasaki, as the title of a book published back in 1972 suggests.[1] The book, translated into English, was entitled *Give me Water: Testimonies of Hiroshima and Nagasaki*. Interviewees Miyake Reiko and Nakamura Kazutoshi also heard this call, which they could not forget.

Memoirs and recollections in literature present atomic bomb victims pleading for water and dying as soon as they could drink. The cry for water in the atomic wasteland: '*mizu wo!*' – is a protest against injustice and in the Catholic context a plaintive cry of faith. As Nakamura and Miyake remember the cry for water they identify an intrinsic part of 'dangerous' memory, 'listening' to those who were literally silenced. The haunting cries for water haunt not only the atomic narrative, but also the public history about persecutions, namely in the experiences of the great-grandmother of interviewee Kataoka Chizuko, Sada. Thus, here, I compare three instances of the cry for water, including the narrative of the persecution, each remembered from Urakami.

People cried out and died in the Urakami River after the bombing but water is simultaneously a symbol of life, replenishment and spiritual well-being. A photograph depicts a tributary of the Urakami river which flows through the Peace Park, as a child plays on the seventieth anniversary of the bombing (Figure 7.1). Today, water flows adjacent to the hypocenter memorial in the Peace Park and a sculpted basin of water is found at the Peace Memorial Hall at the top of the hill, 'containing the water that the victims of the atomic bombing so desperately craved'.[2]

Figure 7.1 Urakami River on the occasion of the seventieth anniversary of the atomic bombing of Nagasaki, photograph used by permission, Fiona McCandless, 25 January 2019.

Water is an elemental symbol of a flourishing environment. Juxtaposed narratives of desecration and purification recall the bodies of the dead clogging waterways and harmonising with the ecosystem, just as bodies melded with Urakami's soil.

Mary! Give me water!

The cry for water in both atomic and persecution narratives questions God's goodness, by its deadening endangering belief. A literary group wrote a poem in 1982 reflecting upon the 'cry for water' with a Catholic-oriented perspective. The Christian faithful call for compassionate 'Mary of Urakami' to rise from her rest and to act, writing in the first line 'Virgin Mary of Urakami, I beg of you, Answer me now…' The poem imitates the composure of biblical Psalms which pursue justice, calling for God to pass judgement on those who unleashed the bomb: '… Are you watching, God … Pass your judgement…' In another stanza, the group reiterate the cry for water: '… Water! Give me water! … Help me sustain the thread of life, Somebody.'[3]

Water! Atomic cries and echoes in the past 131

The writers imagine religious victims complaining about God's silence in the wake of the bombing. The line 'Who made this despicable bomb?' follows pleas to God and Mary as the poet contemplates God's complicity. The poem foreshadows the narratives described in this chapter of the memory of survivors and the bombing as physical threat and spiritual test.

Hell at the river

Interviewee Miyake Reiko arrived at the Urakami River on 10 August 1945 and observed a scene of ghostly chaos. I introduced Miyake's testimony in Chapter 3, when she narrated her memory of the injured and the dead bodies at the devastated school where she taught. Twenty years of age at the time of the bombing, Miyake was a young teacher at Shiroyama *Kokumin Gakkō* (National School). Miyake also recalled the scene at the Urakami river after the bombing. The *Asahi* newspaper printed her recount of the surreal scene of the irradiated and dying who arrived one by one seeking water:

> Burned and blackened people were standing in line for water on the stone steps leading down to the river. Young and old alike were groaning, 'Water, water.' After a person at the front of the line scooped a handful of water from the river and sipped it, that person never lifted his or her head again. All of them would let themselves fall into the river. The next person in line would take a sip and fall into the river. Another and yet another followed in turn. Miyake gazed at this scene for a while.[4]

Miyake reports a discomforting memory of suffering. Her telling of her narrative allows her to confront and, to at least some extent, come to terms with this horrible and difficult experience. The retelling of the experience may push her emotional reactions into the background in favour of explaining what happened. For Miyake and for those reading (or listening), the lack of emergency support for those affected magnifies the memory. The narrative evinces the sentiment of the poem, 'Help me sustain the thread of life. Somebody.' But few people were able to help the injured and suffering in either Nagasaki or Hiroshima in the immediate aftermath. Miyake, too, watched on with a sense of helplessness and confusion.

Miyake's memory is yet more challenging because water, a life-giving element we take for granted, in this case did not give life but accompanied death. People died after drinking, a phenomenon which was and remains shocking.[5] Even when people arrived at the water, drinking likely caused various complications due to injuries caused by irradiation and burns shock. No one at the time knew the properties of the 'new-style' weapon, or realised that water in its irradiated state could expose the victims to even more damage to their internal organs. Water may have actually aggravated blood loss sustained in injuries. After drinking water, burns victims may enter severe shock which results in death. Burns and trauma may affect all organ systems. Increasing fluid intake above a certain range leads to intracranial pressure, pulmonary edema, or heart failure.[6] Thus, the water the people desired was in reality physically dangerous.

There is an attentiveness to suffering in Miyake's narration. She acknowledges the humanity she observed, undercutting 'Catholic' (and other) narratives which over-emphasise the role of graceful death in the face of the atomic bombing.[7] Her observance and memory of human tragedy and environmental ruin is supported by local newspaper reports and historic testimonials.[8] This report stands in contrast to the *hansai* narrative of Junshin Girls' High School in which girls were said to sing 'Christ, the Lamb' as they went to their death in the same river.

It is desperation in the cries Miyake relates, not song. The abruptly silenced cry of the people for water in the atomic narrative is specific 'dangerous' memory, witnessed by Miyake and shared for those who will listen. Creative minds after the Jewish Shoah similarly imagine 'silenced cries' of forgotten suffering. A poem by Jewish German-Swedish poet Nelly Sachs entitled '*Landschaft aus Schreien*' (Landscape of Screams, 1957) describes a landscape where all that remains is human cries. Sachs incorporates Job's and Jesus' screams, depicted as impotent, like 'an insect in crystal'.[9] She connects Job's scream to Jesus' cry as he died recorded in the Christian scriptural narrative: 'My God, why have you forsaken me?'

Likewise, both cries stand at the centre of theology and theodicy for the German theologian Johann Metz.[10] For Metz, the suffering of the Jewish diaspora is a 'landscape of cries' – linking the Jewish suffering to 'early Christianity, whose biography ... ends with a cry...'[11] Sachs and Metz question by their writing who will witness the silent screams, like in the poem quoted earlier.[12] Those who cried for water in Nagasaki succumbed to immobilisation and lifelessness. And, after almost 70 years, it is Miyake who carries the cries at the river, burnt into her memory. By narration and by sharing her discomforting memory, she is a courageous witness. The telling of the story of the forgotten, silenced ones demands our attention – in her re-voicing and re-imagining.

The boy who cried for water

The second mention of a cry for water was by Nakamura Kazutoshi, who discussed his own survival as tribulation or trial. Nakamura told me about an episode he remembered in the aftermath of the bombing.

Soon after the bomb was dropped, 11-year-old Nakamura, searching for his father, found a better view of the destruction from an elevated gravesite southeast of Urakami Cathedral. He came across a boy, lying flat on the ground with terrible burns. In the interview he used a picture drawn by his son to accompany the narrative, showing the scene after he was halted by the boy's parched cry. I draw on two sources in understanding his story: the picture drawn by his son, Kōji (Figure 7.2), and the interview record:

> My eldest son drew this picture for me (Figure 7.2) [...] this is a child who was burnt by the bomb and laid out on the ground. He couldn't handle the

Water! Atomic cries and echoes in the past 133

Figure 7.2 'The boy who cried for water', drawn by his son, Nakamura Kōji, used by permission, Nakamura Kazutoshi, 17 January 2019.

heat of the sun [...] so I put the blanket on [...] here in the cemetery. And the grave stones had fallen over and there was a bright coloured futon which happened to fall out there. So, I took it and laid it over him [...] it [the place] was out of the way, so people were not coming [here] [...] this guy had become alone, without even a single person he knew, it was like he was the only person in the world, I felt [...][13]

Nakamura's narration intensifies the imagery of forsakenness and abandonment: the boy '... was the only person in the world'. He laid a futon blanket over the injured boy in a cemetery, a location which itself epitomises death. The bright colours of the futon in the original colour picture are incongruous when behind is the rubble of vanquished Urakami and a broken tree. Japanese gravestones in the picture are lopsided, blown awry by the bomb, onto the ground. The boy seeks solace and Nakamura is the 'Somebody' in the poem quoted early in this chapter, a witness offering humanity and hope. Nakamura continues:

[...] this was a high place and I could see the sea and I was relieved and thought maybe my father was over there, coming from the station, maybe he was on a road [...] I was thinking I would walk when I heard the [boy's] voice saying, '*Ni-chan, mizu wo chōdai* – water please!' It was a long way to get water [...] and I said, 'I'll definitely come back and give you water, so do your best until then!'[14]

Nakamura subconsciously elides from the discussion his missing family members while the boy's suffering consumes the *kataribe*. The cry for help as a reasonable and urgent need challenged Nakamura to action. He said, 'I'll definitely come back.' However, he also continued his search for his father, who he found. His other family members were also missing, but in his discussion of the boy, Nakamura does not mention them. Nakamura told me later in the interview that together he and his father came across the bodies of his close relatives at home and about the distress of never finding his mother. For now, though, he related:

> This time I ran and joined the back of the column of people and finally I got to meet my father. After that, on the way back to the school, I came past here, near Urakami cathedral [...] Just as I passed this place, I remembered that I had made the promise to the boy and had to bring him water. So, taking my father's container, I went back to where the child was.[15]

Nakamura omits major events within his own narrative by the two words 'after that'. In the interim his underlying trauma of coming across the remains of bodies of family members unfolded. The trauma may have caused him to forget the boy, until he finally walked past the area once more. When he recalled him, Nakamura took a container of water (his father's) and desperately ran the final distance:

> When I got there and approached, there was a mass of black big flies [...] [and] because I was running, *WAAA* [the flies rose up] [PAUSE] I shuddered with a horrible chill. I had a premonition as I saw that the child had his eyes open, staring into the distance, looking at me and I realised that he had died. Even now, I think *I did an awful thing to this boy*. [PAUSE] [...] all the boy wanted until the last was water [...] If only I had gotten him some. Even now when I think of that [...][16]

The memory of the boy's cry threatens Nakamura's sense of identity even as this happened to his 11-year-old self. His dialogue and transcript shows the signs of ongoing emotional responses to the boy's death, including the pauses and sound effects (*WAAA*). I italicised above, 'I did an awful thing to this boy.' Nakamura pronounces himself guilty, juxtaposing the needs of the boy against his own failure to respond. The boy's cry for water is Nakamura's 'dangerous' memory, which he cannot dismiss from his mind.

Survivor guilt

Testimony of trauma is untidy. Neither Miyake nor Nakamura describe an ordered narrative with a beginning and an end.[17] Nakamura put a futon on the boy, talked to him and brought water, but he ultimately remembers his failure to return before the boy's death. His narration implies he is entrapped by a psychological 'survivor guilt'. Summarised simplistically, survivor guilt is a remorse felt by those left alive after extreme events when others, including friends, family and acquaintances have died. Nakamura's perception in the horror of the aftermath, 'I should have done more' or 'tried harder' is complex and ineluctable.

A complication for Nakamura is the likely traumatic link to his (here) unmentioned shock of finding other bodies, including close relatives and the agony of never finding his mother. The consternation of finding the boy's body potentially evokes the unresolved lost body of his family member. He agrees that the search for his father (and mother) was legitimate but suggests by neglecting to return quickly he failed to show sufficient affection or care (*aijō*) to the boy:

> [...] that I couldn't get water for this child demonstrates I did not have enough compassion [...] But maybe that was not the case [...] Apart from finding my father, I was worrying most about finding water for this boy. I could see the river, but this was the top of a mountain, so there was no water [...] The thing I was most afraid of was in the time it took to get water to this boy, my father would have gone away.[18]

Nakamura's narrative exposes his inadequacy and his ongoing struggle with life after the atomic bombing. After his father, his next worry was finding water. Coming upon the boy dead, his actions were made redundant and this in turn may link to the lack of agency he expresses he experienced in his subsequent life. The guilt described here by Nakamura bears some similarity to Ozaki Tōmei's memory of his experiences I will describe in the following chapter. Both, as young men, later struggled with suicidal thoughts. But for Nakamura, like Miyake, sharing his story is the imperative that remains.

Nakamura's sense of futility is a contrast when set beside Miyake's sense of agency after the bombing, by her continuation of her work as a teacher in Shiroyama, alongside Urakami. Compared to those who lived in Urakami, Miyake was privileged because her home was preserved and her family life continued, while Nakamura and other survivors were refugees, forced to seek places to live away from Nagasaki. Nakamura articulates his feelings of impotence in dealing with his experiences. He dwells on this 'dangerous' memory, ambivalent about his perceived failure. His laying of a futon over the boy and bringing water were actions rendered meaningless in view of the boy's death. Later, a refugee, he was unable to take control of his own life, missed out on educational opportunity and contemplated suicide. Further, he had no outlet for at least 60 years to discuss his memory of the boy. For Nakamura, speaking about this 'dangerous' memory reminds him of feelings of ambivalence and impotence. However, his sharing of the distressing experience and his son's drawing of the scene appears as cathartic.

Withheld water as persecution

After a lifetime of hearing of communal ancestral narratives, an Urakami Catholic listening to Nakamura's or Miyake's memory of the 'cry for water' might well be drawn to a comparable story found in the public history of the persecutions. The father of interviewee Kataoka Chizuko, the historian Yakichi, wrote about the persecutions of the late nineteenth century and a semi-autobiographical account of his grandmother's experiences.[19] His grandmother was a mother with four young children who narrates her story even as she was singled out as one of the weakest of those exiled by the Nagasaki magistrate.

This analogous cry in the Fourth Persecution is found in a diary, or experience-record (*taiken-ki*), recorded from the perspective of Sada, Chizuko's great-grandmother. The diary may have been orally committed to paper, an early record of oral history. With her four daughters (aged twelve, nine, five and two years), Sada was exiled to Wakayama, a province found south of Ōsaka on Honshū island in the Kansai region of Japan, departing 6 December 1870 from Honbara-gyō, Ippongi in Urakami. Officials separated the women and men and the youngest children went with their mothers. The women wore an outward sign of their illicit faith, their Catholic baptismal veils (*anima*), as they set out.

The group spent seven days and nights on a boat on the way to Wakayama. Here, officials transferred them to a temple where they saw the men. The journey was arduous and relatives and friends were also often separated from each other. After 20 days, the groups were once again split up on gender lines and Sada, separated on this occasion from her three older children, went with the women with small babies and the older people who were 'unable to work' to a horse stable where the group crammed in. The jailers stripped the Christians of their rosaries and Mary flags.[20] Taking away their holy objects was an attempt to strip the *kirishitan* of any concrete items which helped them retain and practise faith.

Evidence of traumatic experience and the presence of bodies is recorded in Sada's diary. She remembered sordid conditions in the stable that lasted for over six months from June 1871 until January 1872. There was much sickness and with no medicine and precious little water, nine people died from infectious disease. When someone died, the women prayed (*orashio*, the prayers of the hidden Christians) and put an *anima* or veil on the body, which remained there overnight. The veils placed over the corpses went black immediately, due to the presence of lice attacking the bodies. Those who remained in the confined space, remembered Sada, were nauseated by the bodies and their smell.[21]

The next section of the diary described cries for water similar to the atomic narratives described.[22] Water emerges in Sada's narrative as a similarly 'dangerous' element, which could cause death to your souls, or physical death due to deprivation. Sada reported that when the overseer from Urakami came in and saw the dead bodies, he yelled, 'You should give up (renounce your faith)!'

> At the time, even as we cried, 'Water please!', we were told, 'There is none' and were not given any. There were people outside working, who

had apostatised and so we asked, 'Please give us water and we won't tell anyone', but they gave us nothing. The sick cried 'Water, water!' repeatedly, close to death. The children pleaded with their parents, 'I want water!' and 'I'm hungry!' and many of the parents gave up [...] [Later,] on 7 April, in the 6th year of Meiji [1873], we returned home to Urakami.[23]

Fear of deprivation and death is reflected in the 'cries for water'. Even the apostates who had formerly been *kirishitan* betrayed their compatriots and refused to provide relief.

The cry for water in this older narrative, like in Miyake and Nakamura's story, protests unjust treatment. The role of witnessing to the experience truthfully as *kataribe* is essential (although Sada is not a *kataribe* or an *hibakusha*). By recording and retelling memory of all three experiences, Sada, Miyake and Nakamura protest unthinking subjection to dehumanisation and victimhood. A second similarity between the narratives is the significant challenge to the people's religious faith. An implicit challenge in the narratives of 1945 is potential subversion of the faith of the victims. Those who apostatised in the persecutions imagine both God's betrayal and their own betrayal of God. However, the choice for those exiled was stark in Sada's account. They had to choose between death/dehydration or abandonment of faith; physical deterioration or spiritual bereavement. Sada reports of mothers apostatising for the sake of their children.

Among 289 exiles to Wakayama, community historian Urakawa Wasaburō details 96 who died and 152 who renounced their beliefs. If correct, only 41 exiled believers avoided both death and apostasy in the group sent to Wakayama.[24] Those who did not give up faith prayed or beseeched God and Mary, cried 'water!' and some died. Some who apostatised were enrolled in work for the magistrate and some returned early to Urakami village.

The atomic bombing was, like the Fourth Persecution, a threat to Catholic faith and dangerous to their identity, world view and discernment – truly a Fifth Persecution. Water was 'dangerous' to those who called for it. In atomic memory, water was physically dangerous to consume, whereas for Sada, the water was spiritually 'dangerous', representing de-Christianisation, repression and abuse.

The parallel cry for water in the atomic narrative alongside the Catholics' past persecution raises another issue. There is a question around the possibility of hope versus despair. Miyake and Nakamura protest the 'impossibility' of the atomic narrative by telling their own versions of the cry for water. Sada's is also an 'impossible' situation, which she lived through with her two-year-old child. The cry for water in atomic literature is often interpreted as a stark anti-nuclear message or for peace against war. However, the cry for water is doubly a 'dangerous' memory in the Catholic narrative and as reframed by their consciousness of suffering, reflects both physical and spiritual concerns, remembered previously within the Fourth Persecution.

For the survivors, Miyake, Nakamura and Sada, the legacies of trauma continue to manifest long after the originating event.[25] Trauma studies theologian

Flora Keshgegian writes that the key to transforming memories of victimisation is to consolidate instances of resistance and agency for the people involved. In the narration of such memories, the humanity of the dehumanised victims is re-imagined. Victims' cries and actions seeking water before death reanimate memories of agency and their fighting for life. Kataoka Sada was sent with her baby along with the infirm and old and displayed faithfulness and resilience within the modern Catholic narrative. In the rendering of the story by her grandson Yakichi, she is one of 41 believers who returned to Urakami and were granted life. She returned on 7 April 1873, part of the faithful and enduring remnant. The roof of her house was demolished and the walls were falling in, but she endured.[26] Her survival signals resistance and her return, God's faithfulness. Later, grandson Yakichi and great-granddaughter Chizuko survived the atomic bombing while many others lost their lives.

Of pollution and restoration

Many of those who cried for water in 1945 ended their lives enveloped in water which became their grave. The atomic bombing brought grave environmental consequences, not least irradiation. The consequences of the bleeding of radioactivity into oceanic ecosystems since the 2011 Fukushima disaster presents devastation on an even greater environmental scale, threatening water's purifying qualities. The Urakami river gradually returned to its wholesome state. In a blog post entitled: 'For Nagasaki citizens, the river is for the repose of souls', local teacher and illustrator Ejima Tatsuya estimated that between 10,000 and 20,000 bodies were in the Urakami river for at least a year after the bombing.[27] Ejima writes that for the *hibakusha* of the day, the water represented 'life-giving' properties. The water, physically 'dangerous' for those victimised at the time, in death enabled purification and restoration. In Shinto belief, water is a purifying agent.[28] The water was a symbolically appropriate and poignant resting place for the dead, a moving, living ecosystem. The remains lingered in the river for a long period, a 'dangerous' pollution as the bones were washed and washed again. The abandoned dead coalesced into the waterways, absorbed in the ecosystem.

Despite the healing powers of water, the 'silenced' cry for water re-voiced in the interviews and recorded in this collective biography remains jarring and shrill. A lack of resolution is expressed by Nakamura, Miyake and Sada, who recall the 'danger' and the 'hellish' scenes they observed.[29] Physical and spiritual dangers are amalgamated in these narratives.

'Give me water!', a harsh cry of the atomic narrative, is 'dangerous' memory in the *kataribe* voice, protesting the people's harsh treatment. The work of those breaking through silence after the bombing and remembering the cries as the witnesses or *kataribe* allow a release of emotion as described by Nakamura, Miyake and Sada. A sacred moment is identified in the breaking through of grief and lament, to which I will return in Chapter 9.[30] The 'silenced' cry reanimates generationally transmitted experiences of suffering and an ongoing challenge against oppressive and unfair treatment. The *kataribe* tradition channels the Urakami Catholics' knowledge and memory through emotion and subjective experience. The cry for water shows how Urakami and the Catholic remnant were doubly and triply marked by societal oppression, physical pollution and environmental destruction. Yet the bodies of many were graciously enveloped by the element of water, itself a symbol of purification and hope.

Three especially potent symbols emerged in the interviews in the process of considering the atomic bombing: Mary, the Cathedral and the 'cry for water'. Past communal narratives assist in dealing with experiences of atomic desolation and loss. In the final section of this book, I discuss the future of memory and how 'dangerous' memory provides reason for future choices. Even as their time on earth draws short, the *kataribe* continue to imagine their ongoing role as prophets or visionaries. Therefore, in the final section of this book I raise the themes of politics, hopefulness, lament and protest for examination alongside the rich and compelling survivor narratives.

Notes

1 In the days after the bombing, there were some who believed it was not helpful to give water to survivors and others who thought the least they could do was to fulfil someone's dying wish. See, for example, Genbaku taiken o tsutaeru kai, *Give Me Water: Testimonies of Hiroshima and Nagasaki*, trans. Rinjiro Sodei (Tokyo: Citizens Group to Convey Testimonies of Hiroshima and Nagasaki, 1972). Kyoko Iriye Selden and Mark Selden, *The Atomic Bomb: Voices from Hiroshima and Nagasaki* (Armonk, NY: M. E. Sharpe, 1989), 95. Richard H. Minear, *Hiroshima: Three Witnesses* (Chichester: Princeton University Press, 1990), 192.
2 Nagasaki Atomic Bomb Museum, 'Sculpted Basin', Museum website, Nagasaki Atom Bomb Museum, 2017, accessed 27 September 2017, www.peace-nagasaki.go.jp/english/information/i_02.html.
3 Poem read by the *Literati Group for Appealing the Dangers of a Nuclear War*, 3 March 1982 and quoted in Kayoko Yoshida, 'From Atomic Fragments to Memories of the Trinity Bomb: A Bridge of Oral History over the Pacific'. *The Oral History Review* 30.2 (1 July 2003): 74.
4 Gen Okada, 'Memories of Hiroshima and Nagasaki', *Asahi Shinbun*, December 2008, sec. Nagasaki Nōto, accessed 24 May 2016, www.asahi.com/hibakusha/english/shimen/nagasakinote/note01-16e.html.
5 Water is required for casualties, but fluid is not absorbed well by mouth. Shock should be treated in accordance with medical advice. Water assists those who have gone into shock, but in this case the water may have been polluted and the amount they drank is unclear. Leo van Bergen, *Before My Helpless Sight: Suffering, Dying and Military Medicine on the Western Front, 1914–1918* (New York: Routledge, 2016), 233.
6 Pam Wiebelhaus and Sean L. Hansen, 'Managing Burn Emergencies'. *Nursing Management* 32.7 (July 2001): 34.
7 Shijō effectively describes the Catholic narratives in her book: Chie Shijō, *Urakami no genbaku no katari: Nagai Takashi kara Rōma kyōkō e* (Tōkyō: Miraisha, 2015), 108.
8 Miyake's narrative is supported by: Tatsuya Ejima, 'Nagasaki shimin ni totte, kawa wa chingon no basho: Urakami gawa ittai', Blog, Atorie Cho Shigoto nikki, accessed 21 June 2016, http://hayabusa-3.dreamlog.jp/archives/51349615.html. *Genbaku taiken o tutaeru kai, Give Me Water*; Selden and Selden, *The Atomic Bomb*. Nagashuu Shinbun,

'Amari shirarenu ni man tai no ikotsu hibaku ichi nengo ni shuushuu shi maisou', Newspaper, Higashi Honganji Nagasaki, 18 May 2009, accessed 24 June 2016, www.h5.dion.ne.jp/~chosyu/amarisirarenu2manntainoikotu%20hibaku1nenngonisyuusyuusimaisou.html.
9 Sachs refers to the Jewish Shoah as well as Hiroshima and other historic events. Janice Allison Thompson, 'Theodicy in a Political Key: God and Suffering in the Post-Shoah Theology of Johann Baptist Metz' (PhD diss., University of Notre Dame, 2004), 226.
10 Thompson, 'Theodicy in a Political Key', 106–7.
11 Metz is writing of the Christological cry from the cross, reflecting a 'landscape of cries' and of Israel as a people who respond to history through memory in Jewish tradition. Theodicy, he continues, is 'the' question of Christian theology. Johann Baptist Metz and J. Matthew Ashley, 'Suffering Unto God'. *Critical Inquiry* 20.4 (1994): 614.
12 Thompson, 'Theodicy in a Political Key', 227.
13 Kazutoshi Nakamura, interview by Gwyn McClelland, Nagasaki Atomic Bomb Museum, 23 February 2016.
14 Nakamura, 23 February 2016, McClelland.
15 Nakamura, 23 February 2016, McClelland.
16 Nakamura, 23 February 2016, McClelland.
17 Molly Andrews, 'Beyond Narrative: The Shape of Traumatic Testimony', in *We Shall Bear Witness: Life Narratives and Human Rights* (Madison, WI: University of Wisconsin Press, 2014), 43.
18 Nakamura, 23 February 2016, McClelland.
19 Kataoka Yakichi calls the record a 'diary' but it is not clear when Sada wrote it. She probably completed it in the years after 1873 when the survivors returned to Urakami. Yakichi Kataoka, *Urakami yonban kuzure Meiji seifu no kirishitan dan'atsu* (Tokyo: Chikuma Shobo, 1963). Today, the diary is held by the Junshin University library, Megumi no Oka, Nagasaki. Keita Mano, 'Nagasaki: Urakami Kirishitan "yonban kuzure" 150 nen de kikakuten', *Asahi Newspaper online*, 4 September 2017, Digital edition, sec. Culture, accessed 26 August 2017, www.asahi.com/articles/ASK-475W4QK47TOLB00P.html.
20 This is the process referred to previously (Chapter 5), by which 'holy' objects were confiscated by the Nagasaki magistrate. Later, many of these items were transferred as exotic objects to Tokyo, where they remain in the Tokyo National Museum. The various items taken away are carefully listed in Kataoka, *Urakami yonban kuzure*, 170. In 2019, the Catholic community has requested these objects of significance to be returned to Urakami.
21 Kataoka, *Urakami yonban kuzure*, 162–5.
22 Urakawa in his book, *Tabi*, relates that the lack of water during the persecutions especially affected the women and argues that men managed to use bamboo to redirect the water from the roof gutters. Wasaburō Urakawa, *'Tabi' no hanashi* (Nagasaki: Katorikku Urakami Kyoukai, 2005, 1938), 149.
23 An excerpt from Kataoka, *Urakami yonban kuzure*, 166–7.
24 Urakawa, *'Tabi' no hanashi*, 149.
25 Flora A. Keshgegian, *Redeeming Memories: A Theology of Healing and Transformation* (Nashville: Abingdon Press, 2000), 120–1.
26 Kataoka, *Urakami yonban kuzure*, 167.
27 Ejima, 'Nagasaki shimin ni totte, kawa wa chingon no basho: Urakami gawa ittai'. The Higashi Honganji temple's Buddhist ladies' association began cleaning up bodies from March 1946, according to an article which corroborates a figure of approximately 20,000 bodies across Urakami, although the number in the river is unclear. Nagashū Shinbun, 'amari shirarenu'. Southard writes that barrels were placed at intersections in Urakami Valley for the collection of ashes and bones and reports of human

bones collected from the river and buried under trees. Susan Southard, *Nagasaki: Life after Nuclear War* (New York: Viking, 2015), 128.
28 Emiko Namihira describes rituals for the dead as involving washing the bodies with water, as well as those who have encountered the dead. She notes that if 'the pollution of death remains strong even after a fixed time has passed … this is thought to be all the more dangerous'. Emiko Namihira, 'Pollution in the Folk Belief System'. *Current Anthropology* 28.4 (1987): 66.
29 The 'danger' is exerted against the tendency for collective understanding of remembering of the atomic bombing without acknowledging the common humanity observed by these witnesses. They remind us to remember the 'other' and of a hope for the oppressed and vanquished.
30 Theologian Richard Fenn makes the claim that a sacred moment breaks through in lament (not about Nagasaki, but about victims in general) in Richard Fenn, 'Ezra's Lament: The Anatomy of Grief', in *Lament: Reclaiming Practices in Pulpit, Pew, and Public Square*, eds Sally Ann Brown and Patrick D. Miller (Louisville, Kentucky: Westminster John Knox Press, 2005), 139.

References

Andrews, Molly. 'Beyond Narrative: The Shape of Traumatic Testimony'. In *We Shall Bear Witness: Life Narratives and Human Rights*, 147–66. Madison, WI: University of Wisconsin Press, 2014.
Bergen, Leo van. *Before My Helpless Sight: Suffering, Dying and Military Medicine on the Western Front, 1914–1918*. New York: Routledge, 2016.
Ejima, Tatsuya. 'Nagasaki shimin ni totte, kawa wa chingon no basho: Urakami gawa ittai'. Blog. Atorie Cho Shigoto nikki. http://hayabusa-3.dreamlog.jp/archives/51349615.html.
Fenn, Richard. 'Ezra's Lament: The Anatomy of Grief'. In *Lament: Reclaiming Practices in Pulpit, Pew, and Public Square*, eds Sally Ann Brown and Patrick D. Miller. Louisville, Kentucky: Westminster John Knox Press, 2005.
Genbaku taiken o tutaeru kai. *Give Me Water: Testimonies of Hiroshima and Nagasaki*, trans. Rinjiro Sodei. Tokyo: Citizens Group to Convey Testimonies of Hiroshima and Nagasaki, 1972.
Kataoka, Yakichi. *Urakami yonban kuzure Meiji seifu no kirishitan dan'atsu*. Tokyo: Chikuma Shobo, 1963.
Keshgegian, Flora A. *Redeeming Memories: A Theology of Healing and Transformation*. Nashville: Abingdon Press, 2000.
Mano, Keita. Nagasaki: 'Urakami Kirishitan "yonban kuzure" 150 nen de kikakuten'. *Asahi Newspaper online*. 4 September 2017, Digital edition, sec. Culture. www.asahi.com/articles/ASK475W4QK47TOLB00P.html.
Metz, Johann Baptist, and J. Matthew Ashley. 'Suffering Unto God'. *Critical Inquiry* 20.4 (1994): 611–22.
Minear, Richard H. *Hiroshima: Three Witnesses*. Chichester: Princeton University Press, 1990.
Nagasaki Atomic Bomb Museum. 'Sculpted Basin'. Museum website. Nagasaki Atom Bomb Museum, 2017. www.peace-nagasaki.go.jp/english/information/i_02.html.
Nagashuu Shinbun. 'Amari shirarenu 2 man tai no ikotsu hibaku 1 nengo ni shuushuu shi maisou'. Newspaper. Higashi Honganji Nagasaki, 18 May 2009. www.h5.dion.ne.jp/~chosyu/amarisirarenu2manntainoikotu%20hibaku1nenngonisyuusyuusimaisou.html.
Nakamura, Kazutoshi. Interview by Gwyn McClelland, Nagasaki Atomic Bomb Museum, 23 February 2016.

Namihira, Emiko. 'Pollution in the Folk Belief System'. *Current Anthropology* 28.4 (1987): 65–74.

Okada, Gen. 'Memories of Hiroshima and Nagasaki'. *Asahi Shinbun*. December 2008, sec. Nagasaki Nooto. www.asahi.com/hibakusha/english/shimen/nagasakinote/note01-16e.html.

Selden, Kyoko Iriye, and Mark Selden. *The Atomic Bomb: Voices from Hiroshima and Nagasaki*. Armonk, NY: M. E. Sharpe, 1989.

Shijō, Chie. *Urakami no genbaku no katari: Nagai Takashi kara Rōma Kyōkō e*. Tōkyō: Miraisha, 2015.

Southard, Susan. *Nagasaki: Life after Nuclear War*. New York: Viking, 2015.

Thompson, Janice Allison. 'Theodicy in a Political Key: God and Suffering in the Post-Shoah Theology of Johann Baptist Metz'. PhD diss., University of Notre Dame, 2004.

Urakawa, Wasaburō. *'Tabi' no hanashi : Urakami yonban kuzure*. Nagasaki: Katorikku Urakami Kyoukai, 2005.

Wiebelhaus, Pam, and Sean L. Hansen. 'Managing Burn Emergencies'. *Nursing Management* 32.7 (July 2001): 29–35.

Yoshida, Kayoko. 'From Atomic Fragments to Memories of the Trinity Bomb: A Bridge of Oral History over the Pacific'. *The Oral History Review* 30.2 (1 July 2003): 59–75.

Part III
Memory's future

8 Dangerous hope

> *'Yes, gradually as I grew ... the suicidal feelings I had dissipated ... I realised I had been given [much] from God.'*
>
> (Nakamura Kazutoshi)

When faced with an event as momentous as the atomic bombing of Nagasaki, as with executions and other extreme prejudice, it may appear trite to write of the future, or of hope. Themes including lament, anger and protest also speak into the future and I return to them in the final chapter. And yet there is a thread, worn thin in places, of hope. As I began interviewing, I did not know what to expect but many of the survivors with whom I spoke exhibited startling signs of resilience, strength and a concern for the future.

In the process of remembering the martyrs and conceptualising his own experience of the bombing, Ozaki Tōmei (Figure 8.1), the orphan who became a monk, wrote, 'staring at reality ... it was the indestructible [...] God's existence I saw'.[1] In the aftermath of the bombing, he took on the name of a young Christian executed for subversion in 1597. He described how hope had been birthed from within the trauma. His belief in the divine contributed to the public act of renaming himself, an act which Johann B. Metz would surely call political theology. Later, Ozaki discovered the Polish founder of the Nagasaki monastery where he lived after the bombing had perished in Auschwitz during the war. Ozaki travelled to Poland and uncovered the story for himself – authoring a book about the priest, Maximilian Kolbe, and initiating a Kolbe museum in Nagasaki. Ozaki's testimony and the stories of Mine Tōru, Nakamura Kazutoshi and Fukahori Shigemi speak to their varying experiences of hope and public engagement. In the final pages of this chapter, I digress from the testimonies of the collective biography by considering how Catholic memory is especially 'dangerous'. I reflect upon the public actions and speech of a Catholic mayor, who in 1989 made an infamous comment about the Shōwa Emperor.

What is clear despite the atomic bombing is that for the Urakami Catholics, their public and biblical narratives evoke a hopeful political trajectory. In the community's reading of the Christian meta-narrative, the *tabi* (exile) of the late nineteenth century is an Exodus (after the biblical story) and more ancient

146 *Memory's future*

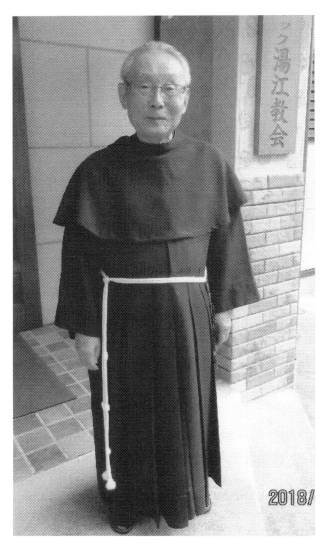

Figure 8.1 Ozaki Tōmei, in his robes, 12 September 2018, supplied and used by permission, 20 January 2019.

martyrdoms are remembered alongside Easter. The community remind us too in the narrative of the atomic bombing not to move over-quickly from the darkness of Easter Saturday to an Easter Sunday hope. Via the survivors' story-telling, I elaborate on how Catholic *hibakusha* memory emerges from a specific matrix of cultural and religious understanding.

The cultural lens

The survivors' interpretation of memory is understood through a specific cultural lens.[2] Ozaki Tōmei (Figure 8.1), whose childhood name was Tagawa Kōichi, discussed his life story utilising popular culture and references to Catholic, *sempuku* (Hidden Christian) and WWII narratives of history. His dialogue emphasises two key concepts: his reconciliation with the memory of his mother and his rediscovery of his Catholic faith.[3]

A Japanese *manga-ka* (cartoon-author) Shiōra Shintarō produced a manga, entitled *yaketa rozario* (*The Burnt Rosary Beads*), based on his own interviews with Ozaki in 2009. Reflections upon Ozaki's Hidden Christian ancestry and redemptive tropes in public narratives are evident in the biographical manga. The illustrator is faithful to the narrative, emphasising through the visual medium of the manga landmarks, sacred places and geography, which recall the public minority narratives of suffering, martyrdom and death.[4]

Ozaki's story of victimisation by the bomb has not achieved the level of fame of better known narratives of the atomic bombing captured in cartoon form, such as Hiroshima's Barefoot Gen.[5] Compared to Barefoot Gen, though, *The Burnt Rosary Beads* adds a unique perspective as an atomic narrative manga, due to the Nagasaki setting and the central protagonist's Catholic faith.

Themes of redemption and hope show continuity within Ozaki's life story. Ozaki became sick, contracting tuberculosis, as a child living in the northern part of Japan's colony of Korea with his mother and the two of them returned to Nagasaki after his father had died to seek medical assistance. Ozaki's mother prayed for his health at the sacred places. In the manga, her pilgrimage into the countryside to pray for his health is accompanied by a map of the Nagasaki region, allowing readers to understand the impact of Christianity on the physical landscape.[6] She travels over Mt Iwaya to Kashiyama Akadake, where she prays facing Kurosaki. The reason for her selection of this location is that Mt Akadake is remembered as Bastian *no kamiyama* (The sacred mountain of Bastian), a site where according to the legend seven Christian martyrs died.[7] Local traditions suggest the mythical Bastian was born at Fukabori, south of Nagasaki and became the gatekeeper to the local Buddhist temple.[8] He converted to Christianity and ministered to the community at Fukabori with another Christian named Juan during the early 1650s. As a seventeenth century prophet of the 'hidden Christians', Bastian purportedly predicted the priests' return to Japan. *Sempuku* Christians and the Catholic community later believed that a spring in the hills of Sotome where Bastian had drunk, called *maruba no ido*, had healing properties and many pilgrims travelled there to collect water for healing. Ozaki's mother also prayed for him in Nagasaki at the Polish monastery, where another spring was located, known as 'Lourdes' in reference to the sacred spring in Europe. This was the monastery to which Ozaki would return after the bombing. He was healed due to his mother's prayers and pilgrimage, according to the manga.[9]

After the bombing Ozaki's voice illustrates his fondness for the concept of 'faithfulness'. A biographical local newspaper article of 2008, entitled 'Last smile of

Mother, as she washed the dishes', incorporates Ozaki's teenage diary in the text. On the day the bomb was deployed, as he left home for work in the Mitsubishi tunnel factory, he prayed with his rosary beads. He quotes from his 17-year-old self:

> About 11 a.m., we were in the tunnel [in Akasakō] building torpedoes, when suddenly the lights went out and it was black. There was a huge sound [Dō-n!] and at the same time, a bomb blast hit us. It was such a large noise that for a while I was deaf.[10]

Speaking of the experience in his interview, Ozaki relates:

> When the bomb was dropped, I was in a tunnel [...] We were no longer able to stay in there as a navy officer told all the healthy people to leave, so for the first time we left the tunnel and saw that the surroundings had changed. The houses were burning; automobiles had rolled over and drivers had lost their clothes. That was what we confronted [as we emerged]. Then, I turned towards home, worrying about what had happened to my mother and house. [...] and I began to walk in that direction.[11]

Further visual sources on Ozaki's blog assist in understanding how he makes sense of his memory and story. His detailed sketch map (Figure 8.2) illustrates his journey from the tunnel in the north towards Nagasaki, crossing the railway line and Urakami River, initially 2.3 kilometres from the hypocenter and ending 500 metres away, at his ruined house. The sketch map incorporates the concentric circles of the wider public narrative, indicating the hypocenter he was headed towards. Red marks highlight the significant landmarks: including Ground Zero; the tunnel; the cathedral; and his home.

I saw, I experienced, I ran away

In the immediate aftermath as he emerged from the tunnel factory, Ozaki's beliefs were sorely tested. The piles of bodies he saw, including the baffling sight of a dead man sitting upright, led him, he wrote, to doubt his faith. The inclusion of the cathedral in the sketch map hints at another reason for concerns. The cathedral in ruins as 'profound negative' undercut the structure's representation of resilience in the Catholic public narratives of past persecutions. Its loss was surely a 'threat to faith'.

During the journey, Ozaki also remembers incidents which haunted him later, his personal 'dangerous' memory. Such incidents stayed with him as a trauma he could not forget, inducing a psychological 'survivor' guilt. They were painful memories of his failure and later drove him to change. He recalls taking five hours to make his way home, a distance which normally took 30 minutes.[12] He summed up his experience as 'I saw, I experienced, I ran away' (*mita, taiken shita, nigeta*), hinting at his fear and turmoil after the bomb, his neglecting of those he met and his regret of his lack of courage. Ozaki's 1996 autobiography,

Dangerous hope 149

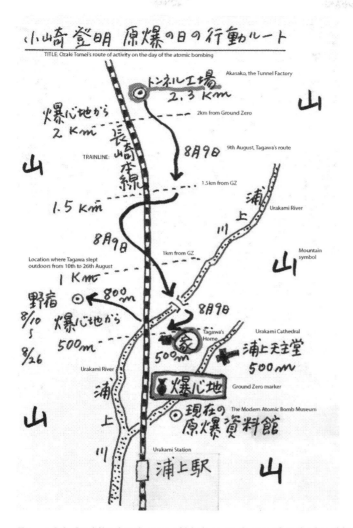

Figure 8.2 Ozaki's sketch map of his journey home after the bombing, with annotations, Ozaki's blog, used by permission, 20 January 2019.

entitled 'A Seventeen year old's summer' (*Jūnanasai no natsu*), contributes to our understanding of his narrative, including the central tenet of his perception that his responses were due to fear and a lack of care for the 'other'.[13] Ozaki deals with this dangerous memory as Nakamura did with his own – by telling his narrative of the difficult encounters which stayed with him.

The first painful memory involved an injured girl. As Ozaki emerged from the tunnel, two or three male factory workers called on him to help free a girl, injured and trapped by the fallen timber of a factory building. With his help, the group then carried her towards the train line.[14] After freeing the girl and carrying her for some time, Ozaki and the others heard an approaching US plane and promptly abandoned her, fearing another bomb. Scholars of emotion and eyewitness memory write that increased arousal or stress causes 'flight or fight' responses, a major consequence of an event of impact.[15] Ozaki wrote simply, 'To help myself, I ran away!'[16]

After abandoning the girl, Ozaki ran off into the woods nearby seeking shelter, only to meet many more seriously wounded people. He averted his eyes and ran on until he encountered someone he knew. It was a colleague from the tunnel factory, Ozaki's *senpai* (senior) by three years. One week prior to the bombing this colleague had hit out physically at Ozaki in anger. As a result, the pair had agreed to fight it out later. Now, though, the man was clearly badly injured, his internal organs spilling out of his belly as he held them with his hands. Ozaki sneered at him and said: 'Guess you're done for, huh?' The man glared, murmured and said, 'Shit.'[17] Ozaki abandoned him and travelled on to the Urakami River, which he needed to forge to find his house on the other side. As he moved through the water, he felt the arm of a 10-year-old boy grab his leg, crying, 'Please help me!' Exclaiming to the boy someone else would help him, Ozaki pulled himself free and fled.[18] Three times Ozaki encountered the 'other', the injured girl, his erstwhile co-worker and a young boy. Each time he averted his gaze and swiftly extricated himself.

Finally, he arrived at the burning remains of his home where he could only find a burnt rosary of his mother's (Figure 8.3). He had nothing left apart from the rosary and an attached cross. Tattered symbol of death, like the church ruins – a threat to his own faith – the burnt rosary was a tangible memory of suffering for Ozaki. He was suddenly an 'orphan without recourse', bereft and alone in the world.[19] Like Mine and Nakamura, he would never find his mother's body.

The manga and Ozaki's autobiography describe his ongoing psychological and existential struggle as he tried to survive living in the open. He was realising the truth that he was alone. He considered suicide at his lowest ebb, shamed by his memory of his unwillingness to help in each of the above incidents – a guilt as strong as that Nakamura described about the boy who cried for water.[20] After making the journey to his home on 9 August, Ozaki spent 16 days living outdoors. He was only about 800 metres from the hypocenter in Urakami.

A new identity

Bereft of mother and home, the ruins of the cathedral and the sight of the dead bodies tested Ozaki's faith and paradoxically compelled him to reconnect with the faith passed down to him. Ozaki and Mine's stories after their orphanhood revolve around a nearby Catholic monastery established by Polish monks in the 1920s, known as *seibo no kishi* (Knights of the Holy Mother). The monastery was protected by mountains from the impacts of the bombing and assisted many

Dangerous hope 151

Figure 8.3 Full page proof from the manga by Shiōra, Ozaki finds the burnt rosary beads of his mother, used by permission, Shiōra Shintarō 2019.

orphans like these two. Ozaki recalls his entry after the bombing to the monastery as an experience like conversion or rebirth.[21] His first encounter on 8 October 1945 is described in an Asahi newspaper article as follows. Having knocked on the door:

> The Polish monk who answered his knock remembered him. Asked about his mother, Ozaki said that she died in the atomic bombing. The monk tried in vain to hold back tears. When Ozaki told another monk that he would like to become a seminarian, the monk embraced him warmly. Thus, he was admitted. He was led to the kitchen where he was served a bowl full of miso soup, which he drained to the last drop.[22]

The narrative records the monk's immediate reaction to Ozaki as empathy. He fed the boy, important for a hungry 17-year-old youth in a state of shock. Physical sustenance represents hoped-for spiritual refreshment, even as attending the monastery was physically a relief. The monks gave Ozaki a bed, clothes and food. Renewed, he found a new beginning.

One and a half months later, Ozaki took a political and outward stance in doubly 'fissured' Nagasaki, deciding to become a monk himself. Formerly known as Tagawa, the novice monk adopted his new name of the child martyr of 1597, identifying him closely with his own communal narrative and his newly deceased mother. By his renaming, Ozaki was marked publicly as a member of a Catholic marginalised minority. The adoption of the name, he wrote, signified a new attitude towards the 'other' (as one who the majority culture marked as 'other'), and a way to deal with his trauma.

In the historical description of the original martyr Ozaki (Kozaki) Tōmei (Thomas) of 1597, a 15-year-old Japanese boy clings to hope in the face of impending disaster. In the middle of winter, the shogun's officials separate the boy from his mother and march the group from Kyoto to Nagasaki for the executions (although they were transported by boat three times along the way). He writes in a letter to his mother, translated into Spanish by Jesuit historian Luis Fróis and later translated back into Japanese:

> The priests and the others who are journeying to be crucified in Nagasaki number in all twenty-four, as testified in the sentence that is carried on a board ahead of us ... I hope to see you both very soon, there in paradise...[23]

The boy continues, 'The world is transient and therefore I strive to achieve the everlasting happiness of heaven.'

Survivor Ozaki was moved by such courage and by the contents of the letter the young martyr wrote to his mother. Significantly, for Ozaki, his own mother first told him the story about this boy, Thomas, when he was a child. The transience of life which the martyr had observed was both observable and recognisable in the disaster of the atomic bomb – and God's transcendent indestructibility a hope against hope for the modern Ozaki. In the face of the destruction and social rejection Ozaki faced – having lost all material things, his family life, all possessions – the promise of God's existence beyond materiality was a great prospect. He wrote:

> The experience of the atomic bombing was exactly like that. Everything in the world is breakable and vanishes. As far as the atom bomb went, there was nothing which cannot be destroyed. We cannot depend on the fragility (breakability) of existence. (*Koware-iku sonzai ni tayotte wa naranai*) Nonetheless, staring at reality, after that, it was the indestructible nature of God's existence which I saw. The Lord God who holds all created things, the source of love and life is the God I know. This is also the source of faith.[24]

As he remembers the aftermath of the bombing in this moment of revelation, developing a new understanding of God, Ozaki took on a new identity to respond to the question explored in the biblical Job: 'Where then is God?' In gutted Urakami, he witnesses to a God who is present to the abandoned.

The path of a martyr

Ozaki employs communal narratives of martyrdom. An orphaned youth, he took on the name of a native Christian boy of 1597, who himself had been executed for subversion. The public nature of Ozaki's stance in post-war Nagasaki invited community prejudice and slander, both inherited (religious and social) and newly emerging (radiation related). Renaming himself after a Japanese Catholic saint was a subversive act in the non-Catholic community, whose members considered the martyrdom of the followers of a non-Japanese religion with ambivalence. For many Japanese, the proscription of Christianity by the Tokugawa authorities was associated with the protection of Japan and with resistance against the imperial powers, who had encroached in Asia. Christianity was portrayed as an 'outside' religion, with no place in Japan, or among the Japanese people. Christian missionaries had failed in their quest to win the Japanese people's hearts.

Even for the Christians, Ozaki's was an abnormal new name. Normally Japanese monks would adopt the name of a Western saint (for example, Nagai 'Paul' Takashi), but Ozaki honoured his ancestors' tradition and faith, taking the 'unexpected' path of selecting a Japanese saint. He associated himself with the saints who had come before, including Bastian. The 1597 executions in Nishizaka were the beginning of many martyrdoms in the Christian (and *sempuku/kakure*) narrative, including the '1622 Great Martyrdom' (Figure 8.1, Chapter 1) and executions in 1635 in Neshiko and Orokunin-sama.[25] Private and communal aspects of the 'dangerous' memory of suffering were understood by others and himself through his new name.

Ozaki refers to the older martyrdoms and persecutions as exemplars of how to understand the ability to accept and bear trials. He moves deftly between narratives of persecutions and personal memory of the atomic bombing:

> [...] the martyrs took the cross as an exemplar for their path to martyrdom. The 26 martyrs walking from Kyoto to Nagasaki [...] imagined Christ's cross [...] When the bomb fell [...] the people who had returned from the time of the Fourth *kuzure* (persecution) [...] [said that] it was one more time [...][26]

Ozaki compares his experiences and his community's exposure in the atomic bombing directly to the 'path to martyrdom', envisaging a 'Fifth Persecution'.

As mentioned, Ozaki's mother was herself born in Urakami, an immediate descendant of the 'hidden Christians'. During the Edo period, the 26 martyrs proceeded past the front door of the house where she was born, below Yamazato Primary School, which was destroyed in the atomic bombing (Chapter 9, Figure

8.3).²⁷ Ozaki thought about the procession of his namesake Ozaki 'Thomas' Tōmei with the 26 martyrs from Kyoto to Nagasaki. He wrote:

> [...] currently my prayer every day is in the way of the martyr, not giving in to wrongdoing, holding a forgiving spirit, pain and adversity may come into my life, but I want to be someone who doesn't run away. The reason is that my name is the name of the martyr, Thomas.²⁸

When he put down the young injured girl, encountered the dying man who had wanted to fight him and was grasped at by a boy, in each case Ozaki remembered and regretted how quickly he ran off. He wished to be a person who 'does not run away'. Seeing the 'other' and engaging with them, he wrote, no matter who they were, was necessary, to disrupt violence and avoid war. His understanding of the 'other' was enhanced by these unsettling encounters, 'dangerous' memories, and his regret about his 'inadequate' responses. In his autobiography, he wrote understanding the hearts of people who suffer is the necessary seeds of peace.²⁹

From Nagasaki to Auschwitz

With renewed faith and a new name, Ozaki came across another example of selflessness. The founder of the monastery, Father Maximilian Kolbe, had returned to Poland in 1936, due to ill health. Ozaki was shocked to hear that in 1941, Kolbe offered up his own life at the Nazi concentration camp of Auschwitz, so another man who had a family could be saved. Ozaki admired Kolbe's offering of his life for the sake of another, and contrasted it with his own memories of abandoning an injured girl after the bombing. This, he wrote, was a true story of Christian service and of how to meet and serve the 'other'. Hope was paradoxically found in following Christ, carrying the cross, like a martyr, even when that path led to death. Ozaki associated his own experience of suffering in Japan with the Polish wartime experience and with those who stand against Nazi brutality.

There were connections, Ozaki noticed, between the experiences of the atomic bombing, the narrative of Father Kolbe, Auschwitz, 'peace', Christianity and the history of the 26 martyrs.³⁰ The Nagasaki monastery which Kolbe had set up was Ozaki's salvation after the hell of the atomic bomb. Kolbe acted out love in both Nagasaki and in Auschwitz. Ozaki resolved to find out more about the priest, Father Kolbe, and travelled to Poland ten times between 1971 and 2004.³¹ His experiences travelling to Poland are also described in Shiōra's manga, which has been translated into Polish. He compared the public history of Nazi violence told by survivors with the experiences of the *hibakusha*. Ozaki wrote two books in Japanese about Kolbe's life, including *Mi gawari no ai* (The Selfless Love of Giving).³² Later, as director of the Kolbe Museum in Nagasaki, where documents about Kolbe were kept from 1986, Ozaki raised the profile of this public history.

Dangerous hope 155

The way Kolbe died in Auschwitz raised questions for Ozaki about the relationship of freedom and domination. Ozaki's recollection of the life and death of Kolbe as 'dangerous' memory breaks the spell of history as owned by the oppressor. For Ozaki the story demonstrated Kolbe's empathy which explicitly disrupted the violent actions of humanity inflicted onto 'others', facing up to death and suffering. It took a stand against any need for war. Kolbe's example illuminated a courageous path for Ozaki, the path of empathising with the 'other'. Johann Metz writes that a 'dangerous' memory of suffering opposes the oblivion of past suffering.[33] The attempted extinguishment of spirit within Auschwitz is of a history which 'presupposes that what is past is past' and 'successfully historicized, it is also forgotten in a sense'. Kolbe's life stands against oblivion, lived in solidarity with the dead and vanquished of Auschwitz, and by association with Nagasaki.[34] Raising Kolbe, Ozaki challenges what Metz might call the 'reason of forgetfulness'. He was standing against atrocity and innocent suffering in Nagasaki and Auschwitz and where-ever else it occurs.[35]

Five siblings

Mine Tōru along with his four siblings was also orphaned by the atomic bomb. Nine years old in 1945, his sisters were aged one, three, five and twelve years. In my interview with him Mine brightens when he discusses the impact of *seibo no kishi* monastery on his and his siblings' life. Like Ozaki, Mine recalls his warm welcome at the monastery, after the loss and abandonment he had suffered. However, due to his young age at the time of the bombing, his elder sister and he were thrust into quasi-parenthood of the three young ones. Because they were so young, the five orphans were vulnerable. Mine's mother had set out for the shops in Nagasaki on the morning of 9 August and had never returned. The five children waited for days and a local policeman insisted, as Mine remembers, they would soon find their mother.

Remembering the monastery, Mine proudly hands me Ozaki's book in the interview, which tells the story of Kolbe. He segues smoothly from his personal story of being assisted at the monastery, to Kolbe's story. For Mine, like Ozaki, the composure of his narrative is assisted by this public narrative about the founder of the monastery, Kolbe, and his self-sacrificial end. The impact this story had upon his own narrative is revealed in the interview.

> After my mother died, I was picked up by *seibo no kishi* [...] the war got crazier and Father Kolbe returned to Poland [...] he was taken to Auschwitz [concentration camp] and [...] he wasn't picked for execution, but the man who was chosen, had a wife and children, he knew, so [...] he offered himself up instead [...] And that was how Father Kolbe died [...][36]

Kolbe is for Mine and Ozaki the human Christ figure, a man who gave up his own life for another. However, there is also the personal connection to this story.

156 *Memory's future*

Mine emphasises the significant impact the Polish brothers in the seminary had upon him.

> Brother Zeno was the first [...] of these Polish people who took me on and you could say it was the warmth [that encouraged me]. I was attracted to that place, I believe. They were people with incredibly healthy nurturing ability and hugged (*haggu*). [...] It was not only words but affection (*aijō*) that made an impact and I felt it strongly. It warmed my heart [...] and encouraged me in my living [...][37]

Brother Zeno (Zenon Zebrowski) and the monks clothed Mine and his siblings, fed them and provided affection. Brother Zeno, whom Mine mentions, was an uneducated Polish monastic, who arrived in Nagasaki in 1930 with Kolbe and stayed in Japan for 51 years until his death in 1981.[38] Zeno worked in relief efforts for the poor in Nagasaki, Tokyo and Hokkaido, continuing Father Kolbe's legacy. Mine suggests his estrangement and loss was met not by the Polish priests' theologising, but by their care – his 'encouragement for living' gifted by *seibo no kishi* monks.

Orphaned Mine lost to the bomb not only his mother, but also most traces of his familial heritage and faith practices. His father was a descendant of the *Kirishitan* and he recalled his maternal grandmother's house, where there was a Christian altar with a cross. However, his own family did not tend to talk about Catholicism. His mother came from the Gotō islands and was a *sempuku* or *kakure* (hidden Christian) by blood relation.

> During the war, I didn't hear about being a *Kirishitan* [...] My father was also a descendant of the *Kirishitan* [...] However, my mother's mother was a passionate *Kirishitan* and when we went to her house, there was an altar [...] and placed on it a Cross and some words [...] but within my own family, I didn't hear much about it.[39]

Due to this gap in his own knowledge, an important part of reconciliation for Mine was to understand Christian belief. He ascribes to religion a personal importance in his own recovery from the atomic bombing.

> [Religion] is helpful [...] [for recovery from the bomb] [...] living day to day, looking to the future [...] religion for [...] working in a company, living in the middle of society [...] as a Catholic [...] [helping me] relate well to people and encouraging my spirit. When I go on Sundays to mass and hear the sermons of the priest [...] [it is good for my] soul. I become calm and healthy [...][40]

Mine describes an everyday faith, which encourages him in societal and occupational relationships. As well as helping him relate to others, Mine considers his spirituality healthy for 'spirit' and 'soul'. His public engagements include work as a *kataribe* (storyteller) at the Nagasaki Atomic Bomb Museum, instructing students and visitors about the atomic bombing.

A gradual hope

For other survivors, torn by psychological and personal torment, hope is equally connected to communal faith culture, though experienced in a less linear fashion to Mine or Ozaki. Nakamura Kazutoshi construes his life ambivalently as a trial but describes a gradual development of new hope due to his own 'growth' and the growth of his children. Nakamura did not attend high school and was at the point of committing suicide.[41] Due to his refugee experiences in Gotō and then Yokohoma after the bombing, he reached a low psychological ebb, experiencing the 'chaos' of post-war Japan in the big city. Later on though, he recounted a gradual transformation:

> Yes, gradually as I grew [I gained in hope] [...] the suicidal feelings I had dissipated [...] it would have been a major sin, to kill myself [...] I realised I had been given [much] from God [...] When [...] I matured [...] found work and got married and had children. The children were cute and we educated [them to] [...] go to university which I could never do [...] These things were an encouragement to me.[42]

Nakamura is psychologically and physically tormented and his past still haunts him, but he believes it was his morality which kept him from suicide. 'If I hadn't been Catholic, I would have jumped from somewhere and wouldn't have made it.' Like the restored Job in the biblical narrative, he understands what he has been given as gifts from God, including work, marriage and children. Morning and night, he prays at a personal shrine to Mary and is proud of his children, of whom two are educated teachers.

The 'other' in Japan

Even as we would rightly expect experiences of faith and hope after the bombing to be different among the Catholic survivors, a similarity is found in the context of their own marginalisation, their categorisation as 'other' in Nagasaki and Japan. Before I introduce some more political dimensions of remembering in Urakami, I comment on an observer's discussion about those found on the margins, in the 'mosaic' of Nagasaki society.

When I interviewed him, Takazane Yasunori (1939–2017) was the non-Catholic academic director of the Oka Masaharu Peace Museum in Nishizaka. He insisted upon the examination of minority perspectives. Takazane explained that a truthful understanding of the bombing history includes the history of discrimination against Christians, but also prejudice against Chinese and Korean people. The museum which Takazane directed is an 'alternative' non-sponsored and volunteer-run institution and reading room, emphasising the colonialist and racist history of Japan. The exhibition highlights the lives of Korean and Chinese minorities in Nagasaki in 1945, indicating an attempt to shift public memorialising to include awareness of Japanese political oppression and the exploitation of colonial subjects during the war. Tyranny expressed against the 'other' includes colonial labourers of foreign extraction and the exacerbation of socioeconomic divisions specific to Nagasaki's own historic development, distinguishing Catholic and *burakumin* (outcaste) communities as 'other'.[43] Takazane said:

> Yes, [Nagasaki] is a real mosaic [...] filled with history [...] there are the 26 martyrs [...] there are various critiques of the indiscretions (*fukenshiki*) of war but I believe that at the centre of the [understanding of the] churches and the church groups is the history of the persecution of Christianity [...] The yon-ban kuzure (fourth persecution) [...] What was that like, what torture did they bear, what happened? [...] So, if it is only the beauty of the churches, or the impressiveness of the religious piety [that we perceive] [...] it is not true history; but ignorance, or 'history held by people'. We need to ask, 'What was the purpose in Japan of such terrible persecutions?'[44]

In Takazane's view, the study of the bombing ought to articulate an understanding of this older history of the Catholic people, as it should consider the wider nature of colonial society prior to the bomb and the suffering of Korean and Chinese minorities. The study of the Catholic community as 'other' sheds significant light on the wider history of Nagasaki and Japan. For Takazane, discussion of the Christian minority should incorporate the story from the narrative of the 26 martyrs and the Catholic discourse of the Fourth Persecution, not so well known in other parts of Japan. 'Touristic' and consumerist history is not the same as 'living memory'. Viewing the beautiful churches and admiring the faith of the hidden Christians does not encapsulate their history. More is required to understand the heritage of the Christians in Japan and to realise the horror of the persecutions, or else, '... the persecuted people will not be able to change'.

Divided loyalties

Catholic groups shied away from post-war politicism, but the practice of Christian faith had its implications for loyalty and there were impacts on the perception of the position of the Emperor. In pre-war and wartime Japan, the Emperor was venerated as god-like in association with Shintō cosmologies by military and nationalistic leaders. Two interviews with Fukahori Shigemi and Ozaki touched upon the theme of divided loyalties.

Fukahori remembers his attendance at a Shintō Shrine. He was compelled by his teachers to visit a shrine as an elementary school student, at a time when Shintō worship was associated with the state and encouraged by the national government as part of its mobilisation efforts.[45] It is likely that his memory is coloured by narratives he became aware of later in life. Fukahori recalls visiting the shrine where he had the powerful perception that his religious identity was being compromised:

> [...] from the 15th year of Showa [1940] [...] the townspeople (*machi no hito*) discriminated against us because of our Catholic faith [...] We were forced to go visit the shrine [...] From school [...] Everyone went [...] because Japan was *Shin-goku* (divine country) [...] we went to a shrine like [...] *Yasukuni Jinja* [...] when we went, we wouldn't go inside, but we would hide! (LAUGHS) Not everyone hid, but just those who took our Catholicism seriously [...] We went to pay homage (Sanpai suru), which made us feel terrible! For small children [...] It was tough [...] We wouldn't go through the *torii* (shrine gate).[46]

Fukahori emphasises his resistance, perhaps due to his understanding of the interviewer, as a foreign theologian. He cites the politically notable shrine in Tokyo, Yasukuni Jinja, possibly for my benefit. Fukahori's home was alongside Urakami Cathedral and his familiarity with the Christian spaces may have given him a particular understanding of sacred spaces in Nagasaki. He was a 14-year-old seminarian at the time of the bombing, living in a dormitory some distance away. He says, nevertheless, that he believed at the time, along with the other students, that entering a *torii*, or Shrine gate, was inappropriate and suggests he showed resistance to the forced visit(s) to the shrine by refusing to enter the grounds through the *torii* and by hiding.

A clash between Christianity and Shintō meant for the Christians an uncomfortable relationship to empire, patriotism and emperor. Like Fukahori Shigemi, Ozaki connects his faith to a form of wartime political resistance in his creation of his narrative. The refashioning of his narrative over time is likely, influenced by publicly disclosed narratives, circulated in media and the community.[47] On a blog post on Shōwa Day 2017, a public holiday remembering the wartime Emperor's birthday, Ozaki wrote about his own memory of an oral examination he had to take to enter Junior High School in northern Korea, where his family was living at the start of the war.[48] He was quizzed about whether his allegiances were to the Emperor's army, or to Christ's army. He answered, 'Christ's army' and burst into tears. Even so, he passed the examination, he wrote on the blog entry. For many years, he thought the teacher who passed him must have made a mistake. By their recollections of such religious and social ambiguities and contradictions, Fukahori and Ozaki referred in their interviews to the difficulties of retaining Christian integrity, even as children during the war.

Dangerous politics

The final example of a public and political stance I wish to mention also concerns the Emperor. The former Catholic Mayor of Nagasaki, Motoshima Hitoshi (1922–2014) suggested that the Shōwa Emperor bore some responsibility for war shortly before the Emperor's death in 1989. A consequent media furore erupted throughout Japan.

Motoshima knew his ancestors as *sempuku Kirishitan*. He observed his grandfather hobbling around his blacksmithing shop, due to an injury resulting from a torture called stone hugging during the Fourth Persecution: the person was forced to sit on a stone slab with legs folded under, kindling wood inserted between calf and thigh and stone pestles piled on his lap until his bones crushed and his skin filled with splinters. Motoshima's remembering of the 'other' included memory of persecutions, but also of Chinese and Korean victims of Japanese aggression. In an interview with Japanese studies scholar Norma Field, he stated, 'I think I have a sensitivity to discrimination because as a Christian I experienced it myself growing up.'[49]

Motoshima rose to public office in Nagasaki with a conservative base of constituents and became mayor of Nagasaki in 1979, serving four terms and 16 years in total, until his retirement in 1995. He was not himself an atomic bomb survivor; he had been in another part of Kyushu island training for military service at the time. Each year, however, Motoshima would write a 'Nagasaki Peace Declaration', to be released on the anniversary of the bombing on 9 August, as had become the custom of the sitting mayor. He became aware the shortcoming of this political action was that it did not recognise, in association with the atomic bombings, that Japan had been the perpetrator of an aggressive war.[50] He had a strong appreciation for the Catholic socio-economic stratification in Nagasaki, but, like Takazane, acknowledged and lamented the 'other' Korean and Chinese victims of the Japanese war in Nagasaki.

Motoshima is best known for the comment he made on 7 December 1988, when Emperor Hirohito was unwell and close to death. In the context of answering a question from a Communist Party representative about his own experiences as a young person enlisted into the army, Motoshima said, 'I think the emperor does bear responsibility for the war. However, by will of the majority of Japanese people and the Allied Powers, he was released from taking responsibility and became the symbol of the new constitution.'[51] The media seized on the first part of this statement and a furore followed. A classmate from his middle school, a Liberal Democratic Party politician at the time, asserted in the media that Motoshima was looking more and more like a mayor for Socialists and Communists. By 21 December, representatives from 62 right-wing groups in 85 vehicles had moved into the city, blaring loud-speakers. Activists demanded Motoshima's death as divine retribution: he was assigned 24-hour police protection and was no longer able to live in his own house.[52] Right-wing groups called for retraction of the original statement, his apology and resignation. Finally, the mayor elaborated:

> I am not saying the emperor alone was responsible for the war. There are many who are responsible, myself included ... I have warm regard and esteem for the emperor as a symbol, but he still bears responsibility for the war.[53]

Despite the stinging right-wing backlash against him for his comments, Motoshima received around 7300 letters, postcards and telegrams from around Japan and overseas in the three months after his 'statement', mostly in support of his stance. He decided it would be best to publish this correspondence and 300 letters were eventually published, although the printer and binder were left unnamed in fear of retribution.[54] The letters were from ordinary people around Japan: housewives, schoolteachers, imperial army veterans, farmers, students and Korean and outcaste communities.[55] Komichi, the publisher, selected a representative selection and noted only 5 per cent of the letters were critical of the mayor. Norma Field summarises the content of these letters in her book *In the Realm of a Dying Emperor* and demonstrates how the public response supported Motoshima's comments. Sorrow and anger were expressed by the public that the Emperor approached the end of his own life without recognising his responsibility.[56] The letter writers were not the only ones who came to the support of Motoshima. In Nagasaki, a 'Committee of citizens of Nagasaki seeking Freedom of Speech' collected 13,784 signatures from around the country between 15 and 22 December 1988. Field met members of this group, including schoolteachers, a truck driver, a high school student and a *burakumin* activist.[57]

The book reached the top 20 best-selling list in one of Tokyo's largest bookshops and 36,000 copies were sold. A total of 25 per cent of Japanese polled after Hirohito's death said they thought he bore responsibility for the war, an increasing number and a sign that the long-standing taboo on criticism of the Emperor had finally been broken. A well-known historian, Carol Gluck, linked the changing public response about the Emperor to the statement originally made by Motoshima.[58]

Motoshima's stance disrupted a powerful political narrative and he personally experienced how threatening his challenge to the history of the war could be. Two years later, in a violent incident extremely rare in Japan, Motoshima was injured when a member of a right-wing group (*seiki juku*) attempted to assassinate him. Motoshima survived with bullet wounds. In a later newspaper interview, he articulated his stance on Japan's war guilt and on the Emperor, in view of the cross of Christ:

> As I've often said, at first, I thought I was dying. For one year before the shooting, I thought I might be killed and I was prepared for it. And I'm old enough now that I don't have to worry about my wife and children. Since I believe in the old Christian ways, I hope to go to heaven when I die. So, at the time of the shooting, I was thinking about what I had done for the poor and troubled people in my lifetime as ordered by God, how much I had practiced the cross of Jesus Christ and how I wanted to completely repent my sins before God.[59]

Motoshima thought he might be killed for his stance. Like Ozaki, he believed laying down his life was a path similar to that of Christ or the martyrs. He linked the assassination attempt to his comments, not only about the Emperor, but about the treatment of Koreans during the war and the need to treat refugees humanely. He saw his own comments as an inherently 'dangerous' political practice, even more so following the 1989 incident, as he slowly moved (in his own estimation) in the political realm from right to left.[60]

Forgetfulness by politicians and the public about Japan's own responsibility for an aggressive war and ensuing atrocities riled Motoshima. Later, after the new Emperor had been inaugurated, Motoshima continued to read and write about the Shōwa Emperor. Increasingly aware of the Japanese war of aggression, Motoshima summarised the issues as he saw them in a short booklet put out in Nagasaki by the *seibo no kishi* (Knights of the Holy Mother) monastery press. He included a summary of Japanese war crimes in the Philippines, China, Singapore, Malaysia, Korea, France, England, Netherlands, Australia, East Timor and the United States. He wrote about the statement of the Emperor in autumn of 1975, after the Emperor returned from the United States. Preparing at the time for the fiftieth anniversary year of his reign, the Emperor told the Japanese Press Club that as the atomic bombing of Japan happened during the war, it could not be helped (*yamu wo enakatta*).[61]

Within the narratives of Ozaki, Mine and Nakamura, the 'dangerous' memory of suffering became a personal and collective motivation for future change. Ozaki's identification with a martyr and his investigation of the story of Maximilian Kolbe contributes to his strong conviction that death is not the end. Ozaki's theology of God is congruent with 'dangerous' memory of a 'crucified God', by which God does not wield war, but is found **with** the bereft and the abandoned, in Auschwitz and Nagasaki. Where divine love seems absent is paradoxically where Ozaki perceived it, even as his own possessions were reduced to a single burnt rosary. Meanwhile, Mine, saved in the same Polish monastery, affirms his identity by his life, work and community and Nakamura credits his new family as hope. Challenged by remembered difficult encounters with the suffering 'other', Ozaki's uncomfortable memories still impact on his life, transforming him on a new post-bomb trajectory. The Catholic survivors are also representative of the 'other' in Nagasaki. Their 'otherness' makes them sensitive to marginalising practices in the public realm. They contradict and undercut a tendency in their own community towards passivity. In a notable public stance, the Catholic mayor, Motoshima Hitoshi, was made famous by his 'dangerous' statement critiquing silences in Japan surrounding the Emperor's war responsibility. The backlash to Motoshima resulted ultimately in a right-wing assassination attempt on his life. This incident transformed Motoshima's understanding of his own identity and pointedly clarified his personal and communal calling as a Christian in Nagasaki and Japan.

For the main protagonists, the *kataribe*, their narration enables their imagination of an alternative future. Yet, even as their stories are imbued by hopefulness, they are equally wrought by lament. How do the complainants' laments exert claims upon the future? Let us consider once more the ongoing lament, anger and protests of the *kataribe*.

Notes

1 Tōmei Ozaki, *Jūnanasai no natsu*, Seibo bunko (Nagasaki: Seibo no kisha-sha, 1996), 57.
2 In oral history, the term 'composure' is used to explain how interviewees interpret memory through a subjective lens. See Penny Summerfield, 'Culture and Composure: Creating Narratives of the Gendered Self in Oral History Interviews'. *Cultural and Social History* 1.1 (1 January 2004): 65–93, https://doi.org/10.1191/1478003804cs0005oa. for a concise discussion of composure and culture in oral history.
3 Tōmei Ozaki, interview by Gwyn McClelland, Francisco-en Hōmu, Sasaki, 27 February 2016.
4 Shintarō Shiōra, *Yaketa rozario: genbaku wo ikinuita shōnen no kiseki na unmei to shinta na kokoro no sekai* (Nagasaki: Seibo no kishasha, 2009). Shiōra explained in a 2017 interview that he completed considerable research to draw the manga, interviewing Ozaki and many other bomb survivors during his research trip around the Nagasaki region. Shiōra hoped for a wider audience than the religious in Japan. Shiōra grew up in a Christian family but does not describe himself as Christian today. He related that Ozaki's biography, *Yaketa rozario*, is selling today in an e-book version to a 'large number' of readers each month. Shintarō Shiōra, Tokyo, interview by Gwyn McClelland, 27 June 2017. Shintarō Shiōra, 'Eiga no peeji he no henshiin', email, 25 May 2017. The manga has not been translated into English, although it has been translated into Polish, reflecting the narrative about Polish priest Kolbe within the story.
5 Keiji Nakazawa, *Barefoot Gen, Vol. 1: A Cartoon Story of Hiroshima*, vol. 1, 10 vols., Barefoot Gen (San Francisco: Last Gasp, 2004).
6 Shiōra, *Yaketa rozario*, 13.
7 Stephen R. Turnbull, *The Kakure Kirishitan of Japan: A Study of Their Development, Beliefs and Rituals to the Present Day* (Richmond, Surrey: Japan Library, 1998), 120.
8 Tagita quoted in Stephen R. Turnbull, *The Kakure Kirishitan of Japan*, 117.
9 Shiōra, *Yaketa rozario*.
10 Tōmei Ozaki, 'Shokki arau haha saigo no hohoegao', *Asahi Shimbun*, 29 December 2008, sec. Nagasaki Nōto.
11 Ozaki, 27 February 2016, McClelland.
12 Ozaki, 27 February 2016, McClelland.
13 Ozaki, *Jūnanasai no natsu*, 17.
14 Ozaki, *Jūnanasai no natsu*, 21.
15 See for example, Sven-Ake Christianson, ed., *The Handbook of Emotion and Memory: Research and Theory*, 1st ed. (Hillsdale, NJ: Psychology Press, 1992), 203.
16 Ozaki, *Jūnanasai no natsu*, 22.
17 Gen Okada, 'Christmas in the year of the A-bomb', *Asahi Shimbun*, December 2008, am edition.
18 Okada, 'Christmas'.
19 Shiōra, *Yaketa rozario*, 75.
20 Ozaki, *Jūnanasai no natsu*, 60.
21 Ozaki, *Jūnanasai no natsu*, 46.
22 Gen Okada, 'Memories of Hiroshima and Nagasaki' *Asahi Shimbun*, December 2008, section Nagasaki nōto, accessed 24 May 2016, www.asahi.com/hibakusha/english/shimen/nagasakinote/note01-16e.html.
23 The number changed from 24 to 26, when those who were marching the Christians were added to their number. Renzo De Luca SJ, '26 Martyrs Monument', 26 Martyrs Monument Website, *Museum Website* (blog), 2017, accessed 9 September 2017, www.26martyrs.com/.
24 Ozaki, *Jūnanasai no natsu*, 57, author's translation.

25 See Stephen R. Turnbull, 'Martyrs and Matsuri: The Massacre of the Hidden Christians of Ikitsuki in 1645 and Its Relationship to Local Shintō Tradition'. *Japan Forum* 6.2 (1 October 1994): 159–74, https://doi.org/10.1080/09555809408721511.
26 Ozaki, 27 February 2016, McClelland.
27 Ozaki, *Jūnanasai no natsu*, 47.
28 Ozaki, *Jūnanasai no natsu*, 62, author's translation.
29 Ozaki, *Jūnanasai no natsu*, 23.
30 Tōmei Ozaki, 'Sei korube kinenkan to korube shinpu – ozaki tomei no heya', Blog, *Ozaki Tōmei no heya* (blog), nd, accessed 27 September, 2016, https://sites.google.com/site/tomaozaki/Home/03-korube.
31 Tōmei Ozaki, 'Sotsuja no tanjoubikai. Tabi no nakama tonin ni kakomarete yorokobi no Toma', *Ozaki Tōmei No Heya* (blog), 2 March 2018, accessed 4 March 2018, http://tomaozaki.blogspot.com.au/2018/03/blog-post_2.html.
32 Tōmei Ozaki, *Mi gawari no ai*, 2nd ed. (Nagasaki: Seibo no kisha-sha, 1994).
33 Eduardo Mendieta, *The Frankfurt School on Religion: Key Writings by the Major Figures* (Hoboken: Taylor & Francis Ltd, 2004), 287.
34 Johann Baptist Metz, *Faith in History and Society: Toward a Practical Fundamental Theology* (London: Burns & Oates, 1980), 169.
35 Candace Kristina McLean, '"Do This in Memory of Me": The Genealogy and Theological Appropriations of Memory in the Work of Johann Baptist Metz' (PhD diss., University of Notre Dame, 2012), 83.
36 Tōru Mine, interview by Gwyn McClelland, Nagasaki Atomic Bomb Museum, 24 February 2016. Ten men were selected to be starved to death in an underground bunker by the Nazi soldiers after three escaped, as an example to the inmates. Kolbe volunteered to be in the group in the place of a man who cried out that he had children and a wife. Kolbe was the only man to survive in the bunker for two weeks and was executed by use of lethal injection. He died on 14 August 1941. Ozaki, *Mi gawari no ai*, 210–41.
37 Mine, 24 February 2016, McClelland.
38 Ozaki, *Mi gawari no ai*, 205.
39 Mine, 24 February 2016, McClelland.
40 Mine, 24 February 2016, McClelland.
41 Kazutoshi Nakamura, interview by Gwyn McClelland, Nagasaki Atomic Bomb Museum, 23 February 2016.
42 Nakamura, 23 February 2016, McClelland.
43 The systematised abuses of colonial labour developed between the first and second world wars are described in a book reviewed by Andrew Gordon, 'The Proletarian Gamble: Korean Workers in Interwar Japan. (Book Review)'. *Journal of Social History* 44.1 (2010): 296–98, https://doi.org/10.1353/jsh.2010.0004. Michael Weiner has also summarised Korean migration to Japan, including a phase from 1939 to 1945 when Korean workers were mobilised by the Japanese rulers. Michael A. Weiner, *Race and Migration in Imperial Japan* (London; New York: Routledge, 1994).
44 Yasunori Takazane, interview by Gwyn McClelland, Oka Masaharu Museum, 25 February 2016.
45 Shigemi Fukahori, interview by Gwyn McClelland, Urakami Cathedral, 23 February 2016. After 1932 the government required all school personnel to attend ceremonies at Shintō shrines. Some denominations of Christianity went along with this requirement and others did not. The Methodist and Catholic Christians compromised and accepted the government description of the ceremonies as 'non-religious'. Fukahori's memory of these events is likely coloured by subsequent discussion, especially in the Catholic community, of what occurred. See Sung-Gun Kim, 'The Shinto Shrine Issue in Korean Christianity under Japanese Colonialism', *Journal of Church and State* 39.3 (1997): 503–21.
46 Shigemi Fukahori, 23 February 2016, McClelland.

47 Alistair Thomson, 'Anzac Memories Revisited: Trauma, Memory and Oral History'. *The Oral History Review* 42.1 (1 April 2015): 28, https://doi.org/10.1093/ohr/ohv010.
48 Tōmei Ozaki, 'Shōwa no hi. Shōwa tennō no tanjōbi. Haran ni michita shōwa', Blog post, Ozaki Tōmei no nikki (blog), accessed 29 April 2017, http://tomaozaki.blogspot.com.au/2017/04/blog-post_29.html.
49 Norma Field, *In the Realm of a Dying Emperor: Japan at Century's End* (New York: Vintage, 1993), 249.
50 Hitoshi Motoshima, 'Gembaku tōka wa tadashikatta ka', pamphlet (Nagasaki: Seibo no kisha-sha, 2005), 1–3.
51 Field, *In the Realm of a Dying Emperor*, 178.
52 Field, *In the Realm*, 180–5.
53 Press conference, 12 December 1988, quoted in Field, *In the Realm*, 184.
54 Field, *In the Realm*, 189–91.
55 Ian Buruma, 'Against the Japanese Grain', *The New York Review of Books*, 5 December 1991.
56 Field, *In the Realm*, 191–202.
57 Field, *In the Realm*, 235.
58 Carol Gluck, 'The Idea of Showa'. *Daedalus* 119.3 (1990): 16.
59 Brian Covert, 'The Conscience of Japan: Nagasaki's Mayor Motoshima Talks with Brian Covert'. *Kyoto Journal*, 15 April 1991. www.inochi-life.net/archives_motoshima_interview.html.
60 Sugawara quotes a statement by Motoshima about being called a 'leftist' and not feeling he was either left or right on the political spectrum. However, he added, if he 'blew in the wind', he believed he would remain on the left in the end. Jun Sugawara, 'Nagasaki kara Fukushima he: Motoshima Hitoshi ni yoru Urakami hansai setsu no kaishaku wo meguru – kousatsu'. *Nagasaki Daigaku Sougou Kankyou Kenkyu* 17.1 (2014): 21.
61 Hitoshi Motoshima and Nobuto Hirano, *Motoshima Hitoshi no shisō: genbaku/sensō/hyumanizumu* (Nagasaki: Nagasaki shinbunsha, 2012), 25.

References

Buruma, Ian. 'Against the Japanese Grain'. *The New York Review of Books*, 5 December 1991.
Christianson, Sven-Ake, ed. *The Handbook of Emotion and Memory: Research and Theory*. 1st ed. Hillsdale, NJ: Psychology Press, 1992.
Covert, Brian. 'The Conscience of Japan: Nagasaki's Mayor Motoshima Talks with Brian Covert'. *Kyoto Journal*, 15 April 1991. www.inochi-life.net/archives_motoshima_interview.html.
De Luca SJ, Renzo. '26 Martyrs Monument'. 26 Martyrs Monument Website. *Museum Website* (blog), 2017. www.26martyrs.com/.
Field, Norma. *In the Realm of a Dying Emperor: Japan at Century's End*. New York: Vintage, 1993.
Fukahori, Shigemi. Interview by Gwyn McClelland, Urakami Cathedral, 23 February 2016.
Gluck, Carol. 'The Idea of Showa'. *Daedalus* 119.3 (1990): 1–26.
Gordon, Andrew. 'The Proletarian Gamble: Korean Workers in Interwar Japan. (Book Review)'. *Journal of Social History* 44.1 (2010): 296–98. https://doi.org/10.1353/jsh.2010.0004.
Kim, Sung-gun. 'The Shinto Shrine Issue in Korean Christianity under Japanese Colonialism'. *Journal of Church and State* 39.3 (1997): 503–21.

McLean, Candace Kristina. '"Do This in Memory of Me": The Genealogy and Theological Appropriations of Memory in the Work of Johann Baptist Metz'. PhD diss., University of Notre Dame, 2012.
Mendieta, Eduardo. *The Frankfurt School on Religion: Key Writings by the Major Figures*. Hoboken: Taylor & Francis Ltd, 2004.
Metz, Johann Baptist. *Faith in History and Society: Toward a Practical Fundamental Theology*. London: Burns & Oates, 1980.
Mine, Tōru. Interview by Gwyn McClelland, Nagasaki Atomic Bomb Museum, 24 February 2016.
Motoshima, Hitoshi, and Nobuto Hirano. 'Gembaku tōka wa tadashikatta ka'. Pamphlet. Nagasaki: Seibo no kisha-sha, 2005.
Motoshima, Hitoshi, and Nobuto Hirano. *Motoshima Hitoshi no shiso: genbaku/senso/hyumanizumu*. Nagasaki: Nagasaki shinbunsha, 2012.
Nakamura, Kazutoshi. Interview by Gwyn McClelland, Nagasaki Atomic Bomb Museum, 23 February 2016.
Nakazawa, Keiji. *Barefoot Gen, Vol. 1: A Cartoon Story of Hiroshima*, vol. 1. 10 vols. Barefoot Gen. San Francisco: Last Gasp, 2004.
Okada, Gen. 'Christmas in the Year of the A-bomb'. *Asahi Shimbun*. December 2008, am edn.
Okada, Gen. 'Memories of Hiroshima and Nagasaki'. *Asahi Shinbun*. December 2008, sec. Nagasaki Nōto. www.asahi.com/hibakusha/english/shimen/nagasakinote/note01-16e.html.
Ozaki, Tōmei. *Mi gawari no ai*. 2nd ed. Nagasaki: Seibo no kisha-sha, 1994.
Ozaki, Tōmei. *juunanasai no natsu*. Seibo bunko. Nagasaki: Seibo no kisha-sha, 1996.
Ozaki, Tōmei. 'Shokki arau haha saigo no hohoegao'. *Asahi Shimbun*. 29 December, 2008, sec. Nagasaki Nooto.
Ozaki, Tōmei. 'Sei korube kinenkan to korube shinpu – ozaki tomei no heya'. Blog. *Ozaki Tōmei no heya*, n.d. https://sites.google.com/site/tomaozaki/Home/03-korube.
Ozaki, Tōmei. 'Shōwa no hi. showa tenno no tanjoubi. haran ni michita showa'. Blog. *Ozaki Tōmei no hey*, 29 April 2017. http://tomaozaki.blogspot.com.au/2017/04/blog-post_29.html.
Ozaki, Tōmei. 'Sotsuja no tanjoubikai. tabi no nakama gonin ni kakomarete yorokobi no Toma'. Blog. *Ozaki Tōmei No Heya*, 2 March 2018. http://tomaozaki.blogspot.com.au/2018/03/blog-post_2.html.
Shiōra, Shintarō. *Yaaketa rozario: genbaku wo ikinuita shonen no kiseki na unmei to shinta na kokoro no sekai*. Nagasaki: Seibo no kishasha, 2009.
Shiōra, Shintarō. Interview by Gwyn McClelland, Tokyo, 27 June 2017.
Sugawara, Jun. 'Nagasaki kara fukushima he: Motoshima Hitoshi ni yoru Urakami hansai setsu no kaishaku wo meguru – Kousatsu'. *Nagasaki Daigaku Sougou Kankyou Kenkyu* 17.1 (2014): 19–30.
Summerfield, Penny. 'Culture and Composure: Creating Narratives of the Gendered Self in Oral History Interviews'. *Cultural and Social History* 1.1 (1 January 2004): 65–93. https://doi.org/10.1191/1478003804cs0005oa.
Takazane, Yasunori. Interview by Gwyn McClelland, Oka Masaharu Museum, 25 February 2016.
Thomson, Alistair. 'Anzac Memories Revisited: Trauma, Memory and Oral History'. *The Oral History Review* 42.1 (1 April 2015): 1–29. https://doi.org/10.1093/ohr/ohv010.
Turnbull, Stephen R. 'Martyrs and Matsuri: The Massacre of the Hidden Christians of Ikitsuki in 1645 and Its Relationship to Local Shintō Tradition'. *Japan Forum* 6.2 (1 October 1994): 159–74. https://doi.org/10.1080/09555809408721511.

Turnbull, Stephen R. *The Kakure Kirishitan of Japan: A Study of Their Development, Beliefs and Rituals to the Present Day*. Richmond, Surrey: Japan Library, 1998.
Weiner, Michael A. *Race and Migration in Imperial Japan*. London New York: Routledge, 1994.

9 Lament, anger and protest

We are angry. All of us. Everyone is angry. We are angry, but [...] may this kind of thing never again occur [...]

(Matsuo Sachiko, 2014)

[...] the cultural site of empowerment in the midst of the ancestors – deceased parents and generations of enslaved women and men [...] such sites are spirit filled, conjuring or mediating spaces of empowerment between the living and the dead.

(Joan M. Martin)[1]

Introduction

The storytellers, the *kataribe*, stand up against the tidying over and forgetting of the silenced people and landscape. As we have seen, they voice the silenced cries of the dying and here I suggest their lament transforms into anger.[2] The narration constitutes an ultimate protest incorporating a concern for the future and the survivors' prophetic call. Returning to the Urakami Valley, site of Fukahori Jōji's narrative about his siblings, I elaborate on how the survivors' protests develop from lament.[3] Embracing the task of disentangling words from the dead bodies they try to hide, storytellers of lament like Fukahori 'scripturally embalm' the long-dead (Paul Ricœur's phrase) by speaking of the past.[4] Theirs is an honouring process, of remembering and mourning. The *kataribe* show creativity in their story-telling, seeking prophetic 'opportunities of redirecting and refashioning the force of collective life'.[5] The protests which rise out of their lament anticipate future horrors and seek ways to prevent their realisation.[6]

The rhetoric of protest common to this collective biography troubles observers' assumption Nagasaki is characterised by prayer, not anger.[7] For many years, though, Catholic Urakami avoided lament and protest about the atomic destruction as taboo. Today's survivors threaten spiritualised understandings such as the *hansai-setsu*, which resulted in passivity and silence.[8] The interviewees directly protest the US perpetrators of the bomb and the Japanese authorities who led them into war. Memories of injustice and defeat, writes Johann Metz, preserve the identity of the subjects of suffering,

Lament, anger and protest 169

even those long-dead. Metz is acutely aware of the Jewish Holocaust in German history, arguing that radical suffering, as imagined in the Biblical text of Job, must be protested to God as pure negativity by believers. The Urakami Catholics draw upon Job to understand their own experiences. I examine by theological critique two parallels comparing the speech of Job to that of the *kataribe*. There are implicit challenges of all this to 'official' histories. Less obviously in the interviews, but important nonetheless, protest is tentatively and ambiguously directed to God, just as Biblical psalms and apocryphal writings indicate a long tradition of protest by the faithful directed towards the divine.[9]

Kōji, Akio and Machiko

Fukahori Jōji's narrative metaphorically cradles his sister Machiko and brothers, Kōji and Akio (Chapter 6 Figure 6.2). He experienced the atomic bombing when he was 15 years old in 1945, losing his three younger siblings and his mother. Since 2009, he has pieced together the story of what happened on 9 and 10 August, referring to the public atomic narrative, his own memories and the Atomic Bomb Museum resources. In broader public narratives of the atomic bombing, the death of his siblings is not remembered. No one apart from Fukahori has told or narrated the story of these children until now, nor do others commemorate Machiko, Kōji and Akio. Present-day interviews represent some of the last chances for these

Figure 9.1 Fukahori Jōji, photograph, the author, 2016.

170 *Memory's future*

memories to be discussed.[10] Fukahori's naming of his siblings does not bring them back, but it demonstrates a reverence to their memory.

The hypocenter of the atomic bombing for Fukahori and the Nagasaki Catholics is a 'black hole' of trauma which obliterated family members. Theologian and trauma studies writer Flora Keshgegian suggests trauma may be experienced metaphorically as a 'black hole', from which there is no escape, only utter darkness and hopelessness.[11] In physics, a black hole is a 'space in the universe which emits no light, from whose gravitational field nothing can escape and in which time does not pass'.[12] Trauma and grief lead to relative silence. Fukahori's personal silence lasted 65 years before he took on the role of *kataribe*.

The 'Nagasaki Archive' (project of the *Nagasaki Shinbun*), which I introduced in Chapter 1, is a fascinating witness record, incorporating online photos, video and audio of survivors of Nagasaki.[13] Despite this, in the kilometre circle around the hypocenter, only two testimonies are recorded and within two kilometres there are only 13 testimonies listed. The hypocenter in Urakami, where the drama including Fukahori's siblings unfolded, is a place of myriad silences and forgotten figures. The material in this chapter emerges from the spaces and silences evident on the Nagasaki Archive; in the veritable 'black hole' between 500 and 1000 metres of the hypocenter.

The Urakami 'Landscape of Silence' represents a traumatic 'black hole' with little to do with statistics. This remembered space is disorderly and emblematic of numbing trauma. Fukahori's mother's body and other bodies are elements which he reincorporates by his testimony. The photograph of Fukahori's home location (Figure 9.2) represents a public history of the atomic bombings describing an 'objective' scientific and clinical post-mortem, a history destabilised by his memory which enacts claims on the photograph as personal.

Illogical death

Unable to make sense of the black hole, Fukahori lives with his memories of anomalies and the unknown; the impossibility of composure and the 'illogical' nature of deaths. His insights about 'illogical' or irregular (Fukahori uses the words 差 斑 *sa/mura*[14]) death in Nagasaki raise his own protest and challenges an indistinct history of statistics and the modern myth of 'precision' warfare.[15]

The photograph of his siblings (see Chapter 6, Figure 6.2) is more than an image for Fukahori: it is a treasured object. His father died, circa 1942 in Shimonoseki and Fukahori's family moved to live with his father's family in Nagasaki. Initially they lived near the harbour city but one year prior to the bombing, they moved to Urakami where a photograph of the children was taken (Chapter 6, Figure 6.2). They moved due to a perception of safety in the suburbs and because they had relatives there. The scene incorporates foliage on the left-hand side and the landscape is oriented on an angle. The children are dressed in school uniforms apart from Machiko and the photograph was

Lament, anger and protest 171

Figure 9.2 'Hashigachi-machi and environs seen from Yamazato National School', taken by Shigeo Hayashi, used by permission, Nagasaki Atomic Bomb Museum, 23 January 2019, Tomihisa Taue (Nagasaki mayor): Fukahori's home location is highlighted by the box outline on the photograph. This is where he found his mother.

taken at the beginning of the school year in April 1944. There is the hint of a smile on Fukahori's and the older brother, Kōji's, faces. The children's mother, who died in the bombing, is an invisible presence, likely behind the lens of the camera.

A jarring memory

Some of the grief Nakamura Kazutoshi and Ozaki Tōmei experienced was due to not finding their mothers' bodies, but for Fukahori the most miserable experience of the atomic bombing was finding his mother's body entirely exposed and discoloured (at the ruins of his house, Figure 9.2). Fukahori was somewhat reassured that his siblings did not die in the bombing as his mother did, burnt in the ruins of his home.

The memory of his mother's body is disconcerting and troubling; jarring in our sanitised re-imagining of the silent landscape. Fukahori's unanswered questions are reflected in his choice of two words to describe the memory of death. Because of the difficulty of translating the words, I include the original Japanese in the transcription.

172 *Memory's future*

> There was an inconsistency [*mura*], a differentiation [*sa*]. So, my mother was burnt up. Her whole body had been exposed. She had become scorched black and nothing remained except the elastic [from her pants] [...] However, at the time I wondered whether this had happened to my mother due to the explosion of the bomb, or because of the house-fires which came later. I don't know![16]

Fukahori seeks to fill in the details. He cannot be sure how his mother's death happened. This is a missing element from the picture, representing her forfeited life and Fukahori's loss – a perplexing tale.

Seeking refuge

Fukahori describes what he understands happened to his two brothers and sister on the day of the bombing (see Figure 9.3):

> Basically, those three [Akio, Machiko and Kōji] had gone shopping to the nearby shop. And that was when the atomic bomb exploded [...]
> [Akio] had gone in and made them wait in front [...] to do the shopping, the bomb fell and he was buried, but the other brother [Kōji] managed to free himself and they [Kōji and Machiko] found each other, apparently. They had been waiting in front of the shop. So, my sister was calling his name, '*Onīchan!*' and [Kōji] ran over to her.[17]

Re-listening to the story, I wonder how Fukahori pieced it together. This is an imaginative exploration of what became of his brother and sister, using the resources available in the intervening 70 years to reconstruct in his mind an ostensibly 'irretrievable' event. He may have heard the story from Kōji's point of view, although Kōji's memory would also have been problematic. Other community members who encountered his brother and sister may have informed Fukahori of aspects of what happened. In any case, what Fukahori understands from the narrative is today more important than what may have occurred because of its ongoing impact.[18] He continues:

> Then, 'Oh, thank goodness', joining hands, again the girl [Machiko] called the name of the older brother [Akio] and they searched the area, but he didn't come. They couldn't see him. But gradually, flames developed into fire and they couldn't stay there anymore. So [...] my little brother [Kōji] took my little sister [Machiko] and found that this bridge [See Figure 9.5] had fallen in. Then they crossed over through the river to the other side and came to our home. It was already in flames so not knowing what else to do, they fled further to a place where there was no fire, here beside the cemetery, the main refuge.[19]

As an anti-redemptory narrative, Fukahori's is a 'dangerous' memory with potential to challenge other historiographies of the atomic bomb in Nagasaki.[20]

His discussion of his siblings adds to the unsettling narratives in earlier chapters about the memories of Ozaki Tōmei and Nakamura Kazutoshi and descriptions of bodies in the aftermath. The survivors' memories introduce alternative interpretations, questions and resist our need for closure, as Saul Friedländer has argued in the context of the Shoah. Thus, the historical record may be deepened.[21] Oral history within atomic narratives includes alternative understandings and questioning narratives. Listening to those traumatised is, according to philosopher Susan Brison, a lesson in 'unlearning'.[22] In his specific memory of trauma, Fukahori contests the validity of previously received narratives and unravels resolved meaning taken for granted, including scientific discussions which refer to clinical and instantaneous warfare.

In the above discussion, three children became two. Fukahori describes Machiko and Kōji's ordeal with active verbs: words such as 'managed to free himself ... found each other ... searched ... crossed over the river ... fled' – emblematic of their efforts and agency. Fukahori imagines his brother and sister seeking refuge, resisting victimhood and showing determination. Their efforts towards life continued after the bombing. Fukahori does not achieve closure, but as his narrative unfolds, his memory envisions an alternative imagined future.[23] He remembers his brothers and sister not only as bomb victims, but in their struggle to survive. He relates:

> And I had been searching myself and had at last come to this place. But when I struggled to this place, it was already dark and I had no idea that these two [children] were here. There were so many people and it was frantic. I couldn't even enter [...] it was awful and I straight away left the place and came down to my own house [*wagaya*]. And that's when I found my mother [her remains]. But I didn't see the remains of the three children down there, so I was wondering where on earth they had gone. Just then, my little brother [Kōji] came down and I met him and realised he had fled with my little sister. Unfortunately, in the middle of the night, while she was sleeping she died. Anyway, I met my little brother here [on the slope beside the school] [...][24]

Fukahori reverts to his own memory, recalling his desperate search and the darkness of the refuge. He revisits the finding of his mother once more; a disruptive memory. Two other moments are palpably emotional as Fukahori relates. One is the (temporary) relief of meeting his brother and the other the regret of having missed his little sister, who died during the night.

In the narrative about his siblings and mother, Fukahori determinedly revisits his own trauma and there are moments when he appears overwhelmed. However, without memories such as Fukahori's, narratives of self and community remain incomplete.[25] On a tour of Jewish Berlin, Austrian-American historian Gerda Lerner reflected that the Jews were now a museum piece, to be 'admired, stared at, have graves honoured, memorials marked'. The culture was dead and the dead people were reified into something different from what they had been.

'...they are deader than dead', she wrote.[26] In remembering the past, pain, failure, suffering and ugliness are hidden from sight. Traumatic events are repressed, denied or remembered belatedly.[27] Fukahori's unfinished lament for his siblings allows the construction of a 'truer', 'more complete' story and a prophetic moment.[28] After his long silence, recollecting the deaths of his mother and siblings in the event of the bombing of Nagasaki, Fukahori reimagines his family members' lives, inviting a previously unexpressed grief and the acknowledgement of wrongs.

Social entombment by story-telling

Rather than as museum pieces or as objects of dark tourism, the lives of his siblings as agents of change are re-animated: and Fukahori as storyteller participates in the scriptural 'act of sepulchre'. Fukahori gives life back to the memory of his dead siblings in his embalming testimony, even as he confirms their presence, death's presence among the living.[29] Ricœur writes the representation of the past as the kingdom of the dead may be escaped by considering the historiographical operation as a social ritual of entombment or sepulchre.[30] But entombing implies putting to rest, whereas the *kataribe* disturb complacency and the laying down of lazy histories. Ricœur's metaphor suggests a finalising entombment, but historical determinism is fractured by Fukahori's reintroduction of contingency to history in his story – the past as the 'return' of buried possibilities. In the 'black hole' of the chaos left by the atomic bombing Fukahori experiences the haunting presence of the past. Plagued by his incapacity to forget and a powerlessness to remember clearly at a distance from the event, his imaginative narrative is his gift; a re-storying and reanimation of his silenced siblings.

The task of speech for the *kataribe* challenges and unsettles the narratives of the past, showing an attentiveness to silences. Machiko and Kōji's resistance against death was cut short and Fukahori's imaginative narrative humanises them from victimhood in appreciating their struggle. The sepulchre envisioned by Ricœur, writes philosopher David Leichter, is not final, but an enduring work of mourning, assigning to writing (and narrating?) the role of a burial rite, which 'exorcises death by inserting itself into discourse' and transforms death to life.[31] In Nagasaki we know so many loved ones were left unburied. Leichter interprets Ricœur as transmitting two roles for testimony: the first is to say what happened and the second to 'bear witness to something which cannot be seen or reduced to facts of what happened'.[32] Here, Fukahori achieves both aims, confronting the difficult past, then soothing, pacifying and mourning in his lament of the loss of his loved ones.

Fukahori's prophetic role subtly interacts with and challenges public remembrance. Using visual aids such as photographs and maps, his narration represents the interaction between private memory and more public arenas. Some of the photographs are held today at the Nagasaki Atomic Bomb Museum, although they were taken by US Army representatives. As the interview

Lament, anger and protest 175

continued, Fukahori begins a more esoteric discussion of the illogical nature of atomic bomb death, hinted at by the earlier comments on the body of his mother.

Locating disjuncture

A slope, on the eastern side of the school, is a central site for Fukahori's re-imagining of bodies scattered in the landscape. This is the location where he met his younger brother Kōji after the bombing. Fukahori recalls this place before the bomb as a 'normal' space, where people walked, talked and lived near home.

The following photograph (Figure 9.3) presents the aftermath of the bombing, an overhead image taken as part of the United States' survey of the damage. This photograph was used by the US surveyors in their historiographical brief to demonstrate how the bombing destroyed most buildings, apart from large concrete structures such as the Yamazato *Kokumin Gakkō* (National School). The bridge over the river, which the children used to go to the shops, was demolished and a microcosm of Nagasaki's hilly topography is partially visible.

Figure 9.3 Yamazato Kokumin Gakkō (Yamazato State School): photograph used by permission of the Nagasaki Atomic Bomb Museum, Tomihisa Taue (mayor) 23 January 2019 (USSBS) – the dot in the upper left-hand corner is where Fukahori slept on the first night; the dot in the lower left-hand corner shows where Akio was cremated on 11 August; the farthest dot on the right-hand side is where the family house was, the dot to the left of this is the slope where Fukahori met his brother Kōji before he died. US army, public domain.

Fukahori overlays onto the image the dates and markers of his personal narrative, challenging the post-mortem assertion that death came immediately to all (on which I elaborate later in this chapter). Fukahori details his home, the children's place of refuge (where his sister died), the slope where he met his brother Kōji on 10 August and the location where his other brother Akio was cremated.

The US bombing transformed Fukahori's neighbourhood into a place of death, abnormality and disjuncture. Fukahori revisits the discussion of bodies in Chapter 3 of this book, comparing his understanding of the deaths of his own family members with his memory of encounters with other bodies, construing a jagged differentiation in death. Where bodies are largely elided from modern sanitised narratives, memorials of the atomic bombing which recall the bodies challenge the unquestioned support of the use of 'nuclear warfare'. He describes those who had died:

> Anyway, basically for me, the biggest thing about the atom bomb which I find weird – [is] [...] an inconsistency [*mura*], there is a major differentiation [*sa*] [...] for example, [...] from the top of this slope. [...] On the side, there were two people who had died. [...] They weren't far apart. [...] One of them was still wearing a kimono beautifully, without a single burn or injury [visible], lying there like she was asleep, but dead. [...] But just one metre and a half, or two metres away, there was a person who was completely yellow, burnt all over, his/her whole body was yellow and hair was all over the place, neck to the side and the head had fallen off and he/she had died.[33]

Fukahori contrasts his memory of two bodies of unknown victims he remembers near the place he met his brother. One of the bodies is 'beautiful' in death, in a kimono, 'asleep' and the other one is horribly dehumanised, discoloured, torn apart, his or her body parts strewn nearby. His memory eschews explanation.

> This was the kind of inconsistency [*mura ga [...] sa ga arun desu yo*] that there was. [...] I didn't know about radiation at the time, so I [thought that the difference in death was caused by] the heat rays and the bomb blast's irregularities. Added to this, there was the radiation.[34] [...] In that case, [putting these] three together, there was a lot of irregularity [*mura*]. [...] right here, where I met my little brother.[35]

Fukahori met his younger brother on the same slope where he saw the bodies, tying his discussion of variability into his own narrative and memory. His finding of his own family members, three dead, but one alive, witnesses to abnormalities. Of his own family, although his mother's body was visually desecrated, his brother and sister's bodies were less visibly affected.

Internal injuries and residual radiation experienced by survivors meant trauma would continue for months and years to come. Fukahori's indignant voice in the audio reveals his dissatisfaction in his appraisal of the scientific evidence:

Lament, anger and protest 177

> So, now, looking at various materials [...] this [pointing at map] was 500 metres from the centre and this one kilometre. So, [...] [where the siblings were at the shop] was around one kilometre [...] right? So, what do you think the temperature was in this place? 3000 or 4000 degrees[36] [at the hypocenter]. [...] Then, the wind created by the explosive force was about 280 [km per hr?] However, here [at the shop] would have been about 1000 degrees they say.[37]

Attempting to make sense of his memory alongside the public history of the bombing of Nagasaki is a difficult or nigh impossible task for Fukahori, as he cites the approximate temperatures which scientific reports suggest. The numbers impact his personal story.

> But if it was 1000 degrees, what about my little brother [Kōji]? You would have thought everyone would be burnt black. But they had all come up here, my brother and sister were fine.[38]

He cannot make sense of the science. There is an absolute incongruity between the public history and his own attempts to understand it.

Machiko died within 24 hours, but Kōji died a lingering death around one week after 9 August. Fukahori remembered, in his interview, walking to their aunt's house in the hot ash with his brother, who had no shoes. When he found a doctor, he asked him for medicine for Kōji's pain and the doctor told him, 'What do you think I can do?' Twelve-year-old Kōji became weaker little by little, but Fukahori reported he stayed mentally strong. Kōji complained, 'I'm so hot!' He said to his brother, 'I'm dying', and about an hour later, passed away.[39] Fukahori's lament subtly protests official myths and public narratives about the bombing of Nagasaki, including scientific and generic pronouncements.

Parallels to Job

Expanding to the wider collective biography, I will suggest that the wider narrative of Job provides a useful literary source for showing how lament leads to protest for the surviving Urakami Catholics today, just as Johann Metz also envisaged 'dangerous' memory as a Job-like protest. Since 1945, the Urakami Catholics have drawn deeply on the tale of Job, an archetypal survivor of trauma and tended to understand what had happened as a trial of God.

Just as the interpretation of the Catholic experience of the bombing has been understood differently in Nagasaki over time, there is a progression or change evident in the character portrayed in the book of Job. Some traditional readings of Job have (mis)understood the protagonist ultimately as a patient sufferer, submissive and pious. In this understanding, Job demonstrates a passive, but legitimised religious response to undeserved suffering: apposite to the Japanese proverb equating Nagasaki with prayer.[40]

There are, however, two sides to the eponymous protagonist, comparable to the evolution of the Urakami survivors from the early years after the bombing, to the transformed reaction of those remaining alive today. The first Job submits to God, silent and avoiding vocalised question and complaint. Reading Job in the full biblical narrative, however, reveals a second confused character with doubts, who experiences the full extent of despair, crying out in anguish. One scholar, Katharine Dell, in 1991 supported a new reading of Job, reinterpreting the book of Job as explicitly sceptical literature.[41] Urakami Catholics today similarly show scepticism of traditional doctrines and dogma in the light of their experiences.

Catholic survivors lived through multiple traumas (and were recipients of generationally transmitted trauma). Job's questioning of God is commensurate with the exasperated speech of the Nagasaki survivors. The survivors' lament may be compared to that of the biblical character, highlighting how protest develops from lament. Two parallels are fruitful. One contributor to lament and protest in Urakami with a parallel in Job is the interviewees' consciousness of ongoing sickness and injury. A second is their strong consciousness of social exclusion and class. Subsequently emerges the survivors' protests and pleas for justice.

In the early years, survivors read Job and tended to submit and (try to) get on with their lives, avoiding any questioning of God's will. Historian Itō Akihiko remembered Fukahori Masaru, a school teacher in Ōura and an Urakami survivor. Masaru quoted a phrase from the book of Job as he struggled to absorb the loss of his parents, his neighbours and the levelling of his neighbourhood. 'The Lord gave, the Lord has taken away. Blessed be the name of the Lord' (Job 1:21). He concluded his living was itself a trial from God.[42] Itō wrote the only family member who remained alive after the bombing was Masaru's younger sister. Masaru said, 'She [my sister] was an amazing woman. I didn't think there was another girl like her ... if only my sister was there, I did not need anything else. I had to do my best and live with her.' However, one month after the bombing, his sister succumbed to her injuries and passed away.[43] Like Job, Masaru had nothing he loved spared – it was all taken away.

Later, though, a gradual transformation to scepticism is evident among at least some of the Catholic survivors of the atomic bombing. The second Job in the narrative is a sceptic who questions God. Job wrestles with God; he protests and laments.[44] Laid low with terrible sores, his children are killed by a tornado and he curses the day of his birth. 'Why did I not die at birth, come forth from the womb and expire?' (3:11) and 'I have no peace, no quietness, I have no rest, but only turmoil' (3:26 TNIV). In Chapter 30, he complains:

> I cry out to you, God, but you do not waver. I stand up, but you merely look at me [...] Yet when I hoped for good, evil came, when I looked for light; then came darkness. The churning inside me never stops; days of suffering confront me. I go about blackened, but not by the sun [...] my skin grows black with peels; my body burns with fever.
>
> (vs. 20, 26–30 TNIV)[45]

Bodily lament

It is striking in the interviews that Catholic survivors in Nagasaki have ongoing experiences of pain and injury which lead to their protest. The body's ailments incite a metaphoric vision of physical, spiritual, emotional and existential extirpation – the black hole of ongoing suffering. Survivor Nagase Kazuko was unable to use her legs from birth and the atomic bombing multiplied her experiences of bodily dysfunction. When I ask Nagase how she would summarise her testimony, she speaks like Job of her unceasing pain and ever-suffering body:

> To the present, how many years has it been since the atomic bomb? I'm alive but I cannot say if that is a good thing. I'm alive and my body (bones) is sapped (*boroboro*) [Cries] It's true, my body (bones) is exhausted (*boroboro*). Look at me, I cannot take it [...] I lie down, I use pillows, but [...] I hurt, my body [...] Even when I take medicine, despite that, I am in pain, I distrust [the medicine].[46]

Nagase echoes the archetypal survivor's words. Her suffering continues when she lies down. She is not convinced that survival, her 'aliveness', is a good thing. Job cries out, 'I am not at ease, nor am I quiet; I have no rest; but trouble comes' (3:26). He wishes he could be free of his body – disembodied. Nagase's lament cites her tired body: 'I'm alive, but I cannot say if that is a good thing.' Job continues:

> And now my life drains out, as suffering seizes and grips me hard. Night gnaws at my bones; the pain never lets up [...] (verse 16–17) My stomach's in a constant churning, never settles down. Each day confronts me with more suffering [...] (verse 27) I'm black and blue all over, burning up with fever.
>
> (Verse 30, The Message ver.)

Job's pains never stop; his inside churning does not cease. Nagase, like Job, calls her bones, representative of her body, exhausted (*boroboro* means old or broken). Nagase's medicine does not halt the relentless pain. Her bodily lament is infused with doubt about her ability to continue. Dissimilar to *kataribe* Nakamura and to Job, Nagase is not blessed at the end of her life with more children and renewed wealth – instead she is tormented by her past, her lost family and cornered by her tragedy.

There was a pious assumption of the *hansai* interpretation in Urakami that survival indicated sinfulness and death purity (related to the *hansai* or sacrificial narrative). In Nagase's lament, though, like Job, she does not accept that she is deserving of her suffering – she strongly protests her innocence. Job's disease and disability enable new insight for the protagonist, according to theologian Amy Erickson. Job's friends surmise his ailments show his guilt, but he reinterprets his ill health, overturning the assumption of his friends that his sickness shows his sinfulness.[47]

180 *Memory's future*

Other survivors speak too of their pain and suffering. Nakamura Kazutoshi laments his own experience of physical sickness and mental anguish and the loss of family members. Nakamura found the bodies of his little brothers and his sister's two young daughters outside his house, where they had been playing and assisted his father in their cremation and never found his mother. His elder sister experienced the bombing at Shōwa-chō, had skin covered with red blotches and died in September 1945. She was the sixth member of his immediate family who did not survive.[48] In the biblical narrative, God blesses Job and his family is renewed. Likewise, Nakamura perceives hope through the new family granted to him and as a result of his children's education (Chapter 8). Yet, neither Nakamura nor Job's physical healing is complete in old age.[49] Nakamura and Nagase are pained by ongoing ill health. Liberation from suffering is not yet achieved.

Prejudice and exclusion

A second parallel between *hibakusha* complaints and scriptural narrative is the ongoing painfulness of social exclusion; enemies loom large. Job complains about how young children of the neighbourhood despise him, and his friends and family are estranged.[50] Commentators write Job likely sat upon an ash-heap outside town reserved for outcasts and people with infectious diseases. His skin disease may have been leprosy, eczema, smallpox, syphilis or scurvy.[51] The complaints of the Urakami Catholics are contextualised by social 'fissure' and estrangement. Matsuo Sachiko (Figure 9.4) describes her life after the bombing as sharply marked by discrimination and poverty. Matsuo, as we saw in Chapter 3, experienced the bomb as a girl and was particularly haunted by the sight of the decomposing corpses of a woman and her unborn baby. She remembers family life prior to the calamity as being rich (*yūfuku*). The family returned from exile in 1873 to build a business despite losses and through hard work. Her father and family were involved in trade, the second and third generation since the Urakami Fourth Persecution. They were model citizens in Catholic Urakami, developing a business for 30 years, managing up to eight horse carriages. Before the bombing, the Matsuos employed live-in employees in a large house of 20, approximately 600–700 metres from the future hypocenter.[52]

Due to her father's death and a subsequent loss of income, Matsuo's family was left destitute. In summer 1945, Matsuo's father had built a shelter on the hill behind their house (see Map in Chapter 1) and instructed them to stay there after the United States army dropped leaflets warning of a new bomb. Fulfilling community duties at a lookout tower in town, her father did not join the family in the mountainside shelter. He was badly injured by the bomb and died within a month on 28 August. Matsuo reflects:

> [Due to the bomb] Everyone died. All the houses were demolished, so that only the land remained, so we made a small house [...] For a short while things were okay, but as I got bigger, my life got worse. My father died, so we became poor, little by little. For a long time, living in the burnt remains of our own house, where people had died [...] As a child, in all these places,

Lament, anger and protest   181

Figure 9.4 Matsuo Sachiko, photograph, the author, December 2014.

I felt like they [their spirits] were all around me. I didn't want to be around our house, because that was where they died.[53]

The family land remained but all possessions and buildings were levelled after the impact, in the Ōhashi region in the Urakami valley. On top of the loss of home and possessions, Matsuo suffered the deaths of eight family members and lived on in the 'dark face' of Urakami. She experienced a life of discrimination, poverty and sickness. Her family members rebuilt a small house and Matsuo lived with her mother and grandmother.[54] She did not return to school until the following year, as was common for children in the Urakami region and her family had little food in 1945.[55]

> We would go up to the mountains and find [something to eat], we received no support from payments, but took what we could [...] and grew food in the paddocks [...][56]

Matsuo experienced the added discrimination of being tainted by what she (or others) called *kin* (菌), or germs, from radiation. She says:

> It wasn't so much the bombing, though, as germs (*kin)*, [and] a feeling that the germs would be spread. [...] from the atomic bombing and the radiation [...] 'Urakami *hibakusha* have it [the germs] [...] So you shouldn't go near them' [...] they said. [...] for the people [*hibakusha*] who were pregnant, it was unjust. The children would have disabilities, they thought. Even now, when women are having babies, it is still a worry. I also worried [...] about the radiation.[57]

Matsuo is marked by poverty, her *hibakusha* status and social difference. She continues, 'I had no house, no books ... Barefoot, I went back to school.'[58] Despite entrenched poverty in Urakami, the first assistance from the government for atomic bomb victims was provided after 12 years in 1957. Life following the bombing for Matsuo constituted a fall from relative prosperity to poverty; and was marked by a life of stigma and exclusion.

From lament to explicit protest

Lament engages with emotions like anger to rise to the surface and stimulates explicit protest. Describing her grievances which relate to her social exclusion, Matsuo responds to the commonly heard trope of Nagasaki as prayer and Hiroshima as anger. She remonstrates:

> We are angry. [*okotte imasu yo*] All of us. Everyone is angry. We are angry, but [...] Never again, may this kind of thing never again occur [...] [let it not happen ever again] [...] But I don't think the United States has understood yet [...] The impact of the radiation [...] Using a lot of atomic power immediately the air is dirty [*dame*] [...] Radiation and living in amongst the radiation is not right [...] But we are in pain [*kurushimu*], it is too painful [...] for *hibakusha* the pain continues and they are disappearing (dying). This feeling is still strong [...][59]

Lament, anger and protest 183

Most Urakami Catholics lost many family members in the bombing and Matsuo is no different. As well as her father, the atomic bomb killed her two younger brothers, two older brothers, an older sister, a sister-in-law and two aunts. Matsuo is unapologetically emotional as she speaks. She proclaims: 'We are all angry', reclaiming agency and self-hood. She decries the American 'official' lack of recognition of the lifelong impacts of radiation and its effect. Matsuo wishes for deeper understanding and is sceptical about the ability of the 'United States' to understand her life and the damages sustained. She laments her personal torment, the impacts of radiation and the continuing deaths of the *hibakusha*.

Matsuo's grandmother, Nishio Waki (Chapter 6), one of the *hibakusha* who bridged back to an older history of suffering, was a survivor of the *yon-ban kuzure* (Fourth Persecution) of Urakami.[60] Nishio, like the initial submissive Job, avoided protest when she discussed her own suffering caused by the bombing of Nagasaki. Formed by earlier experiences of marginalisation, Nishio spoke to her granddaughter of the need to move on and to not hold grudges. Matsuo, however, contrasted her grandmother's attitude to her own:

> [...] anyway, my grandma didn't hold a grudge against America. 'This world we live in, given to us by God, we live here, by God's grace' [she said] [...] but angry people were still angry [laughs].[61]

In Catholic Urakami, the elder survivors skirted over protest, but those who were children in 1945 have begun to vocalise their anger. Matsuo's anger is haunted by her knowledge of previous trauma in her community: 'dangerous' memory for the surrounding city. Her intimate knowledge of the earlier maltreatment of her grandmother, Nishio, by Japanese authorities is background and context for her experience of the atomic bombing. Matsuo is conscious not only of the wrongs of the atomic bomb but also the complications of localised prejudices.

Matsuo's lament, attentive to silences and the downtrodden, leads to protest. Her anger disrupts oppressive silences, empowers by her self-affirmation and demands God's intervention.[62] Fukahori in narrating the drama of his siblings moves from what he understands, to the inexplicable (the illogical bomb effects), affirming himself and his siblings by his speech. The survivors lament their pain, social exclusion and traumas of loss. The protest of Matsuo against the injustice of the bombing and of Nagase against the pain is consistent with the 'second' sceptical Job. Other Biblical sources including one-third of the book of Psalms are located within the genre of grievance, using hyperbolic, regressive language, contending with the power of cosmic negation and the power of death.[63]

I have mentioned some challenges due to protest, but against whom is the protest of the *hibakusha* directed? For whom is this memory 'dangerous'? There are four main reverberations. The *kataribe* challenge official Catholic Church silences about the bombing of Nagasaki.[64] Protests are levelled at the United States perpetrators of the bomb, at Japanese militarism and aggression and finally, implicitly, at the divine, or God.

184 *Memory's future*

The survivors protest the perceived injustices of the US deployment of the atomic bombing, disputing the legitimacy and appropriateness of the action. When I ask Nagase Kazuko about the perpetrators of the bombing, she is unequivocal:

> *yurusu beki ja nai desu. genbaku desu ne. yurusanai.* This is not something that one should forgive. The atomic bomb, you mean? I don't forgive it.[65]

By her protest Nagase proclaims her innocence – she is angry about her experience which froze time for her at 9 August 1945.

Nishida Kiyoshi calls the atomic bomb indiscriminate and disproportionate:

> Really, the atomic bomb did not perform a purpose. It was indiscriminate [*musabetsu*] […] they shouldn't have used it on Hiroshima/Nagasaki […] that kind of bombing.[66]

Fukahori Jōji, after remembering his siblings, similarly decries the use of the bomb. He does not condemn 'all Americans', but the governmental figures who caused the bombing.

> Yes […] The United States at the time, dropping the bomb, I don't forgive that action. I don't want to forgive [the USA]. On the other hand, I do not mean in respect of all Americans. Einstein said until the end not to drop the bomb […] to the government. But despite that they dropped it. […] However, it's not that I hate the United States of today […] It shouldn't have happened, but the atomic bombing was really a bit different, I think.[67]

Nakamura, who wondered if his mother joined Mother Mary, specifically directs his anger at United States President Truman:

> For myself, I don't hate Americans. On the other hand, no matter what I can't forgive the US president. In the end, the order to drop the atomic bomb wouldn't have happened without the president […] Therefore, I can't forgive this even now.[68]

Further to the general protests against the US leadership, the discussion is made more specific by examining claims about casualties of women and children and comparing with the narratives explored in this collective biography. The stories from the survivors destabilise official and clinical histories of the atomic bombing. In 2015 in an analysis of American war, John Curatola, a historian at the US Army Command in Kansas, described the Nagasaki atomic bomb blast: 'Within a radius of 1 km from hypocenter men [sic] and animals died almost instantaneously from the blast and pressure and heat […]'[69] Fukahori's knowledge of his young siblings' deaths describes a much more illogical and unpredictable suffering. His mother and three siblings were exposed in the region between 500 metres and 1 kilometre from the hypocenter and two died immediately, his five-year-old sister around 18 hours later and his other brother at least a week later. Nagase's narrative also contradicts the above account of instantaneous death sharply. In 1945, she was located only 700–800 metres from the blast in her house and survived, badly traumatised, to continue to tell her near-death experience more than seven decades later. Fukahori's tale of his siblings and Nagase's life evidence a gradual and painful death fought against and protested by the survivors to the present day.[70]

Kataribe collective claims about their family members who died constitute a specific challenge to the American narrative of the atomic bombing. American secretary of war Henry Stimson, considering 'the targeting issue', discussed the likely effects of an atomic bomb on 'surrounding communities' and implications for 'the killing of women and children'. Stimson repeatedly suggested he wanted to hold the Air Force to 'precision' bombing and may have deceived himself that he was not intentionally targeting civilians for mass killing.[71] Some leaders such as Stimson stated their desire to avoid killing women and children, but the survivors' experiences show that this desire was not carried out. By his testimony, Fukahori laments and publicises the treatment of Akio, Machiko and Kōji, representing countless other children and those caught up in Urakami.

Children and women made up a disproportionate number of the victims of the atomic bomb of Nagasaki.[72] The loss of their mothers experienced as a collective trauma has ongoing psychological impacts upon Nakamura, Fukahori, Nagase and Ozaki. Emotion rises to the surface as Nagase speaks about the death and consequent cremation of her mother (Chapter 5). Nakamura discusses his own loss of the mother he never found:

> I was eleven years old at the time, so [...] No matter how you say it, I still, still long for the time I was with my mother you see. That was the biggest shock for me: the death of my mother.[73]

A lament for Ozaki Tōmei's mother (Figure 9.5) is found on his blog, final statement on a post that is dated 9 August 2012. Ozaki writes in short sentences:

> My sadness is the morning farewell on the day of the atomic bomb. 'I'll be back soon!' Mum does not reply. A sad bidding bye. That was her last silhouette. Clara Tagawa Wasa, 1945, 67 years ago. I'm now an old man of 84.[74]

By their memory of and lament for lost siblings, relatives and mothers the survivors show the long-felt implications of the violence they experienced. Protesting their mothers' and siblings' treatment, the *kataribe* show an unwillingness to accept what happened, a compassion for the weak and their holding on to a hope in the possibilities of future justice. Johann Vento, feminist theologian, draws on Metz's concept of 'dangerous' memory to suggest hope by

Figure 9.5 Ozaki Tōmei's mother, Clara Wasa Tagawa, photograph used by permission, 20 January 2019.

memory and lament is held out for 'defeated and long dead women who never experienced healing in their own lifetimes' and as resistance to the victimisation of all women, past and present.[75]

The second spur of protest relates to the Japanese actions that contributed to the wartime situation. The atomic bombings of Japan occurred after Japan's violent and aggressive treatment of neighbouring countries and prisoners-of-war. Nagasaki's civil society includes movements which work to remember the colonial context of war, including the impacts on Korean workers. Motoshima Hitoshi, the Catholic mayor of Nagasaki, famously protested Japanese colonialism and mistreatment of the 'other', going so far as publicly questioning the Shōwa Emperor's complicity in the war.

Nagai Tokusaburō, grandson of Nagai Takashi, does not consider the war and the bombing solely the United States' responsibility. He allocates responsibility for what happened to the actions of both the United States and Japan.

> No, I don't think the US is responsible. Well, I can't say there is nothing, but when you are in a war with your neighbour, you can't say anyone particularly takes responsibility. Both have responsibility and both are damaged, so I don't think you can assign responsibility to the US [...] Japan is not just a victim (*yareppanashi*).[76]

Tokusaburō remembers his grandfather's legacy and how Nagai tended to avoid blaming the United States for the Nagasaki bombing. He points out that the Japanese army was itself involved in violence in war.

Fukahori Jōji's anger rises to the surface as he speaks about the *tokkōtai* (Special Forces), also known as kamikaze. Fukahori does not relate the atomic bombing to Japanese actions, but has a nuanced understanding that war trauma was also inflicted on the Japanese people by his own government. His personal knowledge of the vagaries of the Japanese war machine is due to his own work as a teenager in Mitsubishi instalments in Nagasaki. Fukahori laboured, making screens for the *tokkōtai* boats. As he remembers his work here, he uses strong language, *baka* (stupid), about the experience. The boats were made as they had run out of the materials to construct aeroplanes, for flying suicide missions into American warships. Fukahori may have become a torpedo *kamikaze*, if the war had lasted any longer.

> Well, 3 km away [from here], beyond that hill was my school and [...] due to the war, there was a big Mitsubishi factory [...] Anyway, at that stage, we were 15 years old, in junior high 3rd year [...] [we made] it was stupid (*baka*) [...] Japan's *tokkōtai* [...] [*kamikaze* special forces] [...] Plastic boats, little plastic boats [[...]] they put explosives in and [...] and were told to drive them into American ships, towards the end [...] People my age had already gone to war. They went from 15 years of age.
> (Fukahori Jōji, Nagasaki Atom Bomb Museum, 2014)

Fukahori is scathing of the plastic boats sent to sea with young boys on board, as *kamikaze*, to die and he protests Japan's role in the war and the use of these young men and boys in suicide missions.

The final implication of their protest is as a grievance raised against God. Nagase and Nakamura are exasperated about ongoing sickness and many of the survivors continue to mourn for beloved family members. Four said they considered suicide. While some claim prayer as the right response to the memory of the atomic bombing, others are not content with prayer alone, demonstrating anger and protest. The main protagonist in this chapter, Fukahori, is both ambivalent and sceptical about God:

> I'm not very religious [*bushinjin*]. I don't have much faith so I don't really think about it [...] But basically, during mass at church, I sit and think and you might call it transcendence [*chōshizen*] [...] You might say God but I would not want to say God. Rather, transcendence [...] And then there is another problem [...] I was born a Catholic, due to where I was born [...] so I was baptised by my parents [...] So, I say transcendence is important [...] [laughs][77]

Fukahori calls himself a non-believer and is evasive about the use of the name God. He experiences 'transcendence', or a supernaturality. He may go to Catholic mass because he was baptised by his parents but is ambivalent – and implicitly questions God's presence. In the literary book of Job, the character too expressively protests his own birth.

> Then Job broke the silence. He spoke up and cursed his fate:
> Obliterate the day I was born.
> Blank out the night I was conceived!
> Let it be a black hole in space.
> May God above forget it ever happened. Erase it from the books!
> (Job 3:1–4, The Message paraphrase)

Unlike Job's, the *kataribe* protest to God is not definitive. Those who 'cried for water' after the bombing, like those in the persecution, hoped for assistance and in both cases their hopes were dashed. Survivors' protest arises from lament and anger, but some still demonstrate an ultimate hope in God's faithfulness.

By the methodology I have employed, I have aimed to ask new questions of those on the margin, to recover the '"dangerous memories" of those who have placed the authority of God's house above the powers and principalities of this world', as M. Shawn Copeland puts it.[78] In Catholic Nagasaki, God's memory is symbolised by personifying statues of Mary and a communally reinvigorated cathedral. The Catholic *kataribe* hold a hope in an ongoing memory of the forgotten, represented by the image of the forgiving God, who expunges the guilt of those who seek help. Ozaki Tōmei 'saw', despite the atomic wasteland, an indestructible God of providence and future hope. Ozaki discusses the peasant-mother Mary and her intrinsic 'mother' image, reflecting:

> The archdiocese of Nagasaki has especially believed in Mary. That is, in Mary's gentleness (*yasashisa*) they especially love. Her gentleness. Christianity has the suffering of the Cross, [which is] a father image. Mary is the 'mother' image. That is why the *kakure kirishitan* had *Maria kannon* and Mary images[...] the connection from this Mary is where faith came from and developed.[79]

Ozaki's hero, priest Maximilian Kolbe, is remembered today in Poland for his veneration of Mary. For Ozaki, the liberative image of Mary is an encouraging sign of a gentle memory, God's mother-image, in the aftermath of the bombing.

As they recover their anger the *kataribe* today protest injustice. By an attentiveness to silences around Ground Zero, the collective biography of the survivors presented reaches beyond this small group to the vast suffering of the bombing of Nagasaki, including the forgotten dead and the dehumanised. They raise their angry protest from lament based in concrete experience – railing against the US decision to drop the atomic bomb, against the Japanese authorities' militarism, against a culture of official Catholic silence and inarticulately against God. Given ongoing sickness, disability, the loss of loved ones and mental torment added to social exclusion, the *kataribe* cry: 'I will not keep silent!' like Job (Job 7:11, NIV). Despite long years of suffering, they are not granted forgetfulness. They are compelled to speak of difficult and illogical 'dangerous' memories, mediated by wider public narratives of their ancestors' suffering. Their rhetoric of protest is built on past communal narratives of liberating miracles, reminding them to hold on to hope of redemption even as they cry out to the divine. This writing began by drawing attention to a 'black hole' of death and trauma around the hypocenter of the atomic bombing. The survivors' memory of suffering emanates from this space, refusing to fall away from the silent landscape and dissolve. Their protests remain jagged, asymmetrical and determined.

Notes

1 Joan M. Martin, 'A Sacred Hope and Social Goal: Womanist Eschatology', in *Liberating Eschatology: Essays in Honor of Letty M. Russell*, eds Serene Jones and Margaret A. Farley (Louisville, Kentucky: Westminster John Knox Press, 1999), 216.
2 As explained in Chapters 1 and 3, the *kataribe* are traditional Japanese storytellers. In modern parlance, the survivors of the atomic bombing have been commonly called *kataribe*, who tell the story of the bombing.
3 Barbara Lai describes how lament develops protest in Hebrew testament psalms and how she therefore understands an act of protest as developing from the practice of lament. Barbara M. Leung Lai, 'Psalm 44 and the Function of Lament and Protest'. *Old Testament Essays* 20.2 (1 January 2007): 424.
4 Ricœur uses the term in describing the historiographical operation as a scriptural equivalent of the social ritual of entombment. Paul Ricœur, *Memory, History, Forgetting* (Chicago: London: University of Chicago Press, 2009), 365.
5 Enrique Martínez Celaya, 'The Prophet'. *Psychological Perspectives* 59.2 (2016): 157–66 (161).
6 Celaya, 'The Prophet', 162.
7 As I noted earlier, Hiroshima has been characterised by anger and Nagasaki prayer, casting Nagasaki survivors as passive. In a recent example of writing which assumes the passivity of the Nagasaki survivors, Otsuki Tomoe writes, '... forgiveness, reconciliation and prayers have shaped the historical consciousness of Urakami Catholic bomb survivors over subsequent decades'. She quotes a survivor who was filmed in a 2000 documentary made by Nagasaki Broadcasting Company: 'I can't join a movement or cry out in protest. All we can do [...] is pray for peace.' Tomoe Otsuki, 'The Politics of Reconstruction and Reconciliation in US–Japan Relations – Dismantling the Atomic Bomb Ruins of Nagasaki's Urakami Cathedral'. *The Asia-Pacific Journal: Japan Focus* 13.32 (2015): 1–33. Another scholar in a recent book, Matthew Edwards, cites the 'Hiroshima is anger; Nagasaki is prayer' proverb and states that 'the atomic bombing survivors in Nagasaki are reported to be more inclined to reconcile to their

190 Memory's future

own fate than their counterparts in Hiroshima'. *The Atomic Bomb in Japanese Cinema: Critical Essays* ed. Matthew Edwards (Jefferson, NC: McFarland, 2015), 195.
8 Narita writes that while passivity in Nagasaki is often blamed upon Nagai and his book, *The Bells of Nagasaki*, Nagai did not think that Christians could only be passive and prayerful, as may be seen from his work in the recovery of Urakami. Fumiki Narita, 'Seeing Nagasaki: A Tale', trans. Wallace Gray, *Comparative Civilizations Review*, Manassas, 68 (2013): 102.
9 See William S. Morrow, *Protest Against God: The Eclipse of a Biblical Tradition* (Sheffield England: Sheffield Phoenix Press Ltd, 2007).
10 As a *kataribe*, Fukahori also speaks into civil society at the Atomic Bomb Museum and occasionally at transnational meetings, such as for the 'Peaceboat', a boat which conducts voyages raising awareness about and campaigning against nuclear proliferation. *Fukahori Johji, Nagasaki Survivor at the UN International School*, Nuclear Family website (New York: United Nations, 2016), accessed 24 October 2016, www.facebook.com/hibakushavoices/videos/1610762982560200/.
11 Flora A. Keshgegian, *Time for Hope: Practices for Living in Today's World* (New York: Bloomsbury, 2008), 108.
12 Keshgegian, *Time for Hope*, 99.
13 Nagasaki Shinbun, *Nagasaki Archive*, Archive (Nagasaki: Nagasaki Shinbun, 2016), http://e.nagasaki.mapping.jp/p/nagasaki-archive.html.
14 It was a complex process to interpret what Fukahori intended by these two words. Dr Jeremy Breaden at Monash University assisted me in rethinking the language he intended. I interpreted in the context of Fukahori's composure of his narrative, examining the way he was describing the situation and his memory of coming across dead bodies including his mother's in the landscape. *Mura* is usually written in kana characters rather than kanji and might mean in English capricious, inconsistent or uneven. *Sa* refers to a differentiation, or variation. I have notated throughout in the block quotes from interviews where Fukahori used the word *mura* and where he used *sa*. In most cases he used both words, so I have attempted to interpret them contextually as 'illogical' or 'inconsistent'.
15 Barton J. Bernstein described the War Secretary of the United States in 1945, Henry Stimson, as a man overcome with ambivalence about the casualties caused by the US bombings of Japan and seeking refuge in the untenable idea that the air force was engaged in 'precision bombing'. Stimson discussed the problem with President Harry Truman on 6 June and the two resolved to remove Kyoto from the target list of cities for the sake of its 'relics'. Truman approved a final list of atomic bomb targets, with Nagasaki and Kokura instead of Kyoto and wrote, 'I have told Sec. of War … Stimson to use it so that military objectives and soldiers and sailors are the target and not women and children … [t]he target will be a purely military one.' It is unclear from this record whether the issue of 'relics' in Kyoto, or that of precision bombing which avoided killing women and children was at the forefront of their minds. Barton J. Bernstein, 'The Atomic Bombings Reconsidered'. *Foreign Affairs* 74.1 (1 February 1995): 135–52. Whatever the case, precision bombing during the Second World War which was attempted against Germany was 'spectacularly imprecise'. In 57 US raids against three German synthetic oil plants, only 2 per cent did any damage to the intended targets. Geoffrey Ward, 'Roosevelt and Auschwitz; "Precision Bombing" was spectacularly imprecise. It could not have stopped the trains or the killings.' *Wall Street Journal (Online); New York*. Arts section, 18 September 2015.
16 Jōji Fukahori, interview by Gwyn McClelland, Nagasaki Atomic Bomb Museum, 22 February 2016.
17 Fukahori, 22 February 2016, McClelland.
18 James E. Young, 'Between History and Memory: The Voice of the Eyewitness', in *Witness and Memory: The Discourse of Trauma*, eds Ana Douglass and Thomas A. Vogler, 1st ed. (New York: Routledge, 2003), 275–84, 281.

19 Fukahori, 22 February 2016, McClelland.
20 Young in Douglass and Vogler, 'Between History and Memory', 276.
21 Young in Douglass and Vogler, 'Between History and Memory', 278.
22 Susan Brison quoted in Elizabeth O'Donnell Gandolfo, 'Remembering the Massacre at El Mozote: A Case for the Dangerous Memory of Suffering as Christian Formation in Hope'. *International Journal of Practical Theology* 17.1 (2013): 62–87 (71).
23 Gandolfo, 'Remembering the Massacre', 79.
24 Fukahori, 22 February 2016, McClelland.
25 E. Byron Anderson, 'Memory, Tradition, and the Re-Membering of Suffering'. *Religious Education* 105.2 (30 March 2010): 134–5.
26 Gerda Lerner, *Why History Matters: Life and Thought* (New York: Oxford University Press, 1996), 25–6.
27 Dominick LaCapra, *History and Memory after Auschwitz*, 1st ed. (Ithaca, NY: Cornell University Press, 1998), 9.
28 Anderson, 'Memory, Tradition and the Re-Membering', 137.
29 Candace Kristina McLean, ' "Do This in Memory of Me": The Genealogy and Theological Appropriations of Memory in the Work of Johann Baptist Metz' (unpublished doctoral dissertation, University of Notre Dame, 2012), 314.
30 Ricœur, *Memory, History, Forgetting*, 365, 382.
31 David Leichter, 'The Dual Role of Testimony in Paul Ricœur's Memory, History, Forgetting'. *Phenomenology 2010* 5.Part 1 (2010): 373–99 (390).
32 Leichter, 'The Dual Role of Testimony', 395.
33 Fukahori, 22 February 2016, McClelland.
34 As Fukahori suggests, radiation was a significant issue caused by the atomic bombing. According to the report put together by the Manhattan Engineer District of the United States Army, 'light' radiation travelled at the speed of light, intense enough to kill people within a certain distance from the explosion and including ultra-violet rays, with a wave length shorter than visible light, causing flash burn and ultra-short wave length gamma rays. Radiation comes in two bursts – one intense about three milliseconds long and a less intense one of longer duration over several seconds. Carrie Rossenfeld, 'Total Casualties: The Atomic Bombings of Hiroshima and Nagasaki', *Atomic Archive*, (USA, National Science Foundation, 2015), accessed 18 August 2017, www.atomicarchive.com/Docs/MED/med_chp11.shtml.
35 Fukahori, 22 February 2016, McClelland.
36 The museum website cites the temperature 3000 to 4000 degrees at the hypocenter. Nagasaki Atomic Bomb Museum, '11:02 Nagasaki City Peace/Atomic Bomb', *Nagasaki Atom Bomb Museum* (2017) http://nagasakipeace.jp/japanese/atomic/record/scene/1102.html, accessed 18 August 2017.
37 Fukahori, 22 February 2016, McClelland.
38 Fukahori, 22 February 2016, McClelland.
39 This aspect of his story Fukahori explains on a video speaking at the UN peace school and released on social media, New York 'Fukahori Johji, Nagasaki Survivor at the UN International School', *Nuclear Family* [Facebook post] (New York: United Nations, 22 October 2016), accessed 24 October 2016, www.facebook.com/hibakushavoices/videos/1610762982560200/.
40 Katharine Julia Dell, *The Book of Job as Sceptical Literature* (Berlin New York De Gruyter, 1991), 6–22.
41 See for example, Dell, *The Book of Job as Sceptical Literature*; Dan Mathewson, 'Between Testimony and Interpretation: The Book of Job in Post-Holocaust, Jewish Theological Reflection'. *Studies in the Literary Imagination* 41.2 (22 September 2008): 17–40.
42 Akihiko Itō, *Genshiya no 'yobu ki': katsute kaku sensō ga atta* (Tōkyō: Komichi Shōbō, 1993), 232.
43 Itō, *Genshiya no 'yobu ki'*, 240–2.

44 Mathewson, 'Between Testimony and Interpretation', 18.
45 Dell, *The Book of Job as Sceptical Literature*, 48.
46 Sachiko Matsuo, interview by Gwyn McClelland, Nagasaki Atomic Bomb Museum, 5 December 2014.
47 Amy Erickson, '"Without My Flesh I Will See God": Job's Rhetoric of the Body'. *Journal of Biblical Literature* 132.2 (2013): 295–313 (297).
48 Nagasaki Shinbun, 'Shōnen ni mizu yarezu kōhai', *Nagasaki Peace Site*, (Nagasaki, 2011), accessed 25 April 2017, www.nagasaki-np.co.jp/peace/hibaku/date/757.html.
49 Katharine J. Dell, 'What was Job's Malady?'. *Journal for the Study of the Old Testament* 41.1 (2016): 61–77, 75–6.
50 See Chapter 19 of Job: especially v. 13–19. Dell, 'What was Job's Malady?', 71.
51 Dell, 'What was Job's Malady?', 62.
52 Sachiko Matsuo, 'Itaitengari yake nobara', *Nagasaki Peace Site* (Nagasaki, 1997), accessed 16 September 2017, www.nagasaki-np.co.jp/.
53 Matsuo, 5 December 2014, McClelland.
54 Matsuo, 5 December 2014, McClelland.
55 The ability to return to school was another aspect which sharply divided the children of Nagasaki, depending on whether they lived in the Urakami valley or not. Miyake Reiko said Inasa Elementary School, near her home, was opened up to students again in September 1945, but she initially had no idea when Shiroyama, the school in Urakami where she worked, would be able to start operating again. Reiko Miyake, interviewed by Gwyn McClelland, Nagasaki Atomic Bomb Museum, 19 July 2008. Eventually, Miyake coordinated with the Nagasaki city office to rent rooms from Inasa so that some students from Shiroyama could meet there from November, after conducting outdoor classes before that. Gen Okada, 'A Graduation Ceremony for Fourteen Students', *Asahi Shimbun* October 2008, am ed., accessed 16 September 2017, www.asahi.com/hibakusha/english/shimen/nagasakinote/note01-08e.html.
56 Matsuo, 5 December 2014, McClelland.
57 Matsuo, 5 December 2014, McClelland.
58 Matsuo, 5 December 2014, McClelland.
59 Matsuo, 5 December 2014, McClelland.
60 See Chapters 2 and 6, where I initially introduced Matsuo's grandmother, the double survivor. Nishio's photograph is included in Chapter 6, Figure 6.2. Kazuo Takagi, *Meiji katorikku kyōkai shi* (Tōkyō: Kyōbunkan, 2008), 285.
61 Matsuo, 5 December 2014, McClelland.
62 Lai, 'Psalm 44', 428.
63 Brueggemann, 'The Hope of Heaven', 102.
64 In this collective biography six of the Catholic survivors participated in their interviews at the public Nagasaki Atomic Bomb Museum and three met me at Catholic institutions.
65 Kazuko Nagase, interview by Gwyn McClelland, Genbaku Hōmu, Megumi no Oka, 24 February 2016.
66 Kiyoshi Nishida, interview by Gwyn McClelland, Nagasaki Atomic Bomb Museum, 19 July 2008.
67 Jōji Fukahori, interview by Gwyn McClelland, Nagasaki Atomic Bomb Museum, 1 October 2014.
68 Kazutoshi Nakamura, interview by Gwyn McClelland, Nagasaki Atomic Bomb Museum, 23 February 2016.
69 John M. Curatola, *Bigger Bombs for a Brighter Tomorrow: The Strategic Air Command and American War Plans at the Dawn of the Atomic Age, 1945–1950* (Jefferson, NC: McFarland, 2015), 9.
70 Johann M. Vento, 'Violence, Trauma, and Resistance: A Feminist Appraisal of Metz's Mysticism of Suffering unto God'. *Horizons*, 29.1 (2002): 7–22 (9).

71 Sean Malloy refers to Stimson's pleas for the atomic bombing to avoid civilian casualties, although the move by the United States to target cities would clearly mean that 'the killing of women and children' would occur. Sean L. Malloy, 'Four Days in May: Henry L. Stimson and the Decision to Use the Atomic Bomb'. *Asia-Pacific Journal: Japan Focus* 7.14 (4 April 2009), http://apjjf.org/-Sean-Malloy/3114/article.html.
72 Susan Southard, 'What US Citizens Weren't Told about the Atomic Bombing of Japan', *Los Angeles Times*, 7 August 2015, sec. Opinion Editorial.
73 Nakamura, 23 February 2016, McClelland.
74 Author's translation, Tōmei Ozaki, *Ozaki Tōmei no heya* (online blog) '67 nen mae no kanashimi', accessed 19 September 2016, https://sites.google.com/site/tomaozaki/Home/08-rurudo.
75 Vento, 'Violence, Trauma and Resistance', 19.
76 Tokusaburō Nagai, interview by Gwyn McClelland, Nyokodō Museum, 29 September 2014.
77 Fukahori, 1 October 2014, McClelland.
78 M. Shawn Copeland, 'Journeying to the Household of God: The Eschatological Implications of Method in the Theology of Letty Mandeville Russell', in *Liberating Eschatology: Essays in Honor of Letty Russell*, eds Serene Jones and Margaret A. Farley (Louisville, KY: Westminster John Knox Press, 1999), 41.
79 Tōmei Ozaki, interviewed by Gwyn McClelland, Francisco-en Hōmu, Sasaki, 27 February 2016.

References

Anderson, E. Byron. 'Memory, Tradition, and the Re-Membering of Suffering'. *Religious Education* 105.2 (30 March 2010): 124–39.

Bernstein, Barton J. 'The Atomic Bombings Reconsidered'. *Foreign Affairs* 74.1 (1 February 1995): 135–52.

Brueggemann, Walter. 'The Hope of Heaven … on Earth'. *Biblical Theology Bulletin* 29.3 (1 August 1999): 99–111. https://doi.org/10.1177/014610799902900302.

Celaya, Enrique Martínez. 'The Prophet'. *Psychological Perspectives* 59.2 (2 April 2016): 157–66. https://doi.org/10.1080/00332925.2016.1170452.

Copeland, M. Shawn. 'Journeying to the Household of God: The Eschatological Implications of Method in the Theology of Letty Mandeville Russell'. In *Liberating Eschatology: Essays in Honor of Letty Russell*, eds Serene Jones and Margaret A. Farley. Louisville, KY: Westminster John Knox Press, 1999.

Curatola, John M. *Bigger Bombs for a Brighter Tomorrow: The Strategic Air Command and American War Plans at the Dawn of the Atomic Age, 1945–1950*. Jefferson, NC: McFarland, 2015.

Dell, Katharine J. *The Book of Job as Sceptical Literature*. Berlin New York: De Gruyter, 1991.

Dell, Katharine J. 'What Was Job's Malady?'. *Journal for the Study of the Old Testament* 41.1 (1 September 2016): 61–77. https://doi.org/10.1177/0309089216628418.

Edwards, Matthew. *The Atomic Bomb in Japanese Cinema: Critical Essays*. Jefferson, NC: McFarland, 2015.

Erickson, Amy. '"Without My Flesh I Will See God": Job's Rhetoric of the Body'. *Journal of Biblical Literature* 132.2 (2013): 295–313. https://doi.org/10.2307/23488013.

Fukahori, Jōji. Interview by Gwyn McClelland, Nagasaki Atomic Bomb Museum, 10 January 2014.

Fukahori Joji, *Nagasaki Survivor at the UN International School. Nuclear Family* website. New York: United Nations, 2016. www.facebook.com/hibakushavoices/videos/1610762982560200/.

Fukahori, Jōji. Interview by Gwyn McClelland, Nagasaki Atomic Bomb Museum, 22 February 2016.

Gandolfo, Elizabeth O'Donnell. 'Remembering the Massacre at El Mozote: A Case for the Dangerous Memory of Suffering as Christian Formation in Hope'. *International Journal of Practical Theology* 17.1 (2013): 62–87. https://doi.org/10.1515/ijpt-2013-0006.

Ito, Akihiko. *Genshiya no 'Yobu ki': katsute kakusenso ga atta*. Tokyo: Komichi Shobo, 1993.

Keshgegian, Flora A. *Time for Hope: Practices for Living in Today's World*. New York: Bloomsbury, 2008.

LaCapra, Dominick. *History and Memory After Auschwitz*. 1st ed. Ithaca, NY: Cornell University Press, 1998.

Lai, Barbara M. Leung. 'Psalm 44 and the Function of Lament and Protest'. *Old Testament Essays* 20.2 (1 January 2007): 418–31.

Leichter, David. 'The Dual Role of Testimony in Paul Ricœur's Memory, History, Forgetting'. *Phenomenology 2010* 5.Part 1 (1 February 2010): 373–99. https://doi.org/10.7761/9789731997742_17.

Lerner, Gerda. *Why History Matters: Life and Thought*. New York: Oxford University Press, 1996.

Malloy, Sean L. 'Four Days in May: Henry L. Stimson and the Decision to Use the Atomic Bomb'. *Asia-Pacific Journal: Japan Focus* 7.14 (4 April 2009). http://apjjf.org/-Sean-Malloy/3114/article.html.

Martin, Joan M. 'A Sacred Hope and Social Goal: Womanist Eschatology'. In *Liberating Eschatology: Essays in Honor of Letty M. Russell*, eds Serene Jones and Margaret A. Farley. Louisville, KY: Westminster John Knox Press, 1999.

Mathewson, Dan. 'Between Testimony and Interpretation: The Book of Job in Post-Holocaust, Jewish Theological Reflection'. *Studies in the Literary Imagination* 41.2 (22 September 2008): 17–40.

Matsuo, Sachiko. 'Itaitengari yake nobara'. *Nagasaki Shinbun Archive*. Nagasaki Peace Site, 29 May 1997. www.nagasaki-np.co.jp/.

Matsuo, Sachiko. Interview by Gwyn McClelland, Nagasaki Atomic Bomb Museum, 5 December 2014.

McLean, Candace Kristina. '"Do This in Memory of Me": The Genealogy and Theological Appropriations of Memory in the Work of Johann Baptist Metz'. PhD diss., University of Notre Dame, 2012.

Miyake, Reiko. Interview by Gwyn McClelland, Nagasaki Atomic Bomb Museum, 19 July 2008.

Morrow, William S. *Protest Against God: The Eclipse of a Biblical Tradition*. Sheffield England: Sheffield Phoenix Press Ltd, 2007.

Nagai, Tokusaburō. Interview by Gwyn McClelland, Nyokodō Museum, 29 September 2014.

Nagasaki Atomic Bomb Museum. '11:02 Nagasaki City Peace/Atomic Bomb'. Nagasaki City. Nagasaki Atom Bomb Museum, 2017. http://nagasakipeace.jp/japanese/atomic/record/scene/1102.html.

Nagasaki Shinbun. 'Shōnen ni mizu yarezu kōhai'. Archive. Nagasaki Peace Site, 29 November 2011. www.nagasaki-np.co.jp/peace/hibaku/date/757.html.

Nagasaki Shinbun. 'Nagasaki Archive'. Archive. Nagasaki: Nagasaki Shinbun, 2016. http://e.nagasaki.mapping.jp/p/nagasaki-archive.html.

Nagase, Kazuko. Interview by Gwyn McClelland, Genbaku Hōmu, Megumi no Oka, 24 February 2016.

Nakamura, Kazutoshi. Interview by Gwyn McClelland, Nagasaki Atomic Bomb Museum, 23 February 2016.

Narita, Fumiki. 'Seeing Nagasaki: A Tale', trans. by Wallace Gray. *Comparative Civilizations Review*, Manassas, 68 (2013): 98–105.

Nishida, Kiyoshi. Interview by Gwyn McClelland, Nagasaki Atomic Bomb Museum, 19 July 2008.

Okada, Gen. 'A Graduation Ceremony for Fourteen Students'. *Asahi Shimbun*. October 2008, am ed. www.asahi.com/hibakusha/english/shimen/nagasakinote/note01-08e.html.

Otsuki, Tomoe. 'The Politics of Reconstruction and Reconciliation in US–Japan Relations – Dismantling the Atomic Bomb Ruins of Nagasaki's Urakami Cathedral'. *The Asia-Pacific Journal: Japan Focus* 13.32 (2015): 1–33.

Ozaki, Tōmei. '67 nen mae no kanashimi'. Blog. *Ozaki Tōmei No Heya* (blog), n.d. https://sites.google.com/site/tomaozaki/Home/08-rurudo.

Ozaki, Tōmei. Interview by Gwyn McClelland, Francisco-en Hōmu, Sasaki, 27 February 2016.

Ricœur, Paul. *Memory, History, Forgetting*. Chicago and London: University of Chicago Press, 2009.

Rossenfeld, Carrie. 'Total Casualties: The Atomic Bombings of Hiroshima and Nagasaki'. Archive. Atomic Archive, 2015. www.atomicarchive.com/Docs/MED/med_chp11.shtml.

Southard, Susan. 'What US Citizens Weren't Told about the Atomic Bombing of Japan'. *Los Angeles Times* 7 August 2015, sec. Opinion Editorial.

Takagi, Kazuo. *Meiji katorikku kyōkai shi*. Tōkyō: Kyōbunkan, 2008.

Vento, Johann M. 'Violence, Trauma, and Resistance: A Feminist Appraisal of Metz's Mysticism of Suffering unto God'. *Horizons* 29.1 (2002): 7–22. https://doi.org/10.1017/S0360966900009695.

Ward, Geoffrey. 'Roosevelt and Auschwitz; "Precision Bombing" Was Spectacularly Imprecise. It Could Not Have Stopped the Trains or the Killings'. *Wall Street Journal (Online), New York.* 18 September 2015, sec. Arts.

Young, James E. 'Between History and Memory: The Voice of the Eyewitness'. In *Witness and Memory: The Discourse of Trauma*, eds Ana Douglass and Thomas A. Vogler, 1st ed., 275–84. New York: Routledge, 2003.

10 Conclusion

Inside present-day Urakami Cathedral, a stained-glass window depicts the 'dangerous' memory of the ruined cathedral. Catholics have not forgotten the mortifying scene, nor the long suffering they experienced in the surrounding spaces. The glass shows the fractured form of the building and rubble lying in front with the exposed dark-brown earth segments. At first, it seems the scene portrayed is by night. Ozaki Tōmei remembered contemplating the cathedral at night, the scene lit by fire, in the weeks after the bombing. But the sky in the window scene is ripped into shards of blue, purple and grey, and the one star visible suggests the possibility of a new day. Breaking through the night, a light in the east rises above the west-facing cathedral once more – and for those who gather here in a

Figure 10.1 Urakami Cathedral stained-glass window, photograph, Richard Flynn 2006, used by permission, 7 January 2019.

Conclusion 197

reclaimed and repurposed building, there is a suggestion of hope and a brighter future. Each December, the liturgical year reframes the star above the ruins, and the people remember another dark night in which was heralded the birth of baby Christ by Mother Mary, a new life, promising the overcoming of deathly structures and global violence.

The survivors' narratives as collective biography are like the stained-glass window of the ruined cathedral – incorporating shards and brokenness – yet, adding colour and shade due to the provision of a vital historical perspective on what we already know about Nagasaki and the atomic bombing. Dori Laub[1] suggests, '… the listener has to let these trauma fragments make their impact both on him [sic] and on the witness …' Later in the same passage she writes that for the survivor as they rebuild their own life following trauma, '… in the center of this massive dedicated effort remains a danger, a nightmare, a fragility, a woundedness that defies all healing'.

The use of the term 'dangerous' memory in the Catholic context illuminates a political and future-focused understanding of memory and how older public narratives of resistance and resilience contribute to recovery and healing for survivors in this project.

The Urakami Catholic story of the *hibakusha* is composed of at times overwhelming memory of disempowerment, marginalisation and seemingly unbearable losses; and simultaneously of resilience. Their memory is unique in atomic history because of the nuances within survivor stories of distinct religious, social and cultural connections due to combined European and Japanese influences. Stories are stilted and the survivors' memories haunted – not only by their attempts to come to terms with trauma but by their ancestors' own heritage of suffering and survival. Returnees from persecution built the cathedral at the place where they remembered their ancestors' forced apostasy and humiliation. Pilgrims travel annually to locations of exile where they remember their ancestors' travails.

In this book ordinary people tell the Catholic narrative of the atomic bombing. Atomic survivors of Urakami make connections to the community's public history of persecution and link such remembering to the devastation of the atomic bomb. The ordinary *kataribe* – spokespeople of memory – are drawn to similarly difficult stories of their predecessors, remembering persecutions, hidden churches and martyrdoms and succinctly connect them to their own resilience.

The agency of seemingly 'ordinary' women in the public history is notable, adding a gendered element to 'dangerous' remembering in Nagasaki. Women and children suffered some of the worst of the atomic bombing and Clara Wasa, Nishio Waki, Kataoka Sada and Iwanagi Tsuru are some of the heroines remembered here. Nagase Kazuko, Kataoka Chizuko, Matsuo Sachiko and Miyake Reiko are strong and courageous women who contribute vibrantly to this biography. Those who were lost are celebrated for their legacy.

The US action of deployment of the atomic bomb known as 'Fatman' made the language of *kuzure* (crushing) used by the Japanese magistrate on behalf of the *bakufu* about the earlier persecutions an actuality here. Martyrdoms and the 'crushing' of ancestral hidden Christian cells by the Tokugawa shogunate occurred from time to time through the centuries until the Catholic community was forcefully crushed by the American wartime actions in the atomic bombing of 1945. The so-called Fifth Persecution devastated the community.

Figures of fractured Mary were like the cathedral ruins, a reminder of the destruction and the approximate 8500 deaths the community experienced due to the atomic bombing. Yet Christians of Nagasaki and the world perceived the Christian figure of Mary with keloid scars over time as raising sacred and secular protest against the atomic bombing. Making sense of a modern *hibakusha* Mary of Urakami is only possible in conjunction with the *sempuku* hidden Christian Mary, even as the subtle and major differences between the two are understood. Maria/Maruya, a 'dangerous' figure of faith for the historic Catholic community in Japan, is an icon which recalls suffering. She was trampled, confiscated and 'crumbled', just as the broken Mary was found after the *kuzure* of the atomic bombing. Urakami Mary recalls the narrative of Christ's birth, life and death, even as Mary was remembered in other forms by *sempuku* communities as Buddhist *kannon* or archetypal mother.

Survivor memory of the cry 'Water! Give me Water!' articulates a protest against the American crushing of the community, recalling those who died in horrific circumstances. The cry for water was also a cry to the divine, echoed in the community's public history of the nineteenth century. Children's cries for water to their mothers could not be fulfilled leading some to apostasy, and after the bombing of Nagasaki many Christians similarly gave up faith. Catholic remembering of suffering upholds these protests as silenced screams.

The *kataribe* protest is not only symbolic but addressed overtly against both the United States' bombing action and Japanese mistreatment of the 'other', including Christian and multiple minorities. The memory of bodies viewed after the bombing haunted survivors, and their narration testifies to a United States' unwitting 'persecution' of the Christian community. Bodies melded with exposed soil and others washed away in waterways. As the bodies haunt the memory of the modern survivors, those left behind after executions or discarded as bones in the Tokugawa period haunted Christians and apostates in earlier years. The survivors lament their losses, channelling emotion into anger and protest against the actions of the United States military and government and also the Japanese aggressive and militaristic actions which led up to the devastation.

'Dangerous' memory also suggests change for the Catholic community itself. The force of the atomic bomb left a 'black hole' of confusion and traumatisation, and a silencing characterised the community which gradually returned to the scarred area around the hypocenter. Into this silence Nagai Takashi spoke of *hansai*, a holy sacrifice. The atomic bomb as sacrifice was initially accepted by many of the faithful and the official Church. Survivors today, though, increasingly challenge the spiritualised idea of the sacrifice of the 'unblemished' Catholic victims as necessary for the people of Japan. An implication is a gradual emergence of alternative theologies allowing survivors and their descendants resistance against the atomic bombing. The Catholic *hibakusha*, after many years of silence, have found their voice as *kataribe* tribal storytellers.

There are meaningful connections between two of the most cataclysmic and distinct events of the twentieth century: the Jewish Shoah and the atomic bombings of Japanese cities. Despite dissimilarities, both wartime phenomena represent the tendency of the perpetrators to exert 'god's' judgement upon the 'other'. The intent of the Nazi regime and the US atomic bombing was to damage, disable and to kill, to punish and to eliminate: and both were chillingly successful. Survivors of both experiences are angry at the perpetrators, but also protest their treatment to 'God'.

'Dangerous' memory threatens 'national' summations of history and exclusivist theological interpretations, but is also 'dangerous' for the individual narrator. As Flora Keshgegian writes, for those who experienced trauma, the process of remembering is ambiguous and painful. There are signs that discomforting memory signals profoundly negative psychological and physical entrapment. A traumatic 'black hole' in memory can become an utter negative, which re-traumatises and damages, rather than assisting recovery.

Despite such equivocacy, the *kataribe*'s extraordinary courage is evident. Revisiting the past, the survivors' narration embraces a scriptural sepulchre of hope for the defeated and the dead. With the ongoing possibility of re-traumatisation from the spectre of past violence, the participants in this project allude to their own grasp of an often-tenuous faith – sitting alongside their lament and protest – and a still held hope for the future. As *kataribe*, the survivors take on the role of storytellers, and educators, and mention children to whom they tell their stories.

The narration of the Urakami Catholic survivors of the atomic bomb is haunted by their communal narratives of trauma, 'dangerous' memory transmitted across generations spanning Edo, Meiji, Taishō, Shōwa, Heisei and Reiwa periods. The Meiji period was not immediately emancipatory nor revolutionary for the Catholics, who languished in multiple detention camps around Japan when the Tokugawa regime was overthrown. After a few years, the persecutions eased, but a stigma pursued the group in the Taishō and Shōwa periods, and overt discrimination lingered.

The Catholic *kataribe* upset the stereotype of passivity in this town, Nagasaki, demonstrating resistance to ongoing suffering and asserting the right of remembrance of common humanity with the suffering 'other'. They offer testimony for the dead, seeking assurance and change for the future. Today, in Urakami Cathedral, the symbolic picture formed in stained glass depicts the broken-down ruins of the cathedral. The representation of the broken cathedral as 'dangerous' memory is not the only icon to be observed in this kaleidoscopic image. The hope of the people is also evidenced in the shining, sparkling rising star.

A postscript

On the sixty-seventh anniversary of the bombing of Nagasaki in 2012, Ozaki Tōmei wrote on his blog (author's translation):

> There was a story of a frog I heard from my mother.
> Once there was a selfish frog.
> It wouldn't listen to anything.
> If you said 'go to the mountain', it went to the river.
> If you said 'study!' it would go and play.
> 'Your mother is growing old, so if I die, where will you bury me?
> If I say the river, you will bury me on the safer mountain I guess.'
> So, the mother frog said, 'If I die, the river! Right?'
> It was the first time that this selfish frog took any notice of death.
> Anyway, it buried her in the river.
> When the typhoon came, or the river flooded, oh! The mother would be carried away and the frog would cry out,
> *'Ribit, ribit'.*

Ozaki continued: My mother didn't go in a flood, she passed away surrounded in a sea of flames of the atomic bomb. The mother frog, believing that her son would continue in his contrary ways, asked to be buried in the river, thinking he would do the opposite and bury her in a safe location on the mountain. However, realizing his selfishness for the first time, and taking her word for it, the frog buried the mother frog in the river.[2]

Notes

1 Shoshana Felman and Dori Laub, *Testimony: Crises of Witnessing in Literature, Psychoanalysis and History* (New York, London: Routledge, 2013), 71–3.
2 Tōmei Ozaki, 'Ozaki Tomei No Nikki: Gembaku No Hi. 67nenmae No Kanashimi. Haha to No Tsunagari. Wasurenai', Blog, *Ozaki Tomei No Nikki* (blog), 8 September 2012, http://tomaozaki.blogspot.com.au/2012/08/blog-post_3765.html.

References

Felman, Shoshana, and Dori Laub. *Testimony: Crises of Witnessing in Literature, Psychoanalysis and History*. New York, London: Routledge, 2013.
Ozaki, Tōmei. 'Ozaki Tomei No Nikki: Gembaku No Hi. 67nenmae No Kanashimi. Haha to No Tsunagari. Wasurenai'. Blog. *Ozaki Tomei No Nikki* (blog), 8 September 2012. http://tomaozaki.blogspot.com.au/2012/08/blog-post_3765.html.

Appendix
Notes on sources

Archives, memoirs and popular history

There is a need to set the major literature consulted for this project against the wider literature in the field. Hiroshima University's bibliography of 'Atomic bomb literature' assists, recording the generations of post-war writers online and showing Hiroshima authors far outnumber Nagasaki writers.[1] Included are several memoirs from Nagasaki which informed this book extensively. These sources include online oral records available through the Nagasaki Archive; the early memoirs of the Junshin University archive; and the Nagasaki *Gembaku hōmu taikenki (Memoirs from the Atom Bomb Elderly People's Home of Nagasaki)*. All assist in understanding Catholic recollections of the bomb from Nagasaki.[2]

The complicated historic emergence of the city has partially led to Nagasaki atomic bomb literature's marginalisation in comparison to Hiroshima. I have only touched on this aspect of marginalisation in this book. I restricted myself to a sample summary of the Nagasaki and Hiroshima *hibakusha* literature at large and closely considered the Nagasaki memoirs and literature. Where relevant, I consulted literature from the Edo, Meiji, Taishō and early Shōwa periods, although I focused on the post-war period.

Within published literature, the most significant records for this project are narratives composed in Japanese by survivors interviewed, such as Ozaki Tōmei and Kataoka Chizuko. Ozaki's books include his own autobiography, a book about Father Kolbe and a biographical manga written by Shiōra Shintarō.[3] Kataoka has written about the French Priest Bernard Petitjean who arrived in Nagasaki in the nineteenth century and the Catholic seminaries and colleges in the region. However, it is the collection of essays she wrote and edited with her sister, Rumiko, entitled *Hibakuchi Nagasaki no saiken* (The reconstruction of atomic Nagasaki), which was of particular interest for the purposes of this book.[4]

In addition, interviewees for this book such as Miyake Reiko, Mine Tōru, Fukahori Jōji and Matsuo Sachiko have previously participated in video interviews, publicly available online.[5] Further, journalists have interviewed many survivors for newspaper articles over the years, the records of which assist in gleaning more information about their lives and their composure of their individual narratives. A variety of online reports and public accounts were also useful for my research.[6] Social media provided helpful supplementary sources.

Popular history books describe survivor narratives in English, although authors tended to brush over the socially complex historiography of Nagasaki or largely ignore issues of Catholic public remembering. See Susan Southard's *Life after Nuclear War* and Craig Collie and Paul Ham's histories entitled respectively: *Nagasaki: The Massacre of the Innocent and Unknowing* and *Hiroshima Nagasaki*. Southard's book certainly challenges the popular American historiography that an atomic bombing of Nagasaki was inevitable, but does not clearly describe the city's historical distinctiveness, partially eliding the narratives of the Catholics.[7]

Hibakusha (survivor) memoir has a high status in atomic literature in Japan, but there is a lack of sources about atomic memory from the Catholic perspective. While there is a variety of scholarship which engages with the *sempuku* (secret) Christians, little research has connected understandings of the atomic bombing to the ancestral historic background of the Catholics. Systematic marginalisation of this specific group has occurred, so I employ the strategy of making inferential connections between different and sometimes incomplete sources in order to understand largely undocumented experiences in Urakami.

Nagai Takashi

Given that the research on Christian recovery and the atomic experience in Nagasaki post-1945 is limited, discussion of the Catholic experience usually begins with the memoirs of Nagai Takashi, a prominent Catholic doctor who wrote extensively about the bomb and died in 1951. Nagai Takashi's sacrificial interpretation of the bombing in 1945–51 proved increasingly controversial over time and I elaborated upon the importance of this understanding in Chapter 5. Nagai was a prolific writer, producing a best-selling memoir entitled *The Bells of Nagasaki* (1949) and many other books and documents, illustrating his ideas in painting and drawing, calligraphy and poems, until he died of radiation sickness in May 1951.[8]

Although religious and philosophical academic critiques of the historical figure of Nagai have emerged, Shijō Chie argues that what is needed now is a historico-sociological critique, which the present account goes some way to providing.[9] Yamada Kan, Takahashi Shinji, Nishimura Akira and Shijō are prominent critics of Nagai in Japanese scholarship and their views are discussed extensively in Chapter 5.[10] Yuki Miyamoto's work examining religious understandings of the atomic bomb impacts, from Buddhist and Catholic points of view (Nagai's), discusses Nagai's legacy in an admiring fashion.[11] Kevin Doak or Narita Fumiki offer a generally positive assessment, as does Australian priest Paul Glynn whose popular biography on Nagai's life, *A Song for Nagasaki*, was published in 1988 and translated into a number of languages.[12] I interviewed Glynn in Sydney about his work in 2014.

There are a number of other sources in which writers mention the Catholic survivors in Nagasaki. Nagai Takashi's *We of Nagasaki* was published in 1951 and told the stories of survivors, including a number of Catholics.[13] The survivors who testified in Nagai's book did not refer, except in passing, to their faith. In *Death in Life: Survivors of Hiroshima* (1991), Robert Lifton examines psychological responses of survivors to the atomic bombing and discusses interviews with several Nagasaki survivors, including a Nun who employed religious responses.[14] A 1981 essay by Kamata Sadao, entitled 'Nagasaki no inori to ikari (the prayers and wrath of Nagasaki)', challenged the image of Nagasaki as prayer (rather than Hiroshima as wrath), noting the labelling of the bombing as a 'Fifth Persecution' by some Catholics, after the four historic persecutions.[15] Itō Akihiko and Takahashi Shinji are two local writers who since 1981 have considered some aspects of Catholic interpretations of the bomb.[16] Just as Metz envisages 'dangerous' memory as a Job-like protest against suffering, Itō was influenced by the idea of the Old Testament Job as a survivor. Itō's work writing about biblical Job was a way of understanding the Catholic interpretation of the atomic bomb, and has been particularly useful for this book. Itō compiled many testimonies of *hibakusha* from Urakami, and his book was entitled *Genshiya no 'Yobu ki': katsute kaku sensō ga atta* (Job of the atomic field: the time there was an atomic war).[17] Itō also refers to the community-based literature reporting on the government crackdowns (*kuzure*) and describing the narrative of the people out of exile in the 1870s. By incorporating pictures of the survivors of the 'fourth persecution of Urakami' and associated family trees, Itō relates the devastation of the earlier trials to the atomic bombing.

In a dissertation which Chad Diehl turned into a 2018 book describing the recovery of Nagasaki, designated an 'International Cultural City' after the bombing, he reflects on the renewal of the Urakami Cathedral and the work of Nagai Takashi and shows that the cathedral is contested as a symbol of 'atomic ruin'.[18] Diehl's interest is in the Nagasaki community's recovery from the bombing. He conceptually separates the 'Catholics' and *hibakusha*.[19] Journalist Yokote Kazuhiko, Takase Tsuyoshi and scholar Ōtsuki Tomoe claim that the Christian rebuilding of the cathedral was the origin of silences in Nagasaki atomic memory.[20] However, the historiography written by Urakami Catholic community members, such as Wasaburō Urakawa and Kataoka Yakichi, elevate the importance of alternative meanings applied to the cathedral. The Catholic *hibakusha* discussed in this book contribute further to the debate about this material symbol, re-examining the memory of the cathedral and ruins from the Catholic survivors' perspective (see Chapter 5).[21]

Catholic narratives

A crucial manuscript for this project proved to be the Japanese language book *Urakami no gembaku no katari* (The telling of the atomic bomb in Urakami), published in 2015 by researcher Shijō Chie.[22] Her methodology of history and narration (*rekishi to katari*) re-evaluates narratives of the atomic bomb in Urakami. She did not conduct interviews but used written records extensively to uncover the Catholic voice. Shijō included personal memoirs of survivors at the *Gembaku Hōmu* (Atom Bomb Elderly People's home) and the Junshin Girls' School, newspaper reports and Catholic publications. Shijō's narration of a 'rupture' experienced by the community who survived in the irradiated rubble is illuminative and helpful. She shines the spotlight on interpretations of the atomic bomb in Nagasaki, focused upon its contextual background as an originally Christian city and addressing the invisibility of the Catholic community in the record of the bombing. Shijō writes that Catholicism in Nagasaki was still regarded with suspicion into the twentieth century and the war against the 'Christian United States' from 1941 added to the lingering 'dangerous-ness' with which the Christian Japanese minority were regarded.[23] I was able to interview Shijō shortly after her book was published in 2016.

Other Japanese sources of importance in the post-war literature about Catholic narratives include the writings of Akizuki Tatsuichirō and Motoshima Hitoshi, which I analysed in relation to my interviews.[24] Akizuki, a doctor and later critic of Nagai Takashi's interpretation of the bombing, converted to Catholicism in 1953 and became a rare Catholic writer-activist among the *hibakusha* of Nagasaki.[25] He published *Nagasaki Genbaku-ki: hibaku ishi no shōgen* (Record of the Nagasaki atomic bombing: Memoirs of a survivor doctor) in 1966 and *Shi no Dōshinen* (Concentric circles of Death) in 1972.[26] Motoshima Hitoshi, a Christian and a descendant of the *sempuku Kirishitan* was Mayor of Nagasaki, from 1979–95. Originally a politician with a conservative base, aspects of his public role included making a 'Peace Declaration' on 9 August and Motoshima became more circumspect about Japan's war history over the years. In 1988, during the Shōwa Emperor's final illness, the Mayor became embroiled in a controversy over a statement he made that the Emperor bore responsibility for the war (see Chapter 8). Norma Field usefully evaluated the significance of his remarks for Japanese public narratives of the emperor, war and nation.[27]

Notes

1 Styczek, Ursula, Nakamura, Tomoko, and Nakamura, Toko, 'Atom Bomb Literature: A Bibliography', in *Atomic Bomb Literature: A Bibliography* (Hiroshima, Hiroshima Peace Memorial Museum, 2017), accessed 31 July 2013, http://home.hiroshima-u.ac.jp/bngkkn/database/English data/BibliographyonAtomic bombLit.html.
2 Itō, *Genshiya no 'Yobu-ki'*; Megumi no Oka Genbaku Hōmu, *genbaku taiken ki*, 2nd ed. (Nagasaki: Megumi no oka Genbaku Hōmu, 2005); *Nagasaki Shinbun*, 'Nagasaki Archive' (Nagasaki: 2016), accessed 17 October 2016, http://e.nagasaki.mapping.jp/p/nagasaki-archive.html.
3 Tōmei Ozaki, *mi gawari no ai*, 2nd ed. (Nagasaki: Seibo no kishasha, 1994); Tōmei Ozaki, *Jūnanasai no natsu*, Seibō bunkō (Nagasaki: Seibo no kisha-sha, 1996); Shintarō Shiōra, *Yaketa rozario: genbaku wo ikinuita shōnen no kiseki na unmei to arata na kokoro no sekai* (Nagasaki: Seibo no kishasha, 2009).
4 Kataoka and Kataoka, *Hibakuchi saiken*.

Sources 205

5 *Fukahori Jōji, UN School in New York,* 'Fukahori Johji, Nagasaki Survivor at the UN International School, Nuclear Family' [Facebook post] (New York: United Nations, 22 October 2016), accessed 24 October 2016, www.facebook.com/hibakushavoices/videos/1610762982560200/; Hiroshima Peace Culture Foundation, 'Hibakusha Testimony Videos' (Hiroshima: Peace Culture Foundation, 1986), accessed 29 March 2016, www.pcf.city.hiroshima.jp/virtual/VirtualMuseum_e/visit_e/est_e/panel/A6/6204.htm; Comprehensive Nuclear-Test-Ban Treaty Organisation, *Nagasaki Atomic Bomb Survivor Tells Her Story* trans. Thomas Shingō Baier [YouTube video] (Vienna: CTBTO Preparatory Commission, 2013), accessed 3 March 2017, www.youtube.com/watch?v=2aLU-3Z-r-g.
6 *Nagasaki Shinbun,* 'Nagasaki Archive'.
7 Craig Collie and Paul Ham have written histories of Nagasaki which neglect the Catholic minority around the hypocenter. See my review of Susan Southard at: Gwyn McClelland, 'Nagasaki: Life after Nuclear War'. *Rethinking History* 20.0 (2016): 1–2.
8 Takashi Nagai, *The Bells of Nagasaki* (Tōkyō: Kodansha International, 1994). Also, for a variety of Nagai publications see Takashi Nagai, *Takashi Zenshū* (Takashi Compendium) (Tōkyō: Kodansha, 1971); Takashi Nagai, *We of Nagasaki: The Story of Survivors in an Atomic Wasteland* (New York: Duell, Sloan and Pearce, 1951); Takashi Nagai, *Rozario no kusari* (Tōkyō: Romansusha, 1948); Takashi Nagai, *Atomic Bomb Rescue and Relief Report* (Nagasaki: Nagasaki Association for Hibakushas' Medical Care, 2000), accessed 27 April 2016, www.nashim.org/e_pdf/atomic_bomb/.
9 Shijō aims to provide a historico-sociological critique, by the use of documentary evidence. Chie Shijō, *Urakami no genbaku no katari: Nagai Takashi kara rōma kyōkō e* (Tōkyō: Miraisha, 2015), 56.
10 Kan Yamada, 'gizensha: Nagai Takashi e no kokuhatsu'. *Ushio* (1972): 231–7; Shinji Takahashi, *Nagasaki ni atte tetsugakusuru: kakujidai no shi to sei,* Shōhan (Tōkyō: Hokuju Shuppan, 1994); Akira Nishimura, 'Inori no Nagasaki: Nagai Takashi to genbaku shisha' (Tōkyō University, 2002), Tōkyō University Repository http://repository.dl.itc.u-tokyo.ac.jp/dspace/handle/2261/26039; Shijō, *Urakami no genbaku*; Chizuko Kataoka and Rumiko Kataoka, *hibakuchi Nagasaki no saiken* (Nagasaki: Nagasaki Junshin Daigaku, 1996).
11 Yuki Miyamoto, 'Rebirth in the Pure Land or God's Sacrificial Lambs? Religious Interpretations of the Atomic Bombings in Hiroshima and Nagasaki'. *Japanese Journal of Religious Studies* 32.1 (2005): 131–59.
12 Kevin M. Doak, 'Hiroshima Rages, Nagasaki Prays: Nagai Takashi's Catholic Response to the Atomic Bombing', in *When the Tsunami Came to Shore,* ed. Roy Starrs (Leiden: Brill, 2014), 249–71; Paul Glynn, *A Song for Nagasaki* (Grand Rapids, MI: Eerdmans, 1990); Fumiki Narita, 'Seeing Nagasaki: A Tale', trans. Wallace Gray, *Comparative Civilizations Review,* Manassas, 68 (2013): 98–105.
13 Nagai, *We of Nagasaki.*
14 Robert Jay Lifton, *Death in Life: Survivors of Hiroshima* (Chapel Hill: The University of North Carolina Press, 1991).
15 Kamata Sadao, 'Nagasaki no inori to ikari', in *Nihon no genbaku bungaku 15: hiron/essei,* vol. 15, 15 vols., Nihon no genbaku bungaku (Tōkyō: Horupu Shuppan, 1983), 408–17.
16 Kataoka and Kataoka, *Hibakuchi Nagasaki*; Akihiko Ito, *Genshiya no 'yobu ki': katsute kaku sensō ga atta* (Tōkyō: Komichi Shōbō, 1993); Shijō, *Urakami no genbaku*; Takahashi, *Nagasaki ni atte*; Hitoshi Motoshima and Nobuto Hirano, *Motoshima Hitoshi no shisō: genbaku/sensō/hyūmanizumu* (Nagasaki: Nagasaki shinbunsha, 2012); Hitoshi Motoshima, *genbaku tōka wa tadashikatta ka* (Nagasaki: Seibo no kishasha, 2005).
17 Itō, *Genshiya no 'yobu ki'.*
18 Carla Montane, *Sacred Space and Ritual in Early Modern Japan: The Christian Community of Nagasaki (1569–1643)* (PhD diss., University of London, 2012); Chad

Richard Diehl, 'Resurrecting Nagasaki: Reconstruction, the Urakami Catholics, and Atomic Memory, 1945–1970' (PhD diss., Columbia University, 2011), accessed 8 June 2014, http://academiccommons.columbia.edu/catalog/ac:162775.
19 I reviewed Diehl's dissertation and two other works in a review essay published in 2015: Gwyn McClelland, 'Guilt, Persecution, and Resurrection in Nagasaki: Atomic Memories and the Urakami Catholic Community'. *Social Science Japan Journal* 18.2 (2015): 233–40.
20 Kazuhiko Yokote, *Nagasaki kyū Urakami tenshudō 1945–58: ushinawareta hibaku isan* (Tōkyō: Iwanami Shoten, 2010). Tomoe Otsuki has also recently written about the loss of the ruins as a loss of atomic memory. Tomoe Otsuki, 'The Politics of Reconstruction and Reconciliation in US–Japan Relations – Dismantling the Atomic Bomb Ruins of Nagasaki's Urakami Cathedral'. *The Asia-Pacific Journal: Japan Focus* (2015): 1–33, accessed 29 March 2016, http://apjjf.org/2015/13/32/Tomoe-Otsuki/4356.html. Tsuyoshi Takase, *Nagasaki kieta mō hitotsu no 'genbaku dōmu'* (Tōkyō: Heibonsha, 2009).
21 Wasaburō Urakawa, *Urakami Kirishitan shi* (Tōkyō: Kokusho Kankōkai, 1973). Yakichi Kataoka, *Urakami yonban kuzure Meiji seifu no kirishitan dan'atsu.* (Tōkyō: Chikuma Shōbō, 1963).
22 Shijō, *Urakami no genbaku.* See my own review of her book in Gwyn McClelland, 'Shijō Chie, Urakami no genbaku no katari: Nagai Takashi kara Rōma kyōkō e (The Narration of the Atomic Bomb in Urakami: From Nagai Takashi to the Pope)'. *Japanese Religions* 41.1, 2 (2016): 102–5.
23 I discussed Shijō's book with her at an interview in Nagasaki. Shijō Chie, interview by Gwyn McClelland, Nagasaki City Library, 20 February 2016.
24 Tatsuichirō Akizuki, *Nagasaki genbaku-ki: hibaku ishi no shōgen* (Tōkyō: Nihon zushō sentā, 1972); Tatsuichirō Akizuki, *shi no dōshinen: Nagasaki hibaku ishi no kiroku* (Tōkyō: Kodansha, 1972); Motoshima and Hirano, *Motoshima Hitoshi no shisō*.
25 Kenichiro Yamaguchi, *kokusaku to gisei: gembaku gempatsu soshite gendai iriyō no yukue* (Tōkyō: Shakai Hyoronsha, 2016), 301–16.
26 Akizuki, *Nagasaki genbaku-ki* (Tokyo: Nihon zusho senta, 1972), Akizuki, *shi no dōshinen.* (Tokyo: Kodansha, 1972).
27 Norma Field, *In the Realm of a Dying Emperor: Japan at Century's End* (New York: Vintage, 1993).

References

Akizuki, Tatsuichiro. *Nagasaki genbaku-ki: hibaku ishi no shogen.* Tokyo: Nihon zusho senta, 1972.
Akizuki, Tatsuichiro. *Shi no doshinen: Nagasaki hibaku ishi no kiroku.* Tokyo: Kodansha, 1972.
Chie, Shijo. Interview by Gwyn McClelland, Nagasaki City Library, 20 February 2016.
Diehl, Chad Richard. 'Resurrecting Nagasaki: Reconstruction, the Urakami Catholics, and Atomic Memory, 1945–1970'. PhD diss., Columbia University, 2011.
Doak, Kevin M. 'Hiroshima Rages, Nagasaki Prays: Nagai Takashi's Catholic Response to the Atomic Bombing'. In *When the Tsunami Came to Shore*, ed. Roy Starrs, 249–71. Leiden: Brill, 2014.
Field, Norma. *In the Realm of a Dying Emperor: Japan at Century's End.* New York: Vintage, 1993.
Fukahori Johji, *Nagasaki Survivor at the UN International School.* Nuclear Family website. New York: United Nations, 2016. www.facebook.com/hibakushavoices/videos/1610762982560200/.

Genbaku Hōmu, Megumi no Oka. *Genbaku taiken ki*. 2nd ed. Nagasaki: Megumi no oka Genbaku Homu, 2005.
Glynn, Paul. *A Song for Nagasaki*. Grand Rapids, MI: Eerdmans, 1990.
Higashibaba, Ikuo. 'Historiographical Issues in the Studies of the "Christian Century" in Japan'. *Japanese Religions* 24.1 (1999): 29–50.
Hiroshima Peace Culture Foundation. 'Hibakusha Testimony Videos', 1986. www.pcf.city.hiroshima.jp/virtual/VirtualMuseum_e/visit_e/est_e/panel/A6/6204.htm.
Itō, Akihiko. *Genshiya no 'yobu ki': katsute kakusenso ga atta*. Tokyo: Komichi Shobo, 1993.
Kamata Sadao. 'Nagasaki no inori to ikari'. In *Nihon no genbaku bungaku 15: hiron/essei* 15: 408–17. Nihon no genbaku bungaku. Tōkyō: Horupu Shuppan, 1983.
Kataoka, Chizuko, and Rumiko Kataoka. *Hibakuchi Nagasaki no saiken*. Nagasaki: Nagasaki Junshin Daigaku, 1996.
Kataoka, Yakichi. *Urakami yonban kuzure Meiji seifu no kirishitan dan'atsu*. Tokyo: Chikuma Shobo, 1963.
Lifton, Robert Jay. *Death in Life: Survivors of Hiroshima*. Chapel Hill: The University of North Carolina Press, 1991.
McClelland, Gwyn. 'Guilt, Persecution, and Resurrection in Nagasaki: Atomic Memories and the Urakami Catholic Community'. *Social Science Japan Journal* 18.2 (2015): 233–40. https://doi.org/10.1093/ssjj/jyv018.
McClelland, Gwyn. 'Nagasaki: Life after Nuclear War'. *Rethinking History* 20.0 (15 August 2016): 1–2. https://doi.org/10.1080/13642529.2016.1218623.
McClelland, Gwyn. 'Shijō Chie, Urakami No Genbaku No Katari: Nagai Takashi Kara Roma Kyoko e (The Narration of the Atomic Bomb in Urakami: From Nagai Takashi to the Pope)'. *Japanese Religions* 41.1, 2 (2016): 102–5.
Miyamoto, Yuki. 'Rebirth in the Pure Land or God's Sacrificial Lambs? Religious Interpretations of the Atomic Bombings in Hiroshima and Nagasaki'. *Japanese Journal of Religious Studies* 32.1 (2005): 131–59.
Montane, Carla. 'Sacred Space and Ritual in Early Modern Japan: The Christian Community of Nagasaki (1569–1643)'. University of London, 2012.
Motoshima, Hitoshi. *genbaku touka wa tadashikatta ka*. Nagasaki: Seibo no kisha-sha, 2005.
Motoshima, Hitoshi, and Nobuto Hirano. *Motoshima Hitoshi no shiso: genbaku/senso/hyumanizumu*. Nagasaki: Nagasaki shinbunsha, 2012.
Nagai, Takashi. *Rozario no kusari*. Tokyo: Romansusha, 1948.
Nagai, Takashi. *We of Nagasaki: The Story of Survivors in an Atomic Wasteland*. New York: Duell, Sloan and Pearce, 1951.
Nagai, Takashi. *Nagai Takashi Zenshu*. Tokyo: Kodansha, 1971.
Nagai, Takashi. *The Bells of Nagasaki*. Tokyo: Kodansha International, 1994.
Nagai, Takashi. *Atomic Bomb Rescue and Relief Report*. Nagasaki: Nagasaki Association for Hibakushas' Medical Care, 2000. www.nashim.org/e_pdf/atomic_bomb/.
Nagasaki Atomic Bomb Survivor Tells Her Story. Video. Vienna: CTBTO Preparatory Commission, 2013. www.youtube.com/watch?v=2aLU-3Z-r-g.
Nagasaki Shinbun. 'Nagasaki Archive'. Archive. Nagasaki: Nagasaki Shinbun, 2016. http://e.nagasaki.mapping.jp/p/nagasaki-archive.html.
Narita, Fumiki. 'Seeing Nagasaki: A Tale', trans. Wallace Gray. *Comparative Civilizations Review*, Manassas, 68 (2013): 98–105.
Nishimura, Akira. 'Inori no Nagasaki: Nagai Takashi to genbaku shisha'. Tokyo University, 2002. Tokyo University Repository. http://repository.dl.itc.u-tokyo.ac.jp/dspace/handle/2261/26039.

Otsuki, Tomoe. 'The Politics of Reconstruction and Reconciliation in US–Japan Relations – Dismantling the Atomic Bomb Ruins of Nagasaki's Urakami Cathedral'. *The Asia-Pacific Journal: Japan Focus* 13.32 (2015): 1–33.
Ozaki, Tōmei. *Mi Gawari no Ai*. 2nd ed. Nagasaki: Seibo no kisha-sha, 1994.
Ozaki, Tōmei. *juunanasai no natsu*. Seibo bunko. Nagasaki: Seibo no kisha-sha, 1996.
Shijō, Chie. *Urakami no genbaku no katari: Nagai Takashi kara Rōma kyōkō e*. Tōkyō: Miraisha, 2015.
Shiōra, Shintarō. *Yaketa rozario: genbaku wo ikinuita shonen no kiseki na unmei to shinta na kokoro no sekai*. Nagasaki: Seibo no kishasha, 2009.
Styczek, Ursula, Nakamura, Tomoko, and Nakamura, Toko. 'Atom Bomb Literature: A Bibliography'. Archive. Atomic Bomb Literature, 2017. http://home.hiroshima-u.ac.jp/bngkkn/database/Englishdata/BibliographyonA-bombLit.html.
Su-lan Reber, Emily A. 'Buraku Mondai in Japan: Historical and Modern Perspectives and Directions for the Future'. *Harvard Human Rights Journal* 12 (1999): 297–360.
Takahashi, Shinji. *Nagasaki ni atte tetsugakusuru: kakujidai no shi to sei*. Shohan. Tōkyō: Hokuju Shuppan, 1994.
Takase, Tsuyoshi. *Nagasaki kieta mō hitotsu no 'genbaku dōmu'*. Tōkyō: Heibonsha, 2009.
Urakawa, Wasaburō. *Urakami Kirishitan shi*. Tōkyō: Kokusho Kankōkai, 1973.
Yamada, Kan. 'Gizensha: Nagai Takashi e no kokuhatsu'. *Ushio* (1972).
Yamaguchi, Kenichiro. *Kokusaku to gisei: gembaku gempatsu soshite gendai iriyou no yukue*. Tokyo: Shakai Hyoronsha, 2016.
Yokote, Kazuhiko. *Nagasaki kyū Urakami tenshudō 1945–58: ushinawareta hibaku isan*. Tōkyō: Iwanami Shoten, 2010.

Glossary
Japanese and theological terms

anamnesis		remembering that which was lost
anima	アニマ	religious veil
bakufu	幕府	feudal military government, or shogunate
bugyō	奉行	magistrate's office in Nagasaki
buraku(min)	部落（民）	*buraku literally referred to a hamlet or village. However, buraku (min)* refers to people who were historically during the Tokugawa era mainly known pejoratively as *eta* and *hinin*, but known by their own communities as *kawaya*, because of their dealing with animal skins. *Buraku* means literally 'hamlet' or 'community', but to distinguish outcast communities from others, the euphemistic term *tokushū buraku* (special hamlet) came to be commonly used. Emily A. Su-lan Reber, 'Buraku Mondai in Japan: Historical and Modern Perspectives and Directions for the Future', *Harvard Human Rights Journal* 12 (1999): 299. The Catholics of Urakami were also called *buraku* during the early twentieth century. *Buraku* discrimination is still a problem in Japan and nowadays those who have come to be associated with *burakumin* have also been discriminated against, linked by kinship, place of residence and occupation. Su-lan Reber, 300.
chōkata	帳方	leader of a hidden Christian community, with various roles
chūshincchi	中心地	Japanese name for the hypocenter or Ground Zero of the bomb blast

eta	穢多	lit. 'filth', used as a name for lower class people in Tokugawa society
fumi-e/e-fumi	踏み絵、絵踏み	religious images, usually of Christ or Mary, which the authorities forced people to step on to demonstrate that they were not Christian during the period when Christianity was outlawed
hansai	燔祭	burnt offering, from Old Testament usage. Often translated as holocaust.
hibakusha	被爆者	survivor of the atomic bomb, or person exposed to irradiation
hinin	非人	lit. non-human (not considered a part of society)
hisabetsu	被差別	discriminative (usually used with buraku to show those discriminated against)
hypocenter		location above which the atomic bomb exploded in Nagasaki, also known as the hypocenter. Designated with US spelling as this is the spelling used in Nagasaki
ikinokori	生き残り	survivor (used about those who returned from exile)
jakyō	邪教	heathen, foreign beliefs
kakure	隠れ	hidden – this term was applied to the communities of former 'secret' Christians who remained separated from the Catholics after the Christian ban was lifted. In academia today, this is the term applied to those who still follow a syncretistic form of faith developed over the many years of seclusion
kannon	観音	Buddhist deity, Guanyin (Chinese), Goddess of Compassion
kataribe	語り部	tribal storyteller
katorikku	カトリック	Catholic believer, Catholic faith
kawaya(chō)	皮屋(町)	the area of the town where people worked with leather (associated with buraku by the Meiji period)

Glossary 211

keloid			A keloid scar is scar tissue caused by atomic burns on humans, and many survivors in both Hiroshima and Nagasaki had such scars from the atomic bombing, which were often prominent
kin	菌		germ(s), fungus: a term used to denote people impacted by radiation from the atomic bombing in Nagasaki
kirishitan	キリシタン 吉利支丹		kanji used during Tokugawa period, *katakana* script used frequently
kunchi	くんち		Shinto festival instituted in Nagasaki in 1625, alongside the Suwa Shrine with the support of the *bakufu* as a part of a push to de-Christianise the region
kurisuchan	クリスチャン		modern word for Christian believer
kurō/kurōshū	クロー・クローシュー		from Cross. Derogatory names for Christians/hidden Christians
kuzure	崩れ		lit. crushing, crumbling. Referred to the finding, persecuting and crushing of hidden Christians (i.e. by the magistrate)
Meiji Period	明治時代		1868–1912
memoria passionis			memory of Christ associated with his death on the cross
memoria resurrectionis			memory of the resurrection
Nichiren Buddhist			branch of Mahayana Buddhism based on the teachings of the thirteenth-century monk Nichiren
nijūkōzō	二重横造		Takahashi Shinji's term: two regions, side by side
orashio	オラシオ		prayers, from the Latin of the hidden Christians
paraiso	パライソ		heaven (paradise)
sakoku	鎖国		period of seclusion within Japan from outside influences
seibo no kishi	聖母の騎士		monastery, 'Knights of the Holy Mother' in Nagasaki

sempuku	潜伏	(concealed, latent or dormant) refers to the hidden Christians during the time of persecution, known by historians as the sempuku jidai (1640–1873) Ikuo Higashibaba, 'Historiographical Issues in the Studies of the "Christian Century" in Japan', *Japanese Religions* 24, no. 1 (1999): 29. Stephen Turnbull notes that Tagita Kōya was the only writer to apply the term *sempuku Kirishitan* to the communities who remained separated from the Catholics, while Turnbull chose to apply the term *kakure* 隠れ instead, following Kataoka Yakichi and later Miyazaki Kentarō. (Turnbull). Therefore, in this publication, I follow the more frequently used term for the separated communities: *kakure*.
sempuku jidai	潜伏時代	'Secret period' while Christianity was proscribed.
(go)setsuri	ご摂理	providence
shinbun	新聞	newspaper
shiren	試練	trials
Showa Period	昭和時代	1926 to 1989
shūdan	宗団	cult/religious group
shugendō	修験道	amalgam of religious influences including Buddhist and Shinto beliefs
tabi	旅	lit. trip – the Hidden Christians called their exile *tabi*
Taisho Period	大正時代	1912 to 1926
tennō	天皇	The Emperor of Japan
Tokugawa Period	徳川時代	1603 to 1868
yaso	耶蘇	Christ
zenchō	ゼンチョー	From the Portuguese for gentile/Name the Christians called townsfolk of Nagasaki

Index

26 martyrs 21, 117, 123, 153–4, 158, 26 Martyrs' Museum 91; monument 7, 11

Adam and Eve 92
Akizuki Tatsuichirō 12, 70–1, 204
American occupation 42, 70, 77
Anan, Shigeyuki 38, 40
apostasy 43, 49, 93, 103, 114–16, 124, 137, 197–8
atomic bomb dome 13, 122
Atomic Bomb Home *see Gembaku Hōmu*
Auschwitz 13–14, 98, 145, 154–5, 162; *see also* Holocaust

baby Christ 91, 197
Barefoot Gen 147
Bastian 147, 153
The Bells of Nagasaki 62, 74
Bishop Yamaguchi 121
black hole 170, 174, 179, 188–9, 198–9
Brison, Susan 173
Buddhism 10, 22, 38, 40–4, 46, 48, 70, 80, 87, 91–3, 95–6, 116, 119, 147, 198
burakumin 7, 9–10, 21, 37, 40, 43, 49, 78, 115–16, 158
burnt offering 59–60, 63, 66, 74, 80

Catholic Center, Nagasaki 96, 118, 123
cherry trees 43, 46, 59
Chinatown, Nagasaki 36, 96
Chinese 91, 96, 157–8, 160
collective biography 4, 13, 19, 24, 27, 138, 145, 168, 177, 184, 189, 197
communism 68–9, 160
Copeland, M. Shawn 188
'crippling memories' 110, 118
cross of Christ 161
cultural hybridity 91

Daggers, Jenny 23
dance 37
dark tourism 120, 174
dehumanisation 137–8, 176, 189
Diehl, Chad 63, 119, 203

Emperor Hirohito 160–1
Enju, Toshio 19, 22
environmental consequences 13, 130, 132, 138–9
exile 6, 11, 21–2, 40, 43–5, 48, 77–8, 93, 95, 103, 111, 113–19, 122, 136–7, 145, 180, 197

feminist theology 23, 88, 90, 185; *see also* Daggers, Jenny; Johnson, Elizabeth; Ruether, Rosemary; Vento, Johann; Yee, Gale
Field, Norma 160–1
Fifth Persecution 35, 45, 87, 98, 110–11, 115–17, 119, 124, 137, 153, 198
fissure 3–4, 7, 12, 30, 35–7, 48, 62–3, 71–2, 87, 118, 124, 152, 180
flagellation 93
Fourth Persecution 6, 13, 21–2, 35, 43–4, 46, 48–9, 59, 61, 77, 95, 98, 111–12, 114–17, 120, 136–7, 158, 160, 180, 183
French 43–4, 48, 95
Friedländer, Saul 173
frog 200
Fukahori, Jōji 9, 19–21, 23–4, 26–7, 68, 78–9, 88, 112, 116, 118, 122, 168–77, 183–5, 187–8
Fukahori, Masaru 178
Fukahori, Shigemi 22, 26–8, 37, 48, 89, 98, 118, 158–9
fumi-e 12, 87, 93–7, 103, 116, 118, 122

Gembaku Hōmu 22, 68, 74

214 Index

germs 3, 182
Glynn, Paul 113
go-ban kuzure see Fifth Persecution
Ground Zero 9–10, 13, 19–22, 27, 101, 103, 124, 148, 189; *see also* hypocenter
Guernica, Spain 14, 97–8
guilt 63, 65, 68, 70, 72, 80, 96, 150, 161, 179, 188; survivor 12, 134–5, 148

hansai 59, 63, 65–9, 75, 78–80, 103, 132, 179, 198; critique of 69–70; *hansaisetsu* 59, 64, 74, 77, 79, 168
Hansen's disease 38
Hasegawa, Gonroku 42
Heisei 199
Hideyoshi, Toyotomi 38, 40, 119
Holocaust 19, 24, 27, 30, 59, 67, 98, 169
Holy Mother in Nagasaki 101
hypocenter 4–5, 9–11, 19–20, 25–6, 62, 64, 66, 129, 150, 170, 177, 180, 184–5, 198; *see also* Ground Zero

Ikeda, Toshio 119
ikinokori 45, 113–15, 122
illogical suffering 170, 175, 183–4, 189
indiscriminate 47, 88, 97, 184
intersubjectivity 24–5
Itō Akihiko 45–6, 178
Iwanagi, Tsuru 113, 116–17, 123, 197
Izumo Shinto shrine 61

Jewish Shoah 59, 132, 173, 199; *see also* Holocaust
Jews 67, 88, 132, 173
Job (biblical) 13–14, 45–6, 59, 132, 153, 157, 169, 177–80, 183, 188–9
Johnson, Elizabeth 90, 93
Johnston, William 62–3

Kagoshima 44, 114
kamikaze 187
karma 70
Kataoka, Chizuko 13, 19, 22, 24, 28, 64, 67, 72–5, 77–9, 129, 136, 138, 197
Kataoka, Sada 129, 136–8, 197
Kataoka, Tsuyo 64
Kataoka, Yakichi 72, 121, 138
kataribe 12–13, 19, 23–4, 49, 64, 79–80, 124, 137–9, 162, 168–70, 174, 183, 185, 188–9, 197–9
Keller, Helen 62
keloid scars 64, 77, 87, 102–3, 198
Keshgegian, Flora 117–18, 138, 170, 199
Kichizō, Hayashi no 95

Kiku 98
Knights of the Holy Mother (*seibo no kishi*) 24, 28, 75, 77, 150, 155–6, 162
Kolbe, Maximilian 145, 154–6, 162, 188
Konishi, Shin'ichi 6–7, 19, 22, 26–7, 59, 79, 89, 90, 100, 115, 122
Korea 21, 38, 147, 159, 162
Korean 38, 42, 157–8, 160–2, 186

LaCapra, Dominick 37
Landscape of Silence 170
Lerner, Gerda 173
Lourdes 147
low-caste 37, 40, 116; *see also* outcaste

Manchuria 61, 72, 78–9
manga 147, 150–1, 154
mariology 90–1
Mary: *hibaku-Maria* 87, 89, 91, 97–8; keloid Madonna 102; *Maria Kannon* 87, 91–3, 95–6, 103, 188; Mother of Christ 12, 87; statues 12, 27–8, 48, 87–90, 95, 97–8, 102–3, 113, 115, 123; of Urakami 96, 101, 103, 130, 198
Matsuo, Sachiko 3, 19, 21, 24, 26–7, 35–7, 47–9, 67, 71, 88–9, 101, 113–18, 121–2, 168, 180–3
Matsuzono, Ichijirō 35–7, 48, 96–7
memorial 13, 42, 46, 116, 119, 122–4, 129, 173, 176; memorialisation 5, 11–12, 48, 66, 103, 158
Meiji 6, 10, 21, 44, 137, 199, 201
Metz, Johann Baptist 67, 80, 90, 117, 132, 145, 155, 168–9, 177, 185
Mine, Tōru 19, 21, 23, 26, 28, 35, 42, 49, 67, 145, 150, 155–7, 162
Misericordia 38, 40, 42
mission 38, 40, 43–4, 48, 95, 153
Miyake, Reiko 20, 24, 26–7, 35, 46–7, 49, 79, 129, 131–8, 197
Miyazaki, Yoshio 96–7, 118
Morisaki cape 38, 40
mother God 96
Motoshima, Hitoshi 65, 159–62, 186
Munsi, Roger 93

Nagai, Midori 59–62
Nagai, Takashi 11–12, 20, 25–6, 45–6, 59–80, 89, 98, 113, 117–18, 123–4, 153, 187, 198
Nagai, Tokusaburō 24, 26, 64–5, 75, 187
Nagasaki Archive 5, 170
Nagasaki Atomic Bomb Museum 5, 10, 174

Index

Nagasaki, Jinzaemon 38
Nagasaki Peace Declaration 160
Nagase, Kazuko 19–20, 22, 24, 26–7, 37, 87, 99–100, 179–80, 183–5, 187, 197
Nakamura, Kazutoshi 13, 18–19, 21–4, 26–9, 67–9, 79, 98–9, 129, 132–8, 145, 149–50, 157, 162, 171, 173, 180, 184–5, 187
Napoleon III 44
Nelson, Katherine 27
Nichiren Buddhist 43
Nishida, Kiyoshi 19, 20, 27, 79, 184
Nishio, Waki 48, 114–17, 183, 197
Nishizaka: Hill 11; martyrdoms 40, 42, 46, 91, 153; region of 7, 12, 25, 36, 38, 40, 42–3, 46, 49; slopes of 3–4, 12, 37–8, 40, 43

Oka Masaharu Peace Museum 157
Ōmura, Sumitada 38
oral history 4, 30, 136, 173; 'composure' or subjectivity of 24, 29
orphan 13–14, 19, 27–8, 38, 64, 88, 116, 145, 150–1, 153, 155–6
'other' 67, 80, 88, 98, 103, 120, 149–50, 152, 154–5, 157–8, 160, 162, 187, 198–9
Otsuki, Tomoe 61, 79
Ōura 22, 79, 95; Ōura Cathedral 22, 27, 44
outcaste 7, 9, 21, 43, 49, 78, 115, 158, 161
Ozaki, Tōmei 13–14, 19, 21, 24, 27–8, 35–6, 41–2, 49, 64, 67, 75, 77–8, 98, 110, 117, 121, 135, 145–55, 157–9, 161–2, 171, 173, 185, 188, 196, 200

peace activists 28, 89, 122
Pearl Harbour 121
Petitjean, Bernard 95
pietá 93, 101, 103
Poland 145, 154–5, 188
Polish 14, 28, 147, 150–1, 154, 156, 162
Pope John Paul II 12, 64, 75–80
Pope Pius XI 113
Portelli, Alessandro 19
Portuguese 38, 40
providence 26, 28–9, 59, 63–6, 70, 74–5, 77–9, 120, 188; *see also* Nagai, Takashi
psalms 64, 130, 169, 183

radiation 124, 131, 153, 176; sickness 23, 27, 62, 70, 182–3
Reiwa 199
religious hybridity 93

Research Center for Nuclear Weapons Abolition, Nagasaki 60
Requiem Mass 37, 120
Ricœur, Paul 90, 168, 174
right-wing 160–2
rosary beads 44, 59, 88, 147–8, 150, 162
Ruether, Rosemary 90

sacred spaces 4, 38, 43, 48–9, 119, 159
St Clara 44, 48, 119
St Ludoviko Ibaraki 123
St Paul, Minnesota 121
San Joao Bautista 38–9
San Lazaro 38–9
Santa Clara 42, 48
Sao Lorenzo 42
Sao Miguel 42
Sawanobu, Yoshi 44
Schwab, Gabriele 48–9
shadowy face 7, 37
Shigeyuki, A'nan 38
Shijō, Chie 6, 9, 60, 65, 67–8, 72
Shintoism 10, 28, 38, 43, 61, 93, 138, 158–9
Shiōra, Shintarō 147, 151, 154
shiren 28–9, 59, 63, 65–6, 69, 78
Shiroyama 20, 26, 135
Shōwa period 48, 159, 199, 201
Shōwa Emperor 13, 62, 145, 159, 162, 187
Shugendō Shinto 43
social exclusion 43, 178, 180, 182–3, 189
Spanish: Catholic 14, 113; language 152; statue 97–8
stained-glass windows 110, 117, 196–7
star 196–7, 199
Stimson, Henry 185
suicide 20, 23, 27, 64, 67, 69–70, 135, 145, 150, 157, 187
Suwa Shrine 5, 29, 36, 37; *o-kunchi* Festival 5, 36–7, 120
syncretism 10, 91

Tagawa, Clara Wasa 21, 185–6
Tagawa, Tsutomu 121
Taishō 199, 201
Takagi, Sen'emon 44, 46, 59, 61
Takahashi, Shinji 7, 59, 61, 72, 77, 79
Takazane, Yasunori 157–8, 160
Tanaka, Chikao 102–3
tanka 66
Third Persecution 95
Thomson, Alistair 29,
Tokugawa: era 6–7, 35, 37, 44; authorities 18, 42, 91, 93, 95, 114, 153, 198–9

216   *Index*

Tokugawa, Ieyasu 40
Tokyo National Museum 95, 120
torture stone 116–17, 123
transcendence 28, 80, 102, 152, 188
transformation 64, 75, 97, 116, 157, 178
trauma studies 111, 117, 137, 170; *see also* Keshgegian, Flora; Vento, Johann
Treat, John W. 10
trials *see shiren*
Tsuru 113, 116–17, 123, 197
Tsuwano 48, 98, 114–15

Ueno, Makoto 101
Urakami Cathedral 7, 11, 28, 88–90, 97–8, 110, 113, 116–20, 159, 196, 199; as monument 13, 25, 113, 124; rebuilding of 69, 78, 101, 121, 124; *see also* Fifth Persecution
Urakami River 9–11, 13, 48, 66, 124, 129–31, 138, 148, 150
Urakami valley 4–5, 9, 12, 22, 46, 62–3, 72, 118, 168, 181

United States 3–4, 7, 70, 72, 79, 121, 162, 175, 180, 182–4, 187, 198, 204

Vento, Johann 185
Vilela, Gaspar 38
village headman 113, 118

Wakabayashi, Chiyo 101
Whelan, Christal 92–3

Yamada, Kan 70, 72
Yamazato schools 11, 153, 171, 175
Yasukuni Jinja 159
Yee, Gale 88
Yokohama 114
yon-ban kuzure see Fourth Persecution
Yoneyama, Lisa 28
Yow, Valerie Raleigh 27

Zebrowski, Zenon 156